Other Books and Series by Jeff Bowen

Applications for Enrollment of Chickasaw Newborn Act of 1905
Volumes I thru VII

Visit our website at **www.nativestudy.com** to learn more about these and other books and series by Jeff Bowen

CHEROKEE INTERMARRIED WHITE 1906 VOLUME I

TRANSCRIBED BY
JEFF BOWEN
NATIVE STUDY
Gallipolis, Ohio
USA

Other Books and Series by Jeff Bowen

1901-1907 Native American Census Seneca, Eastern Shawnee, Miami, Modoc, Ottawa, Peoria, Quapaw, and Wyandotte Indians (Under Seneca School, Indian Territory)

1932 Census of The Standing Rock Sioux Reservation with Births And Deaths 1924-1932

Census of The Blackfeet, Montana, 1897- 1901 Expanded Edition

Eastern Cherokee by Blood, 1906-1910, Volumes I thru XIII

Choctaw of Mississippi Indian Census 1929-1932 with Births and Deaths 1924-1931 Volume I
Choctaw of Mississippi Indian Census 1933, 1934 & 1937, Supplemental Rolls to 1934 & 1935 with Births and Deaths 1932-1938, and Marriages 1936-1938 Volume II

Eastern Cherokee Census Cherokee, North Carolina 1930-1939 Census 1930-1931 with Births And Deaths 1924-1931 Taken By Agent L. W. Page Volume I
Eastern Cherokee Census Cherokee, North Carolina 1930-1939 Census 1932-1933 with Births And Deaths 1930-1932 Taken By Agent R. L. Spalsbury Volume II
Eastern Cherokee Census Cherokee, North Carolina 1930-1939 Census 1934-1937 with Births and Deaths 1925-1938 and Marriages 1936 & 1938 Taken by Agents R. L. Spalsbury And Harold W. Foght Volume III

Seminole of Florida Indian Census, 1930-1940 with Birth and Death Records, 1930-1938

Texas Cherokees 1820-1839 A Document For Litigation 1921

Choctaw By Blood Enrollment Cards 1898-1914 Volumes I thru XVII

Starr Roll 1894 (Cherokee Payment Rolls) Districts: Canadian, Cooweescoowee, and Delaware Volume One
Starr Roll 1894 (Cherokee Payment Rolls) Districts: Flint, Going Snake, and Illinois Volume Two
Starr Roll 1894 (Cherokee Payment Rolls) Districts: Saline, Sequoyah, and Tahlequah; Including Orphan Roll Volume Three

Cherokee Intruder Cases Dockets of Hearings 1901-1909 Volumes I & II

Indian Wills, 1911-1921 Records of the Bureau of Indian Affairs Books One thru Seven;
Native American Wills & Probate Records 1911-1921

Other Books and Series by Jeff Bowen

Turtle Mountain Reservation Chippewa Indians 1932 Census with Births & Deaths, 1924-1932

Chickasaw By Blood Enrollment Cards 1898-1914 Volume I thru V

Cherokee Descendants East An Index to the Guion Miller Applications Volume I
Cherokee Descendants West An Index to the Guion Miller Applications Volume II (A-M)
Cherokee Descendants West An Index to the Guion Miller Applications Volume III (N-Z)

Applications for Enrollment of Seminole Newborn Freedmen, Act of 1905

Eastern Cherokee Census, Cherokee, North Carolina, 1915-1922, Taken by Agent James E. Henderson
    Volume I (1915-1916)
    Volume II (1917-1918)
    Volume III (1919-1920)
    Volume IV (1921-1922)

Complete Delaware Roll of 1898

Eastern Cherokee Census, Cherokee, North Carolina, 1923-1929, Taken by Agent James E. Henderson
    Volume I (1923-1924)
    Volume II (1925-1926)
    Volume III (1927-1929)

Applications for Enrollment of Seminole Newborn Act of 1905 Volumes I & II

North Carolina Eastern Cherokee Indian Census 1898-1899, 1904, 1906, 1909-1912, 1914 Revised and Expanded Edition

1932 Hopi and Navajo Native American Census with Birth & Death Rolls (1925-1931) Volume 1 - Hopi
1932 Hopi and Navajo Native American Census with Birth & Death Rolls (1930-1932) Volume 2 - Navajo

Western Navajo Reservation Navajo, Hopi and Paiute 1933 Census with Birth & Death Rolls 1925-1933

Cherokee Citizenship Commission Dockets 1880-1884 and 1887-1889 Volumes I thru V

Copyright © 2013
by Jeff Bowen

ALL RIGHTS RESERVED
No part of this publication may be reproduced
or used in any form or manner whatsoever
without previous written permission from the
copyright holder or publisher.

Originally published:
Baltimore, Maryland
2013

Reprinted by:

Native Study LLC
Gallipolis, OH
www.nativestudy.com
2020

Library of Congress Control Number: 2020917307

ISBN: 978-1-64968-070-9

Made in the United States of America.

This series is dedicated to
Jerry Bowen
the Brave and the Strong.

DEPARTMENT OF THE INTERIOR

Commissioner to the Five Civilized Tribes
Muskogee, Indian Territory, March 9, 1907.

NOTICE IS HEREBY GIVEN that the undersigned, the Commissioner to the Five Civilized Tribes, has been designated by the Secretary of the Interior, as the official to make and approve appraisals of the value of improvements upon land in the Cherokee Nation which were made prior to November 5, 1906, by white persons who intermarried with Cherokee citizens prior to December 16, 1895, and who have the right under the Act of Congress approved March 2, 1907 (Public 180), to sell improvements.

NOTICE IS FURTHER GIVEN that former claimants to citizenship by intermarriage who have made permanent and valuable improvements on lands of the Cherokee Nation and who claim the right to sell the same under and by virtue of said Act of Congress of March 2, 1907 (Public 180), must appear before the Commissioner to the Five Civilized Tribes prior to April 1, 1907, and designate the land upon which are located the improvements which they claim the right to sell by virtue of said Act; and if any such intermarried citizen shall fail to appear before the Commissioner to the Five Civilized Tribes prior to April 1, 1907, it will be considered that he makes no claim to the benefits conferred by said Act. Such appearance and designation of improvements must be made before the Commissioner at his office in Muskogee, Indian Territory, at any time between Monday, March 11th, 1907, and Saturday, March 30th, 1907, inclusive, or at any of the following named places between the dates named at which places the Commissioner will have a representative to receive said designations and hear testimony relative thereto:

Bartlesville, Ind. Ter., Monday March 18th, 1907, to Saturday March 23rd, 1907, inclusive.
Tulsa, Ind. Ter., Monday March 25th, 1907, to Saturday March 30th, 1907, inclusive.
Claremore, Ind. Ter., Monday March 18th, 1907, to Saturday March 23rd, 1907, inclusive.
Nowata, Ind. Ter., Monday March 25th, 1907, to Saturday March 30th, 1907, inclusive.
Vinita, Ind. Ter., Monday March 18th, 1907, to Saturday March 23rd, 1907, inclusive.
Pryor Creek, Ind. Ter., Monday March 25th, 1907, to Saturday March 30th, 1907, inclusive.
Tahlequah, Ind. Ter., Monday March 18, 1907, to Saturday March 23rd, 1907, inclusive.
Sallisaw, Ind. Ter., Monday March 25th, 1907, to Saturday March 30th, 1907, inclusive.

Designations must be made in person by the intermarried white claimant, or in case proper proof is made that he is physically unable to appear, by some adult member of his immediate family, or in case proper proof is made of the fact that the intermarried white claimant is physically unable to appear and has no adult member of his immediate family, by a person holding a properly executed power of attorney; provided, that in every case the designation must be made by a party familiar with the character, ownership, location and value of the improvements to be designated. At the time of said designation the testimony of any competent person will be taken by the Commissioner as to the location, character and value of said improvements.

No former intermarried white claimant will be permitted to designate improvements upon more land than he would have been entitled to take in allotment for him self had he been admitted to citizenship. If any intermarried white claimant has made a tentative selection of a full allotment he will not be allowed to designate improvements upon other land.

NOTICE IS FURTHER GIVEN that if any citizen of the Cherokee Nation entitled to select an allotment shall claim that the improvements on land tentatively selected by a former intermarried white claimant, or held by him, do not belong to said intermarried white claimant, or makes any adverse claim to said improvements, or to the right of the intermarried white claimant to sell said improvements under the Act approved March 2, 1907 (Public 180), said citizen must appear before the Commissioner to the Five Civilized Tribes either at Muskogee, Indian Territory, prior to April 1, 1907, or at one of the places above designated and within the dates above designated and make formal complaint before the Commissioner to the Five Civilized Tribes of his contention. At Muskogee, Indian Territory, between March 11th and March 30th, 1907, inclusive, and at the other places herein named during the hearings at said places at times fixed, plats will be open for inspection showing the location of tentative allotments made by former claimants to citizenship by intermarriage and all other land on which such claimants claim improvements, so far as indicated by the records of this office.

All persons interested should take careful note of the limitation of time herein provided for, within which designations and complaints may be made, and that they must be made by appearance before the Commissioner.

TAMS BIXBY,
Commissioner.

This particular notice concerns the appraisals of improvements on properties held by Cherokee intermarried whites. You would have found notices like this throughout the Nation to bring in people to finalize the allotment question, of who belonged and who did not.

E.C.M.

Cherokee 58.

DEPARTMENT OF THE INTERIOR,
COMMISSIONER TO THE FIVE CIVILIZED TRIBES.

In the matter of the application for the enrollment of ALBERTIN HAMPTON as a citizen by intermarriage of the Cherokee Nation.

D E C I S I O N

THE RECORDS OF THIS OFFICE SHOW: That at Fairland, Indian Territory, July 9, 1900, Albertin Hampton appeared before the Commission to the Five Civilized Tribes, and made application for the enrollment of himself as a citizen by intermarriage, and for the enrollment of his wife, Jane E. Hampton, et al. as citizens by blood of the Cherokee Nation. The application for the enrollment of the said Jane E. Hampton et al. as citizens by blood of the Cherokee Nation has been heretofore disposed of, and their rights to enrollment will not be considered in this decision. Further proceedings in the matter of said application were had at Muskogee, Indian Territory, September 3, 1902, October 14, 1902, and January 2, 1907.

THE EVIDENCE IN THIS CASE SHOWS: That the applicant herein, Albertin Hampton, a white man, was married, in accordance with Cherokee law, January 20, 1874, to his wife, Jane E. Hampton, nee Thomas, who was at the time of said marriage a recognized citizen by blood of the Cherokee Nation, and whose name appears on the approved partial roll of citizens by blood of the Cherokee Nation, opposite No. 195; that since said marriage the said Albertin Hampton and Jane E. Hampton have resided together as husband and wife, and have continuously lived in the Cherokee Nation. Said Albertin Hampton is identified on the Cherokee authenticated tribal roll of 1880, and the Cherokee census roll of 1896, as "Bert Hampton", an intermarried citizen of the Cherokee Nation.

IT IS, THEREFORE, ORDERED AND ADJUDGED: That in accordance with the decision of the Supreme Court of the United States, dated November 5, 1906, in the case of Daniel Red Bird et al. vs. the United States,

E.C.M.   - 2 -   Cherokee 58.

under the provisions of Section twenty-one, of the Act of Congress approved June 28, 1898 (30 Stat., 495), Albertin Hampton is entitled to enrollment as a citizen by intermarriage of the Cherokee Nation, and his application for enrollment as such is accordingly granted.

                                                    Commissioner.

Dated at Muskogee, Indian Territory, this JAN 18 1907

The above is an accepted decision of the Commissioner to the Five Civilized Tribes. The Attorney for the Cherokee Nation had fifteen days after the date of Commissioner's decision in which to protest.

Cherokee
58.

W. W. HASTINGS, ATTORNEY
OFFICE OF
H. M. VANCE, SECRETARY

Attorney for the Cherokee Nation,
MUSKOGEE, I. T.   January 18, 1907.

The Commissioner to the Five Civilized Tribes,

    Muskogee, Indian Territory.

Sir:

    Receipt is acknowledged of the testimony and of your decision enrolling Albertin Hampton, as a citizen by intermarriage of the Cherokee Nation. Time for protesting said decision is waived and I consent that said person may be placed upon the schedule immediately.

                      Yours very truly,

                      W. W. Hastings

                      Attorney for Cherokee Nation.

The above is a notice of the Attorney waiving the time for protesting the Commissioner's decision (on the two previous pages) concerning Albertin Hampton's application and consenting to place the applicant upon schedule immediately.

INTRODUCTION

The *Cherokee Intermarried White*, National Archive film M-1301, Rolls 305-307, are found under the heading of Applications for Enrollment of the Commission to the Five Civilized Tribes. The genealogical value of this series concerning the relationships between many Cherokee tribesman and their marriages among another race is very important and virtually a treasure trove of information long sought after. While on the other hand what these cases are really about are the efforts of many to attain Cherokee land allotments. Referenced from the Supreme Court Decision, Cherokee Intermarriage Cases – 203 U.S. 76 (1906).

This collection of Intermarried claims involves two hundred and eighty-eight separate cases with a variety of scenarios from the divorced to the widowed to the deserving to the deceptive. During these times there were many that wanted what was rightfully only the Cherokees. You will see each case will be headed by the title from the first folder as an example: *Intermarried White I, Trans from Cher. 34*, the transfer number is the Dawes Commission number from the claimants spouse.

These cases are fascinating because of the generational bloodlines that can be verified by documentation rather than just word of mouth. From Kent Carter's book, *The Dawes Commission*, "The tribe also, continued to oppose the enrollment of whites who had married into the Cherokee tribe. That controversy dragged through the U.S. Court of Claims and then the Supreme Court, which finally ruled in favor of the tribe on November 05, 1906. The court upheld the Cherokee citizenship laws that denied rights to any white who had married into the tribe after November 1, 1877. It also upheld an 1839 law which stated that anyone who moved out of the nation lost their citizenship unless they were readmitted. The applications of 3,341 persons were rejected as a result of this ruling, and the allotment clerks were forced to undo a great deal of their work. With the issue finally settled by the courts, the commission was able to send the first schedule of Cherokees by intermarriage, containing fifty-five names, to the secretary of interior on June 10, 1907. Eventually only 286 people were enrolled as intermarried whites----far fewer than the number put on the rolls of the Choctaw and Chickasaw tribes, which had much more liberal laws on rights based on marriage." [1]

---

[1] The Dawes Commission and the Allotment of the Five Civilized Tribes, 1893-1914 by Kent Carter, pg. 121

In Cohen's Handbook of Federal Indian Law he states, "In the *Cherokee Intermarriage Cases,* the Supreme Court considered the claims of certain white persons, intermarried with Cherokee Indians, who wanted to participate in the common property of the Cherokee Nation. Such persons were permitted by tribal law to be tribal citizens with limited rights in tribal property. The tribe had also provided for the revocation of citizenship rights of a white person who intermarried with a Cherokee if the Cherokee spouse were abandoned or if a widower or widow married a non-Cherokee. The Court found that the Cherokee Nation had authority to qualify the rights of citizenship which it offered to its "naturalized citizens. Such tribal action defeated the claims of the plaintiffs:

The laws and usages of the Cherokees, their earliest history, the fundamental principles of their national policy, their constitution and statutes, all show that citizenship rested on blood or marriage; that the man who would assert citizenship must establish marriage; that when marriage ceased (with a special reservation in favor of widows or widowers) citizenship ceased; that when an intermarried white married a person having no rights of Cherokee citizenship by blood it was conclusive evidence that the tie which bound him to the Cherokee people was severed and the very basis of his citizenship obliterated."[2]

An important footnote that Cohen published within his pages for the above paragraph also needs to be studied. He noted, "Under Cherokee law white persons intermarrying with Cherokees before 1875 were tribal citizens for most purposes, including allotment of tribal land, but had no interest in tribal funds except those funds derived from tribal lands. A Cherokee law that became effective in 1875 provided that whites marrying Cherokees had no rights to tribal property but could obtain full citizenship by the payment of $500 to the tribe. In 1877 the tribe provided that no intermarried citizen could obtain any rights to tribal land or funds."[3]

During many years of study this author has found cases that should have been been accepted, especially with the particular documentation presented. All in all the outcome of the decision made should have rendered a different result. Also there have been many that numb the mind as to how they their cases were even considered. The years have given many the hopes that their ancestors were one of those that had a decent claim and an honest consideration. Like any time in history there are political struggles

---

[2] Felix S. Cohen's Handbook of FEDERAL INDIAN LAW 1982 ED. pgs 20-21.
[3] Felix S. Cohen's Handbook of FEDERAL INDIAN LAW 1982 ED. pg 21 footnote16.

and the human factor that points out man is not perfect. These pages were transcribed with the wish that another person somewhere along the line will find their relation from the past and give them the answers long hoped for.

Jeff Bowen
Gallipolis, Ohio
NativeStudy.com

Cherokee Intermarried White 1906
Volume I

Cher Intermarried White 1
Trans from Cher 34

◇◇◇◇◇

E.C.M.

DEPARTMENT OF THE INTERIOR,
COMMISSIONER TO THE FIVE CIVILIZED TRIBES.

In the matter of the application for the enrollment of

GEORGE W. ELLIOTT

as a citizen by intermarriage of the Cherokee Nation.

CHEROKEE 34.
◇◇◇◇◇

Commission to the Five Civilized Tribes,
Muskogee, Indian Territory,
May 11th, 1900.

In the matter of the application of Anna E. Elliott for enrollment as a member of the Cherokee Tribe of Indians: being sworn and examined by Commissioner McKennon she testifies as follows:

Q What is your name? A Anna E. Elliott.
Q How old are you? A Fifty.
Q Are you on the 1880 roll? A Yes sir.
Q What was your name then? A The same.
Q Your post-office address is Muskogee? A Yes sir.
Q Have you children? A I have only one at home single.
Q What is her age? A Twenty-four.
Q What is her name? A Mary, they call her Mamie. And my husband, George Elliott, he is a white man.
Q How old is he? A Sixty-four.

Department of the Interior,
Commission to the Five Civilized Tribes

I hereby certify, upon my official oath as stenographer to above named Commission, that this transcript is a true, full and correct translation of my stenographic notes.

M.D. Green

◇◇◇◇◇

Cherokee Intermarried White 1906
Volume I

"R"

Cherokee straight case No. 34.

Department of the Interior,
Commission to the Five Civilized Tribes,
Muskogee, I. T., January 9, 1902.

SUPPLEMENTAL TESTIMONY, in the matter of the application of George W. Elliott et al for enrollment as Cherokee citizens.

Appearances:
Applicant in person.

GEORGE W. ELLIOTT, being sworn and examined, testified as follows:

BY COMMISSION:
Q What is your name? A George W. Elliott.
Q How old are you? A 66 years old.
Q What is your post-office address? A Muskogee.
Q Are you a recognized citizen by intermarriage of the Cherokee Nation? A Yes sir.
Q How long have you resided in and been recognized as a citizen of the Cherokee Nation? A Since 1865.
Q Have you made the Cherokee Nation your home continuously since that time? A Yes sir.
Q What is the name of your wife? A Before she married. Yes. A Annie E. Kerr.
Q What was the name of her father? A Frederick A. Kerr.
Q What was the name of her mother? A Laurena.
Q Does she claim the right to enrollment through her father or mother? A Through her mother, her mother was a Cherokee.
Q Your wife is living? A Yes sir.
Q Is your name on the roll of 1880? A Yes sir.
Q Is the name of your wife on that roll? A Yes sir.
Q Does she appear on that roll as your wife? A Yes sir.
Q Has she lived in the Cherokee Nation continuously? A Yes sir.
Q She has always been recognized as a citizen by blood? A Yes sir.

1880 authenticated roll of citizens of the Cherokee Nation examined and applicant and wife identified on
page 15 No. 395, G.W.Elliott, Canadian District, adopted white.
page 15 No. 397, A.E.Elliott, Canadian District, native Cherokee.
1896 census roll of citizens of the Cherokee Nation examined and applicants identified on
page 303 No. 326 George W. Elliott, Cooweescoowee District;
page 151 No. 1556 Annie E. Elliott, Cooweescoowee District.

Cherokee Intermarried White 1906
Volume I

Q Do you own property in the Cherokee Nation? A Yes sir.
Q How long have you been residing in the Creek Nation? A Well quite a little while, off and on I have been here for several years.
Q Have you ever exercised the right of suffrage as a citizen of any other state or territory since you were married to your wife under Cherokee law? A No sir.
Q When were you married to her? A 1865, March 8th.

BY COMMISSION: On the 11th day of May, 1900, application was made for the enrollment of George W. Elliott and his wife Anna E Elliott as citizens of the Cherokee Nation. Said George W. Elliott making application as a citizen by intermarriage and his wife as a citizen by blood. The testimony taken at that time is found to be incomplete, and said George W. Elliott this day appears before the Commission and gives further testimony as regards his application and that of his wife to be enrolled as citizens of the Cherokee Nation. He is duly identified on the authenticated roll of 1880 and the census roll of 1896, as an adopted white. His wife is duly identified on the said rolls as a native Cherokee; satisfactory proof has been made as to their residence of the applicant and his wife in the Cherokee Nation, and they will be listed for enrollment as citizens of the Cherokee Nation, his wife as a citizen by blood and the applicant as a citizen by intermarriage.

----****----

MARY ELLIOTT, appearing before the Commission on this same day, to be enrolled as a Cherokee citizen, and being sworn and examined, testified as follows:

BY COMMISSION:
Q What is your name? A Mary Elliott.
Q Do you desire to be listed for enrollment as Mary or Mamie? A Mary I suppose.
Q How old are you? A 26.
Q What is your post-office address? A Muskogee.
Q Your mother made application for your enrollment in May 1900 as a citizen of the Cherokee Nation? A Yes sir.
Q What is the name of your father? A George W. Elliott.
Q And your mother's name? A Annie E. Elliott.
Q You claim the right to enrollment as a citizen by blood through your mother? A Yes sir.
Q Have you always resided in and claimed it as your home? A Yes sir.
Q Have you always been enrolled on the tribal rolls made by the authorities of the Cherokee Nation? A I have.

1880 authenticated roll of citizens of the Cherokee Nation examined and applicant identified on
page 15 No. 402 Mary Elliott, Canadian District, native Cherokee;
1896 census roll of citizens of the Cherokee Nation examined and applicant identified on
page 151 No. 1555 Mary Elliott, Cooweescoowee District.

Cherokee Intermarried White 1906
Volume I

BY COMMISSION: On the 11th day of May, 1900, application was made for the enrollment of Mary Elliott as a citizen by blood of the Cherokee Nation. By reason of the fact that she had reached her majority, and for the further eason[sic] that the testimony taken at that time was found to be incomplete, she was requested to again appear before the Commission. She this day appears and gives further testimony as regards her application to be enrolled as a citizen by blood of the Cherokee Nation. She is duly identified on the authenticated roll of 1880 and the census roll of 1896. She makes satisfactory proof as to her residence, and will be listed for enrollment as a Cherokee by blood.

--**--

M.D. Green, being first duly sworn, states that as stenographer to the Commission to the Five Civilized Tribes he correctly recorded the testimony and proceedings in this case and that the forgoing is a true and complete transcript of his stenographic notes thereof.

M.D. Green

Subscribed and sworn to before me this January 10, 1902.

T.B. Needles
Commissioner.

◇◇◇◇◇

DEPARTMENT OF THE INTERIOR.
Commission to the Five Civilized Tribes.
Muskogee, Indian Territory, September 30th, 1902.

In the matter of the application of George W. Elliott for the enrollment of himself as a citizen by intermarriage of the Cherokee Nation and for the enrollment of his wife Anna E. Elliott and his daughter Mary Elliott as citizens by blood of the Cherokee Nation.

Supplemental to #34.

Appearances:
Applicant appears in person.
Cherokee Nation by J. C. Starr.

GEORGE W. ELLIOTT, being duly sworn, testified as follows:
Examination by the Commission.
Q What is your name, please? A George W. Elliott.
Q What is your age at this time? A 66.

4

Cherokee Intermarried White 1906
Volume I

Q What is your post office? A Muskogee.
Q Are you the same George W. Elliott that made application to the Commission for enrollment on May 11th, 1900, as an intermarried citizen? A Yes, dir.
Q What is your wife's name? A Anna E.
Q When were you and she married? A In 1865.
Q Were you ever married prior to your marriage to this wife? A No, sir.
Q Was she ever married prior to her marriage to you? A No, sir.
Q You are her first husband? A Yes, sir.
Q She is your first wife? A Yes, sir.
Q Have you lived together continuoulsy[sic] since your marriage yp[sic] to the present time? A Yes, sir.
Q Were you living together as husband and wife on the first day of September, 1902? A Yes, sir.
Q How long have you resided in the Cherokee Nation? A I have been here about 43 years.
Q Have you lived here for the last 43 years? A Yes, sir.
Q How long has your wife lived in the Cherokee Nation? A She was born here.
Q Has she lived in the territory all her life? A Yes, sir.
Q Have you a daughter living at home? A Yes, sir.
Q What is her name? A Mary Elliott.
Q How long has she lived in the Territory? A Since she was born?
Q Lived here all her life? A All her life.
Q Is your wife Anna E. and daughter Mary living at this time? A Yes, sir.
Q You have never been married to any other woman except this wife? A No, sir.
Q Never was separated from her? A No, sir.

    Jesse O. Carr, being first duly sworn, states that as stenographer to the Commission to the Five Civilized Tribes he reported the above entitled case and that the foregoing is a true and complete transcript of his stenographic notes thereof.

Jesse O. Carr

Subscribed and sworn to before me this 15th day of October, 1902.

BC Jones
Notary Public.

◇◇◇◇◇

Cherokee Intermarried White 1906
Volume I

Cherokee No.
34.

DEPARTMENT OF THE INTERIOR,

COMMISSIONER TO THE FIVE CIVILIZED TRIBES,

MUSKOGEE, INDIAN TERRITORY, JANUARY 4, 1907.

IN THE MATTER OF THE APPLICATION of George W. Elliott for enrollment as a citizen by intermarriage of the Cherokee Nation.

GEORGE W. ELLIOTT, being first duly sworn by Walter W. Chappell, Notary Public, for the Western District of the Indian Territory, testified as follows:

EXAMINATION

ON BEHALF OF THE COMMISSIONER:

Q What is your name age and postoffice address?
A George W. Elliott, 70 years old, Santa Anna, California, Box 94.
Q You claim to be a citizen by intermarriage of the Cherokee Nation, do you?
A Yes sir.
Q Through whom? A Anna E. Kerr.
Q Is Anna E. Kerr living at the present time? A Yes sir.
Q What is her citizenship? A Cherokee by blood.
Q Is she a native born citizen of the Cherokee Nation? A Yes sir.
Q When were you and Anna E. Kerr married? A March 7, 1865.
Q Under a Cherokee license? A Yes sir.
Q Where was the license procured? A From Webbers Falls.
Q What District is that in? A Canadian District.
Q That license was issued by the authorities in the Canadian District? A Yes sir.
Q Who performed the marriage ceremony? A Mr. Willie.
Q What was his office? A He was a minister.
Q Were either you or your wife married prior to your marriage in 1865? A No sir.
Q She was a citizen of the Cherokee Nation at the time of your marriage, was she?
A Yes sir; her mother was a niece of Chief John Ross.
Q Have you lived together continuously since your marriage? A Yes sir.
Q Where have you resided during that time? A Part of the time in the Cherokee Nation, part of the time in the Creek Nation, and two years out in California.
Q Up until two years ago, you lived continuously in the Indian Territory since your marriage? A Yes sir.
Q When did you leave the Indian Territory for California? A My wife left February 17th three years ago next February; and I left two years ago September 15th, - taken my son-in-law out there for his health, got consumption, - Mr. Bozeman.
Q You left the Cherokee Nation subsequent to September 1, 1902? A Yes sir.

Cherokee Intermarried White 1906
Volume I

Q Have you a certified copy of the marriage license issued you? A No sir; they were returned to me and I gave them to the minister, and he returned them back to the court, I suppose.
Q Who issued the license under which you were married? A The clerk of the court; I don't know who was the clerk of the court at that time, been so long ago.
Q Was that in the Canadian District A Yes sir, Webbers Falls.
Q Did you secure the license in person at Webbers Falls? A I sent down for them. It was right after the war, and it wasn't safe to go very far from the fort.
Q Were you living in the Illinois District at Fort Gibson? A Yes, living right at Fort Gibson, what is called old town now.

ON BEHALF OF THE COMMISSIONER:

On Page 9, Book A, "Record of Marriage certificates Illinois District, Cherokee Nation," appears the following:
"1865, February,
Elliott-Kerr"

Issued license of marriage to George Elliott to marry Anna Kerr (license issued by Amos Thornton, Clerk of the District Court)."

Said Anna E. Elliott (nee Kerr) is included in an approved partial roll of Cherokees by blood, opposite No. 126.
The applicant, George W. Elliott, is identified on the authenticated Cherokee tribal roll of 1880, Canadian District and the Cherokee census roll of 1896, Coowees Coowee District, opposite Nos. 395 and 326, respectively, as an intermarried white.

(Witness dismissed).

I, S. T. Wright, stenographer to the Commissioner to the Five Civilized Tribes, on oath, state that I recorded the testimony and proceedings had in the above entitled cause on January 4, 1907, and that the above and foregoing is a true and correct transcript of my stenographic notes thereof taken on said date.

S.T. Wright

Subscribed and sworn to before me this January 5th, 1907.

Edward Merrick
NOTARY PUBLIC.

**Cherokee Intermarried White 1906
Volume I**

C.F.B.   Cherokee 34.

DEPARTMENT OF THE INTERIOR,
COMMISSIONER TO THE FIVE CIVILIZED TRIBES.

In the matter of the application for the enrollment of GEORGE W. ELLIOTT as a citizen by intermarriage of the Cherokee Nation.

D E C I S I O N

THE RECORDS OF THIS OFFICE SHOW: That on May 11, 1900, application was received by the Commission to the Five Civilized Tribes for the enrollment of George W. Elliott as a citizen by intermarriage of the Cherokee Nation. Further proceedings in the matter of said application were had at Muskogee, Indian Territory, January 9, and September 30, 1902, and January 4, 1907.

THE EVIDENCE IN THIS CASE SHOWS: That the applicant herein, George W. Elliott, a white man, was married in accordance with Cherokee law March 7, 1865, to his wife, Anna E. Elliott, nee Kerr, who was at the time of said marriage a recognized citizen by blood of the Cherokee Nation, who is identified on the Cherokee authenticated tribal roll of 1880, Canadian District, No. 397, as a native Cherokee, and whose name is included in the approved partial roll of citizens by blood of the Cherokee Nation, opposite No. 126. It is further shown that from the time of said marriage the said George W. Elliott and Anna E. Elliott resided together as husband and wife, and continuously lived in the Cherokee Nation up to and including September 1, 1902. Said applicant is identified on the Cherokee authenticated tribal roll of 1880, and the Cherokee census roll of 1896, as an intermarried citizen of the Cherokee Nation.

IT IS, THEREFORE, ORDERED AND ADJUDGED: That in accordance with the decision of the Supreme Court of the United States, dated November 5, 1906, in the cases of Daniel Red Bird et al. vs. the United States, Nos. 125, 126, 127 and 128, the said applicant, George W. Elliott is entitled, under the provisions of Section twenty-one, of the Act of Congress approved June 28, 1898 (30 Stats., 495), to enrollment as a citizen by intermarriage of the Cherokee Nation, and his application for enrollment as such is accordingly granted.

Tams Bixby
Commissioner.

Dated at Muskogee, Indian Territory,
this JAN 19 1907

Cherokee Intermarried White 1906
Volume I

DEPARTMENT OF THE INTERIOR.
COMMISSIONER TO THE FIVE CIVILIZED TRIBES.

CHIEF CLERK,
CHEROKEE LAND OFFICE.

DEAR SIR:

The records of this office show   George W Elliott

listed on Cherokee card No.   #34
to be prima facie entitled to enrollment as   *(Illegible)* intermarriage   of the Cherokee Nation for the following reason, viz: Is on Schedule for Departmental Approval

Respectfully,

Commissioner.

Dated   Jany 28 1907

◇◇◇◇◇

Cherokee
34

Muskogee, Indian Territory, December 22, 1906.

George W. Elliott,
Box 94,
Santa Ana, California.

Dear Sir:

November 6, 1906, the United States Supreme Court held that white persons who intermarried with Cherokee citizens according to Cherokee law prior to November 1, 1875, are entitled to enrollment and allotments of land as citizens of the Cherokee Nation.

You are advised that to properly determine your right to enrollment as a citizen by intermarriage of the Cherokee Nation, it will be necessary for you to appear before the Commissioner for the purpose of giving testimony as to the date of your marriage and whether or not your wife, by reason of your marriage to whom you claim the right to enrollment as a citizen of the Cherokee Nation, was a recognized citizen of the Cherokee Nation at the time of your marriage to her, and whether or not you were married to her in accordance with Cherokee laws.

Cherokee Intermarried White 1906
Volume I

You are, therefore, directed to appear before the Commissioner at Muskogee, Indian Territory, at 9 o'clock A. M., on Wednesday, January 2, 1907, and give testimony as above indicated.

Respectfully,

J.M.H.
Commissioner.

Acting

D.C. 510-1907.

Santa Ana, Cal
Dec 29 1906.

Mr Wm O Beall
Acting Commissioner

Dear Sir:

Yours of the 22nd inst. received to-day and will say that I will start day after to morrow.

Respectfully,
G. W. Elliott.

Cherokee
34.

Muskogee, Indian Territory, January 19, 1907.

W. W. Hastings,
Attorney for Cherokee Nation,
Muskogee, Indian Territory.

Dear Sir:

There is enclosed herewith a copy of the decision of the Commissioner to the Five Civilized Tribes dated January 19, 1907, granting the application for the enrollment of George W. Elliott, as a citizen by intermarriage of the Cherokee Nation.

Respectfully,

Commissioner.

Incl-C-14
LMC

Cherokee Intermarried White 1906
Volume I

Cherokee 34.

W.W. HASTINGS.
ATTORNEY.

OFFICE OF

H.M. VANCE.
SECRETARY.

Attorney for the Cherokee Nation,
MUSKOGEE, I. T.

January 19, 1907.

The Commissioner to the Five Civilized Tribes,
Muskogee, Indian Territory.

Sir:

Receipt is acknowledged of the testimony and of your decision enrolling George W. Elliott as a citizen by intermarriage of the Cherokee Nation. Time for protesting said decision is waive[sic] and I consent that said person may be placed upon the schedule immediately.

Respectfully,
W. W. Hastings
Attorney for Cherokee Nation.

◇◇◇◇◇

Cherokee
34

Muskogee, Indian Territory, January 21, 1907.

George W. Elliott,
Santa Ana, California. Box 94.

Dear Sir:

There is enclosed herewith copy of the decision of the Commissioner to the Five Civilized Tribes, dated January 19, 1907, granting the application for your enrollment as a citizen by intermarriage of the Cherokee Nation.

You will be advised when your name has been placed upon the schedule of citizens of the Cherokee Nation and approved by the Secretary of the Interior.

Respectfully,

Enc M - 11
M.T.M.

Commissioner.

Cherokee Intermarried White 1906
Volume I

Cher I W 2
Trans from Cher Card #58
3/12/07

E.C.M.

DEPARTMENT OF THE INTERIOR,
COMMISSIONER TO THE FIVE CIVILIZED TRIBES.

In the matter of the application for the enrollment of

ALBERTIN HAMPTON

as a citizen by intermarriage of the Cherokee Nation.

CHEROKEE 58.

DEPARTMENT OF THE INTERIOR,
COMMISSION TO THE FIVE CIVILIZED TRIBES,
FAIRLAND, I.T. JULY 7, 1900.

In the matter of the application of Jane Elizabeth Hampton et al for enrollment as Cherokee citizens, said Hampton being sworn by Commissioner Breckenridge[sic], testified as follows:

Q What is your name? A Jane Elizabeth Hampton.
Q Qhat[sic] is your age? A 40.
Q What is your postoffice address? A Grove.
Q Where do you live? A At Cowskin Prairie four miles east of Grove.
Q Is that your permanent home? A Yes.
Q How long have you lived there? A 15 years.
Q Have you lived there continuously for the past 15 years? Are you a Cherokee? A Yes.
Q Yiu[sic] make application then as a Cherokee by blood? A Yes.
Q What is the name of your father? A Tholiver[sic] Thomas.
Q Was your father of Indian origin? A No sir.
Q Your mother, was she of Indian origin? A Yes.
Q When did your father die? A In '61.
Q Are you married? A Yes.
Q When did you marry? A In '74.
Q Does your name appear upon any of the official rolls? A Yes.
Q And your maiden name was what? A J. E. Thomas.
Q Your name is on the roll of '80 as J. E. Hampton? A Yes.

Cherokee Intermarried White 1906
Volume I

Q What is your township or district? A Deleware[sic].
Q I see on the roll of '80 an Elizabeth Hampton from Going Snake District? A Yes, I lived there at that time.
    Applicant,s[sic] name is found duly recorded on the Cherokee roll of 1880, page 440, number 864, Goingskane[sic] district.
Q Is your father living? A No sir.
Q Is you mother living? A Yes.
Q When did your father die? A In '61.
Q Have you children? A Yes.
Q How many children? A 8.
Q How many of them are under 21 years of age and unmarried? A 5.
Q Your husband is not an Indian? A No sir.
Q Will you please state respectively the names and ages of your children-- what is the name of the eldest one of your unmarried children? A Pearl, 18 years old. (who appears on the '96 roll).
Q The next one? A Mary, 16. (This child appears duly recorded on the roll of 1896.)
Q Your next child? A Dewitt, 12 years old. (This child is found duly recorded on the roll of 1896.)
Q Your next one? A Gracie, 9 years old. (This child is found duly recorded on the roll of 1896.)
Q Your next child? A Edgar, 5 years old. (This child is duly recorded on the '96 roll.)
Q None of them dead? A No sir.

    Brown McDonald being duly sworn by Commissioner C. R. Breckenridge[sic], says as Stenographer to the Commission to the Five Civilized Tribes, he reported in full the testimony of the above named witness, and that the foregoing is a full, true and correct transcript of his notes.
                                                Brown McDonald

Sworn to and subscribed before me this 10th day of July, 1900, at Fairland, I.T.

                                       Clifton R. Breckinridge
                                             Commissioner.

◇◇◇◇◇

DEPARTMENT OF THE INTERIOR,
COMMISSION TO THE FIVE CIVILIZED TRIBES,
FAIRLAND, I.T. JULY 9, 1900.

    In the matter of the application of Albertin Hampton for enrollment as a citizen of the Cherokee Nation, said Hampton being first sworn by Commissioner Breckenridge[sic] testified as follows:

A What is your name? A Albertin Hampton.
Q What is your age? A 47.
Q What is your postoffice address? A Grove.
Q Where do you live? A Near Grove in Deleware[sic] district.

Cherokee Intermarried White 1906
Volume I

Q That is your permanent home? A Yes.
Q How long have you lived there? A About 12 or 13 years.
Q Where did you live before that time? A In Flint District.
Q Where were you born? A In North Carolina.
Q Are you a Cherokee? A No sir.
Q Adopted citizen? A Intermarried citizen.
Q Are you on any of the rolls of the Cherokee Nation? A Yes, I guess on most all of them that have ever been taken here.
Q Are you on the roll of 1880? A Yes.
Q Where did you live in 1880? A In Going Snake District right on the line in the corner of the two districts.
Q A Burt Hampton who is recorded on the 1880 roll is the same as yourself? A Yes, I am the man.

This applicant is duly recognized as recorded on the roll of 1880 as Burt Hampton, page 440, number 863.

Q You do not wish to make application for any members of your family? A No sir, my wife has already applied for my children and herself and they have been admitted.

Brown McDonald, being first duly sworn by Commissioner Breckenridge[sic], says as Stenographer to the Commission to the Five Civilized Tribes, he reported in full the testimony of the above named witness and that the foregoing is a full, true and correct transcript os[sic] his stenographic notes.

Brown McDonald

Sworn to and subscribed before me this 10th day of July, 1900, at Fairland, I.T.

Clifton R Breckinridge
Commissioner.

◇◇◇◇◇

DEPARTMENT OF THE INTERIOR.
Commission to the Five Civilized Tribes.
Muskogee, Indian Territory, October 14th, 1902.

In the matter of the application of Albertin Hampton for the enrollment of himself as a citizen by intermarriage and for the enrollment of his wife, Jane E. Hampton, and his children, Pearl, Mary, Dewitt, Gracie and Edgar Hampton, as citizens by blood of the Cherokee Nation.

Supplemental to #58.

Cherokee Intermarried White 1906
Volume I

ALBERTIN HAMPTON, being duly sworn, testified as follows:

Examination by the Commission.
Q. What is your name? A. Albertin Hampton.
Q. How old are you? A. 47 years old.
Q. What is your post office? A. Groves.
Q. Are you a white man? A. Yes sir.
Q. You are on the eighty roll as a white man? A. Yes, sir.
Q. What is your wife's name? A. She signs her name J. E.
Q. Jane E.? A. Yes, sir.
Q. Have you and your wife lived together ever since 1880? A. Yes, sir.
Q. Made your home since 1880 in the Cherokee Nation? A. Yes, sir.
Q Never lived out? A. No, sir.
Q. Were you and your wife living together on the first of last September? A. Yes, sir.
Q. How many children have you? A. Eight.
Q How many living at home with you? A. I have five at home.

IIIIIIIIIIIIIIIIIIIIIIIIII

Jesse O. Carr, being first duly sworn, states that as stenographer to the Commission to the Five Civilized Tribes he reported the above entitled case and that the foregoing is a true and complete transcript of his stenographic notes thereof.

Jesse O. Carr

Subscribed and sworn to before me this 3rd day of January, 1903.

John O Rosson
Notary Public.

◇◇◇◇◇

C. 58

DEPARTMENT OF THE INTERIOR,
COMMISSIONER TO THE FIVE CIVILIZED TRIBES.

Muskogee, Indian Territory. January 2, 1907.

In the matter of the application for the enrollment of Alberten[sic] Hampton as a citizen by intermarriage of the Cherokee Nation.

Alberten Hampton, being first duly sworn by W. W. Chappell, Notary Public, testified as follows:

Cherokee Intermarried White 1906
Volume I

BY THE COMMISSIONER:

Q State your name, age and postoffice address? A My postoffice address is Grove; my age is 54 years old; Alberten Hampton.
Q You claim to be a citizen by intermarriage of the Cherokee Nation do you? A Yes, sir.
Q Through whom do you claim? A My wife.
Q What is her name? A Her name is Jane Elizabeth Hampton.
Q What is her citizenship? A Citizen by blood of the Cherokee Nation.
Q Is she living at the present time? A Yes, sir, she is still living.
Q Has she been enrolled? A Yes, sir.
Q Received her allotment? A Yes, sir.

The applicant, together with his wife, Jane E. Hampton, are identified on Cherokee Straight Card No. 58 as citizens by intermarriage and by blood of the Cherokee Nation, respectively. Also on the Cherokee authenicated[sic] tribal roll of 1880 and Cherokee Census roll of 1896 as an intermarried white citizen and by blood, respectively. The said Jane E. Hampton is on the approved roll of citizens by blood of the Cherokee Nation opposite No. 195.

Q When were you married to your present wife? A It was in January, I think it was the 20th day, 1874.
Q Had you ever been married prior to that time? A No, sir.
Q Had your wife been married prior to that marriage? A No, sir.
Q Where were you married, Mr. Hampton? A Flint District, Cherokee Nation.
Q Were you married under a Cherokee license? A Yes, sir.
Q Have you a copy of that license with you? A No, sir.
Q Have you made any effort to secure a copy of that license? A No, sir, I haven't.
Q Who issued this Cherokee license that you were married under? A Warren Adair. He was the clerk, and we was married by the judge up there.
Q Warren Adair was clerk of Flint District? A Yes, sir, and we was married by the District Judge, Sam Adair.
Q At the date of your marriage your wife was a citizen of the Cherokee Nation, was she? A Yes, sir.
Q Since your marriage where have you lived? A Right in the Cherokee Nation here.
Q What was your wife's name at the time of your marriage? A Thomas.

Page 124, book "B" "marriage record Flint District" now in possession of this office shows that on January 19, 1874, James W. Adair, Clerk District Court, Cherokee Nation, issued a Cherokee ~~license~~ marriage license to the applicant, A. B. Hampton, "to marry Miss Elizabeth Thomas, a Cherokee by birth", the said A. B. Hampton having complied with the requirements of the law regulating intermarriage with white men". That on the 20th day of January 1874, the marriage of the above named parties was solemnized by Samuel Adair, Judge District Court, Flint District, Cherokee Nation.

WITNESS EXCUSED.

Cherokee Intermarried White 1906
Volume I

F. Elma Lane, upon Oath, states that as stenographer for the Commissioner to the Five Civilized Tribes, she reported the proceedings in the above entitled cause, and that the foregoing is a true and correct transcript of her stenographic notes therein.

F. Elma Lane

Subscribed and sworn to before me this 3rd day of January, 1907.

Warren W. Chappell
Notary Public.

◇◇◇◇◇

E.C.M.

E.C.M.
Cherokee 58.

DEPARTMENT OF THE INTERIOR,

COMMISSIONER TO THE FIVE CIVILIZED TRIBES.

In the matter of the application for the enrollment of ALBERTIN HAMPTON as a citizen by intermarriage of the Cherokee Nation.

D E C I S I O N

THE RECORDS OF THIS OFFICE SHOW: That at Fairland, Indian Territory, July 9, 1900, Albertin Hampton appeared before the Commission to the Five Civilized Tribes, and made application for the enrollment of himself as a citizen by intermarriage, and for the enrollment of his wife, Jane E. Hampton, et al. as citizens by blood of the Cherokee Nation. The application for the enrollment of the said Jane E. Hampton et al. as citizens by blood of the Cherokee Nation has been heretofore disposed of, and their rights to enrollment will not be considered in this decision. Further proceedings in the matter of said application were had at Muskogee, Indian Territory, September 3, 1902, October 14, 1902, and January 2, 1907.

THE EVIDENCE IN THIS CASE SHOWS: That the applicant herein, Albertin Hampton, a white man, was married, in accordance with Cherokee law, January 20, 1874, to his wife, Jane E. Hampton, nee Thomas, who was at the time of said marriage a recognized citizen by blood of the Cherokee Nation, and whose name appears on the approved partial roll of citizens by blood of the Cherokee Nation, opposite No 195; that since said marriage the said Albertin Hampton and Jane E. Hampton have resided together as husband and wife, and have continuously lived in the Cherokee Nation. Said Albertin Hampton is identified on the Cherokee authenticated tribal roll of 1880, and the

Cherokee Intermarried White 1906
Volume I

Cherokee census roll of 1896, as "Bert Hampton", an intermarried citizen of the Cherokee Nation.

IT IS, THEREFORE, ORDERED AND ADJUDGED: That in accordance with the decision of the Supreme Court of the United States, dated November 5, 1906, in the case of Daniel Red Bird et al. vs. the United States, under the provisions of Section twenty-one, of the Act of Congress approved June 28, 1898 (30 Stat., 495), Albertin Hampton is entitled to enrollment as a citizen by intermarriage of the Cherokee Nation, and his application for enrollment as such is accordingly granted.

Tams Bixby
Commissioner.

Dated at Muskogee, Indian Territory,
this   JAN 18 1907

◇◇◇◇◇

Cherokee
58

Muskogee, Indian Territory, December 22, 1906.

Albertin Hampton,
    Grove, Indian Territory.

Dear Sir:

November 6, 1906, the United States Supreme Court held that white persons who intermarried with Cherokee citizens according to Cherokee law prior to November 1, 1875, are entitled to enrollment and allotment of land as citizens of the Cherokee Nation.

You are advised that to properly determine your right to enrollment as a citizen by intermarriage of the Cherokee Nation, it will be necessary for you to appear before the Commissioner for the purpose of giving testimony as to the date of your marriage and whether or not your wife, by reason of your marriage to whom you claim the right to enrollment as a citizen of the Cherokee Nation, was a recognized citizen of the Cherokee Nation at the time of your marriage to her, and whether or not you were married to her in accordance with Cherokee laws.

You are, therefore, directed to appear before the Commissioner at Muskogee, Indian Territory, at 9 o'clock A. M., on Wednesday, January 2, 1907, and give testimony as above indicated.

Respectfully,

J.M.H.

◇◇◇◇◇

Acting Commissioner.

Cherokee Intermarried White 1906
Volume I

Cherokee
58.

Muskogee, Indian Territory, January 18, 1907.

W. W. Hastings,
    Attorney for the Cherokee Nation,
        Muskogee, Indian Territory.

Dear Sir:

    There is enclosed herewith a copy of the decision of the Commissioner to the Five Civilized Tribes, dated January 18, 1907, granting the application for the enrollment of Albertin Hampton, as a citizen by intermarriage of the Cherokee Nation.

Respectfully,

Encl. H-40.
HJC

Commissioner.

◇◇◇◇◇

Cherokee
58.

W.W. HASTINGS.
ATTORNEY.

OFFICE OF

H.M. VANCE.
SECRETARY.

Attorney for the Cherokee Nation,
Muskogee, I. T.

January 18, 1907.

The Commissioner to the Five Civilized Tribes,
    Muskogee, Indian Territory.

Sir:

    Receipt is acknowledged of the testimony and of your decision enrolling Albertin Hampton, as a citizen by intermarriage of the Cherokee Nation. Time for protesting said decision is waived and I consent that said person may be placed upon the schedule immediately.

Yours very truly,
W.W. Hastings
Attorney for Cherokee Nation.

◇◇◇◇◇

Cherokee Intermarried White 1906
Volume I

Cherokee
58

Muskogee, Indian Territory, January 21, 1907.

Albertin Hampton,
    Grove, Indian Territory.

Dear Sir:

    There is enclosed herewith copy of the decision of the Commissioner to the Five Civilized Tribes, dated January 18, 1907, granting the application for your enrollment as a citizen by intermarriage of the Cherokee Nation.

    You will be advised when your name has been placed upon the schedule of citizens of the Cherokee Nation and approved by the Secretary of the Interior.

Respectfully,

Enc M - 5

M T M   Commissioner.

Cher I W 3
Trans from Cher 79 7-10-07

◇◇◇◇◇

E.C.M.

DEPARTMENT OF THE INTERIOR,

COMMISSIONER TO THE FIVE CIVILIZED TRIBES.

In the matter of the application for the enrollment of

AUGUSTUS C. SAGER

as a citizen by intermarriage of the Cherokee Nation.

CHEROKEE 79.

◇◇◇◇◇

Cherokee Intermarried White 1906
Volume I

DEPARTMENT OF THE INTERIOR.
COMMISSION TO THE FIVE CIVILIZED TRIBES.
FAIRLAND, I. T., JULY 10th, 1900.

IN THE MATTER OF THE APPLICATION OF A. C. Sager et al for enrollment as citizens of the Cherokee Nation, and A. C. Sager, being sworn by Commissioner, C. R. Breckenridge[sic], testified as follows:

Q What is your name? A A. C. Sager.
Q What is your age? A Sixty-four.
Q What is your Postoffice address? A Grove.
Q In what District to you live? A Delaware.
Q How far do you live from Grove? A Just a mile.
Q How long have you lived there? A About eighteen years.
Q Have you lived there continuously for the last eighteen years? A Yes sir.
Q Have you been out of the Territory? A Just visiting around.
Q Just visiting? A Yes sir.
Q Where were you born? A In Germany.
Q So you are not a Cherokee by blood? A No sir.
Q Have you ever been enrolled by the Cheroke[sic] tribal authorities? A Yes sir.
Q Does your name appear on the 1880 authenticated roll of citizens of the Cherokee Nation? A Yes sir.
(Records examined, and applicant's name found on Page 319, #2450, 1880 Roll)
Q Is your name on the 1896 census Roll? A Yes sir.
(Records examined, and applicants[sic] name found on Page 589, #504, as Augusta Sager, Delaware District)
Q Are you married? A Yes sir.
Q Under what law were you married? A Cherokee law.
Q Have you your marriage liscence[sic] and certificate? A I have not here; I have at home.
Q Is your wife living? A Yes sir.
Q Is she here? A No sir.
Q Where were you living at the time of your marriage? A In the State of Arkansas; I was married in Delaware District in 1870.
Q What was your wife's name before marriage? A Amelia A. Tittle.
Q When were you married? A In 1870.
Q Does your wife's name appear on the Roll of 1880? A Yes sir.
(Roll of 1880 examined, the name of applicant' wife appears on Page 319 thereof, #2451, as Amelia Sager)
Q Your wife is still living? A Yes sir.
Q What is the name of your wife's father? A Tittle.
Q Is he living? A No sir.
Q Is he on the Roll of 1880? A Yes sir.
Q What is his full name? A D. M. Tittle, is the way he signs it.
Q Is your wife's mother - what is her name? A Rosa Tittle.
Q Is she living? A No sir.
Q When did she die? A This Spring.

Cherokee Intermarried White 1906
Volume I

Q Is she on the Roll of 1880? A Yes sir.
Q Have you any children? A Yes sir.
Q Any children under twenty one years of age? A Yes sir.
Q Do you want to apply for them here to be enrolled? A Yes sir.
Q How many such children have you? A Threee[sic].
Q Three under twenty one years of age? A Yes sir.
Q What are their names and ages? A Lewis H. Sager, 16 years old. (Roll of 1896 examined, and on Page 534 thereof, #2898, appears the name of Louis Sager - 12 years of age at that time)
Q You[sic] next child? A James Sager.
Q Age? A Thirteen.
Q Age at the time he was enrolled? A Nine.
(Roll of 1896 examined, and on Page 534, #2899 appears the name of James F. Sager)
Q What is the next child? A Myrtle Sager.
Q How old is she? A Ten years.
(Roll of 1896 examined, and on Page 534, #2900 thereof, appears the name of Ollie M. Sager)
Q Is that all of your minor children? A Yes sir.
Q Have you had any children to die since 1880?, that were on the Roll of 1880? A Yes sir, one.
Q Was that child a boy or a girl? A Boy; he died fourteen years ago.
Q What was his name [sic] Robert Newton Sager.
Q How old was he when he died? A Five or six years old.
Q Your wife is living? A Yes sir
Q Where is your wife; here? A No sir.
Q How far from here do you live? A Ten miles.
Q Why did you not bring your wife in and enroll her? A They said it was not necessary.
Q Under what law were you married? A Cherokee law.
Q You say you have not your liscence[sic] or certificate with you? A No sir.
Q Does your wife's name appear on the Roll of 1880? A Yes sir.
(Examination of the Roll shows that his wife, Amelia Sager is o the Roll of 1880, Page 319, #2451)
Q Is her father living? A No sir.
Q Is he[sic] mother living? A No sir.
Q You are now living with your wife? A Yes sir/[sic]
Q When did you marry? A 1870.
Q Have you lived continuously with your wife all that time? A Yes sir.
Q And she is a Cherokee? A Yes sir.
Q What proportion of Cherokee blood does your wife claim? A Her mother was one eighth and her father a white man.
Q She claims one sixteenth, does she? A No; her mother was one fourth, and my wife claims one eighth.
(The names of A. C. Sager, his wife, Amelia A. Sager and his minor children, Lewis H. Sager, James F. Sager, and Ollie Myrtle Sager all appearing duly recorded on the authenticcated[sic] rolls of the Cherokee Nation, including the Rolls of 1880 and 1896, are identified as the persons thereon enrolled, and are enrolled by this Commission.

Cherokee Intermarried White 1906
Volume I

R. R. Cravens, being first duly sworn, states that as stenographer to the Commission to the Five Civilized Tribes, he reported the foregoing case, and that the above and foregoing is a true, full and correct transcript of his stenographic notes in said case.

R. R. Cravens

Sworn to and subscribed before me this 11th day of July, 1900.

Clifton R Breckinridge
COMMISSIONER.

◇◇◇◇◇

AAD

Cherokee Card 79

DEPARTMENT OF THE INTERIOR,

COMMISSION TO THE FIVE CIVILIZED TRIBES,

Muskogee, I. T., September 3, 1902.

In the matter of the application of Augustus C. Sager et. al. for enrollment as Cherokee citizens.

SUPPLEMENTAL STATEMENT.
o-o-o-o

An examination of the Cherokee census roll of 1896 for Delaware District shows that Augustus C. Sager is identified thereon, at page 589, No. 504, as "Augusta;" and that Amelia A. Sager is identified on that roll, at page 534 No. 2897.

C. R. Breckinridge
Commissioner.

◇◇◇◇◇

DEPARTMENT OF THE INTERIOR.
Commission to the Five Civilized Tribes.
Muskogee, Indian Territory, September 30th, 1902.

In the matter of the application of Augustus C. Sager for the enrollment of himself as a citizen by intermarriage of the Cherokee Nation and for the enrollment of his wife Amelia A. Sager and his children Lewis H., James F. and Ollie Myrtle Sager as citizens by blood of the Cherokee Nation.

Supplemental to #79.

Cherokee Intermarried White 1906
Volume I

J. C. STARR, being duly sworn, testified as follows:
Examination by the Commission.
Q. What is your name? A. J. C. Starr.
Q. Are you acquainted with Mr. Augustus C. Sager.[sic] A Yes, sir.
Q. How long have you known Augustus C.? A. Since 1880.
Q. Where has he lived since you have known him? A. Lived in the Cherokee Nation.
Q. Are you acquainted with his wife, Amelia A.? A. Yes, sir.
Q. How long have you known her? A. For the same length of time.
Q. Have they lived together as husband and wife since 1880 up to the present time?
A. Yes, sir.
Q. Never have been separated? A. No, sir, living together as husband and wife at this time.
Q. And were on the first of September, 1902? A. Yes, sir.
Q. Have they both lived in the Cherokee Nation from 1880 up to the present time?
A. Yes, sir.
Q. He has never married any other woman since you have known him?
A. He has never married any other woman since I have known him in 1880.

Jesse O. Carr, being first duly sworn, states that as stenographer to the Commission to the Five Civilized Tribes he reported the above entitled case and that the foregoing is a true and complete transcript of his stenographic notes thereof.

Jesse O. Carr

Subscribed and sworn to before me this 16th day of October, 19o2[sic].

BC Jones
Notary Public.

⋄⋄⋄⋄⋄

JOR.
Cher. 79.

Department of the Interior.
Commission to the Five Civilized Tribes.
Tahlequah, I. T., October 20, 1902.

SUPPLEMENTAL TESTIMONY in the matter of the application for the enrollment of AUGUSTUS C. SAGER as a citizen by intermarriage of the Cherokee Nation.

AUGUSTUS C. SAGER, being first duly sworn, and being examined, testified as follows:
BY COMMISSION: What is your name? A Augustus C. Sager.
Q How old are you? A Sixty-seven.

Cherokee Intermarried White 1906
Volume I

Q What is your post office address? A Grove.
Q Are you a white man? [sic]
Q Has application been made to this Commission for your enrollment as a citizen by intermarriage of the Cherokee Nation? A Yes sir.
Q Who made that application, did you or your wife? A I made it.
Q What is the name of your wife? A Amelia A. Sager.
Q Is she living? A Yes sir.
Q Is she a Cherokee by blood? A Yes sir.
Q Do you claim your right to enrollment by reason of your marriage to her? A Yes sir.
Q When were you and she married? A In 1870.
Q Were you married to her at that time according to Cherokee law? A Yes sir.
Q Does your name appear upon the roll of 1880? A Yes sir.
Q Were you ever married before you married her? A Yes sir.
Q What was the name of your first wife? A Mary Shelly.
Q Is she living? A No sir.
Q Was she living at the time you married your present wife? A No sir.
Q Was that the only woman you ever married before you married your present wife? A Yes sir.
Q Was your present wife ever married before she married you? A No.
Q You are her first husband and she is your second wife? A Yes sir.
Q Have you and she lived together continuously since your marriage? A Yes sir.
Q Were you living together on the 1st day of September, 1902? A Yes sir.
Q Never been separated at all? A No sir.
Q Have you resided in the Cherokee Nation continuously since you married her? A Yes sir.
Q Has she also? S[sic] Yes sir.
Q You have how many children that you made application for? A Three
Q Are all of those children living at this time? A Yes sir.

    This testimony will be filed with and made a part of the record in the matter of the application for the enrollment of Augustus C. Sager as a citizen by intermarriage of the Cherokee Nation, Cherokee straight card field No. 79.

Wm. Hutchinson, being first duly sworn, states that as stenographer to the Commission to the Five Civilized Tribes he correctly recorded the testimony and proceedings in this case, and that the foregoing is a true and complete transcript of the stenographic notes thereof.

                                                Wm Hutchinson

Subscribed and sworn to before me this 30th day of October, 1902.

                                                John O Rosson
                                                Notary Public.

Cherokee Intermarried White 1906
Volume I

Cherokee 79.

DEPARTMENT OF THE INTERIOR,
COMMISSIONER TO THE FIVE CIVILIZED TRIBES.
MUSKOGEE, I. T., January 2, 1907.

In the matter of the application for the endrollment[sic] of Augustus C. Sager as a citizen by intermarriage of the Cherokee Nation.

AUGUSTUS C. SAGER, being first duly sworn by Frances R. Lane, a Notary Public for the Western District of Indian Territory, testified as follows:

By the Commissioner:
Q What is your name? A Augusta C. Sager.
Q How old are you? A Seventy-one.
Q What is your postoffice address? A Grove, I. T.
Q You claim to be a citizen by intermarriage of the Cherokee Nation? A Yes sir..
Q Through whom do you claim to derive your rights as a citizen of the Cherokee Nation? A Amelia A. Tittel[sic]
Q When were you married to her? A In 1870.
Q What time of the year? A April.
Q Were you married under a Cherokee license? A Yes sir.
Q Have you got that license with you? A Yes sir.
Q Do you desire to offer this license in evidence? A Yes sir.
    Applicant offers in evidence certificate of marriage showing his marriage to Amelia A. Tittel[sic] on April 3, 1870, under a license issued by T. J. McGhee on March 26, 1870, the clerk of Delaware District, Cherokee Nation. Same is marked Exhibit A. and made a part of the record herein.
Q Were you ever married efore[sic] you were married to Amelia A. Tittle? A Yes sir.
Q To whom? A Mary Shalley.
Q Was she living at the time of your marriage to Amelia A. Tittel[sic]? A No, she died; she didn't live but about six months.
Q Was Amelia A. Tittel ever married before she married you? A No sir.
Q Where were you married? A In the Cherokee Nation.
Q Have you lived together continuously as man and wife in the Cherokee Nation since your marriage in 1870? A Yes sir.
Q Was your wife a citizen of the Cherokee Nation at the time you married her in 1870? A Yes sir.
Q Been on all the rolls of the Cherokees since that time? A Yes sir.
    The applicant is identified on the 1880 Cherokee roll opposite No. 2450.
    His wife, through whom he claims his rights to citizenship is identified on said roll opposite No. 2451. She is also identified on the final roll of citizens by blood of the Cherokee Nation opposite No. 257.

Frances R. Lane being first duly sworn states that as stenographer to the Commissioner to the Five Civilized Tribes she reported the testimony in the above entitled cause and that the above and foregoing is a true and correct transcript of her stenographic notes thereof.

Cherokee Intermarried White 1906
Volume I

Frances R Lane

Subscribed and sworn to before me this 4th day of January, 1907.

Edward Merrick
Notary Public.

◇◇◇◇◇

(The Marriage License and Certificate below typed as given.)

Exhibit a.

Cherokee Nation)
)
Delaware District)

To any Regular Admister of the Gospel to Execute and Return Greeting
You are Here By Command to Solemnize the Rites of Matrimony of marriages Between the Parties the following names August Sager a citizen of the United States and Mela Arline Tittle a Female Citizen of the Cherokee Nation.

Here in fail Not
Given Under My Hand offically This the 26th day March A.D. 1870

T.G.McGhee
(Clerk D C D D
(Cherokee Nation

This is to certefy that I joined in maridge the above maned persans Before witnesses according to the rules of my church on this the third day of April A D.1870

A.J.Farthing Minister of the Gospel

this is to certify By me that the within is a true copy from the Record on this the 7th Day nov 1887

T.J.McGhee
Clerk Del Dist C N

Lucas Isude to August Sager.

The undersigned being duly sworn states that as stenographer to the Commissioner to the Five Civilized Tribes, she made the above copy, and that the same is a true and correct copy of the instrument now on file in this office.

Mary Tabor Mallory

Cherokee Intermarried White 1906
Volume I

Subscribed and sworn to before me this the 15 day of January 1908

Chas E. Webster
Notary Public.

◇◇◇◇◇

E.C.M.   Cherokee 79.

DEPARTMENT OF THE INTERIOR,

COMMISSIONER TO THE FIVE CIVILIZED TRIBES.

In the matter of the application for the enrollment of AUGUSTUS C. SAGER as a citizen by intermarriage of the Cherokee Nation.

D E C I S I O N

THE RECORDS OF THIS OFFICE SHOW: That at Fairland, Indian Territory, July 10, 1900, Augustus C. Sager appeared before the Commission to the Five Civilized Tribes, and made application for the enrollment of himself as a citizen by intermarriage, and for the enrollment of his wife, Amelia A. Sager, et al., as citizens by blood, of the Cherokee Nation. The application for the enrollment of the said Amelia A. Sager, et al. as citizens by blood of the Cherokee Nation has been heretofore disposed of and their rights to enrollment will not be considered in this decision. Further proceedings in the matter of said application were had at Muskogee, Indian Territory, September 3, 1902, and September 30, 1902, at Tahlequah, Indian Territory, October 20, 1902, and at Muskogee, Indian Territory, January 2, 1907.

THE EVIDENCE IN THIS CASE SHOWS: That the applicant herein, Augustus C. Sager, a white man, was married, in accordance with Cherokee law, April 3, 1870, to his wife, Amelia A. Sager, nee Tittle, who was at the time of said marriage a recognized citizen by blood of the Cherokee Nation, and whose name appears on the approved partial roll of citizens by blood of the Cherokee Nation, opposite No. 257; that previous to said marriage the said Augustus C. Sager had been married to one Mary Shelly who died a short time thereafter, and before his marriage to the said Amelia A. Sager; that since said marriage the said Augustus C. Sager and the said Amelia A. Sager have resided together as husband and wife and have continuously lived in the Cherokee Nation. Said Augustus C. Sager is identified on the Cherokee authenticated tribal roll of 1880, and the Cherokee census roll of 1896, as an intermarried citizen of the Cherokee Nation.

IT IS, THEREFORE, ORDERED AND ADJUDGED: That in accordance with the decision of the Supreme Court of the United States, dated November 5, 1906, in the case of Daniel Red Bird et al. vs. the United States, under the provisions of Section twenty-one, of the Act of Congress approved June 28, 1898 (30 Stats., 495), Augustus C. Sager

Cherokee Intermarried White 1906
Volume I

is entitled to enrollment as a citizen by intermarriage of the Cherokee Nation, and his application for enrollment as such is accordingly granted.

                                           Tams Bixby
                                              Commissioner.

Dated at Muskogee, Indian Territory,
this JAN 17 1907

Cherokee
79

                              Muskogee, Indian Territory, December 22, 1906.

Augustus C. Sager,
        Grove, Indian Territory.

Dear Sir:

    November 6, 1906, the United States Supreme Court held that white persons who intermarried with Cherokee citizens according to Cherokee law prior to November 1, 1875, are entitled to enrollment and allotments of land as citizens of the Cherokee Nation.

    You are advised that to properly determine your right to enrollment as a citizen by intermarriage of the Cherokee Nation, it will be necessary for you to appear before the Commissioner for the purpose of giving testimony as to the date of your marriage and whether or not your wife, by reason of your marriage to whom you claim the right to enrollment as a citizen of the Cherokee Nation, was a recognized citizen of the Cherokee Nation at the time of your marriage to her, and whether or not you were married to her in accordance with Cherokee laws.

    You are, therefore, directed to appear before the Commissioner at Muskogee, Indian Territory, at 9 o'clock A. M., on Wednesday, January 2, 1907, and give testimony as above indicated.

                                            Respectfully,

J.M.H.   Acting Commissioner

Cherokee Intermarried White 1906
Volume I

Cherokee
79

Muskogee, Indian Territory, January 17, 1907.

W. W. Hastings,
    Attorney for the Cherokee Nation,
    Muskogee, Indian Territory.

Dear Sir:

    There is enclosed herewith copy of the decision of the Commissioner to the Five Civilized Tribes, dated January 17, 1907, granting the application for the enrollment of Augustus C. Sager as a citizen by intermarriage of the Cherokee Nation.

Respectfully,

Commissioner.

Enc I-21

RPI

◇◇◇◇◇

Cherokee 79.   W.W. HASTINGS.   OFFICE OF   H.M. VANCE.
                        ATTORNEY.   SECRETARY.

Attorney for the Cherokee Nation,
MUSKOGEE, I. T.

January 18, 1907.

The Commissioner to the Five Civilized Tribes,
    Muskogee, Indian Territory.

Sir:

    Receipt is acknowledged of the testimony and of your decision enrolling Augustus C. Sager as a citizen by intermarriage of the Cherokee Nation. Time for protesting said decision is waived and I consent that said person may be placed upon the schedule immediately.

Yours very truly,
W. W. Hastings
Attorney for Cherokee Nation.

◇◇◇◇◇

Cherokee Intermarried White 1906
Volume I

Cherokee
79

Muskogee, Indian Territory, January 19, 1907.

Augustus C. Sager,
    Grove, Indian Territory.

Dear Sir:

    There is enclosed herewith a copy of the decision of the Commissioner to the Five Civilized Tribes, dated January 17, 1907, granting your application for enrollment as a citizen by intermarriage of the Cherokee Nation.

    You will be advised when your name has been placed upon a schedule of citizens of the Cherokee Nation and approved by the Secretary of the Interior.

                  Respectfully,

Encl. H-86   Commissioner.
JMH

◇◇◇◇◇

Cherokee
I . W. 3

Muskogee, Indian Territory, April 8, 1907.

Augustus C. Sager,
    Grove, Indian Territory.

Dear Sir:

    Your marriage license and certificate, filed in connection with your application for enrollment as a citizen by intermarriage of the Cherokee Nation, is returned to you herewith, copies of the same being retained in this office.

                  Respectfully,

L M B   Acting Commissioner

Encl. B-*(?)*9

Cherokee Intermarried White 1906
Volume I

Cher I W 4
Trans from Cher 82 7-10-07

DEPARTMENT OF THE INTERIOR,
COMMISSION TO THE FIVE CIVILIZED TRIBES.
FAIRLAND, I. T., JULY 10th, 1900.

IN THE MATTER OF THE APPLICATION OF Solon James et al, for enrollment as citizens of the Cherokee Nation, and Solon James, being sworn by Commissioner, C. R. Breckenridge[sic], testified as follows:

Q What is your name? A Solon James.
Q What is your age? A Fifty-eight.
Q What is your Postoffice address? A Fairland?[sic]
Q How far do you live from Fairland? A About eight miles south.
Q How long have you lived there? A Twenty-three years.
Q Where were you born? A In Missouri.
Q Where did you live before you lived in the Territory? A In Missouri.
Q When did you come to the Territory? A When I was about eight years old.
Q Are you a Cherokee? A No sir.
Q What is your District? A Delaware.
Q Have you lived continuously in the Territory since you have been at you[sic] present residence? A Yes sir.
Q Have you ever been enrolled by the Cherokee tribal authorities? A Yes sir.
Q Does your name appear on the roll of 1880? A Yes sir.
Q Are you a Cherokee by inter-marriage? A Yes sir.
(1880 Roll examined, and on Page 271, thereof, #1367 appears the name of Solon James, Delaware District.)
Q Are you married at this time? A Yes sir.
Q Under what law were you married? A Cherokee law.
Q When were you married? A In 1866.
Q Is your wife still living? A Yes sir.
Q You and she are living together? A Yes sir.
Q Have you a liscense[sic] and certificate of your marriage? A No sir.
Q What was your wife's name before marriage? A Tennessee A Lane.
Q Is your wife present? A Yes sir.
Q Your wife's name is on the Roll of 1880? A yes sir.
(Applicant's wife's name, which applicant gives as Tennesee[sic] A. James on the Roll of 1880 as P. J. James, Page 271, #1868.
Q Your wife is here? A Yes sir.
Mrs. James being sworn, testified as follows:

Q What is your name? A Tennesee[sic] A. James.
Q What is your age? A Fifty-one.
Q Are you the wife of Solon James? A Yes sir.

Cherokee Intermarried White 1906
Volume I

Q You name appears on the records of 1880 as P. J. James? A It has been done through a mistake, I support; my name is Tennessee James (Tennessee A. James).
Q The record indicated you in every other particular; were you ever called by any other name? A No sir.
Q You think that it is simply a clerical error? A Yes sir.
Q You acknowledge that that is a record of your name? A I am Solon James' wife; he never had any other wife that I know of.

Mr. James re-examined, testified under oath as follows:

Q Have you any children under twenty one years of age? A Yes sir.
Q How many? A Four.
Q Please give their names and ages? A I have one that is living with me older than that that I want to give in.
Q Deal with the youngest ones first?
A Lula Bell James, 19 years old (Roll of 1896 examined, and on age 486 thereof, #1592, appears the name of Lula Bell James, Delaware District.
    Cornelia Jane James, 15 years old. On 1896 Roll, Page 486, #1593, Delaware District.
    Jesse Lamar James, thirteen years old. (Roll of 1896 examined, and on Page 486 thereof, #1594 appears the name of Jesse Lamar James Delaware District.)
    Claud James, ten years old. (On 1896 Roll as Claud Frank James, Page 486, #1595, Delaware District)
Q How old is your oldest child? A Twenty-six.
Q Girl? A Yes sir.
Q What is her name? A Clara Bell.
Q Unmarried? A Yes sir.
Q Has never been married? A No sir.
(Roll of 1880 examined, and on Page 272 thereof, #1372 appears the name of Clara D. James)
Q She is unmarried and living with you? A Yes sir.
Q Makes that her home? A Yes sir.
Q You give her name as Clara Dell James? A Yes sir.
Q Have you had any children to die that were enrolled in 1880? A No sir.
    Mr. James, your name and the name of your wife and the names of your children have been duly authenticated upon the rolls, as indicated in the evidence, as citizens of the Cherokee Nation: You will be enrolled by this Commission as an inter-married citizen, and the others as citizens by blood.

R. R. Cravens, being first duly sworn, states that as stenographer to the Commission to the Five Civilized Tribes, he reported the foregoing case, and that the foregoing and above is a true, full and correct transcript of his stenographic notes in said case.

                                                     R. R. Cravens

Cherokee Intermarried White 1906
Volume I

Sworn to and subscribed before me this 11th day of July, 1900.

          Clifton R. Breckinridge
          COMMISSIONER.

Cherokee 82.

      Department of the Interior,
      Commission to the Five Civilized Tribes,
      Muskogee, Indian Territory I. T., September 22, 1902.

In the matter of the application of Solon James for enrollment as a citizen by intermarriage of the Cherokee Nation.
Cherokee Nation appears by W. W. Hastings.

  Francis M. Conner, being duly sworn and examined by the Commission, testified as follows:
Q What is your name, age and postoffice address? A Francis M. Conner, Fairland, I. T., 50 years old.
Q Are you acquainted with Solon James, the applicant in this case? A Yes sir.
Q How long have you known him? A Twenty-five years.
Q Is he a white man or Cherokee by blood? A White man.
Q Do you know his wife? A Yes sir.
Q What is her name? A I don't know whether I can give her given name. I can't think of it.
Q Where does Solon James live? A He lives about between six and seven miles southeast of Fairland.
Q In the Cherokee Nation? A Yes sir.
Q Has he always lived in the Cherokee Nation since you learned to know him? A Yes sir.
Q Do you know whether or not he has been married more than once? A No sir, he hasn't been married more than once since I knew him.
Q Is he living with the same wife that he was living with when you first learned to know him? A Yes sir.
Q Living together at the present time? A Yes sir.

  The undersigned, being duly sworn, states that as stenographer to the Commission to the Five Civilized Tribes he correctly recorded the testimony and proceedings in this case, and that the foregoing is a true and correct transcript of his stenographic notes thereof.
          EG Rothenberger

Cherokee Intermarried White 1906
Volume I

Subscribed and sworn to before me this 24th day of September, 1902.

BC Jones
Notary Public.

◇◇◇◇◇◇

AAD

Cherokee Card 82

DEPARTMENT OF THE INTERIOR,
COMMISSION TO THE FIVE CIVILIZED TRIBES,
Muskogee, I. T., September 3, 1902.

In the matter of the application of James Solon et. al. for enrollment as Cherokee citizens.

SUPPLEMENTAL STATEMENT.
o-o-o-o

An examination of the Cherokee census roll of 1896 for Delaware District shows that James Solon is identified thereon, at page 578, No. 280: that Tennessee A. James is identified on that roll, at page 486, No. 1588; and that Clara Dell James is also identified on that roll, at page 486, No. 1590.

C.R. Breckinridge
Commissioner.

◇◇◇◇◇◇

C.F.B.

Cherokee 82

DEPARTMENT OF THE INTERIOR,
COMMISSIONER TO THE FIVE CIVILIZED TRIBES.
MUSKOGEE, IND. TER. JANUARY 2, 1907.

In the matter of the application for the enrollment of SOLON JAMES is[sic] a citizen by intermarriage of the Cherokee Nation.

Applicant appears in person;
APPEARANCES: Cherokee Nation represented by H.M. Vance, on behalf of W. W. Hastings, Attorney.

SOLON JAMES being duly sworn by John E. Tidwell, a Notary Public, testified as follows:

Q. What is your name? A. Solon James.
Q. What is your age? [sic] Sixty-five; will be Sixty-six next Saturday.
Q. What is your postoffice address? A. Fairland, I.T.

Cherokee Intermarried White 1906
Volume I

Q. Are you an applicant for enrollment as a citizen by intermarriage of the Cherokee Nation? A. I am.
Q. You have no Cherokee blood? A. No sir.
Q You claim solely by reason of your marriage to a citizen of the Cherokee Nation? A. Yes sir.
Q. What is the name of the person through whom you claim the right to enrollment? A. Tennessee A. James.
Q. When were you married to her? A. Well, we were first married-Now understand-- the first time on the 16th day of October, 1866.
Q. She was your first wife? A. Yes sir.
Q. You were her first husband? A. Yes sir.
Q. You say you were first married to her in 1866, when were you married to her the second time, of you were married a second time
Q.[sic] Well, we moved to the Cherokee Nation from the Neutral Ground in Kansas; the Cherokee country there, you understand, and we moved down here after the treaty of '66; and we were married here in '69, under a license I got here.
Q. Have you any documentary evidence to show that marriage? A. No sir, I have not.
Q. Did you secure a marriage license here? A. Yes sir, I did.
Q. Was your wife a recognized citizen of the Cherokee Nation at the time you married her? A. Yes ir.
Q. Since your marriage have you and she continuously resided together and in the Cherokee Nation? A. Yes sir. Well- no- I went up to Baxter Springs, moved part of our things, and stayed there about three months once, when I was sick; came back when I got well.
Q. Any absence that you have made from the Cherokee Nation has been of a temporary nature? A. Yes sir, the Nation has always been my home.
Q To whom did you go get your marriage license? A. I went to the Clerk.
Q. In what District? A. Delaware District.
Q. Cherokee Nation? A. Cherokee Nation.
Q. The Clerk of Delaware District issued you a marriage license to marry a citizen of the Cherokee Nation? A. Yes sir.
Q. The license was in due form? A. I suppose so.
Q. You have not got it with you? A. No sir, I returned them as I was required to do and I never got a certificate.
Q. What was the date of your marriage under Cherokee license? A. I could not give the exact date; it was in September I think.
Q. In what year? A. In 1869.

The original Marriage Record of the Cherokee Nation for Delaware District is now in the possession of this office, and the same shows that on October 29, 1869, a license was issued Solon James to marry Tanasse Lane, a Cherokee citizen, in accordance with Cherokee law, and that the same was returned for record on November 7, 1869.

The applicant, Solon James, is identified on the Cherokee authenticated tribal roll of 1880, Delaware District, No. 1367. His wife, Tennessee A. James, is

Cherokee Intermarried White 1906
Volume I

included in an approved partial roll of Citizens by Blood of the Cherokee Nation opposite Number 266.

The undersigned being first duly sworn, states that as stenographer to the Commissioner to the Five Civilized Tribes she correctly recorded the testimony taken in the above case and that the above and foregoing is a full, true and correct transcript of her stenographic notes thereof.

Lucy M Bowman

Subscribed and sworn to before me this 3rd day of January, 1907.

B.P. Rasmus
Notary Public.

◇◇◇◇◇

E.C.M.

E.C.M.   Cherokee 82.

DEPARTMENT OF THE INTERIOR,

COMMISSIONER TO THE FIVE CIVILIZED TRIBES.

In the matter of the application for the enrollment of SOLON JAMES as a citizen by intermarriage of the Cherokee Nation.

D E C I S I O N

THE RECORDS OF THIS OFFICE SHOW: That at Fairland, Indian Territory, July 10, 1900, Solon James appeared before the Commission to the Five Civilized Tribes, and made application for the enrollment of himself as a citizen by intermarriage, and for the enrollment of his wife, Tennessee A. James, et al., as citizens by blood of the Cherokee Nation. The application for the enrollment of the said Tennessee A. James et al. as citizens by blood of the Cherokee Nation has been heretofore disposed of, and their rights to enrollment will not be considered in this decision. Further proceedings in the matter of said application were had at Muskogee, Indian Territory, September 22, and September 3, 1902, and January 2, 1907.

THE EVIDENCE IN THIS CASE SHOWS: That the applicant herein, Solon James, a white man, was married, in accordance with Cherokee law in the year 1869, to his wife, Tennessee A. James, nee Lane, who was at the time of said marriage a recognized citizen by blood of the Cherokee Nation, and whose name appears on the approved partial roll of citizens by blood of the Cherokee Nation, opposite No. 266; that

Cherokee Intermarried White 1906
Volume I

since said marriage the said Solon James and Tennessee A. James have resided together as husband and wife, and have continuously lived in the Cherokee Nation. Said Solon James is identified on the Cherokee authenticated tribal roll of 1880, and the Cherokee census roll of 1896, as an intermarried citizen of the Cherokee Nation.

IT IS, THEREFORE, ORDERED AND ADJUDGED: That in accordance with the decision of the Supreme Court of the United States, dated November 5, 1906, in the case of Daniel Red Bird et al. vs. the United States, under the provisions of Section 21, of the Act of Congress approved June 28, 1898 (30 Stat., 495), Solon James is entitled to enrollment as a citizen by intermarriage of the Cherokee Nation, and his application for enrollment as such is accordingly granted.

Tams Bixby
Commissioner.

Dated at Muskogee, Indian Territory,
this JAN 18 1907

◇◇◇◇◇

Cherokee
82

Muskogee, Indian Territory, December 22, 1906.

Solon James,
    Fairland, Indian Territory.

Dear Sir:

November 6, 1906, the United States Supreme Court held that white persons who intermarried with Cherokee citizens according to Cherokee law prior to November 1, 1875, are entitled to enrollment and allotments of land as citizens of the Cherokee Nation.

You are advised that to properly determine your right to enrollment as a citizen by intermarriage of the Cherokee Nation, it will be necessary for you to appear before the Commissioner for the purpose of giving testimony as to the date of your marriage and whether or not your wife, by reason of your marriage to whom you claim the right to enrollment as a citizen of the Cherokee Nation, was a recognized citizen of the Cherokee Nation at the time of your marriage to her, and whether or not you were married to her in accordance with Cherokee laws.

You are therefore directed to appear before the Commissioner at Muskogee, Indian Territory, at 9 o'clock A. M., on Wednesday, January 2, 1907, and give testimony as above indicated.

Respectfully,

J.M.H.   Acting Commissioner

◇◇◇◇◇

Cherokee Intermarried White 1906
Volume I

Cherokee
82.

Muskogee, Indian Territory, January 18, 1907.

W. W. Hastings,
    Attorney for the Cherokee Nation,
        Muskogee, Indian Territory.

Dear Sir:

    There is enclosed herewith a copy of the decision of the Commissioner to the Five Civilized Tribes, dated January 18, 1907, granting the application for the enrollment of Solon James as a citizen by intermarriage of the Cherokee Nation.

                Respectfully,

Encl. HJ-39.
HJC
                                                  Commissioner.

<><><><><>

Cherokee   W.W. HASTINGS,   OFFICE OF   H.M. VANCE.
82.   ATTORNEY.   SECRETARY.

Attorney for the Cherokee Nation,
MUSKOGEE, I. T.

                                                        January 18, 1907.

The Commissioner to the Five Civilized Tribes,
    Muskogee, Indian Territory.

Sir;

    Receipt is acknowledged of the testimony and of your decision enrolling Solon James, as a citizen by intermarriage of the Cherokee Nation. Time for protesting said decision is waived and I consent that said person may be placed upon the schedule immediately.

                                  Yours very truly,
                                    W. W. Hastings
                                Attorney for Cherokee Nation.

Cherokee Intermarried White 1906
Volume I

Cherokee
82

Muskogee, Indian Territory, January 21, 1907.

Solon James,
    Fairland, Indian Territory.

Dear Sir:

There is enclosed herewith copy of the decision of the Commissioner to the Five Civilized Tribes, dated January 18, 1907, granting the application for your enrollment as a citizen by intermarriage of the Cherokee Nation.

You will be advised when your name has been placed upon the schedule of citizens of the Cherokee Nation and approved by the Secretary of the Interior.

Respectfully,

Enc M - 6

M.T.M.   Commissioner.

Cher I W 5
Trans from Cher 91 7-10-07

◇◇◇◇◇

DEPARTMENT OF THE INTERIOR,

COMMISSIONER TO THE FIVE CIVILIZED TRIBES.

In the matter of the application for the enrollment of

ROXIE S. FREEMAN

as a citizen by intermarriage of the Cherokee Nation.

CHEROKEE 91.

◇◇◇◇◇

Cherokee Intermarried White 1906
Volume I

DEPARTMENT OF THE INTERIOR,
COMMISSION TO THE FIVE CIVILIZED TRIBES,
FAIRLAND, I.T. JULY 10, 1900.

In the matter of the application of D. W. Freeman et als[sic]., for enrollment as Cherokee citizens, said Freeman being sworn by Commissioner Breckenridge[sic], testified as follows:

Q What is your name? A D. W. Freeman.
Q What is your age? A 47.
Q What is your postoffice address? A Fairland.
Q Where do you live? A Fairland.
Q Is that your permanent residence? A Yes.
Q How long have you lived here? A Seven years.
Q Delaware is your district? A Yes.
Q Where were you born? A In Delaware district.
Q Have you lived in this district all your life? A No sir.
Q You have lived in this locality seven years? A Yes.
Q Where did you live immediately before that? A Maysville, Ark.
Q How long did you live there? A 10 or 12 years.
Q Where did you live before that? A Down at Tahlequah.
Q Did you live all your life previous to this residence you speak of in Arkansaw[sic] in the Territory? A Yes, I was in the Choctaw Nation then.
Q Do you make application as a Cherokee by blood? A Yes.
Q Do you apply through your father or mother? A Mother.
Q Is your father living? A No sir.
Q Is he enrolled on he roll of '80? A No sir.
Q Is your mother living? A No sir.
Q Does your name appear upon the roll of 1880? A Yes sir.
    The record shows that Mr. Freeman's name appears duly enrolled on the roll of '80, page 255, number 992.
Q Mr. Freeman, are you married? A Yes.
Q What percentage of Cherokee blood do you claim? A About 1/16.
Q Under what law were you married? A Under the Arkansaw[sic] law in Arkansaw.
Q When were you married? A In '75.
Q Is your wife now living? A Yes sir.
Q Is she on the roll of 1880? A Yes.
Q What is her name? A Roxie Levania.
Q What is her age? A 42 years.
Q You say that your wife is on the roll of '80? A Yes sir.
    The roll being consulted his wife is identified as R. S. Freeman, page 255, number 993.
Q Mr. Freeman, you are living with your wife at this time? A Yes sir.
Q Have you any children under 21 years of age which you want to enter? A Yes. William Clyde Freeman, 16 years old. (This child is duly identified on the roll of '96 as Clyde Freeman, page 472 number 1218.)

Cherokee Intermarried White 1906
Volume I

[sic] Mr. Freeman, your name and the name of your wife being duly identified on the roll of 1880, as indicated in the testimony, and your child, Clyde Freeman, properly, William Clyde Freeman, being duly identified on the roll of 1896, as indicated in the testimony, you will all three be enrolled upon the roll now being prepared by the Dawes Commission.

Brown McDonald, being sworn by Com'r. Breckenride[sic], says that as Stenographer to the Commission to the Five Civilized Tribes, he reported in full the testimony of the above named witness, and that the foregoing is a full, true and correct transcript of his notes.

Brown McDonald

Sworn to and subscribed before me this 11th day of July, 1900, at Fairland, I. T.

Clifton R. Breckinridge
Commissioner.

◇◇◇◇◇

Filed With Cherokee No. 91.

Department of the Interior,
Commission to the Five Civilized Tribes,
Muskogee, I. T. February 26, 1902.

4850.

In the matter of the application for identification as Mississippi Choctaws of Roxanna Freeman for herself and her minor son, William Clyde Freeman.

Applicants represented by attorney J. G. Ralls; No appearances.

Roxanna Freeman being first duly sworn testifies as follows:

Examination by the Commission.

Q What is your name? A Roxanna Freeman.
Q What is your age? A Forty-five.
Q What is your postoffice address? A Fairland, Indian Territory.
Q How long have you lived there? A We have lived there eight years I believe.
Q Where did you live before that? A Maysville, Arkansas.
Q Where were you born? A Sherman Texas.
Q How long did you live in Texas? A I was twelve years old when we left Texas.
Q And went to Arkansas? A Yes sir.
Q And lived there until nine years ago? A I lived in the Territory part of the ime[sic].
Q But for nine years continuously you have lived in the Territory? A Yes sir.
Q Is your father living? A No, sir; he is dead.
Q Is your mother living? A Yes sir.

Cherokee Intermarried White 1906
Volume I

Q What is your father's name? A Jackson D. Dumas.
Q What is your mother's name? A Lucinda Dumas.
Q That is her name now? A Yes, sir.
Q Has she a middle initial? A Lucinda Caroline.
Q You claim through your father or money[sic]? A Through my father.
Q How much Choctaw blood do you claim? A One-sixteenth.
Q Has your father ever been recognized in any way or enrolled as a member of he Choctaw tribe of Indians by the Choctaw tribal authorities or the United States authorities in Indian Territory? A No, sir.
Q When, and where, if your[sic] remember, were your father and mother married? A They were married in fifty-three and I believe they were married at Ripley, Mississippi; I am not sure about that.
Q By a minister and under a license? A I could not tell you.
Q You think you could produce evidence of their marriage later? A my[sic] brother has sent for it.
    A reasonable time will be allowed for that purpose.

Q Have you a husband living? A Yes sir.
Q What is your husbands[sic] name? A D. W. Freeman.
Q You make any claim for him as having Choctaw Indian blood? A No sir.
Q His blood is white is it? A No sir, it is Cherokee.
Q You make the claim then that he has Cherokee blood? A Yes sir.
Q But not Choctaw? A No sir.
Q Have you any children under 21 years of age and unmarried? A One.
Q You want to make application for that one? A Yes sir.
Q What is the Child's name? A William Clyde Freeman.
Q How old is he? A He is eighteen.
Q And he is the son of D. W. Freeman? A Yes sir.
Q And lives with you at your home? A Yes sir.
Q Has your husband been enrolled as a Cherokee? A Yes sir.
Q Do you know whether or not he has made application for the enrollment of this son? A Yes sir.
Q As a Cherokee? A Yes sir.
Q Has the son been enrolled? A Yes sir.
Q Have you been enrolled as a Cherokee? A Yes sir as an adopted citizen.

> It appears from an examination of the records of the Commission that the applicant and her minor child William Clyde Freeman have been listed for enrollment by the Commission as citizens of the Cherokee Nation; the applicant in chief under the name of Roxie L. Freeman as a citizen by intermarriage of the Cherokee Nation and her minor son as a citizen by blood of the Cherokee Nation and their names appear on Cherokee roll card field number ninety-one. The name of the applicant in chief is found upon the 1880 authenticated roll of the Cherokee Nation as a citizen of the Cherokee Nation the Delaware District, number 993 as R. S. Freeman and the name of her son William Clyde Freeman is found upon the 1896 census roll as a citizen of the Cherokee Nation, Delaware District, number 1218.

Cherokee Intermarried White 1906
Volume I

At this point in the examination it developing that the applicant Roxanna Freeman and her minor child William Clyde Freeman having been listed for enrollment as citizens of the Cherokee Nation the examination, at the request of the applicant in chief, is discontinued.

G. Rosenwinkel being duly sworn on his oath states that as stenographer to the Commission to the Five Civilized Tribes he reported in full all the proceedings had in the above entitled cause on February 26, 1902, and that the above and foregoing is a full, true and correct transcript of his stenographic noted in said cause on said date of February 1902.

G. Rosenwinkel.

Subscribed and sworn to before me this 1st day of March 1902.

Clara Mitchell Wood.
Notary Public.

I, Maragret[sic] Crutsinger, do hereby certify that as stenographer to the Commission to the Five Civilized Tribes I made the foregoing copy and that same is a true and complete copy of the original transcript.

Margaret Crutsinger

◇◇◇◇◇

AAD

Cherokee Card 91

DEPARTMENT OF THE INTERIOR,

COMMISSION TO THE FIVE CIVILIZED TRIBES,

Muskogee, I. T., September 3, 1902.

In the matter of the application of Daniel W. Freeman et. al. for enrollment as Cherokee citizens.

SUPPLEMENTAL STATEMENT.
o-o-o-o

An examination of the Cherokee census roll of 1896 for Delaware District shows that Daniel W. Freeman is identified thereon, at page 472, No. 1217, as "Daniel Webster Freeman;" and that Roxie L. Freeman is identified on that roll at page 572, No. 174.

C. R. Breckinridge
Commissioner.

◇◇◇◇◇

Cherokee Intermarried White 1906
Volume I

DEPARTMENT OF THE INTERIOR.
Commission to the Five Civilized Tribes.
Muskogee, Indian Territory, October 1st, 1902.

In the matter of the application of Daniel W. Freeman for the enrollment of himself as a citizen by blood of the Cherokee Nation; for the enrollment of his wife, Roxie L. Freeman, as a citizen by intermarriage of the Cherokee Nation, and for the enrollment of his son, William Clyde Freeman, as a citizen by blood of the Cherokee Nation.

Supplemental to #91.

W. W. HASTINGS, being duly sworn, testified as follows:
Examination by the Commission.

Q. What is your name? A. W. W. Hastings.
Q. What is your age? A. 35.
Q. Post office? A. Tahlequah.
Q. Are you acquainted with Daniel W. Freeman? A. Yes, sir.
Q. Are you acquainted with his wife, Roxie L. Freeman, who is an applicant before the Commission for enrollment as an intermarried citizen? A. Yes, sir.
Q. How long have you known Daniel W. Freeman? A. Well, I will say 30 years. Ever since I can remember.
Q. How long have you known his wife? A. The same.
Q. Did you know them before they were married? A. Yes, I knew them. I was a child.
Q. Is Daniel W. Freeman a citizen by blood? A. Yes, sir.
Q. Is his wife Roxie a citizen by blood? A. She is a white woman.
Q. Was Daniel W. ever married prior to his marriage to Roxie L.? A. No, sir.
Q. Was she ever married before? A. No, sir.
Q. Living together on the first of September, 1902? A. Yes, sir.
Q. Has Daniel W. Freeman resided in the Cherokee Nation all the time since 1880? A. No, I think he was in the mercantile business in Arkansas, just across the line.
Q. How many years? A. I don't remember just how many years he was there, but in '94 or 5 he moved up to Fairland. My recollection is that he has been living there since then.
Q. Was he residing in the Cherokee Nation June 28th, 1898? A. Yes, sir.
Q. Was his wife living with him June 28th, 1898, in the Cherokee Nation? A. Yes, sir.
Q. Have they lived in the Cherokee Nation since 1880 except for the year or so they were in Arkansas? A. Yes, sir.

Jesse O. Carr, being first duly sworn, states that as stenographer to the Commission to the Five Civilized Tribes he reported the above entitled case and that the foregoing is a true and complete transcript of his stenographic notes thereof.

Jesse O. Carr

Cherokee Intermarried White 1906
Volume I

Subscribed and sworn to before me this 24th day of October, 1902.

BC Jones
Notary Public.

◇◇◇◇◇

Cher-91

DEPARTMENT OF THE INTERIOR.
Commission to the Five Civilized Tribes,
Muskogee, I.T., October 23, 1902.

In the matter of the application of Roxie L. Freeman for enrollment as a citizen of the Cherokee Nation, and for the enrollment of her husband, Daniel W. Freeman, and her child William Clyde Freeman, as citizens by blood of the Cherokee nation[sic].

Roxie L. Freeman being first duly sworn, and examined by the Commission, testified as follows:

Q Your name is Roxie L. Freeman? A Yes sir.
Q How old are you? A 46 years.
Q What is your postoffice? A Fairland, I.T.
Q Is your name on the 1880 roll as an adopted citizen? A Yes sir.
Q What is your husband's name? A Daniel W. Freeman.
Q Is he a Cherokee by blood? A Yes sir.
Q Is he the husband through whom you are claiming citizenship rights? A Yes sir.
Q Was he your husband in 1880? A Yes sir.
Q You and your husband have been living together ever since 1880? A Yes.
Q You have never been separated? A No sir.
Q Has the Cherokee nation[sic] been your home all that time? A Yes sir.
Q You and your husband are living together now? A Yes sir.
Q How many children have you? A I have one dead and one living.
Q William Clyde, is that all the child that is living? A Yes sir.
Q He has lived in the Cherokee nation[sic] all his live? A Yes sir.

Frances R. Lane upon oath states that as stenographer to the Commission to the Five Civilized Tribes she correctly reported the testimony in the above entitled cause, and that the foregoing is an accurate transcript of her stenographic notes thereof.

Frances R Lane

Subscribed and sworn to before me this October 29th, 1902.

BC Jones
Notary Public.

◇◇◇◇◇

Cherokee Intermarried White 1906
Volume I

CHEROKEE - 91.

DEPARTMENT OF THE INTERIOR,
COMMISSIONER TO THE FIVE CIVILIZED TRIBES.
Muskogee, Indian Territory, January 2, 1907.

In the matter of making proof of the marriage of Roxie L. Freeman to her Cherokee husband, prior to November 1, 1875.

Roxie L. Freeman, having been first duly sworn by B. P. Rasmus, a Notary Public, testified as follows:

COMMISSIONER:

Q. What is your name? A. Roxie L. Freeman.
Q. What is your age? A. 49.
Q. Your post office address? A. Fairland.
Q. Do you claim rights as a citizen by intermarriage of the Cherokee Nation? A. Yes sir.
Q. Through whom do you claim the right to enrollment as an intermarried citizen of the Cherokee Nation? A. Daniel W. Freeman.
Q. When were you married to Daniel W. Freeman? A. We were married on the 14th. of February, 1874.
Q. Where were you living at the time of your marriage? A. In Arkansas.
Q. What place? A. Maysville -- right on the line. Part of the town is in the state and part in the Territory.
Q. Where was Mr. Freeman living at that time? A. In the same town, but he lived in the Territory part of it.
Q. Did you move to the Territory upon your marriage to Mr. Freeman? A. Yes sir.
Q. At once? A. Yes sir.
Q. Have you lived together continuously in the Nation since your marriage? A. Part of the time we lived in the State.
Q. How long did you live in Maysville? A. I don't know.
Q. What time was it you lived in Maysville? A. In about '77 I guess.
Q. How many years did you liv there? A. I don't know just how long we did live there.
Q. Had Mr. Freeman ever been married before he married you? A. No sir.
Q. Had you ever been married before you married him? A. No sir.
Q. Have you lived together continuously since your marriage? A. Yes sir.
Q. Was Daniel W. Freeman a citizen of the Cherokee Nation at the time you married him? A. Yes sir.
Q. Had he been admitted to citizenship prior to that time? A. He was born and raised right here in the Territory.
Q. Was he voting as a citizen at that time? A. Yes sir?[sic]

Cherokee Intermarried White 1906
Volume I

Q. Is he here today? A. No, he is not here. He has always voted in the Territory.
Q. Are you and Daniel W. Freeman living together at the present time? A. Yes sir.

(Commissioner -- The applicant is identified upon the 1880 Roll, opposite No. 993, and her husband is identified upon said roll opposite No. 992. The applicant is also identified upon the 1896 Census roll opposite No. 174, on page 572.)

Q. Were you married under a license? A. No sir.
Q. Have you a certificate? A. We got one two or three weeks ago He wrote to the man that married us.
Q. Do you want to file it? A. It is not fit to file. The man is old.

(Commissioner-- The applicant offers in evidence the certificate of J. M. McCraw, to the effect that he married her to D. W. Freeman, on February 14, 1874. The same is marked exhibit "A", and made a part of the record in this case.)

WITNESS EXCUSED.

Eula Jeanes Branson, being sworn, states that she correctly reported he proceedings had in the above and foregoing on the 2nd. day of January, 1907.

Eula Jeanes Branson

Subscribed and sworn to before me, this the 3rd day of January, 1907.

Walter W. Chappell
Notary Public.

(The Marriage Certificate below typed as given.)

febeuary the 14,1874
this is to certifie that I did solmonize & publish the writes of matrimony betwen
D W freeman & Roxie Dumas at or nere Maysville   Benton Co   Ark
revernt J M. Mc.Crow

Exhibit A.

The undersigned being duly sworn states that as stenographer to the Commissioner to the Five Civilized Tribes, she made the above copy, and that the same is a true and correct copy of the instrument now on file in this office.

Mary Tabor Mallory

Cherokee Intermarried White 1906
Volume I

Subscribed and sworn to before me the 15 day of January 1907

            Chas E Webster
             Notary Public.

◇◇◇◇◇

              Cherokee 91.

DEPARTMENT OF THE INTERIOR,

COMMISSIONER TO THE FIVE CIVILIZED TRIBES.

  In the matter of the application for the enrollment of ROXIE L. FREEMAN as a citizen by intermarriage of the Cherokee Nation.

D E C I S I O N

  THE RECORDS OF THIS OFFICE SHOW: That at Fairland, Indian Territory, July 10, 1900, Daniel W. Freeman appeared before the Commission to the Five Civilized Tribes and made application for the enrollment of his wife, Roxie L. Freeman, as a citizen by intermarriage, and for the enrollment of himself and his minor child, William Clyde, as citizens by blood of the Cherokee Nation. The application for the enrollment of the said Daniel W. Freeman and William Clyde Freeman as citizens by blood of the Cherokee Nation has been heretofore disposed of, and their rights to enrollment will not be considered in this decision. Further proceedings in the matter of said application were had at Muskogee, Indian Territory, February 26, 1902, September 3, 1902, October 1, 1902, October 23, 1902, and January 2, 1907.

  THE EVIDENCE IN THIS CASE SHOWS: That the application herein, Roxie L. Freeman, married February 14, 1874, in the State of Arkansas, one Daniel W. Freeman, who was at the time of said marriage a recognized citizen by blood of the Cherokee Nation, and whose name appears on the approved partial roll of citizens by blood of the Cherokee Nation, opposite No. 284; that shortly after said marriage the said Daniel W. Freeman and the said Roxie L. Freeman removed to the Cherokee Nation, where they continuously resided together as husband and wife up to and including September 1, 1902. The said Roxie L. Freeman is identified on the Cherokee authenticated tribal roll of 1880, and the Cherokee census roll of 1896, as an intermarried citizen of the Cherokee Nation.

  IT IS, THEREFORE, ORDERED AND ADJUDGED: That in accordance with the decision of the Supreme Court of the United States, dated November 5, 1906, in the case of Daniel Red Bird, et al., vs. the United States, under the provisions of Section twenty-one, of the Act of Congress approved June 28, 1898 (30 Stat., 495), Roxie L. Freeman is entitled to enrollment as a citizen by intermarriage of the Cherokee Nation, and her application for enrollment as such is accordingly granted.

Cherokee Intermarried White 1906
Volume I

Tams Bixby
Commissioner.

Dated at Muskogee, Indian Territory,
this JAN 18 1907

⋄⋄⋄⋄⋄

Cherokee
91

Muskogee, Indian Territory, December 22, 1906.

Roxie L. Freeman,
    Fairland, Indian Territory.

Dear Madam:

    November 6, 1906, the United States Supreme Court held that white persons who intermarried with Cherokee citizens according to Cherokee law prior to November 1, 1875, are entitled to enrollment and allotments of land as citizens of the Cherokee Nation.

    You are advised that to properly determine your right to enrollment as a citizen by intermarriage of the Cherokee Nation, it will be necessary for you to appear before the Commissioner for the purpose of giving testimony as to the date of your marriage and whether or not your husband, by reason of your marriage to whom you claim the right to enrollment as a citizen by intermarriage of the Cherokee Nation, was a recognized Cherokee citizen at the time of your marriage to him.

    You are, therefore, directed to appear before the Commissioner at Muskogee, Indian Territory, at 9 o'clock A. M., on Wednesday, January 2, 1907, and give testimony as above indicated.

                              Respectfully,

J.M.H.   Acting
Commissioner.

⋄⋄⋄⋄⋄

Cherokee Intermarried White 1906
Volume I

Cherokee
91.

Muskogee, Indian Territory, January 18, 1907.

W. W. Hastings,
    Attorney for the Cherokee Nation,
        Muskogee, Indian Territory.

Dear Sir:

There is enclosed herewith a copy of the decision of the Commissioner to the Five Civilized Tribes, dated January 18, 1907, granting the application for the enrollment of Roxie L. Freeman as a citizen by intermarriage of the Cherokee Nation.

Respectfully,

Encl. HJ-45.
HJC   Commissioner.

◇◇◇◇◇

Cherokee   W.W.HASTINGS.   OFFICE OF   H.M. VANCE.
                       ATTORNEY.   SECRETARY.
91
          Attorney for the Cherokee Nation,
                        MUSKOGEE, I. T.

January 18, 1907.

The Commissioner to the Five Civilized Tribes,
        Muskogee, Indian Territory.

Sir:

Receipt is acknowledged of the testimony and of your decision enrolling Roxie S[sic]. Freeman, as a citizen by intermarriage of the Cherokee Nation. Time for protesting said decision is waived and I consent that said person may be placed upon the schedule immediately.

Yours very truly,
W. W. Hastings
Attorney for Cherokee Nation.

◇◇◇◇◇

Cherokee Intermarried White 1906
Volume I

Cherokee
91

Muskogee, Indian Territory, January 21, 1907.

Roxie L. Freeman,
    Fairland, Indian Territory.

Dear Madam:

    There is enclosed herewith copy of the decision of the Commissioner to the Five Civilized Tribes, dated January 18, 1907, granting the application for your enrollment as a citizen by intermarriage of the Cherokee Nation.

    You will be advised when your name has been placed upon the schedule of citizens of the Cherokee Nation and approved by the Secretary of the Interior.

                  Respectfully,

Enc M - 12
M.T.M.   Commissioner.

◇◇◇◇◇

Cherokee
I.W. 5

Muskogee, Indian Territory, April 6, 1907.

Roxie L. Freeman,
    Fairland, Indian Territory.

Dear Madam:
    Your certificate of marriage, filed in connection with your application for enrollment as a citizen by intermarriage of the Cherokee Nation, is returned to you herewith, copies of the same having been retained in this office.

                    Respectfully,

L M D   Acting
Commissioner.

Encl. B-81

Cherokee Intermarried White 1906
Volume I

Cher I W 6
Trans from Cher 171 3-13-07

C.E.W.

DEPARTMENT OF THE INTERIOR,

COMMISSIONER TO THE FIVE CIVILIZED TRIBES.

In the matter of the application for the enrollment of

JAMES C. YEARGAIN

as a citizen by intermarriage of the Cherokee Nation.

CHEROKEE 171

DEPARTMENT OF THE INTERIOR.
COMMISSION TO THE FIVE CIVILIZED TRIBES.
FAIRLAND, I. T., JULY 13th, 1900.

IN THE MATTER OF THE APPLICATION OF Mary Jane Yeargain et al, for enrollment as citizens of the Cherokee Nation, she being sworn by Commissioner, T. B. Needles, testified as follows:

Q What is your name? A Mary Jane Yeargain.
Q What is your age? A Fifty two.
Q What is your Postoffice address? A Maysville, Arkansas.
Q Where do your reside? A Delaware District.
Q How long have your lived there? A Thirty three years.
Q What part of Delaware District? A In the north east corner I recon.
Q Have you lived there for the last thirty three years concinuously[sic]? A Yes sir.
Q You have never lived out of the Territory during that time? A No sir.
Q Are you a Cherokee? A Yes sir.
Q Make application as a Cherokee by blood? A Yes sir.
Q What is the name of your father? A George Kenney.
Q Is he living? A No sir.
Q What is the name of your mother? A Carrie Williams.
Q Is she living? A No sir, she is dead.
Q Are they on the Rolls of the Cherokee Nation, either of them?
Q[sic] They were on the rolls before the war.

Cherokee Intermarried White 1906
Volume I

Q When did they die? A They died before the war.
Q In what District do you claim residence? A Delaware.
Q You are on the Rolls of 1880? A Yes sir.
Q Under your present name? A Yes sir. (Roll of 1880 examined and on Page 345 thereof, #3111, Delaware District, appears the name of Mary J. Yeargain.
Q Do you know James Yeargain? A Yes sir; he is my husband/[sic]
Q Is he living? A Yes sir.
Q Where is he? A At home; he is not very well.
Q Does your name appear on the Rolls of 1896? A Yes sir. (Rolls of 1896 examined, and on Page 562 thereof, #3695 appears the name of Mary J. Yeargain) (Delaware District)
Q What proportion of Cherokee blood do you claim? A My mother was one sixteenth; I would be about one eighth.
Q Was your father a white man? A Yes sir.
Q Are you married? A Yes sir.
Q Under what law were you married? A Territory laws.
Q Have you a marriage liscence[sic] or certificate? A I have a liscence, but they are at home.
Q Where were you living at the time of your marriage? A Near Bentonville.
Q Have you any children under twenty one years of age living with you? A Yes sir, two.
Q What are their names? A Claybe Yeargain.
Q How old is he? What is hi proper name? A Turner Alvin Yeargain. (Roll of 1896 examined, and on Page 562 thereof, #3697, appears the name of Turner Alvin Yeargain)
Q What is the name of the other one? A Robert Percey Yeargain. (Roll of 1896 examined, and on Page 562 thereof, #3698, appears the name of Robert P. Yeargain.
Q They are the only two you have at home with you? A Yes sir.
Q Do you apply or the admission of your husband? A Yes sir.
Q What is his name? A James C. Yeargain.
Q How old is he? A Fifty eight.
Q What is his Postoffice address? A Maysville, Arkansas.
Q Where does he reside? A In Delaware District, close to Maysville.
Q How long has he been living there? A Thirty three years.
Q Living there continuously? A Yes sir.
Q Never lived out during that time? A No sir.
Q Is he your husband? A Yes sir.
Q Is his name on any Roll of the Cherokee Nation? A Yes sir?[sic]
Q Roll of 1880? A Yes sir.
(Roll of 1880 examined, and on Page 345 thereof, #3110, Delaware District, appears the name of James C. Yeargain) (Roll of 1898 also examined, and on Page 595, #612, appears the name of James C. Yeargain)
Q Turner Alvin Yeargain and Robert Percy Yeargain; are they his children? A Yes sir.
Q Are these children living with you and your husband now at this time? A Yes sir.
Q James Yeargain is living? A Yes sir..

James C. Yeargain's name appearing on the Roll of 1880, and satisfactory proof having been made as to his legal residence in this Territory, he being also identified on the Roll of 1896, appearing on both rolls as per page and number given in this testimony,

Cherokee Intermarried White 1906
Volume I

is ordered admitted to citizenship in the Cherokee Nation, as an intermarried citizen, and his name will be put on the Rolls now being made by this Commission. The name of his wife, Mary Jane Yeargain also appearing upon the Rolls of 1880, and satisfactory proof being made as to her residence, and that she is a Cherokee by blood; she being also identified on the Roll of 1896, as per page and number given in the testimony, and the names of Robert Percy Yeargain and Turner Alvin Yeargain, their children, being found on the Rolls of 1896, and being duly identified as the children of the said James C. Yeargain and Mary Jane Yeargain; satisfactory proof being made as to their legal residence in the Indian Territory; all of these persons are declared admitted as Cherokee citizens; their names will be enrolled on the rolls now being made by this Commission.

R. R. Cravens, being first sworn, states that as stenographer to the Commission to the Five Civilized Tribes, he reported the foregoing case, and that the foregoing and above is a true, full and correct transcript of his stenographic notes in said case.

R R. Cravens

Sworn to and subscribed before me this 13 day of July, 1900.

T.B. Needles
COMMISSIONER.

◇◇◇◇◇

SUPPLEMENTAL: CHEROKEE #171.

Department of the Interior,
Commission to the Five Civilized Tribes,
Vinita, I. T., October 17, 1901.

In the matter of the application of James Yeargain et al., for enrollment as Cherokee Indian citizens.

STATEMENT AND ORDER.

COMMISSIONER BRECKINRIDGE: On review of Cherokee straight case #171, the same being at present entitled James Yeargain et al., it is found upon consulting the rolls of 1880 and of 1896 that James Yeargain is upon both of said rolls as an adopted white, which conforms to statement made in the field judgment of his being an intermarried citizen of the Cherokee Nation, which statement appears to have been left out of the direct testimony.

It is further found that James Yeargain is entered upon the jacket of his case without the initial C., while the testimony and his enrollment uniformly give him as James C. Yeargain, and it is directed that the enrollment of his name be changed to correspond to this.

As regard the child, Robert Percy Yeargain; he is stated in the judgment as being identified on the roll of 1896, but that fact is omitted in the direct testimony. Upon

Cherokee Intermarried White 1906
Volume I

consultation this day of the rolls he is found to be on the roll of 1896, page 562, No. 3698, Delaware District.

It is directed that copies of this statement and order the attached t the copies of the testimony already filed in this case.

----****----

M. D. Green, being first duly sworn, states that as stenographer too the Commission to the Five Civilized Tribes he correctly recorded the testimony and proceedings in this case and that the foregoing is a true and complete transcript of his stenographic notes thereof.

MD Green

Subscribed and sworn to before me this October 17th, 1901.

C.R. Breckinridge

◇◇◇◇◇

Cherokee 171.

Department of the Interior,
Commission to the Five Civilized Tribes,
Muskogee, I.T., September 22, 1902.

In the matter of the of the application of Jams C. Yeargain for enrollment as a citizen by intermarriage of the Cherokee Nation.

W. W. Hastings, being sworn and examined by the Commission, testified as follows:
Q What is your name, age and postoffice address? A W. W. Hastings, Tahlequah, I. T, age thirty-five.
Q Are you acquainted with James C. Yeargain? A Yes sir.
Q How long have you known him? A More than thirty years.
Q Is he a white man? A Yes sir.
Q How long have you known his wife? A For that long any way, more than thirty years any way.
Q She is a Cherokee is she? A Yes sir.
Q Have they been living together continuously as man and wife since you learned to know them? A Yes sir.
Q Are they living together at this time? A Yes sir.
Q Have they always made their home in the Cherokee Nation? A Yes sir.
Q Making this their home at the present tim[sic]? A Yes sir.

The undersigned, being duly sworn, states that as stenographer to the Commission to the Five Civilized Tribes he correctly recorded the testimony and proceedings in this

Cherokee Intermarried White 1906
Volume I

case, and that the foregoing is a true and correct transcript of his stenographic notes thereof.

EG Rothenberger

Subscribed and sworn to before me this 25th day of September, 1902.

BC Jones
Notary Public.

◇◇◇◇◇

Cherokee 171.

DEPARTMENT OF THE INTERIOR,
COMMISSIONER TO THE FIVE CIVILIZED TRIBES.
MUSKOGEE, I. T., DECEMBER 27, 1906.

In the matter of the application for the enrollment of JAMES C. YEARGAIN as a citizen by intermarriage of the Cherokee Nation.

APPEARANCES:
For Applicant, present in person.
For Cherokee Nation, W. W. Hastings.

JAMES C. YEARGAIN, being first duly sworn by B. P. Rasmus, a Notary Public, testified as follows:

ON BEHALF OF THE COMMISSIONER:

Q What is your name? A James C. Yeargain.
Q How old are you? A 64.
Q What is your postoffice? A Maysville, Arkansas.
Q Are you an applicant for enrollment as a citizen by intermarriage of the Cherokee Nation? A Yes sir.
Q What is the name of your wife? A Mary Jane Yeargain.
Q Is she living? A Yes sir.
Q Are you and she living together? A Yes sir
Q Is she a Cherokee by blood? A Yes sir/[sic]
Q When were you married? A Married in 1869.
Q Have you an[sic] documentary evidence of your marriage? A I have got the license there.

Applicant presents a license issued by T. J. McGhee, Clerk of Delaware District, on the 24th day of March, 1869, and a certificate signed by James Neely, a Minister of the Gospel, certifying that he united in matrimony J. C. Yargain[sic] and Mary J. Kinney, the parties mentioned in the license on the 25th day of March, 1869.

Cherokee Intermarried White 1906
Volume I

The original records of marriages of Delaware District, Cherokee Nation, are in the possession of this office and the Record of the marriage of the parties mentioned in the license referred to is found in Book "S" of said records.

Q Are you the identical person mentioned in this license as J. C. Yargain[sic]? A Yes sir, but that name is not spelled right.
Q Is your present wife the identical person who is mentioned in the license as Mary J. Kinney? A Yes sir
Q Have you and she lived together continuously since your marriage? A Yes sir/
Q Were you ever married before you married her? A No sir
Q Was she ever married before she married you? A No sir.
Q Was she a recognized citizen by blood of the Cherokee Nation when you married her? A Yes sir/
Q Has she continuously lived in the Cherokee nation since then? A Yes sir, never lived anywhere else since.

The applicant and his wife are identified on the 1880 Authenticated Roll of citizens of the Cherokee Nation, opposite Nos. 3110 and 3111 respectively, Delaware District. They are isted[sic] for enrollment on Cherokee Field Card No. 171, and his wife as Mary J. Yeargain is identified upon an approved roll of citizens by blood of the Cherokee Nation opposite No. 560.

-----------------------oOo-----------------------

Geo. H. Lessley, being first duly sworn states that as stenographer to the Commission to the Five Civilized Tribes, he reported the proceedings had in the above entitled cause, and that the above and foregoing is a true and correct transcript of his stenographic notes thereof.

Geo H Lessley

Subscribed and sworn to before me this 10th day of January, 1907.

B.P. Rasmus
Notary Public.

(The below typed as given.)

COPY

This is to certify by me that J. C. Yeargan a white man was licens to marry Mary J. Rinney a female Cherokee on the 24th day March 1869 & the licens executed and return March the 25th 1869 Being with according to the Act past by the National Council bareing date Oct the 15th 1855 in regard to white men marring in this Nation.

T. J. McShee CK D.C.D & C N

Cherokee Intermarried White 1906
Volume I

The undersigned being first duly sworn states that as stenographer to the Commissioner to the Five Civilized Tribes, she made the above copy and that the same is a true and correct copy of the original marriage record now on file in this office.

Lola M Champlin

Subscribed and sworn to before me this 14 day of January 1907.

Chas E. Webster
notary public.

◇◇◇◇◇

C.E.W. Cherokee 171

DEPARTMENT OF THE INTERIOR,

COMMISSIONER TO THE FIVE CIVILIZED TRIBES.

In the matter of the application for the enrollment of James C. Yeargain, as a citizen by intermarriage of the Cherokee Nation.

D E C I S I O N

THE RECORDS OF THIS OFFICE SHOW: That at Fairland, Indian Territory, July 13, 1900, application was received by the Commission to the Five Civilized Tribes for the enrollment of James C. Yeargain, as a citizen by intermarriage of the Cherokee Nation. Further proceedings in the matter of said application were had at Vinita, October 17, 1901, at Muskogee, Indian Territory, September 22, 1902, and December 27, 1906.

THE EVIDENCE IN THIS CASE SHOWS: That the applicant herein, James C. Yeargain, a white man, was married in accordance with Cherokee law March 25, 1869 to Mary J. Yeargain, nee Kinney, who was at the time of said marriage a recognized citizen by blood of the Cherokee Nation, and who is identified on the Cherokee authenticated tribal roll of 1880, Delaware District, page 345, number 3111, as a native Cherokee, and whose name appears upon the approved partial roll of citizens by blood of the Cherokee Nation, opposite number 560; that since said marriage the said James C. Yeargain and Mary J. Yeargain have resided together as husband and wife and have continuously lived in the Cherokee Nation. Said applicant is identified on the Cherokee authenticated tribal roll of 1880, and the Cherokee census roll of 1896 as an intermarried citizen of the Cherokee Nation.

IT IS, THEREFORE, ORDERED AND ADJUDGED: That in accordance with the decision of the Supreme Court of the United States, dated November 5, 1906, in the case of Daniel Red Bird et al. vs. the united[sic] States, Nos 125, 126, 127, and 128, the said applicant James C. Yeargain is entitled, under the provisions of Section 21 of the Act of

Cherokee Intermarried White 1906
Volume I

Congress approved June 28, 1898 (30 Stat., 495), to enrollment, as a citizen by intermarriage of the Cherokee Nation, and his application for enrollment as such is accordingly granted.

                                        Tams Bixby
                                        Commissioner.

Dated at Muskogee, Indian Territory,
this   JAN 19 1907

◇◇◇◇◇

DEPARTMENT OF THE INTERIOR.
COMMISSIONER TO THE FIVE CIVILIZED TRIBES.

CHIEF CLERK,
    CHEROKEE LAND OFFICE.

DEAR SIR:

    The records of this office show   James C. Yeargain

listed on Cherokee card No. #6 to be prima facie entitled to enrollment as   Intermarried   of the Cherokee Nation for the following reason, viz: Is on Schedule for Departmental Approval

                                          Respectfully,

                                          Commissioner.

Dated   Feby 6, 1907

◇◇◇◇◇

Cherokee
171

                                Muskogee, Indian Territory, January 19, 1907.

W. W. Hastings,
    Attorney for the Cherokee Nation,
        Muskogee, Indian Territory.

Dear Sir:

    There is enclosed herewith a copy of the decision of the Commissioner to the Five Civilized Tribes, dated January 19, 1907, granting the application for the enrollment of James C. Yeargain, as a citizen by intermarriage of the Cherokee Nation.

Cherokee Intermarried White 1906
Volume I

Respectfully,

Commissioner.

Incl. C-22
LMC

◇◇◇◇◇

Cherokee 171   W.W. HASTINGS.   OFFICE OF   H.M. VANCE.
               ATTORNEY.   SECRETARY.

Attorney for the Cherokee Nation,
MUSKOGEE, I. T.

January 19, 1907.

The Commissioner to the Five Civilized Tribes,
    Muskogee, Indian Territory.

Sir:

    Receipt is acknowledged of the testimony and of your decision enrolling James C. Yeargain as a citizen by intermarriage of the Cherokee Nation. Time for protesting said decision is waived and I consent that said person may be placed upon the schedule immediately.

Respectfully,
W. W. Hastings
Attorney for Cherokee Nation.

◇◇◇◇◇

Cherokee
171

Muskogee, Indian Territory, January 21, 1907.

James C. Yeargain,
    Maysville, Arkansas.

Dear Sir:

    There is enclosed herewith copy of the decision of the Commissioner to the Five Civilized Tribes, dated January 19, 1907, granting the application for your enrollment as a citizen by intermarriage of the Cherokee Nation.

    You will be advised when your name has been placed upon the schedule of citizens of the Cherokee Nation and approved by the Secretary of the Interior.

Respectfully,

Commissioner.

Enc M - 7
M.T.M.

Cherokee Intermarried White 1906
Volume I

◇◇◇◇◇

Cherokee
    I . W. 6

Muskogee, Indian Territory, April 6, 1907

James C. Yeargain,
    Maysville, Arkansas.

Dear Sir:

    Your marriage license and certificate, filed in connection with your application for enrollment as a citizen by intermarriage of the Cherokee Nation, are returned to you herewith, copies of the same being retained in this office.

    Respectfully,

Encl. B-82   Actin[sic] Commissioner

L M B

Cher I W 7
Trans from Cher 204 3-16-07

◇◇◇◇◇

E.C.M.

DEPARTMENT OF THE INTERIOR,
COMMISSIONER TO THE FIVE CIVILIZED TRIBES.

In the matter of the application for the enrollment of

LEE B. SMITH

as a citizen by intermarriage of the Cherokee Nation.

CHEROKEE 204

◇◇◇◇◇

Cherokee Intermarried White 1906
Volume I

Department of the Interior,
Commission to the Five Civilized Tribes,
Westville, I. T., July 16, 1900.

In the matter of the application of Lee B. Smith et al for enrollment as Cherokee citizens; being sworn and examined by Commissioner Needles he testifies as follows:

Q What is your name? A Lee B. Smith.
Q What is your age? A Fifty-six.
Q What is your post-office? A South-west City, Missouri.
Q Where do you live? A Delaware District.
Q Do you make your residence in Delaware District? A Yes sir.
Q How long have you lived there? A Thirty years last fall.
Q You have lived there continuously? A Yes sir.
Q Are you Cherokee? A No sir.
Q For whom do you make application? A Myself, wife and one child.
Q You are a white man? A Yes sir.
Q Have you ever been enrolled by the Cherokee Tribal authorities? A Yes sir.
Q Your name apear[sic] upon the 1880 roll? A Yes sir.
　　Note: 1880 roll examined, page 312, #2286, L. B. Smith, Delaware District.
Q Does your name appear upon the 1896 roll? A Yes sir.
　　Note: 1896 roll examined, page 88, #492, Lee B. Smith, Delaware District.
Q Did you ever apply to the Cherokee Tribal authorities for citizenship in the Cherokee Nation? A Yes sir.
Q Were you admitted or rejected? A Admitted. I think it was in 1870 or 1871.
Q Did you ever apply to the Dawes Commission? A No sir.
Q Are you married? A Yes sir.
Q Under what law were you married? A The Cherokee Tribal law.
Q Have you a certificate of marriage? A Yes sir.
(Produces paper.)
Q Where were you living at the time you married? A Delaware District, where I live now.
Q What is your wife's name? A Florence C.
Q What is the date of your marriage? A 1980
Q Is your wife's name upon the 1880 roll? A Yes sir.
　　Note: 1880 roll examined, page 312, #2287, Florence C. Smith, Delaware District.
　　1896 roll, page 530, #2788, Florence C. Smith, Delaware District.
Q Is her name also on the 1894 roll? A Yes sir
Q What is the name of her father? A James Perry.
Q Is he a white man? A ~~Yes~~ No sir.
Q What is the name of her mother? A Susan Jane.
Q Is she alive? A No sir.
Q Is she on the 1880 roll? A I don't know; she died before 1880.
Q What proportion of Cherokee blood does your wife claim? A One-eighth.
Q Have you children under twenty-one years of age living with you? A No sir, I have one boy living with me over twenty-one.
Q What is his name? A Emmet B., he will be twenty-four years old soon.

Cherokee Intermarried White 1906
Volume I

Note: 1880 roll examined, page 312, #2291, Delaware District, Emmitt[sic] Smith. 1896 roll examined, page 530, #2790, Emmet B. Smith, Delaware District.

Com'r Needles: The name of L. B. Smith being found upon the authenticated roll of 1880, and also upon the rolls of 1896, according to page and number as indicated in this record, and he having made sufficient proof as to his continuous residence in the Cherokee Nation, and roof having been made that he was married in 1870 to Florence C. Perry; Florence C. Perry's name being found upon the roll of 1880; proof having been made as to her continuous residence in the Cherokee Nation a sufficient length of time to entitle her to citizenship, said L. B. Smith is ordered enrolled as an intermarried citizen and his wife as citizens by blood of the Cherokee Nation citizen by blood, and their names be placed upon the rolls now being made by this Commission. His son, Emmet B. Smith's name being found upon the rolls of 1880 and also the census roll of 1896, and proof being made as to his residence in accordance with law, he is also ordered enrolled and his name placed upon the rolls now being made by this Commission.

M.D. Green, being first duly sworn, states that as stenographer to the Commission to the Five Civilized Tribes he reported the foregoing case and that the above and foregoing is a full true and complete transcript of his stenographic notes in said case.

M.D. Green

Subscribed and sworn to before me this 16th day of July 1900.

TB Needles
Commissioner.

◇◇◇◇◇

Cherokee 204.

Department of the Interior,
Commission to the Five Civilized Tribes
Muskogee, I. T., October 3, 1902.

In the matter of the application of Lee B. Smith for the enrollment of himself as a citizen by intermarriage, and for the enrollment of his wife, Florence C., and child, Emmet B. Smith, as citizens by blood of the Cherokee Nation.

S. T. Lincoln, being sworn and examined by the Commission, testified as follows:
Q Give me your name, age and postoffice? A S. T. Lincoln, Fairland, age forty two.
Q Mr. Lincoln, are you acquainted with Lee B. Smith, an applicant before this Commission for enrollment as an intermarried citizen? Citizens by blood of the Cherokee Nation Yes sir.
Q What is his wife's name? Florence.
Q How long have you known Lee B. Smith? A About eighteen years, fifteen or eighteen.

Cherokee Intermarried White 1906
Volume I

Q Has he and his wife, Florence, lived together as husband and wife for the last eighteen years? A Yes sir.
Q Living together on the first day of September, 1902? A Yes sir.
Q He never has been married to any other woman in the last 18 years has he? A No sir.
Q How long has Lee B. Smith lived in the Cherokee Nation of your knowledge? A About 32 or 3 years.
Q Have Lee B. Smith and his wife, Florence, lived in the Cherokee Nation for the last twenty years? A Yes sir, for the last 32 years.
Q You know their son Emmet B.? A Yes sir.
Q How long has Emmet B. lived in the Cherokee Nation? A He is 26 years old and was born here.
Q Live here all his life? A Yes sir.
Q In the nation? A Yes sir.

The undersigned, being duly sworn, states that as stenographer to the Commission to the Five Civilized Tribes he correctly recorded the testimony and proceedings in this case, and that the foregoing is a true and correct transcript of his stenographic notes thereof.

EG Rothenberger

Subscribed and sworn to before me this 18th day of October, 1902.

BC Jones
Notary Public.

◇◇◇◇◇

JOR.
Cher. 204.

Department of the Interior,
Commission to the Five Civilized Tribes.
Tahlequah, I. T., October 10, 1902.

SUPPLEMENTAL TESTIMONY AND PROCEEDINGS in the matter of the application for the enrollment of LEE B. SMITH as a citizen by intermarriage of the Cherokee Nation.

LEE B. SMITH being first duly sworn, and being examined, testified as follows:

BY COMMISSION: What is your name? A Lee B. Smith.
Q How old are you? A Fifty-eight.
Q What is your post office address? A Southwest City, Missouri.
Q You are a white man, are you? A Yes sir.
Q Have you heretofore made application to the Commission for enrollment as a citizen by intermarriage of the Cherokee Nation? A I have.

Cherokee Intermarried White 1906
Volume I

Q What is the name of your wife? A Florence C. Smith.
Q Is she living? A Yes sir.
Q Is she a Cherokee by blood? A Yes sir.
Q Do you claim your right to enrollment by reason of your marriage to her? A I do.
Q When were you and she married? A That is very indefinite in my mind just now. I think it was in 1870 or 1871.
Q Were you married to her at that time according to Cherokee law? A Yes sir.
Q Have you and she lived together continuously since that time? A Yes sir.
Q Were you living together on the 1st day of September, 1902? A Yes sir.
Q You have never been separated at all? A No sir.
Q Were you ever married before you married her? A Never.
Q Was she ever married before she married you? A Never.
Q You are her first husband and she is your first wife? A Yes sir
Q Have you resided in the Cherokee Nation continuously since you and she were married? A Yes sir.
Q Has she also? A Yes sir.
Q You made application for the enrollment of how many children? A Just one.
Q Is that child living at present? A Yes sir.

This testimony ~~and procee~~ will be filed with and made a part of the record in the matter of the application for the enrollment of Lee B. Smith as a citizen by intermarriage of the Cherokee Nation, Cherokee straight card field No. 204.

Wm. Hutchinson, being first duly sworn, states that as stenographer to the Commission to the Five Civilized Tribes he correctly recorded the testimony and proceedings in this case, and that the foregoing is a true and correct transcript of his stenographic notes thereof.

Wm Hutchinson

Subscribed and sworn to before me this 17th day of October, 1902.

John O Rosson
Notary Public.

Cherokee Intermarried White 1906
Volume I

Cherokee 204.

DEPARTMENT OF THE INTERIOR,
COMMISSIONER T THE.
Muskogee, Ind. Ter., January 2, 1907.

In the matter of the application for the enrollment of LEE B. SMITH as a citizen by intermarriage of the Cherokee Nation.

LEE B. SMITH, being first duly sworn by Frances R. Lane, a Notary Public for the Western District of Indian Territory, testified as follows:

By the Commissioner:
Q What is your name? A Lee B. Smith.
Q How old are you? A Sixty-two years L[sic]
Q What is your postoffice address? A Southwest City, Mo.
Q You claim to be as a citizen by intermarriage of the Cherokee Nation? A Yes sir.
Q Through whom do you claim to derive such right? A Florence C. Perry.
Q When were you married to Florence C. Perry? A In 1870.
Q Where were you married? A Cherokee Nation.
Q Under Cherokee laws? A Yes sir.
Q Get a license from the Cherokee authorities? A Yes sir.

    Applicant offer in evidence marriage license issued to him on March 22, 1870 by T. J. McGhee, Clerk of Delaware District, Cherokee Nation, together with the certificate of his marriage to Florence C. Perry on April 3, 1907.

Q Were you ever married prior to your marriage to Florence C. Perry? A No sir.
Q Was she ever married prior to her marriage to you? A No sir
Q Have you lived together as husband and wife continuously in the Cherokee Nation since 1870 up to the present time? A Yes sir.
Q In the Cherokee Nation? A Yes sir.

    The applicant is identified on the 1880 Cherokee roll opposite No. 2286. His wife, through whom he claims the right to enrollment, is identified on said roll opposite No. 2287. His wife is also identified on the final roll of citizens by blood of the Cherokee Nation opposite No. 22327.

Witness excused.

Frances R. Lane upon oath states that as stenographer to the Commissioner to the Five Civilized Tribes she correctly reported the testimony in the above entitled cause and that the above and foregoing is an accurate transcript of her shorthand notes thereof.

Frances R Lane

Cherokee Intermarried White 1906
Volume I

Subscribed and sworn to before me this January 4, 1907.

                                                                            Edward Merrick
                                                                            Notary Public.

Cherokee Nation (
                         (
Delaware District. (

      To any regular minister of the Gospel or any of the judges of this nation to execute and return:

      You are hereby commanded to solomonize[sic] the rites of matrimony and marriage between L.B. Smith, a citizen of the United States and F.C. Perry, a female citizen of the Cherokee Nation according to the laws of the Cherokee Nation.

                                     Given under my hand officially this, the 22 day of March 1870.
                      Signed,

                                    (T.J. McGhee,
                                    (
                                    (Clerk D.C.D.D.
                                    (C.N.

      This is to certify that the rites of matrimony were celebrated between L.B. Smith and Florence C. Perry, April 3, 1870 by D.B. Cumming.

      The undersigned being duly sworn states that as stenographer to the Commission to the Five Civilized Tribes she made the above copy, and that the same is a true and correct copy of the instrument now on file in this office.

                                                   Mamie Tabor Mallory

Subscribed and sworn to before me this 10 day of January 1907.

                                                         Chas E Webster
                                                         Notary Public.

Cherokee Intermarried White 1906
Volume I

E C M   Cherokee 204

DEPARTMENT OF THE INTERIOR,
COMMISSIONER TO THE FIVE CIVILIZED TRIBES.

In the matter of the application for the enrollment of Lee B. Smith as a citizen by intermarriage of the Cherokee Nation.

D E C I S I O N .

THE RECORDS OF THIS OFFICE SHOW: That at Westville, Indian Territory, July 16, 1900, Lee B. Smith appeared before the Commission to the Five Civilized Tribes, and made application for the enrollment of himself as a citizen by intermarriage, and for the enrollment of his wife, Florence C. Smith and their son, Emmett B. Smith, as citizens by blood of the Cherokee Nation. The application for the enrollment of the said Florence C. Smith and Emmett B. Smith as citizens by blood of the Cherokee Nation has been heretofore disposed of, and their right to enrollment will not considered in this decision. Further proceedings in the matter of said application were had at Muskogee, Indian Territory, October 3, 1902 and October 10, 1902, and January 2, 1907.

THE EVIDENCE IN THIS CASE SHOWS: That the applicant herein, Lee B. Smith, a white man, was married in accordance with the Cherokee law, April 3, 1870, to his wife, Florence C. Smith, who was at the time of said marriage a recognized citizen by blood of the Cherokee Nation, and whose name appears upon the approved partial roll f citizens by blood of the Cherokee Nation, opposite number 22327; that since said marriage the said Lee B. Smith and Florence C. Smith have resided together as husband and wife, and have continuously lived in the Cherokee Nation. Said Lee B. Smith is identified on the Cherokee Authenticated Tribal Roll of 1880, and the Cherokee Census Roll of 1896 as an intermarried citizen of the Cherokee Nation.

IT IS THEREFORE ORDERED AND ADJUDGED: That in accordance with the decision of the Supreme Court of the United States, dated November 5, 1906, in the case of Daniel Red Bird et al. vs. the United States under the provision of Section 21, of the Act of Congress approved June 28, 1898 , (30th. Stat. 495) Lee B. Smith is entitled to enrollment as a citizen by intermarriage of the Cherokee Nation, and his application for enrollment as such is accordingly granted.

                                            Tams Bixby
                                            Commissioner.
Dated at Muskogee, Indian Territory,
this   JAN 16 1907

◇◇◇◇◇

Cherokee Intermarried White 1906
Volume I

Cherokee 204

Muskogee, Indian Territory, January 17, 1907.

W. W. Hastings,
    Attorney for the Cherokee Nation,
        Muskogee, Indian Territory.

Dear Sir:

There is enclosed herewith copy of the decision of the Commissioner to the Five Civilized Tribes, dated January 16, 1907, granting the application for the enrollment of Lee B. Smith as a citizen by intermarriage of the Cherokee Nation.

Respectfully,

Enc I-9

Commissioner.

RPI

◇◇◇◇◇

Cherokee
204

Muskogee, Indian Territory, January 19, 1907.

Lee B. Smith,
    Southwest City, Missouri.

Dear Sir:

There is enclosed herewith a copy of the decision of the Commissioner to the Five Civilized Tribes, dated January 16, 1907, granting your application for enrollment as a citizen by intermarriage of the Cherokee Nation.

You will be advised when your name has been placed upon the schedule of citizens of the Cherokee Nation and approved by the Secretary of the Interior.

Respectfully,

Encl. H-75
JMH

Commissioner.

◇◇◇◇◇

Cherokee Intermarried White 1906
Volume I

Cherokee 204

W.W. HASTINGS．　　OFFICE OF　　H.M. VANCE．
ATTORNEY．　　　　　　　　　　SECRETARY．

Attorney for the Cherokee Nation,
MUSKOGEE, I. T.

January 18, 1907.

The Commissioner
    to the Five Civilized Tribes,
        Muskogee, Indian Territory.

Sir:

    Receipt is acknowledged of the testimony and of your decision enrolling Lee B. Smith as a citizen by intermarriage of the Cherokee Nation. Time for protesting said decision is waived and I consent that said person may be placed upon the schedule immediately.

                                  W. W. Hastings
                                  Attorney for Cherokee Nation.

◇◇◇◇◇

Cherokee
    I. W. 7

                    Muskogee, Indian Territory, April 6, 1907

Lee B. Smith,
    Southwest City, Missouri.

Dear Sir:

    Your marriage license and certificate, filed in connection with your application for enrollment as a citizen by intermarriage are returned to you herewith, copies of the same being retained in this office.

                                  Respectfully,

Encl. B-83　　　　　　　　　　　　　　　　Acting Commissioner

Cher I W 8
Trans from Cher 325　3-18-07

◇◇◇◇◇

Cherokee Intermarried White 1906
Volume I

C.E.M.

DEPARTMENT OF THE INTERIOR,

COMMISSIONER TO THE FIVE CIVILIZED TRIBES.

In the matter of the application for the enrollment of

JOHN F.M. CHRISTIE

as a citizen by intermarriage of the Cherokee Nation.

CHEROKEE 325

Department of the Interior,
Commission to the Five Civilized Tribes,
Westville, I. T., July 18th, 1900.

In the matter of the application of John F. M. Christie for enrollment as an intermarried Cherokee, and for the enrollment of his wife and daughter as Cherokees by blood; being duly sworn and examined by Commissioner Breckenridge[sic], he testified as follows:

Q What is your name? A John F. M. Christie.
Q What is your age? A 66.
Q What is your post office A Westville.
Q Your district? A Going Snake.
Q For whom do you apply besides yourself? A For myself and family, wife and one daughter.
Q Mr. Christie, do you apply as a Cherokee by blood, or intermarriage? A No, sir, by intermarriage.
Q How long have you lived in this district? A I have lived here since 1869.
Q Been your home ever since 1869? A Yes, sir.
Q When were you married? A In 1869.
Q What is your wife's name? A Jane.
(On 1880 roll, page 418, No. 359, John Christie, Going Snake district. On 1896 roll, page 819, No. 49, John Christie, Going Snake district.)
(Jane Christie on roll of 1880, page 418, No. 360, Going Snake district. On 1896 roll, page 736, No. 508, Jane Christie, Going Snake district.)
Q You and your wife are living together at this time? A Yes, sir.
Q Now your daughter, Mr. Christie, what is her name? A Nancy Emma.

Cherokee Intermarried White 1906
Volume I

Q Has she ever been married? A No, sir.
Q What is her age? A 36.
Q Living with you? A Yes, sir.
(On 1880 roll, page 418, No. 363, Emma Christie, Going Snake dist. On 1896 roll, page 736, No. 520, Nancy Christie, Going Snake district.)

Mr Christie, your name and the name of your wife and the name of your daughter all are found on the roll of 1880 and the roll of 1896, You will be enrolled as an intermarried citizen, and your wife and daughter as citizens by blood of the Cherokee Nation.

------o------

Bruce C. Jones, being duly sworn, says that as stenographer to the Commission to the Five Civilized Tribes he reported the testimony of the above names witness, and that the foregoing is a full, true and correct translation of his stenographic notes.

Bruce C. Jones

Sworn to and subscribed before me this the 18th day of July, 1900.

CR Breckinridge
Commissioner.

H.
Cher. 325.

Department of the Interior,
Commissioner to the Five Civilized Tribes.
Tahlequah, I. T., October 7, 1902.

SUPPLEMENTAL TESTIMONY AND PROCEEDINGS in the matter of the application for the enrollment of JOHN F. M. CHRISTIE as a citizen by intermarriage of the Cherokee Nation.

JOHN F. M. CHRISTIE, being first duly sworn, and being examined testified as follows:

BY COMMISSION: What is your name? A John F. M. Christie.
Q How old are you? A Sixty-eight the 19th of last month.
Q What is your post office address? A Westville.
Q Are you a white man? A Yes sir.
Q Have you heretofore made application to this Commission for enrollment as a citizen by intermarriage of the Cherokee Nation? A Yes sir.
Q What is the name of your wife? A Jane Christie.
Q How old is she? A She is sixty-seven.
Q Is she living? A Yes sir.

Cherokee Intermarried White 1906
Volume I

Q Is she a Cherokee by blood? A Yes sir.
Q When were you and she married? A First married in Texas, but after I moved to the Cherokee Nation I had to marry over according to Cherokee law.
Q You made proof of your marriage, did you, according to Cherokee law, at the time you made application for enrollment? A Yes sir.
Q Do you claim your right to enrollment by reason of your marriage to your wife Jane? A Yes sir.
Q Were you ever married before you married her? A No sir.
Q Was she ever married before she married you? A No sir.
Q When did you come to the Cherokee Nation? A I believe it was the fall of 1867, either 1867 or 1868, I don't remember.
Q Have you resided in the Cherokee Nation continuously since the date of your application for enrollment? A Yes sir.
Q Have you and your wife lived together continuously since the date of your marriage? A Yes sir.
Q Are you living together now? A Yes sir.

      This testimony will be filed with and made a part of the record in the matter of the application for the enrollment of John F. M. Christie as a citizen by intermarriage of the Cherokee Nation the Cherokee Nation.

Wm. Hutchinson, being first duly sworn, states that as stenographer to the Commission to the Five Civilized Tribes he correctly recorded the testimony and proceedings in this case, and that the foregoing is a true and complete transcript of his stenographic notes thereof.

                                              Wm Hutchinson

Subscribed and sworn to before me this 10th day of October, 1902.

                                                John O Rosson
                                                      Notary Public.

⋄⋄⋄⋄⋄

C.F.B.   Cherokee 325.

DEPARTMENT OF THE INTERIOR,
COMMISSIONER TO THE FIVE CIVILIZED TRIBES.
MUSKOGEE, I. T., JANUARY 2, 1907.

      In the matter of the application for the enrollment of John F. M. Christie as a citizen by intermarriage of the Cherokee Nation.

    APPEARANCES: Applicant appears in person.
                               Cherokee Nation represented by H. M. Vance,
                               on behalf of W. W. Hastings, Attorney.

Cherokee Intermarried White 1906
Volume I

JOHN F. M. CHRISTIE, being first duly sworn by John E. Tidwell, notary public, testified as follows:

ON BEHALF OF THE COMMISSIONER:

Q What is your name? A John F. M. Christie.
Q What is your age? A 73.
Q What is your post office address? A Christie, Indian Territory.
Q You are an applicant for enrollment as a citizen by intermarriage of the Cherokee Nation, are you? A Yes sir.
Q You possess no Cherokee blood, do you? A No sir, no Cherokee blood.
Q Are you married to a citizen by blood of the Cherokee Nation? A Yes sir.
Q What is your wife's name? A Jane Christie?[sic]
Q When were you married to her? A I have been married to her twice. I first married her before the war in Texas, she was partly raised there, and when I move[sic] to this country, according to the laws of this Nation, I had to marry her again.
Q Were you ever married prior to your marriage to her? A No sir.
Q Was she ever married prior to her marriage to you? A No sir.
Q Was she living in Texas, making that her permanent home at the time you married her? A She was living with her uncle.
Q Where was she born? A She was born in the Cherokee Nation.
Q How long had she been living in Texas at the time you married her? A I suppose some 10 years maybe.
Q How old was she when you married her? A Well, I dont[sic] know that. She was about 12 years old when she left this country; she is 72; she is a year younger than I am; and we was married in '68.
Q When did you and your wife first come to the Cherokee Nation after your marriage? A I lived in Texas, I dont[sic] recollect just how long. I came here two years after the war.
Q You came here then about 1867, along in there? A The way I remember, it was '68.
Q Since your marriage to your wife, have you and she continuously lived together as husband and wife? A Yes sir.
Q She is living at the present time, is she? A Yes sir.
Q Since you came to the Cherokee Nation in 1868, have you continuously lived in the Cherokee Nation? A Yes sir.
Q You have never been absent from the Cherokee Nation for any length of time? A No sir.
Q Your wife, upn[sic] coming to the Cherokee Nation, was recognized as a citizen of the Cherokee Nation, was she, by the Cherokee authorities? A Yes sir, she was admitted.
Q She was admitted, was she, after you came to the Cherokee Nation? A Yes sir.
Q Was that act admitting her passed before you married her the second time? A No sir, it was after we were married the second time.
Q About what year was that act passed admitting your wife to citizenship in the Cherokee Nation? A I believe it was '68.

The applicant presents an original marriage license and certificate showing that on November 23, 1868, he married, in accordance with Cherokee law, Mrs. Jennie Christie

Cherokee Intermarried White 1906
Volume I

(formerly Jennie Starr), and a Cherokee by birth. This marriage license and certificate is filed herewith and made a part of the record in this case.

Q Have you a copy of the admission of your wife to citizenship in the Cherokee Nation?
A No sir.
Q Did she ever have a copy of it? A Not that I know of.
Q You never have seen any evidence that she had, showing that she was admitted to citizenship in the Cherokee Nation after your removal from Texas? A No sir.

The applicant, John F. M. Christie, id identified on the Cherokee authenticated tribal roll of 1880, Going Snake District, No. 359. His wife, Jane Christie, in[sic] included in the approved partial roll of citizens by blood of the Cherokee Nation, opposite No. 993.

The undersigned, being first duly sworn, states that as stenographer to the Commissioner to the Five Civilized Tribes, she correctly reported the above and foregoing testimony, and that the above is a full, true and correct transcript of the stenographic not[sic] es[sic] thereof.

Sarah Waters

Subscribed and sworn to before me this 4th day of Jan, 1906.7

John E. Tidwell
Notary Public.

◇◇◇◇◇

Cherokee Nation)
)
Flint District   )   By the authority in me vested by the law of the Cherokee Nation I do hereby Grant License of marriage to John F. M. Christie, a citizen of the United States and of industrious habits to marry Mrs. Jinnie Christie (formerly Jinnie Starr) and a Cherokee by birth, and a daughter of James Starr Decd. He, (John F. M. Christie) having complied with the requirements of the law regulating intermarriage with white men.

Given from under my hand in office this the 19th. day of Nov. 1868.

James W. Adair Clk
Dist. Ct. Flint.

License fee $5.00

I hereby certify that the above named parties were joined in marriage by me according to the laws of the Cherokee Nation This 23rd. day of Nov A.D. 1868.

W.A. Duncan, Indian Territory
Minister M.E.C. South.

Cherokee Intermarried White 1906
Volume I

The undersigned being duly sworn, states that as stenographer to the Commissioner to the Five Civilized Tribes, she made the above copy, and that the same is a true and correct copy of the instrument now on file in this office.

Mamie Tabor Mallory

Subscribed and sworn to before me this 9 day of Jan. 1907.

Chas E Webster
Notary Public.

◇◇◇◇◇

E.C.M.
Cherokee 325

DEPARTMENT OF THE INTERIOR,
COMMISSIONER TO THE FIVE CIVILIZED TRIBES.

In the matter of the application for the enrollment of John F. M. Christie as a citizen by intermarriage of the Cherokee Nation.

D E C I S I O N.

THE RECORDS OF THIS OFFICE SHOW: That at Westville, Indian Territory, July 18, 1900, John F. M. Christie appeared before the Commission to the Five Civilized Tribes, and made application for the enrollment of himself as a citizen by intermarriage, and for the enrollment of his wife, Jane Christie, et. al. as citizens by blood of the Cherokee Nation has been heretofore disposed of, and their rights to enrollment will not be considered in this decision. Further proceedings in the matter of said application were had at Talequah[sic], Indian Territory, October 7, 1902 and at Muskogee, Indian Territory January 2, 1907.

THE EVIDENCE IN THIS CASE SHOWS: That the applicant herein, John F. M. Christie, a white man, was married in accordance with the Cherokee law, November 23, 1868 to his wife Jane Christie, nee Starr, who was at the time of said marriage a recognized citizen by blood of the Cherokee Nation, and whose name appears upon the approved partial roll of citizens by blood of the Cherokee Nation opposite number 993; that since said marriage the said John F. M. Christie and Jane Christie have resided together as husband and wife and have continuously lived in the Cherokee Nation. Said John F. M. Christie is identified on the Cherokee Authenticated Tribal Roll of 1880 and the Cherokee Census Roll of 1896 as an intermarried citizen of the Cherokee Nation.

IT IS THEREFORE ORDERED AND ADJUDGED: That in accordance with the decision of the Supreme Court of the United States, dated November 5, 1906, in the case of Daniel Red Bird et. al. vs. the United States under the provision of Section 21, of the Act of Congress approved June 28, 1898, (30th. Stat. 495) John F. M. Christie is entitled

Cherokee Intermarried White 1906
Volume I

to enrollment as a citizen by intermarriage of the Cherokee Nation, and his application for enrollment as such is accordingly granted.

              Tams Bixby
                Commissioner.

Dated at Muskogee, Indian Territory,
this   JAN 18 1907

◇◇◇◇◇

REFER IN REPLY TO THE FOLLOWING:
Cherokee
325

DEPARTMENT OF THE INTERIOR,
COMMISSIONER TO THE FIVE CIVILIZED TRIBES.

Muskogee, Indian Territory, December 21, 1906.

John F. M. Christie,
  Westville, Indian Territory.

Dear Sir:

  November 6, 1906, the United States Supreme Court held that white persons who intermarried with Cherokee citizens according to Cherokee law prior to November 1, 1875, are entitled to enrollment and allotments of land as citizens of the Cherokee Nation.

  You are advised that to properly determine your right to enrollment as a citizen by intermarriage of the Cherokee Nation, it will be necessary for you to appear before the Commissioner for the purpose of giving testimony as to the date of your marriage and whether or not your wife, by reason of your marriage to whom you claim the right to enrollment as a citizen of the Cherokee Nation, was a recognized citizen of the Cherokee Nation at the time of your marriage to her, and whether or not you were married to her in accordance with Cherokee laws.

  You are therefore directed to appear before the Commissioner at Muskogee, Indian Territory, at 9 o'clock A. M., on Thursday, January 3, 1907, and give testimony as above indicated.

             Respectfully,
             W^m. O. Beall
H.J.C.   Acting Commissioner.

◇◇◇◇◇

Cherokee Intermarried White 1906
Volume I

Cherokee 325

Muskogee, Indian Territory, January 18, 1907.

W. W. Hastings,
    Attorney for the Cherokee Nation,
        Muskogee, Indian Territory.

Dear Sir:

    There is enclosed herewith a copy of the decision of the Commissioner to the Five Civilized Tribes, dated January 18, 1907, granting the application for the enrollment of John F. M. Christie as a citizen by intermarriage of the Cherokee Nation.

        Respectfully,

Encl. HJ-26.
HJC
                                        Commissioner.

◇◇◇◇◇

Cherokee 325

W.W. HASTINGS.
ATTORNEY.

OFFICE OF

H.M. VANCE.
SECRETARY.

Attorney for the Cherokee Nation,
MUSKOGEE, I. T.

January 18, 1907.

The Commissioner to the Five Civilized Tribes,
    Muskogee, Indian Territory.

Sir:

    Receipt is acknowledged of the testimony and of your decision enrolling John F. M. Christie, as a citizen by intermarriage of the Cherokee Nation. Time for protesting said decision is waived and I consent that said person may be placed upon the schedule immediately.

        Yours very truly,
            W. W. Hastings
            Attorney for Cherokee Nation.

◇◇◇◇◇

Cherokee Intermarried White 1906
Volume I

Cherokee
325

Muskogee, Indian Territory, January 21, 1907.

John F. M. Christie,
    Westville, Indian Territory.

Dear Sir:

    There is enclosed herewith copy of the decision of the Commissioner to the Five Civilized Tribes, dated January 18, 1907, granting the application for your enrollment as a citizen by intermarriage of the Cherokee Nation.

You will be advised when your name has been placed upon the schedule of citizens of the Cherokee Nation and approved by the Secretary of the Interior.

                  Respectfully,

Enc M - 10

M.T.M.   Commissioner.

◇◇◇◇◇

Cherokee
I. W. 8

Muskogee, Indian Territory, April 6, 1907

John F. M. Christie,
    Christie, Indian Territory.

Dear Sir:

    Your marriage license and certificate, filed in connection with your application for enrollment as a citizen by intermarriage of the Cherokee Nation, is returned to you herewith, copies of the same being retained in this office.

                  Respectfully,

Encl. B-84   Acting Commissioner

L M B

Cherokee Intermarried White 1906
Volume I

Cher I W 9
Trans from Cher 344   3-18-07

◇◇◇◇◇

E.C.M.

DEPARTMENT OF THE INTERIOR,

COMMISSIONER TO THE FIVE CIVILIZED TRIBES.

In the matter of the application for the enrollment of

JOHN D. SMITH

AS A CITIZEN BY INTERMARRIAGE OF THE CHEROKEE NATION.

CHEROKEE 344

◇◇◇◇◇

DEPARTMENT OF THE INTERIOR,
COMMISSION TO THE FIVE CIVILIZED TRIBES.
WESTVILLE, I. T., JULY 18th, 1900.

IN THE MATTER OF THE APPLICATION OF John D. Smith et al, for enrollment as citizens of the Cherokee Nation, and he being sworn by Commissioner, C. R. Breckinridge, testified as follows:

Q What is your name? A John D. Smith.
Q What is your age? A Sixty five.
Q What is your Postoffice address? A Oaks.
Q Your district? A Going Snake/[sic]
Q For whom do you make application? A Myself, wife and four children.
Q Do you apply as a Cherokee by blood? A No sir.
Q How long have you lived in this District? A About six years.
Q How long have you lived in this Nation? A Twenty eight years.
Q Been here continuously in the Nation for twenty eight years, have you? A Yes sir.
Q Have you a certificate of marriage? A Yes sir.

Mr. Smith, the paper you have handed me, is a certificate, signed and sealed by Arch Epeers, Deputy Clerk of Tahlequah District, stating that it is duly of record in this office that a liscence[sic] is granted you to marry Miss Sarah Bluebird, a Cherokee; and the rights solemnized by John D. Jones, a Minister of the Gospel, December 23rd, 1872. The certificate to the foregoing effect is dated April 15th, 1897; it is not objected to by the

Cherokee Intermarried White 1906
Volume I

representatives of the Cherokee Nation, and is accepted by this Commission as satisfactory evidence of what it states: I return it to you.
Q You have lived with your wife ever since the marriage indicated? A Yes sir.
(Applicant identified on the roll of 1880, Page 322, #2544, Delaware District, as Jno. D. Smith -- Applicant's wife, on Page 433, #4545, Sarah Smith)
(Applicant identified on the roll of 1896, Page 828, #171, Jno. D. Smith, Going Snake District -- Applicants[sic] wife identified on the roll of 1896, Page 786, #1837, Sarah Smith, Going Snake District)
Q Now your children please; those unmarried and living with you? A I have one son living with me twenty two years old; his name is Walter D. Smith. (Duly identified on the roll of 1880, Page 322, #2548, Walter D. Smith, Delaware District)
(Identified on the roll of 1896, Page 786, #1838, Walter D. Smith)
Q Your next child? A Grover Cleaveland Smith.
Q What is the age of that child? A Fourteen.
(Identified on the roll of 1896, Page 786, #1840, Grover C. Smith, Going Snake District)
Q Next child? A Lucy L. Smith.
(Identified on the roll of 1896, Page 786, #1841, Lucy L. Smith, Going Snake District)
Q Next child? A Floy Lena Smith.
Q Age? A Nine /[sic]
(Identified on the roll of 1896, Page 786, #1842, as Floyd L. Smith)
Q Next one? A Rebecca Ethel Smith?[sic]
Q Age of that child? A Seven. (Identified on the roll of 1896, Page 786, #1843, as Rebecca E. Smith, Going Snake District)
Q What is the next one? A That is all.

Mr. Smith, you name and the name of your wife, both appearing duly of record in the rolls of 1880, and 1896; your son, Walter D. Smith, on the rolls of 1880 and 1896; your other children duly recorded on the roll of 1896; your marriage to your wife is clearly established by the official document cited; your residence has been continuous and satisfactory; Your wife and children will be enrolled as citizens by blood, and you as a citizen by adoption.

R. R. Cravens, being sworn, states that as stenographer to the Commission to the Five Civilized Tribes, he reported the foregoing case, and that the foregoing and above is a true, full and correct transcript of his stenographic notes in said case.

R.R. Cravens

Sworn to and subscribed before me this 19th day of July, 1900.

Tams Bixby
COMMISSIONER.

Cherokee Intermarried White 1906
Volume I

H.
Cher. 344.

Department of the Interior.
Commission to the Five Civilized Tribes.
Tahlequah, I. T., October 6, 1902.

SUPPLEMENTAL TESTIMONY AND PROCEEDINGS in the matter of the application for the enrollment of JOHN D. SMITH as a citizen by intermarriage of the Cherokee Nation.

JOHN D. SMITH?[sic] being first duly sworn, and being examined, testified as follows:

BY COMMISSION: What is your name? A John D. Smith.
Q How old are you? A Sixty-seven.
Q What is your post office address> A Oaks.
Q Are you a white man? A Yes sir.
Q Have you heretofore made application to this Commission for enrollment as a citizen by intermarriage of the Cherokee Nation? A Yes sir.
Q What is the name of your wife? A Sarah.
Q Is she living? A Yes sir.
Q Is she a Cherokee by blood? A Yes sir.
Q When were you and she married? A L872[sic].
Q Have you and she lived together continuously since the date of your marriage? A Yes sir.
Q Are you living together now? A Yes sir.
Q Do you claim your right to enrollment by reason of your marriage to her? A Yes sir.
Q Were you ever married before you married her? A Yes sir.
Q What was the name of your former wife? A Letitia Lester was her maiden name.
Q Is she living? A No sir.
Q Was she a Cherokee by blood? A No, she was a white woman.
Q Is that the only time you were ever married? A That is all.
Q Did you and she live together until the time of her death? A Yes sir.
Q Was your wife ever married before you married her? A No sir.
Q Did you make satisfactory proof of your marriage to your present wife according to Cherokee law at the time you made application for enrollment? A I had the marriage certificate. I presented that to them when I enrolled.
Q Have you resided in the Cherokee Nation continuously since the date of your application for enrollment? A Yes sir.

This testimony will be filed with and made a part of the record in the matter of the application for the enrollment of John D. Smith as a citizen by intermarriage of the Cherokee Nation, Cherokee straight card field No. 344.

Cherokee Intermarried White 1906
Volume I

Wm. Hutchinson, being first duly sworn, states that as stenographer to the Commission to the Five Civilized Tribes he correctly recorded the testimony and proceedings in this case, and that the foregoing is a true and complete transcript of his stenographic notes thereof.

Wm Hutchinson

Subscribed and sworn to before me this 9th day of October, 1902.

John O Rosson
Notary Public.

◇◇◇◇◇

Cherokee No. 344.

DEPARTMENT OF THE INTERIOR,
COMMISSIONER TO THE FIVE CIVILIZED TRIBES.

Muskogee, Indian Territory, January 3, 1907.

In the matter of the application for the enrollment of John D. Smith as a citizen by intermarriage of.

John D. Smith, being first duly sworn and examined, testifies as follows:

BY THE COMMISSIONER:

Q What is your name? A John D. Smith.
Q How old are you? A I am going on 72 years old.
Q What is your postoffice address? A Oakes.
Q Do you claim to be an intermarried citizen of the Cherokee Nation? A Yes, sir.
Q Through whom do you claim your intermarried rights? A Through my wife.
Q What is her name? A Sarah Smith.
Q When were you married to Sarah Smith? A Third day of December, 1872.
Q Were you married under the Cherokee law? A Yes, sir.
Q Got your licence[sic]? A Got my marriage certificate.

Applicant offers in evidence cirtifice[sic] of Arch Spears, Dupety[sic] Clerk, Tahlequah District, dated April 16th, 1897 to the effect of the records of his office show that applicant was married under the Cherokee law to Miss. Sarah Bluebird, A Cherokee citizen, December 23, 1872. An examination of Book "C" of the marriage records of the Tahlequah District showing the licences[sic] issued from 1870 to 1892 shows on page 21 that the applicant was granted a licence[sic] to marry Miss. Sarah Bluebird, and was married on December 23, 1872 by John B. Jones.

Cherokee Intermarried White 1906
Volume I

Q Were you ever married before you married Sarah Bluebird? A Yes, sir.
Q What was the name of your former wife? A Leslie.
Q Was she alive or dead at the time you married Sarah Bluebird.[sic] A Dead.
Q Was Sarah Bluebird married before she married you? A No, sir.
Q Have you lived together continuously since your marriage up to the present time? A Yes, sir.
Q Still living together are you? A Yes, sir.

The applicant is identified on the 1880 Cherokee Roll, Delaware District, opposite 2544. His wife through whom he claims his right to enrollment is identified on said roll opposite No. 2545. She is also identified on the final roll of citizens by blood of the Cherokee Nation opposite No. 1063.

WITNESS EXCUSED.

F. Elma Lane, upon oath, states that she reported the proceedings in the above entitled cause and that the foregoing is a true and correct transcript of her stenographic notes taken therein.

F. Elma Lane

Subscribed and sworn to before me this 4th day of January, 1907.

Chas E Webster
Notary Public.

◇◇◇◇◇

E.C.M.

Cherokee 344

DEPARTMENT OF THE INTERIOR,
COMMISSIONER TO THE FIVE CIVILIZED TRIBES.

In the matter of the application for the enrollment of John D. Smith as a citizen by intermarriage of the Cherokee Nation.

DECISION.

THE RECORDS OF THIS OFFICE SHOW: That at Westville, Indian Territory, July 18, 1900, John D. Smith appeared before the Commission to the Five Civilized Tribes and made application for the enrollment of himself as a citizen by intermarriage, and for the enrollment of his wife, Sarah Smith, et. al. as citizens by blood of the Cherokee Nation. The application for the enrollment of the said Sarah Smith, et. al. as citizens by blood of the Cherokee Nation has been heretofore disposed of, and their rights to enrollment will not be considered in this decision. Further proceedings in the matter of said application were had at Talequah[sic], Indian Territory, October 6, 1902, and at Muskogee, Indian Territory, January 3, 1907.

Cherokee Intermarried White 1906
Volume I

THE EVIDENCE IN THIS CASE SHOWS: That the applicant herein, John D. Smith, a white man, was married in accordance with the Cherokee law December 23, 1872, to his wife Sarah Smith, nee BlueBird, who was at the time of said marriage a recognized citizen by blood of the Cherokee Nation, and whose name appears upon the approved partial roll of citizens by blood of the Cherokee Nation, opposite number 1063; that since said marriage the said John D. Smith and Sarah Smith have resided together as husband and wife, and have continuously lived in the Cherokee Nation. Said John D. Smith is identified on the Cherokee Authenticated Tribal Roll of 1880, and the Cherokee Census Roll of 1896 as an intermarried citizen of the Cherokee Nation.

IT IS THEREFORE ORDERED AND ADJUDGED: That in accordance with the decision of the Supreme Court of the United States, dated November 5, 1906, in the case of Daniel Red Bird et al. vs. the United States under the provision of Section 21, of the Act of Congress approved June 28, 1898, (30th. Stat. 495) John D. Smith is entitled to enrollment as a citizen of the Cherokee Nation, and his application for enrollment as such is accordingly granted.

Tams Bixby
Commissioner.

Dated at Muskogee, Indian Territory,
this   JAN 18 1907

◇◇◇◇◇

Cherokee
344

Muskogee, Indian Territory, December 21, 1906.

John D. Smith,
    Oaks, Indian Territory.

Dear Sir:

November 6, 1906, the United States Supreme Court held that white persons who intermarried with Cherokee citizens according to Cherokee law prior to November 1, 1875, are entitled to enrollment and allotments of land as citizens of the Cherokee Nation.

You are advised that to properly determine your right to enrollment as a citizen by intermarriage of the Cherokee Nation, it will be necessary for you to appear before the Commissioner for the purpose of giving testimony as to the date of your marriage and whether or not your wife, by reason of your marriage to whom you claim the right to enrollment as a citizen of the Cherokee Nation, was a recognized citizen of the Cherokee Nation at the time of your marriage to her, and whether or not you were married to her in accordance with Cherokee laws.

You are therefore directed to appear before the Commissioner at Muskogee, Indian Territory, at 9 o'clock A. M., on Thursday, January 3, 1907, and give testimony as above indicated.

Cherokee Intermarried White 1906
Volume I

Respectfully,

H.J.C.   Acting Commissioner.

Cherokee
344.

Muskogee, Indian Territory, January 18, 1907.

W. W. Hastings,
    Attorney for the Cherokee Nation,
        Muskogee, Indian Territory.

Dear Sir:

    There is enclosed herewith a copy of the decision of the Commissioner to the Five Civilized Tribes, dated January 18, 1907, granting the application for the enrollment of John D. Smith as a citizen by intermarriage of the Cherokee Nation.

Respectfully,

Encl. H.J.-24.
HJC.   Commissioner.

Cherokee 344.   W.W. HASTINGS.   OFFICE OF   H.M. VANCE.
                              ATTORNEY.   SECRETARY.

Attorney for the Cherokee Nation,
MUSKOGEE, I. T.

January 18, 1907.

The Commissioner to the Five Civilized Tribes,
        Muskogee, Indian Territory.

Sir:

    Receipt is acknowledged of the testimony and of your decision enrolling John D. Smith, as a citizen by intermarriage of the Cherokee Nation. Time for protesting said decision is waived and I consent that said person may be placed upon the schedule immediately.

Yours very truly,
W. W. Hastings
Attorney for Cherokee Nation.

Cherokee Intermarried White 1906
Volume I

Cherokee
344

Muskogee, Indian Territory, January 21, 1907.

John D. Smith,
Oaks, Indian Territory.

Dear Sir:

There is enclosed herewith copy of the decision of the Commissioner to the Five Civilized Tribes, dated January 18, 1907, granting the application for your enrollment as a citizen by intermarriage of the Cherokee Nation.

You will be advised when your name has been placed upon the schedule of citizens of the Cherokee Nation and approved by the Secretary of the Interior.

Respectfully,

Enc M - 9

M.T.M.   Commissioner.

Cher I W 10
Trans from Cher 523 3-24-07

◇◇◇◇◇

C.E.W.
DEPARTMENT OF THE INTERIOR,
COMMISSIONER TO THE FIVE CIVILIZED TRIBES.

In the matter of the application for the enrollment of

JAMES M. CLOUD

as a citizen by intermarriage of the Cherokee Nation.

CHEROKEE 523.

◇◇◇◇◇

Cherokee Intermarried White 1906
Volume I

Department of the Interior,
Commision[sic] to the Five Civilized Tribes,
Stilwell, I. T., July 24, 1900.

In the matter of the application of James M. Cloud for th[sic] enrollment of himself and family as Cherokee citizens; being sworn and examined by Commissioner Needles he testifies as follows:

Q What is your name? A James M. Cloud.
Q What is your age? A Sixty-two past.
Q What is your post-office address? A Stilwell.
Q In what district do you live? A Flint.
Q How long have you lived in Flint District? A Going on thirty years.
Q For whom do you make application? A I apply for myself and my wife and one boy.
Q Are you a Cherokee by blood? A No sir.
Q Does your name appear upon the authenticated roll of 1880? A I guess it does.
    Note: 1880 roll examined, page 355, #247, James M. Cloud, Flint District. 1896 roll, Flint District, page 711, #20, James M. Cloud.
Q When were you married? A I have been married- I first married forty years ago, and the second marriage not quite so long as that.
Q Under what law were you married the last time? A Cherokee law.
Q What year was that? A In 1871.
Q Have you a certificate of marriage? A I had it, but I got my house burned yp[sic], and the certificate with it.
Q What is your wife's name? A Martha C. Cloud.
    Note: 1880 roll, M. C. Cloud, page 355, #248, Flint District. 1896 roll, page 655, #462, Martha C. Cloud.
Q Is Martha C. Cloud alive? A Yes sir, she is here present.
Q What is the name of her father? A Charles Ward.
Q Is he living? A No sir.
Q How long has he been dead? A I couldn't tell you.
Q Did he die before 1880? A Yes sir.
Q Is her mother living? A No sir.
Q She die before 1880? A Yes sir.
Q To what district did they belong? A They died back in the Old Country.
Q What proportion of Cherokee blood does your wife claim to have? A One-eighth.
Q Have you any children under twenty-one years of age living with you? A One.
Q What is his name? A William M. Cloud, he is nineteen years old. (On 1896 roll, page 655, #464, William M. Cloud, Flint District.
Q Is this boy living with you at home? A Yes sir.
Q Been living continuously at your house? A Yes sir.

    Com'r Needles: The name of James M. Cloud appearing upon the authenticated roll of 1880 as well as upon the census roll of 1896, as indicated by page and number, and his wife, Martha C.'s name also being found upon the authenticated roll of 1880 and the census roll of 1896, and his son, William M. Cloud's name being found upon the census roll of 1896, and satisfactory proof having been made as to their residence, they are

Cherokee Intermarried White 1906
Volume I

ordered enrolled as Cherokees by blood, and their names will be entered upon the rolls now being made by this Commission.

M.D. Green, being first duly sworn, states that as stenographer to the Commission to the Five Civilized Tribes he reported the foregoing case and that the above and foregoing is a full, true and complete transcript of his stenographic notes in said case.

M D Green

Subscribed and sworn to before me this 24th day of July 1900.

TB Needles
Commissioner.

◇◇◇◇◇

Department of the Interior,
Commission to the Five Civilized Tribes,
Vinita I. T. October 18th 1901.

In the matter of the application of James M. Cloud, Straight Cherokee case No. 523.

Amended Field Judgment

BY COM'R NEEDLES: The name of James M. Cloud appears upon the authenticated roll of 1880 and also the census roll of 1896, as indicated by the page and number in the testimony. And the name of his wife Martha C. also appears on the authenticated roll of 1880 and the census roll of 1896, and the name of his son William M. also appears on the census roll of 1896. They are all duly identified thereby and make satisfactory proof as to residence, consequently the said James M. Cloud will be listed for enrollment as a Cherokee citizen by intermarried[sic], and his wife Martha C. and his son William M. as Cherokee citizens by blood. The former field judgment will be held for naught, having been found incorrect.

============

Chas. von Weise, being first duly sworn, states that as stenographer to the Commission to the Five Civilized Tribes he reported the above proceedings in full and that the foregoing is a true and complete transcript of his stenographic notes therein.

Chas von Weise

Subscribed and sworn to before me this the 21st of October, 1901.

C.R. Breckinridge
Commissioner.

◇◇◇◇◇

Cherokee Intermarried White 1906
Volume I

JOR.
Cher. 523.

Department of the Interior,
Commission to the Five Civilized Tribes.
Tahlequah, I. T., October 13, 1902.

SUPPLEMENTAL TESTIMONY AND PROCEEDINGS in the matter of the application for the enrollment of JAMES M. CLOUD as a citizen by intermarriage of the Cherokee Nation.

JAMES M. CLOUD, being first duly sworn, and being examined, testified as follows:

BY COMMISSION: What is your name? A James M. Cloud.
Q How old are you? A Going on sixty-four.
Q What is your post office address? A Stilwell.
Q You are a white man, are you? A Yes sir.
Q Have you heretofore made application to this Commission for enrollment as a citizen by intermarriage of the Cherokee Nation? A Yes sir.
Q What is the name of your wife? A Martha C. Cloud.
Q Is she living? A Yes sir. She is here present.
Q Is she a Cherokee by blood? A Yes sir.
Q Do you claim your right to enrollment by reason of your marriage to her? A Yes sir.
Q When were you and she married? A First in 1859, then we came her in 1871 and married according to the Cherokee laws in 1871.
Q You married her under state law in 1859? A Yes sir, then under Cherokee law in 1871.
Q At the time you made your application for enrollment, did you make satisfactory proof to the Commission of your marriage to her according to Cherokee law? A Yes sir.
Q Does your name appear upon the roll of 1880? A Yes sir.
Q Were you ever married before you married her? A No sir.
Q Was she ever married before she married you? A No sir.
Q You are her first husband and she is your first wife? A Yes sir.
Q Have you and she lived together continuously since you were married? A Yes sir.
Q Were you living together on the 1st day of September 1902? A Yes sir.
Q Never been separated at all? A Not long at a time.
Q Have you been separated from her? A No sir, not separated at all. I said not long at a time. Sometimes she is out on a visit and knocking around a day or two. You mean separated, quitting? No sir, never been anything of the kind.
Q You have never been separated at all, no more than that she has gone off on a visit? A No sir; that's all.
Q How long is the longest time she has gone at a time? A About a week, I suppose, gone out to see her people.
Q Have you resided in the Cherokee Nation continuously since you and she were married in 1871? A Yes sir.
Q Has she also? A Yes sir.

Cherokee Intermarried White 1906
Volume I

This testimony will be filed with and made a part of the record in the matter of the application for the enrollment of James M. Cloud as a citizen by intermarriage of the Cherokee Nation, Cherokee straight card field No. 523.

Wm. Hutchinson, being first duly sworn, states that as stenographer to the Commission to the Five Civilized Tribes he correctly recorded the testimony and proceedings in this case, and that the foregoing is a true and complete transcript of the stenographic notes thereof.

Wm Hutchinson

Subscribed and sworn to before me this 20th day of October, 1902.
John O Rosson
NP

F.R.   Cherokee-523.

DEPARTMENT OF THE INTERIOR,
COMMISSIONER TO THE FIVE CIVILIZED TRIBES.
Muskogee, I. T., January 11, 1907.

In the matter of the application for the enrollment of James M. Cloud as a citizen by intermarriage of the Cherokee Nation.

James M. Cloud being first duly sworn by Frances R Lane, a Notary Public for Western Disttict[sic] of Indian Territory, testified as follows:

By the Commissioner:
Q What is your name? A James M. Cloud.
Q How old are you? A Going on sixty-eight.
Q What is your postoffice address? A McKey, I. T.
Q Do you claim citizenship by intermarriage in the Cherokee Nation? A Yes sir.
Q Through whom do you claim such citizenship? A I have been married to a Cherokee woman.
Q What was her name before she was married? A Her maiden names used to be Martha C. Ward.
Q That is at the time you married her? A Yes sir.
Q When were you married to Martha C. Ward? A In 1871.
Q Where were you married to her? A In a place called Stilwell, in Flint District.
Q Were you married under a license of the Cherokee Nation? A Yes sir.
Q Have you a copy of that license with you? A No, I havnt[sic] got it with me; its filed at Tahlequah in the office. If I had it I got it burned; my house burned up some years back and it got burned up if I had it.
Q Did you get a certificate of your marriage at that time[sic] A No, my house was burned when I wasn't at home and everything was burned up.
Q Had you ever been married prior to your marriage to Martha C. Ward in 1871?
A Yes.
Q To whom? A Yes, I had been married first to her.

Cherokee Intermarried White 1906
Volume I

Q When were you first married to her? A Back in 1859 in what we called the old country.
Q When did you remove to the Cherokee nation[sic]? A In 1871.
Q Then were you remarried in accordance with the Cherokee laws? A Yes sir.
Q Was she ever married prior to the time she married you in the old country? A No, never was married.
Q She is living at this time? A Yes, this is her right here
Q Have you lived together continuously in the Cherokee nation[sic] as husband and wife since the date of your marriage in 1871? A We have, closely tied together.
Q Martha C. Cloud is a citizen by blood of the Cherokee nation is she? A Yes, she is on the rolls as such.
Q When was she admitted to citizenship, or recognized as a citizen by the tribal authorities? A In 1871. She has always been recognized as a Cherokee. Her father, he came here sometime before and then went back to the old country
Q What do you mean by the old country? A The old territoy[sic] such as North Carolina, Georgia and Tennessee.
Q You say she was admitted to citizenship in 1871? A Yes.
Q Did she apply to any of the Cherokee courts? A Yes, applied to the court at Tahlequah and they testified tht[sic] she was the daughter. Her father's name was already established; his name was on the roll; she was the daughter of Thomas Ward; he was already on the roll.
Q Do you know by whom your Cherokee marriage license was issued? A By a man by the name of James Ward Adair. He might have been acting in the place as a substitute.
Q Who performed the marriage ceremony? A Old gentleman by the name of Ruble.

> In marriage record marked B, Flint District, Page 111 appears the record of marriage license having been issued on April 22, 1871 by James W. Adair, Clerk of the District Court, Flint District, of James Cloud and Mrs. Martha Cloud (formerly Mrs. Martha Ward). Said records further show that James Cloud and Martha Cloud were married under said license by Thomas B. Ruble, minister of the M. E. Church, on April 23, 1871, and said license was filed for record April 24, 1871.
>
> The name of the applicant James M. Cloud, and his wife Martha C. Cloud appear on Cherokee Field Card No. 523, and are included in the 1880 authenticated roll of citizens of the Cherokee Nation, Flint District, opposite Nos. 247 and 248 respectively.
>
> The name of the applicant's wife is also included in the approved partial roll of citizens of the Cherokee nation[sic], opposite No. 1512.
>
> The names of the applicant and his wife are also found upon the 1896 roll, Flint District, opposite Nos. 20 and 462 respectively.

Cherokee Intermarried White 1906
Volume I

Frances R. Lane upon oath states that as stenographer to the Commissioner to the Five Civilized Tribes she reported the testimony in the above entitled cause and that the foregoing is an accurate transcript of her stenographic notes thereof.

Frances R Lane

Subscribed and sworn to before me this 11th day of January 1907.

Edward Merrick
Notary Public.

◇◇◇◇◇

C.E.W. Cherokee 523.

DEPARTMENT OF THE INTERIOR,

COMMISSIONER TO THE FIVE CIVILIZED TRIBES.

In the matter of the application for the enrollment of James M. Cloud, as a citizen by intermarriage of the Cherokee Nation.

D E C I S I O N

THE RECORDS OF THIS OFFICE SHOW: That at Stilwell, Indian Territory, July 24, 1900, application was received by the Commission to the Five Civilized Tribes for the enrollment of James M. Cloud, as a citizen by intermarriage of the Cherokee Nation. Further proceedings in the matter of said application were had at Vinita, Indian Territory, October 18, 1902; at Tahlequah, Indian Territory, October 13, 1902, and at Muskogee, Indian Territory, January 11, 1907.

THE EVIDENCE IN THIS CASE SHOWS: That the applicant herein, James M. Cloud, a white man, was married in accordance with Cherokee law April 23, 1871, to his wife, Martha C. Cloud, nee Ward, who was at the time of said marriage a recognized citizen, by blood of the Cherokee Nation, and who is identified on the Cherokee authenticated tribal roll of 1880, Flint District, page 355, number 248, as an adopted Cherokee, and whose name appears upon the approved partial roll of citizens by blood of the Cherokee Nation, opposite number 1512; that since said marriage the said James M. Cloud and Martha C. Cloud have resided together as husband and wife and have continuously lived in the Cherokee Nation. Said James M. Cloud is identified on the Cherokee authenticated tribal roll of 1880, and the Cherokee census roll of 1896 as an intermarried citizen of the Cherokee Nation.

IT IS, THEREFORE, ORDERED AND ADJUDGED: That in accordance with the decision of the Supreme Court of the United States, dated November 5, 1906, in the cases of Daniel Red Bird et al. vs. the United States, Nos. 125, 126, 127 and 128, the said

Cherokee Intermarried White 1906
Volume I

applicant James M. Cloud is entitled, under the provision of Section 21 of the Act of Congress approved June 28, 1898, (30 Stat., 495), to enrollment, as a citizen by intermarriage of the Cherokee Nation, and his application for enrollment as such is accordingly granted.

Tams Bixby
Commissioner.

Dated at Muskogee, Indian Territory,
this   JAN 19 1907

◇◇◇◇◇

Cherokee
523

Muskogee, Indian Territory, December 22, 1906.

James M. Cloud,
    Stilwell, Indian Territory.

Dear Sir:

November 6, 1906, the United States Supreme Court held that white persons who intermarried with Cherokee citizens according to Cherokee law prior to November 1, 1875, are entitled to enrollment and allotments of land as citizens of the Cherokee Nation.

You are advised that to properly determine your right to enrollment as a citizen by intermarriage of the Cherokee Nation, it will be necessary for you to appear before the Commissioner for the purpose of giving testimony as to the date of your marriage and whether or not your wife, by reason of your marriage to whom you claim the right to enrollment as a citizen of the Cherokee Nation, was a recognized citizen of the Cherokee Nation at the time of your marriage to her, and whether or not you were married to her in accordance with Cherokee laws.

You are therefore directed to appear before the Commissioner at Muskogee, Indian Territory, at 9 o'clock A. M., on Thursday, January 3, 1907, and give testimony as above indicated.

Respectfully,

H.J.C.   Acting Commissioner.

◇◇◇◇◇

Cherokee Intermarried White 1906
Volume I

Cherokee
523.

Muskogee, Indian Territory, January 19, 1907.

W. W. Hastings,
    Attorney for the Cherokee Nation,
        Muskogee, Indian Territory.

Dear Sir:

There is enclose herewith a copy of the decision of the Commissioner to the Five Civilized Tribes, dated January 19, 1907, granting the application for the enrollment of James M. Cloud, as a citizen by intermarriage of the Cherokee Nation.

        Respectfully,

                Commissioner.

Incl. C-25
LMC

◇◇◇◇◇

Cherokee 523.   W.W.HASTINGS. ATTORNEY.   OFFICE OF   H.M. VANCE. SECRETARY.

Attorney for the Cherokee Nation,
MUSKOGEE, I. T.

        January 19, 1907.

The Commissioner to the Five Civilized Tribes,
    Muskogee, Indian Territory.

Sir:

Receipt is acknowledged of the testimony and of your decision enrolling James M. Cloud as a citizen by intermarriage of the Cherokee Nation. Time for protesting said decision is waived and I consent that said person may be placed upon the schedule immediately.

        Respectfully,
        W. W. Hastings
        Attorney for Cherokee Nation.

◇◇◇◇◇

Cherokee Intermarried White 1906
Volume I

Cherokee

523

Muskogee, Indian Territory, January 21, 1907.

James M. Cloud,
    Stilwell, Indian Territory.

Dear Sir:

    There is enclosed herewith copy of the decision of the Commissioner to the Five Civilized Tribes, dated January 19, 1907, granting the application for your enrollment as a citizen by intermarriage of the Cherokee Nation.

You will be advised when your name has been placed upon the schedule of citizens of the Cherokee Nation and approved by the Secretary of the Interior.

    Respectfully,

Enc M - 8

    M.T.M.   commissioner[sic].

Cher I W 11
Trans from Cher 647 3-25-07

◇◇◇◇◇

E.C.M.

DEPARTMENT OF THE INTERIOR,

COMMISSIONER TO THE FIVE CIVILIZED TRIBES.

In the matter of the application for the enrollment of

VICTORIA T. BEAN

as a citizen by intermarriage of the Cherokee Nation.

CHEROKEE 647
◇◇◇◇◇

Cherokee Intermarried White 1906
Volume I

DEPARTMENT OF THE INTERIOR,
COMMISSION TO THE FIVE CIVILIZED TRIBES
STILWELL, I.T. JULY 25, 1900.

In the matter of the application of Mark Bean et als., for enrollment as citizens of the Cherokee nation[sic], said Bean being sworn By Commissioner Needles, testified as follows:

Q What is your name? A Mark Bean.
Q Your age? A 57.
Q Your postoffice? A Evansville, Ark.
Q Have you been recognized as a citizen by the tribal authorities of the Cherokee Nation? A Yes.
Q What district do you live in? A Goingsnake.
Q How long have you lived there? A 57 years.
Q What's is[sic] the name of your father? A Jack.
Q Is he living? A No sir.
Q What's the name of your mother? A Ruth.
Q Is she living? A No sir.
Q These names were upon the rolls of Cherokee Nation: A Yes.
    Mark Bean on '80 roll, page 736, number 159;
    On '96 roll, page 723, number 122;
    On '94 roll, page 622, number 289.
Q Are you married? A Yes.
Q How long have you been married? A '74.
Q What is your wife's name? A Victoria T. Bean.
Q Is she a Cherokee by blood? A No sir.
    On '80 roll, page 736, number 160 as V. T. Bean.
    On '96 roll, page 814, number 14, Page 818
Q How long has your wife lived in the Cherokee Nation? A Since '74 continuously with me.
Q What is the name of your wife's mother? A Levan Wright, a non-citizen.
Q Name of her father? A Wyley P. Wright.
Q Non-citizen? A Yes.
Q Have you any children at home under 21? A No sir.

The name of Mark Bean appearing upon the authenticated roll of '80, as well as upon the census roll of '96 and the pay-roll of '94, and his wife Victoria T. Bean's name appearing upon the authenticated roll of '80 as well as upon the census roll of '96, and satisfactory proof being made as to their residence they are ordered enrolled upon the rolls now being made by this Commission; he, Mark Bean as a Cherokee by blood, and his wife, Victoria T. Bean as a citizen by intermarriage.

Brown McDonald, being duly sworn, says as Stenographer to the Commission to the Five Civilized Tribes, he reported in full the testimony of the above named witness, and the foregoing is a full, true and correct transcript of his notes.

                                                Brown McDonald

Cherokee Intermarried White 1906
Volume I

Sworn to and subscribed before me this 1st day of August, 1900, at Bunch, Indian Territory.

TB Needles
Commissioner.

◇◇◇◇◇

H.
Cher. 647.

Department of the Interior,
Commission to the Five Civilized Tribes.
Tahlequah, I. T., October 6, 1902.

SUPPLEMENTAL TESTIMONY AND PROCEEDINGS IN THE MATTER of the application for the enrollment of VICTORIA T. BEAN as a citizen by intermarriage of the Cherokee Nation.

MARK BEAN, being first duly sworn, and being examined, testified as follows:

BY COMMISSION: What is your name? A Mark Bean.
Q How old are you? A Sixty.
Q What is your post office address? A Evansville, Arkansas.
Q Are you a recognized citizen by blood of the Cherokee Nation? A Yes sir.
Q What is the name of your wife? A Victoria T. bean.
Q Is she living? A Yes sir.
Q Is she a white woman? A Yes sir.
Q Has application heretofore been made to this Commission for her enrollment as a citizen by intermarriage of the Cherokee Nation? A Yes sir.
Q Who made that application? A I did.
Q When were you and she married? A In 1874.
Q Have you and she lived together continuously since the date of your marriage? A Yes sir.
Q Are you living together now? A Yes sir.
Q Does she claim her right to enrollment by reason of her marriage to you? A Yes sir.
Q Were you ever married before you married her? A No sir.
Q Was she ever married before she married you? A No sir.
Q Has she resided in the Cherokee Nation continuously ever since the date of your application for her enrollment? A Yes sir. I lived right on the Arkansas line in the Cherokee Nation.

This testimony will be filed with and made a part of the record in the matter if[sic] the application for the enrollment of Victoria T. bean as a citizen by intermarriage of the Cherokee Nation, Cherokee straight card field No. 647.

Cherokee Intermarried White 1906
Volume I

Wm. Hutchinson, being first duly sworn, states that as stenographer to the Commission to the Five Civilized Tribes he correctly recorded the testimony and proceedings in this case, and that the foregoing is a true and complete transcript of the stenographic notes thereof.

Wm Hutchinson

Subscribed and sworn to before me this 9th day of October, 1902.

John O Rosson
Notary Public.

JOR.
Cher. 647.

Department of the Interior.
Commission to the Five Civilized Tribes.
Tahlequah, I. T., October 30, 1902.

SUPPLEMENTAL TESTIMONY in the matter of the application for the enrollment of VICTORIA T. BEAN as a citizen by intermarriage of the Cherokee Nation.

VICTORIA T. BEAN, being first duly sworn, and being examined, testified as follows:

BY COMMISSION: What ks[sic] your name? A Victoria T. bean.
Q How old are you? A Forty-six.
Q What is your post office address? A Evansville, Arkansas.
Q You are a white woman, are you? A Yes sir.
Q Have you heretofore made application to this Commission for enrollment as a citizen by intermarriage of the Cherokee Nation? A Yes sir.
Q Your husband made application for your enrollment? A Yes sir.
Q What is the name of your husband? A Mark Bean.
Q Is he living? A Yes sir.
Q Is he a Cherokee by blood? A Yes sir.
Q Do you claim your right to enrollment by reason of your marriage to him? A Yes sir.
Q When were you and he married? A 1874.
Q Does you name appear upon the roll of 1880? A Yes sir.
Q Were you ever married before you married him? A Yes[sic] sir.
Q Was he ever married before he married you? A No sir.
Q You are his first wife and he is your first husband? A Yes sir.
Q Have you and he lived together continuously since your marriage? A Yes sir.
Q Were you living together on the 1st day of September, 1902? A Yes sir.
Q Never been separated at all? A No sir.
Q Have you resided in the Cherokee Nation continuously since you married him in 1874? A Yes sir.

Cherokee Intermarried White 1906
Volume I

Q How long has your husband resided in the Cherokee Nation? Has he resided here continuously since he married you? A Yes sir.
Q Have either of you been outside the Cherokee Nation for any purpose, just more than across the line, for the past five years? A No sir.
Q You have no minor children, have you? A No sir.

This testimony will be filed with and made a parr[sic] of the record in the matter of the application for the enrollment of Victoria T. Bean as a citizen by intermarriage of the Cherokee Nation, Cherokee straight card field No. 647.

Wm. Hutchinson, being first duly sworn, states as stenographer to the Commission to the Five Civilized Tribes he correctly recorded the testimony and proceedings in this case, and that the foregoing is a true and complete transcript of the stenographic notes thereof.

Wm Hutchinson

Subscribed and sworn to before me this 17th day of November, 1902.

BC Jones
Notary Public

◇◇◇◇◇

Cherokee 647.

DEPARTMENT OF THE INTERIOR
COMMISSIONER TO THE FIVE CIVILIZED TRIBES.
Muskogee, I. T., January 2, 1907.

In the matter of the application for the enrollment of Victoria T. Bean as a citizen by intermarriage of the Cherokee Nation.

Victoria T. Bean being first duly sworn by Frances R. Lane, a Notary Public for the Western District of Indian Territory, testified as follows:

By the Commissioner:
Q What is your name,[sic] A Victoria T. Bean.
Q How old are you? A Forty-nine on July 6th.
Q What is your postoffice addressM[sic] A Evansville, Ark.
Q You claim to be an intermarried citizen of the Cherokee Nation? A Yes sir.
Q Through whom do you claim to derive your right as such? A Mark Bean.
Q When were you married to Mark Bean? A In 1873.
Q What time of the year? A January.
Q Where were you living at that time? A Evansville, Ark.
Q How long did you live at Evansville, Ark., after you married Mark Bean? A I never did live there after I was married.

Cherokee Intermarried White 1906
Volume I

Q Where did you move to? A Cherokee Nation
Q What part? A Right on the line.
Q You are just across the line from Evansville? A Yes, the line runs right in front of the house. Right in front of our door.
Q Have you been living in the Cherokee Nation ever since you were married to Mark Bean? A Yes sir.
Q Were you ever married prior to your marriage to Mark Bean? A No sir.
Q Was he ever married prior to his marriage to you? A No sir.
Q Have you and Mark Bean lived together continuously in the Cherokee Nation ever since your marriage to him? A He is dead.
Q When did he die? A Two years the 9th day of March next. A year last March.
Q Have you married since his death? A No sir.
Q Was Mark Bean a citizen of the Cherokee Nation? At the time you married him in 1873? A Yes sir.
Q Did you vote in the Cherokee elections at that time? A Yes.
Q And has he been on all the Cherokee rolls since that time? A Yes sir.
Q Did you get a certificate of marriage at the time you married him in 1873? A I don't know whether he did or not. It was under the Cherokee law and he might not have got one.
Q Is there anyone here today that knows that you were married to Mark Bean in 1873?
A There is two ladies here.

The applicant is identified on the 1880 roll opposite No. 160. Her husband through whom she claims her right as a citizen of the Cherokee Nation is identified on said roll opposite No. 159, and is also identified on the final roll of citizens by blood of the Cherokee Nation opposite No. 1850.

Mattie J. Dannenberg, being first duly sworn by Frances R. Lane, a Notary Public for the Western District, testified as follows:

By the Commissioner:
Q What is your name? A Mattie J. Dannenberg.
Q How old are you? A Fifty-four.
Q What is your postoffice address? A Stilwell, I. T.
Q Are you acquainted with Victoria T. Bean? A Yes sir.
Q Did you know her husband in his lifetime? A Yes sir.
Q Do you know when they were married? A Yes sir.
Q When? A 11th day of January, 1873.
Q Were you present at their marriage? A No, but I was with them a few minutes before they got on their horses to go and get married.
Q You have known them ever since they were married in 1873? A Yes sir.
Q Have they lived together continuously as husband and wife in the Cherokee Nation up until the death of Mark Bean in 1905? A Yes sir.
Q Where did they live? A Lived up near the line near Evansville.
Q In the Cherokee Nation? A Yes sir.
                    Witness excused.

Cherokee Intermarried White 1906
Volume I

Frances R. Lane upon oath states that as stenographer to the Commissioner to the Five Civilized Tribes she reported the testimony in the above entitled cause and that the above and foregoing is an accurate transcript of her shorthand notes thereof.

Frances R Lane

Subscribed and sworn to before me this 4th day of January, 1907.

Edward Merrick
Notary Public.

⋄⋄⋄⋄⋄

E.C.M.

Cherokee 647

DEPARTMENT OF THE INTERIOR,
COMMISSIONER TO THE FIVE CIVILIZED TRIBES.

In the matter of the application for the enrollment of Victoria T. Bean as a citizen by intermarriage of the Cherokee Nation.

D E C I S I O N .

THE RECORDS OF THIS OFFICE SHOW: That at Stilwell, Indian Territory, July 25, 1900, Mark Bean appeared before the Commission to the Five Civilized Tribes, and made application for the enrollment of his wife, Victoria T. Bean as a citizen by intermarriage, and for the enrollment of himself as a citizen by blood of the Cherokee Nation. The application for the enrollment of the said Mark Bean as a citizen by blood of the Cherokee Nation has been heretofore disposed of and his right to enrollment will not be considered in this decision. Further proceedings in the matter of the application were had at Talequah[sic], Indian Territory, October 6, 1902 and October 30, 1902, and at Muskogee, Indian Territory, January 2, 1907.

THE EVIDENCE IN THIS CASE SHOWS: That the applicant herein, Victoria T. Bean, a white woman, married in January 1873, one Mark Bean, who was at the time of said marriage a recognized citizen by blood of the Cherokee Nation, and whose name appears upn the approved partial roll of citizens by blood of the Cherokee Nation opposite number 1850; that from the time of said marriage the said Mark Bean and Victoria T. Bean resided together as husband and wife, and continuously lived in the Cherokee Nation up to and including September 1, 1902. Said Victoria T. Bean is identified on the Cherokee Authenticated Tribal Roll of 1880 and the Cherokee Census Roll of 1896 as an intermarried citizen of the Cherokee Nation.

IT IS THEREFORE ORDERED AND ADJUDGED: That in accordance with the decision of the Supreme Court of the United States, dated November 5, 1906, in the case

Cherokee Intermarried White 1906
Volume I

of Daniel Red Bird et al. vs. the United States, under the provisions of Section 21, of the Act of Congress approved June 28, 1898, (30th. Stat. 495) Victoria T. Bean is entitled to enrollment as a citizen by intermarriage of the Cherokee Nation, and her application is accordingly granted.

                                              Tams Bixby
                                                     Commissioner.

Dated at Muskogee, Indian Territory,
this   JAN 18 1907

Cherokee
647.

                                        Muskogee, Indian Territory, December 22, 1906.

Victoria T. Bean,
        Evansville, Arkansas.

Dear Madam:

    November 6, 1906, the United States Supreme Court held that white persons who intermarried with Cherokee citizens according to Cherokee law prior to November 1, 1875, are entitled to enrollment and allotments of land as citizens of the Cherokee Nation.

    You are advised that to properly determine your right to enrollment as a citizen by intermarriage of the Cherokee Nation, it will be necessary for you to appear before the Commissioner for the purpose of giving testimony as to the date of your marriage and whether or not your husband, by reason of your marriage to whom you claim the right to enrollment as a citizen by intermarriage of the Cherokee Nation, was a recognized Cherokee citizen at the time of your marriage to him.

    You are therefore directed to appear before the Commissioner at Muskogee, Indian Territory, at 9 o'clock A. M., on Thursday, January 3, 1907, and give testimony as above indicated.
                                                Respectfully,

H.J.C.   Acting Commissioner.

Cherokee Intermarried White 1906
Volume I

Cherokee
647.

Muskogee, Indian Territory, January 18, 1907.

W. W. Hastings,
    Attorney for the Cherokee Nation,
        Muskogee, Indian Territory.

Dear Sir:

There is enclosed herewith a copy of the decision of the Commissioner to the Five Civilized Tribes, dated January 18, 1907, granting the application for the enrollment of Victoria T. Bean as a citizen by intermarriage of the Cherokee Nation.

        Respectfully,

Encl.HJ-25.
HJC.
                                          Commissioner.

◇◇◇◇◇

Cherokee   W.W. HASTINGS.   OFFICE OF   H.M. VANCE.
647.   ATTORNEY.   SECRETARY.

Attorney for the Cherokee Nation,
Muskogee, I. T.

        January 18, 1907.

The Commissioner to the Five Civilized Tribes,
    Muskogee, Indian Territory.

Sir:

Receipt is acknowledged of the testimony and of your decision enrolling Victoria T. Bean, as a citizen by intermarriage of the Cherokee Nation. Time for protesting said decision is waived and I consent that said person may be placed upon the schedule immediately.

        Yours very truly,
           W. W. Hastings
           Attorney for Cherokee Nation.

◇◇◇◇◇

Cherokee Intermarried White 1906
Volume I

Cherokee
647

Muskogee, Indian Territory, January 21, 1907.

Victoria T. Bean,
    Evansville, Arkansas.

Dear Madam:

    There is enclosed herewith copy of the decision of the Commissioner to the Five Civilized Tribes, dated January 18, 1907, granting the application for your enrollment as a citizen by intermarriage of the Cherokee Nation.

You will be advised when your name has been placed upon the schedule of citizens of the Cherokee Nation and approved by the Secretary of the Interior.

    Respectfully,

Enc M - 4

m t m   Commissioner.

Cher I W 12
Trans from Cher 657 3-26-07

◇◇◇◇◇

E.C.M.

DEPARTMENT OF THE INTERIOR,

COMMISSIONER TO THE FIVE CIVILIZED TRIBES.

In the matter of the application for the enrollment of

REBECCA M. BIGBEY

as a citizen by intermarriage of the Cherokee Nation.

CHEROKEE 657

◇◇◇◇◇

Cherokee Intermarried White 1906
Volume I

Department of the Interior,
Commission to the Five Civilized Tribes,
Stillwell[sic], I. T., July 26, 1900.

In the matter of the application of Thomas W. Bigbey for the enrollment of himself and children as Cherokees by blood, and his wife by intermarriage; beingduly sworn and examined by Commissioner Breckenridge[sic], he testified as follows:
Q What is your name? A Thomas W. Bigbey.
Q What is your age? A 52 years old.
Q What is your post office? A Dutch Mills, Ark.
Q Your district? A Going Snake.
Q How long have you lived there? A I suppose 42 or 43 years.
Q For whom do you make application for enrollment? A Myself and wife and children.
Q Do you apply as a Cherokee by blood? A Yes, sir.
Q Your wife by blood? A No, sir, she is a white woman.
(On 1880 roll, page 410, No. 152, Thomas Bigby, Going Snake dist.
On 1896 roll, page 723, No. 133, Thomas W. Bigbey, Going Snake dist.)
Q Now your wife, is she a white woman? A Yes, sir.
Q What is her age? A She is 53.
Q When were you married? A In 1870, August 18 I believe.
Q What is her name? A Rebecca M.
Q She is enrolled in 1880 under your name? A Yes, sir.
(On 1880 roll, page 410, No. 163, Rachel Bigby, Going Snake dist.
On 1896 roll, page 818, No. 15, Rebecca M. Bigbey, Going Snake dist.)
Q She is living with you at this time? A Yes, sir.
Q Now give me please the names of your children under age and unmarried? A David E. is the first one, he is 20 years old.
Q Is he on the roll of 1880? A I suppose so.
(On 1880 roll, page 410, No. 168, David Bigby, Going Snake dist.
On 1898 roll, page 723, No. 136, David E. Bigbey, Going Snake dist.)
Q Your next child? A Edward C., he is 17.
(On 1896 roll, page 723, No. 137, Edward C. Bigbey, Going Snake dist.)
Q Your next child? A Samuel A., he was born in 1885.
(On 1896 roll, page 723, No. 138, Samuel A. Bigbey, Going Snake dist.)
Q Your next child? A Sarah C. Bigbey, she was born in 1888.
(On 1896 roll, page 723, No. 139, Sarah C. Bigbey, Going Snake dist.)
Q Now your next child? A Minnie ., she was born in 1890.
(On 1896 roll, page 723, No. 140, Minnie C. Bigbey, Going Snake.)
Q Any more? A No, sir, none living.
Q These children are all alive and living with you at this time? A Yes, sir.
Mr. Bigbey, you are duly identified on the roll of 1880, and the roll of 1896, as is your wife also, and your oldest child, David E., and your four younger children, as enumerated in the testimony are duly identified on the roll of 1896; you and your children will be enrolled as Cherokees by blood and your wife as a Cherokee by adoption.

-----0-----

Cherokee Intermarried White 1906
Volume I

Bruce C. Jones, being duly sworn, says that as stenographer to the Commission to the Five Civilized Tribes he reported the testimony of the above named witness, and that the foregoing is a full, true and correct translation of his stenographic notes.

Bruce C Jones

Sworn to and subscribed before me this the 31st day of August, 1900.

CR Breckinridge
Commissioner.

◇◇◇◇◇

JOR.
Cher. 657.

Department of the Interior.
Commission to the Five Civilized Tribes.
Tahlequah, Indian Territory I. T., October 21, 1902.

SUPPLEMENTAL TESTIMONY in the matter of the application for the enrollment of REBECCA M. BIGBEY as a citizen by intermarriage of the Cherokee Nation.

REBECCA M. BIGBEY, being first duly sworn, testified as follows:

BY COMMISSION: What is your name? A Rebecca M. Bigbey.
Q How old are you? A Fifty-six.
Q What is your post office address? A Oak Grove.
Q Are you a whitw[sic] woman? A Yes sir.
Q Has application been made to this Commission for your enrollment as a citizen by intermarriage of the Cherokee Nation? A Yes sir.
Q What is the name of your husband? A Thomas W. Bigbey.
Q Is he living? A Yes sir.
Q Is he a Cherokee by blood? A Yes sir.
Q Do you claim your right to enrollment by reason of your marriage to him? A Yes sir.
Q When were you and he married? A In 1870.
Q Do your name appear upon the roll of 1880? A Yes sir.
Q Were you ever married before you married him? A No sir.
Q Was he ever married before he married you? A No sir.
Q You are his first wife and he is your first husband? A Yes sir.
Q Have you and he lived together continuously since your marriage? A Yes sir.
Q Were you living together on the 1st day of September, 1902? A Yes sir.
Q You have never been separated at all? A No sir.
Q Have you resided in the Cherokee Nation continuously since you and he married? A Yes sir.
Q Has he also? A Yes sir.
Q You have now many minor children that application was made for? A Four or five. There is Ed, Sammy, Sarah and Minnie. I guess that is all the minor children I have. Sone[sic] of the children were enrolled by themselves. two[sic] of them married. Walter

Cherokee Intermarried White 1906
Volume I

and Charles was married, and Thomas enrolled by himself, that just leaves four, I reckon, and David, that is five.
Q Are all five of those children living at this time? A Yes sir.
Q Have you had any children die since you were enrolled? A No sir.

This testimony will be filed with and made a part of the record in the matter of the application for the enrollment of Rebecca M. Bigbey as a citizen by intermarriage of the Cherokee Nation, Cherokee straight card field No. 657.

Wm. Hutchinson, being first duly sworn, states that as stenographer to the Commission to the Five Civilized Tribes he correctly recorded the testimony and proceedings in this case, and that the foregoing is a true and complete transcript of his stenographic notes thereof.

Wm Hutchinson

Subscribed and sworn to before me this 8th day of November, 1902.

BC Jones
Notary Public.

Cherokee 657.

DEPARTMENT OF THE INTERIOR,
COMMISSIONER TO THE FIVE CIVILIZED TRIBES,
Muskogee, I. T. January 2, 1907.

In the matter of the application for the enrollment of Rebecca M. Bigbey as a citizen by intermariage[sic] of the Cherokee Nation.

Thomas W. Bigby[sic], being first duly sworn by Frances R. Lane, a Notary Public for the Western District, testified as follows:

By the Commissioner:
Q What is your name? A Thomas W. Bigbey.
Q What is your age? A Fifty-eight.
Q What is your postoffice adress[sic]? A Dutch Mills, Arkansas.
Q Are you acquainted with Rebecca M. Bigbey? A Yes sir.
Q What relation is she to you? She is my wife.
Q When were you married to Rebecca M. Bigbey? A It was either in 1870 or 1871. I don't remember.
Q Where were you married to her? A In Going Snake District.
Q Did you get a certificate of marriage? A No sir.

Cherokee Intermarried White 1906
Volume I

Q Had you ever been married before you married Rebecca M. Bogbey[sic]?
A No sir.
Q Had she ever been married before she married you? A No sir.
Q have you lived together as husband and wife in the Cherokee Nation, continuously since your marriage in 1870 or 187o[sic], up to and including the present time?
A Yes sir.
Q Were you a citizen of the Cherokee nation[sic] at the time you married Rebecca M. Bigbey? A Yes sir.

> Applicant is identified on the 1880 Cherokee roll, opposite No. 163. Her husband, through whom she claims her right to enrollment is identified opposite No. 162. He is also identified on the final roll of Cherokees by blood, opposite No. 1865.
> Witness excused.

Jane Rider, being first duly sworn by Frances R. Lane, a Notary Public for the Western District, testified as follows:
Q What is your name? A Jane Rider.
Q Your postoffice address? A Evansville, Ark.
Q Are you acquainted with Thomas W. Bigbey and Rebecca M. Bigbey? A Yes sir.
Q Do you know when they were married? A Yes sir.
Q Were you present when they were married? A Yes sir.
Q When? A I think in the month of August, 1870.
Q Where were hey[sic] married? A They were married at this preacher's house where I was married at Gormleys. The same preacher married us.
Q Have they lived together as husband and wife from that time up to the present time?
A Yes sir.
Witness excused.

Frances R. Lane upon oath states that as stenographer to the Commissioner to the Five Civilized Tribes she reported the testimony in the above entitled cause and that the above and foregoing is an accurate transcript of her stenographic notes thereof.

Frances R Lane

Subscribed and sworn to before me this January 4, 1907/[sic]

Edward Merrick
Notary Public.

◇◇◇◇◇

Cherokee Intermarried White 1906
Volume I

E.C.M. Cherokee 657.

DEPARTMENT OF THE INTERIOR,

COMMISSIONER TO THE FIVE CIVILIZED TRIBES.

In the matter of the application for the enrollment of Rebecca M. Bigbey as a citizen by intermarriage of the Cherokee Nation.

D E C I S I O N

THE RECORDS OF THIS OFFICE SHOW: That at Stilwell, Indian Territory, July 26, 1900, Thomas W. Bigbey appeared before the Commission to the Five Civilized Tribes, and made application for the enrollment of himself, et al., as citizens by blood of the Cherokee Nation. The application for the enrollment of the said Thomas W. Bigbey, et al., as citizens by blood of the Cherokee Nation has been heretofore disposed of, and their rights to enrollment will not be considered in this decision. Further proceedings in the matter of said application were had at Tahlequah, Indian Territory, October 21, 1901, and at Muskogee, Indian Territory, January 2, 1907.

THE EVIDENCE IN THIS CASE SHOWS: That the applicant herein, Rebecca M. Bigbey, a white woman, married in August, 1870, one Thomas M[sic]. Bigbey, who was at the time of said marriage a recognized citizen by blood of the Cherokee Nation, and whose name appears on the approved partial roll of citizens by blood of the Cherokee Nation, opposite No. 1865; that from the time of said marriage the said Thomas W. Bigbey and Rebecca M. Bigbey resided together as husband and wife, and continuously lived in the Cherokee Nation up to and including September 1, 1902. Said Rebecca M. Bigbey is identified on the Cherokee authenticated tribal roll of 1880, and the Cherokee census roll of 1896, as an intermarried citizen of the Cherokee Nation.

IT IS, THEREFORE, ORDERED AND ADJUDGED: That in accordance with the decision of the Supreme Court of the United States, dated November 5, 1906, in the case of Daniel Red Bird et al. vs. the United States, under the provisions of Section twenty-one, of the Act of Congress approved June 28, 1899 (30 Stat., 495), Rebecca M. Bigbey is entitled to enrollment as a citizen by intermarriage of the Cherokee Nation, and her application for enrollment as such is accordingly granted.

Tams Bixby
Commissioner.

Dated at Muskogee, Indian Territory,
this JAN 17 1907

Cherokee Intermarried White 1906
Volume I

Cherokee
657.

Muskogee, Indian Territory, December 22, 1906.

Rebecca M. Bigbey,
    Oak Grove, Indian Territory.

Dear Madam:

November 6, 1906, the United States Supreme Court held that white persons who intermarried with Cherokee citizens according to Cherokee law prior to November 1, 1875, are entitled to enrollment and allotments of land as citizens of the Cherokee Nation.

You are advised that to properly determine your right to enrollment as a citizen by intermarriage of the Cherokee Nation, it will be necessary for you to appear before the Commissioner for the purpose of giving testimony as to the date of your marriage and whether or not your husband, by reason of your marriage to whom you claim the right to enrollment as a citizen by intermarriage of the Cherokee Nation, was a recognized Cherokee citizen at the time of your marriage to him.

You are therefore directed to appear before the Commissioner at Muskogee, Indian Territory, at 9 o'clock A. M., on Thursday, January 3, 1907, and give testimony as above indicated.

                Respectfully,

H.J.C.   Acting Commissioner.

Cherokee
657

Muskogee, Indian Territory, January 17, 1907.

W. W. Hastings,
    Attorney for the Cherokee Nation,
        Muskogee, Indian Territory.

Dear Sir:

There is enclosed herewith a copy of the decision of the Commissioner to the Five Civilized Tribes, dated January 17, 1907, granting the application for the enrollment of Rebecca M. Bigbey as a citizen by intermarriage of the Cherokee Nation.

                Respectfully,

Encl.H-39   Commissioner.
JMH

Cherokee Intermarried White 1906
Volume I

Cherokee 657.   W.W. HASTINGS.   OFFICE OF   H.M. VANCE.
                ATTORNEY.   SECRETARY.

Attorney for the Cherokee Nation,
MUSKOGEE, I. T.

January 18, 1907.

The Commissioner to the Five Civilized Tribes,
Muskogee, Indian Territory.

Sir:

Receipt is acknowledged of the testimony and of your decision enrolling Rebecca M. Bigbey as a citizen by intermarriage of the Cherokee Nation. Time for protesting said decision is waived and I consent that said person may be placed upon the schedule immediately.

Yours very truly,
W. W. Hastings
Attorney for Cherokee Nation.

◇◇◇◇◇

Cherokee
657

Muskogee, Indian Territory, January 19, 1907.

Rebecca M. Bigbey,
Oak Grove, Indian Territory.

Dear Madam:

There is enclosed herewith a copy of the decision of the Commissioner to the Five Civilized Tribes, dated January 17, 1907, granting the application for your enrollment as a citizen by intermarriage of the Cherokee Nation.

You will be advised when your name has been placed upon the schedule of citizens of the Cherokee Nation and approved by the Secretary of the Interior.

Respectfully,

Encl.H-90
JMH   Commissioner.

Cherokee Intermarried White 1906
Volume I

Cher I W 13
Trans from Cher 755 3-27-07

E.C.M.

DEPARTMENT OF THE INTERIOR,

COMMISSIONER TO THE FIVE CIVILIZED TRIBES.

In the matter of the application for the enrollment of

JOHN R. ALLISON

as a citizen by intermarriage of the Cherokee Nation.

CHEROKEE 755.

DEPARTMENT OF THE INTERIOR,
COMMISSION TO THE FIVE CIVILIZED TRIBES,
STILWELL, I.T., JULY 27, 1900.

In the matter of the application for the enrollment of John R. Allison et als., for enrollment as citizens of the Cherokee Nation, said Allison being sworn by Commissioner Needles, testified as follows:

Q What is your name? A John R. Allison.
Q Your age? A 59.
Q Your postoffice? A Stilwell.
Q Have you been recognied[sic] by the Cherokee tribal authorities as a citizen of the Cherokee Nation? A Yes.
Q By blood or adoption? A By adoption.
Q Have you ever been enrolled by the Cherokee tribal authorities as a Cherokee citizen? A Yes.
Q Where do you live? A Flint district.
Q How long have you lived there? A About 30 years.
Q What's the name of your father? A Amos.
Q Is he living? A No sir.
Q Is his name upon the rolls of the Cherokee Nation? A No sir.
Q What is your mother's name? A Delaney.
Q Is she living? A No sir.
Q Does her name appear upon the rolls of the Cherokee Nation? [sic] No sir.

Cherokee Intermarried White 1906
Volume I

    Applicant on '80 roll, page 403, number 8 as Rufus Allison.
    On '96 roll, page 711, number 4.
Q Are you married? A Yes.
Q What is your wife's name? A Mildred T. Allison.
Q When were you married? A In '70.
    On '80 roll, page 403, number 9 as W. L. Allison.
    On '96 roll, page 641, number 32;
    On '94 roll, page 510, number '86.
Q What is the name of your wife's father? A John Adair.
Q Is he living? A No sir.
Q What is the name of her mother? A Ann B. Adair.
Q Is she living? A Yes.
Q What proportion of Cherokee blood does your wife claim? A 1/2.
Q Have you any children under 21 years of age? A Two.
Q What are their names? A Edgar G., 19 years old.
    On '96 roll, page 641, number 34, as Edgar J. Allison;
    On '94 roll, page 510, number 89 as Garfield E. Allison
Q What's the next one? A Narcenia, 17 years old.
    On '96 roll, page 641, number 35, as Narcena;
    On '94 roll, page 510, number 90, as Narcena.
Q Are these children alive and living with you? A Yes.
Q Mother of them alive and living with you? A Yes.
Q You and her have lived together continuously as man and wife since marriage?
A Yes.

    The name of John R. Allison appearing upon the authenticated roll of '80 and the census roll of '96, and his wife, Mildred T. Allison's name appearing upon the authenticated roll of '80 as well as the census roll of '96 and the pay-roll of '94, and his children?[sic] Edgar G., and Narcenia, also appearing upon the census roll of '96 and the pay-roll of '94, they being dult[sic] identified, and proof being made as to their residence, they are duly listed for enrollment as Cherokee citizens by blood, with the exception of John R. Allison who will be enrolled as a citizen by intermarriage.

Brown McDonald, being duly sworn, says as Stenographer to the Commission to the Five Civilized Tribes, he reported in full the testimony of the above named witness, and that the foregoing is a full, true and correct transcript of his notes.

                                  Brown McDonald

    Sworn to and subscribed before me this 3rd day of August, 1900, at Bunch, I.T.

                                  TB Needles
                                  Commissioner.

Cherokee Intermarried White 1906
Volume I

Cher # 755

Department of the Interior,
Commission to the Five Civilized Tribes,
Muskogee, I. T., October 10, 1902.

In the matter of the application of JOHN R. ALLISON, for the enrollment of himself as a citizen by intermarriage, his wife MILDRED T. ALLISON, and his two children, EDGAR G. and NARCENIE ALLISON, as citizens by blood, of the Cherokee Nation.

JOHN R. ALLISON, called as a witness, being duly sworn and examined by the Commission, testified as follows:

Q Your full name is John R. Allison ? A Yes sir.
Q How old are you ? [sic] Sixty two years of age.
Q What is your post office address ? A Adair.
Q It used to be Stilwell ? A Yes sir.
Q You are a white man ? A Yes sir.
Q You are on the roll of 1880 as an intermarried white ? A Yes sir.
Q What was the name of your wife at that time ? A The same name as now.
Q The same wife you have now ? A Yes sir.
Q Have you and your wife been living together in the Cherokee Nation ever since 1880 ? A Yes sir.
Q You have never been separated ? A We have never been separated.
Q You have never made your home outside the Cherokee Nation ? A No sir.
Q You and your wife were living together then on the first day of last September ? A Yes sir.
Q Your wife is living ? A Yes sir.
Q Are your children living at home with you ? A Yes sir. There are three living with us, but just two are under age.

E. C. Bagwell, on oath states that as stenographer to the Commission to the Five Civilized Tribes, he correctly recorded the testimony and proceedings in the above entitled cause, and that the foregoing is an accurate transcript of his stenographic notes thereof.

              E.C. Bagwell

Subscribed and sworn to before me this October 17, 1902.

              BC Jones
              Notary Public.

Cherokee Intermarried White 1906
Volume I

Cherokee No. 755

DEPARTMENT OF THE INTERIOR
COMMISSIONER TO THE FIVE CIVILIZED TRIBES

Muskogee, Indian Territory

January 3, 1907

In the matter of the application for the enrollment of John R. Allison as a citizen by intermarriage of the Cherokee Nation.

The applicant being duly sworn by Walter W. Chappell, a Notary Public for the Western District, testified as follows:

Q What is your name? A John R. Allison.
Q What is your age? A 66 years, about that.
Q Your postoffice address? A Adair.
Q You claim to be a citizen by marriage of the Cherokee Nation do you? A Yes sir.
Q Through whom do you claim that right? A My wife, Mildred T. Adair.
Q Is she living at the present time? A She is.
Q What is her citizenship? A She's a Cherokee by blood.
Q Where was she born.[sic] [sic] Born in Georgia.
Q When did she come to the Cherokee Nation? A In 1869 or 1870, I think it was "70, February, 1870, I think it was
Q She was born then a citizen of Georgia? A She was born in the old Nation.
Q Was she admitted to citizenship[sic] when she removed to the Cherokee Nation? A Yes sir She was admitted by the Supreme Court I think in May 1870.
Q Was that the court known as the Daniels Court? A I don't know-- there was a Daniels on the court
Q When were you and she married? A Under the Cherokee law we married first in the old Nation, then came here and again in order to comply with the Cherokee law were married again.
Q When were you married the second time?

The applicant offers in evidence a certificate of "James W Adair Clerk District Court, Flint, Cherokee Nation, under date of March 19, 1870, wherein it is recited that the said James W. Adair granted license of marriage to Mr. John Rufus Allison citizen of the United States to marry Miss Mildred T. Adair, Cherokee by birth. This certificate further shows that the marriage of the above named parties was solemnized by J. T. Adair, Chief Justice of Supreme Court Cherokee Nation on the 23rd day of March, 1870.
Same is filed herewith and made a part of the record in this case.

Q Were either you or your wife married prior to your marriage in Georgia? A No sir.
Q Have you lived together continuously since your marriage in 1870? A Yes sir.

Cherokee Intermarried White 1906
Volume I

Q Where have you resided during that time? A Flint, Cherokee Nation and Cooesscoowee[sic] district.

The said Mildred T. Allison, nee Adair, is identified on the approved partial roll of Cherokees by blood opposite No. 2092.

The applicant is identified on the authenticated Cherokee Tribal roll of 1800 Goingsnake District, and Cherokee Census Roll of 1896, Flint District, opposite numbers 8 and 711, respectively, as an intermarried white.

On Page 106 of Book B, Marriage Records for Flint District is found the record of the license issued to Rufus B. Allison to marry Miss Mildred T. Adair, together with certificate of J. T. Adair Chief Justice of the Supreme Court Cherokee Nation that he had solemnized the marriage of the above named parties.

Witness excused

Gertrude Hanna, being duly sworn, states on oath that as stenographer to the Commissioner to the Five Civilized Tribes she reported the proceedings had in the above case on January 3, 1907, and that the above and foregoing is a true and correct transcript of her stenographic notes taken therein.

Gertrude Hanna

Subscribed and sworn to before me this *(illegible)* the day of January, 1907

Walter W. Chappell
Notary Public

◇◇◇◇◇

Cherokee Nation)
)
Flint District) By the authority in me vested by the law of the Cherokee Nation, I do hereby grant License of Marriage unto Mr. John Rufus Allison a Citizen of the United States and of good moral Character and of industrious habits, to marry Miss Mildred T. Adair, a Cherokee by Birth and a daughter of John Adair, He (Mr. John Rufus Allison), having complyed[sic] with the requirements of the Law regulating intermarriage with white men. Given from under my hand in office this the 19th day of March 1870.

James W. Adair clk.
License fee $5.00. Dist. Ct Flint C.N.

This is to certify that I hav[sic] this day Sollomised[sic] and perform[sic] the rites of ceremony of marriage between Mr. John Rufus Allison and Miss Mildred T. Adair accordent[sic] to Law authorized by the above License.

Given under my hand this, the 23d day March 1870.

Cherokee Intermarried White 1906
Volume I

J. T. Adair,
Chief Justice, S.C.
Cherokee Nation.

This is to certify that the undersigned, being first duly sworn, states that as stenographer to the Commission to the Five Civilized Tribes, she made the above copy, and that the same is a full, true and complete copy of an instrument now on file in this office.

Sarah Waters

Subscribed and sworn to before me this, the 15th day of January, 1907.

John E. Tidwell
Notary Public.

◇◇◇◇◇

E.C.M.   Cherokee 755.

DEPARTMENT OF THE INTERIOR,

COMMISSIONER TO THE FIVE CIVILIZED TRIBES.

D E C I S I O N

THE RECORDS OF THIS OFFICE SHOW: That at Stilwell, Indian Territory, July 27, 1900, John R. Allison appeared before the Commission to the Five Civilized Tribes, and made application for the enrollment of himself as a citizen by intermarriage, and for the enrollment of his wife, Mildred T. Allison, et al., as citizens by blood of the Cherokee Nation. The application for the enrollment of the said Mildred T. Allison, et al., as citizens by blood of the Cherokee Nation has been heretofore disposed of, and their rights to enrollment will not be considered in this decision. Further proceedings in the matter of said application were had at Muskogee, Indian Territory, October 10, 1902, and January 3, 1907.

THE EVIDENCE IN THIS CASE SHOWS: That the applicant herein, John R. Allison, a white man, was married in accordance with Cherokee law March 23, 1870, to his wife, Mildred T. Allison, nee Adair, who was at the time of said marriage a recognized citizen by blood of the Cherokee Nation, and whose name appears on the approved partial roll of citizens by blood of the Cherokee Nation, opposite No. 2092; that since said marriage the said John R. Allison and the said Mildred T. Allison have resided together as husband and wife, and have continuously lived in the Cherokee Nation. Said John R. Allison is identified on the Cherokee authenticated tribal roll of 1880, and the Cherokee census roll of 1896, as an intermarried citizen of the Cherokee Nation.

Cherokee Intermarried White 1906
Volume I

IT IS, THEREFORE, ORDERED AND ADJUDGED: That in accordance with the decision of the Supreme Court of the United States, dated November 5, 1906, in the case of Daniel Red Bird et al. vs. the United States, under the provisions of Section twenty-one, of the Act of Congress approved June 28, 1898 (30 Stat., 495), John R. Allison is entitled to enrollment as a citizen by intermarriage of the Cherokee Nation, and his application for enrollment as such is accordingly granted.

Tams Bixby
Commissioner.

Dated at Muskogee, Indian Territory,
this   JAN 16 1907

◇◇◇◇◇

Cherokee
755

Muskogee, Indian Territory, December 22, 1906.

John R. Allison,
    Adair, Indian Territory.

Dear Sir:

    November 6, 1906, the United States Supreme Court held that white persons who intermarried with Cherokee citizens according to Cherokee law prior to November 1, 1875, are entitled to enrollment and allotments of land as citizens of the Cherokee Nation.

    You are advised that to properly determine your right to enrollment as a citizen by intermarriage of the Cherokee Nation, it will be necessary for you to appear before the Commissioner for the purpose of giving testimony as to the date of your marriage and whether or not your wife, by reason of your marriage to whom you claim the right to enrollment as a citizen of the Cherokee Nation, was a recognized citizen of the Cherokee Nation at the time of your marriage to her, and whether or not you were married to her in accordance with Cherokee laws.

Respectfully,

H J.C.   Acting Commissioner.

◇◇◇◇◇

Cherokee Intermarried White 1906
Volume I

Cherokee 755

Muskogee, Indian Territory, January 17, 1906

W. W. Hastings,
    Attorney for the Cherokee Nation,
        Muskogee, Indian Territory.

Dear Sir:

There is enclosed herewith copy of the decision of the Commissioner to the Five Civilized Tribes, dated January 18, 1907, granting the application for the enrollment of as a citizen by intermarriage of the Cherokee Nation.

        Respectfully,

Enc I7

RPI

        Commissioner.

◇◇◇◇◇

| W.W. HASTINGS,
ATTORNEY. | OFFICE OF | H.M. VANCE,
SECRETARY. | Cherokee 755. |

Attorney for the Cherokee Nation,
MUSKOGEE, I. T.

January 18, 1907.

The Commissioner,
    to the Five Civilized Tribes,
        Muskogee, Indian Territory.

Sir:

Receipt is acknowledged of the testimony and of your decision enrolling John R. Allison as a citizen by intermarriage of the Cherokee Nation. Time for protesting said decision is waived and I consent that said person may be placed upon the schedule immediately.

        W. W. Hastings
        Attorney for Cherokee Nation.

◇◇◇◇◇

Cherokee Intermarried White 1906
Volume I

Cherokee
755

Muskogee, Indian Territory, January 19, 1907.

John R. Allison,
    Adair, Indian Territory.

Dear Sir:

There is enclosed herewith copy of the decision of the Commissioner to the Five Civilized Tribes, dated January 16, 1907, granting the application for your enrollment as a citizen by intermarriage of the Cherokee Nation.

You will be advised when your name has been placed upon the schedule of citizens of the Cherokee Nation and approved by the Secretary of the Interior.

Respectfully,

Enc I-60   Commissioner.

RPI

◇◇◇◇◇

Cherokee
I. W. 13

Muskogee, Indian Territory, April 6, 1907

John R. Allison,
    Adair, Indian Territory.

Dear Sir:

Your marriage license and certificate, filed in connection with your application for enrollment as a citizen by intermarriage, is returned to you herewith, copies of the same being retained in this office.

Respectfully,

L M B   Acting Commissioner.

Encl. B-85

Cherokee Intermarried White 1906
Volume I

Cher I W 14
Trans from Cher 835 3-13-07

E.C.M.

DEPARTMENT OF THE INTERIOR,

COMMISSIONER TO THE FIVE CIVILIZED TRIBES.

In the matter of the application for the enrollment of

TALITHA J. ADAIR

as a citizen by intermarriage of the Cherokee Nation.

CHEROKEE 835

Department of the Interior.
Commission to the Five Civilized Tribes.
Bunch, I. T., July 30th, 1900.

In the matter of the application of Virgil B. Adair et al for the enrollment as Cherokee citizens; being sworn and examined by Commissioner Breckinridge, testified as follows:

Q What is your name? A Virgil B. Adair.
Q Your age? A 58
Q Your post-office? A Dutch Mills, Ark.
Q District? A Goingsnake.
Q How long have you lived in Goingsnake? A About 31 years
Q For whom do you make application now? A Myself, wife and one minor heir.
Q Do you apply as a Cherokee by blood? A Yes sir.
Q Do you apply for your wife as a Cherokee by blood? A No sir.
Q Are you on the roll of 1880? A Yes sir.
Q Goingsnake district? A Yes sir.
Q Also on the roll of 1896? A Yes sir.
Q Give me your wife's full name? A Talitha Jane.
Q How old is she? A 58
Q When were you married? A Married in 1865.
Q Your wife's on the roll of 1880 I suppose? A Yes sir.
Q You and she living together? A Yes sir.
Q Give me the names of your children? A Julius K. Adair.

Cherokee Intermarried White 1906
Volume I

Q How old is he? A 19.
Q Is that child on the rolls of 1894 and 1896? A Yes sir.
Q Is your child living and living with you? A Yes sir.
Note: 1880 roll; page 405, #56, V. B. Adair, Goingsnake Dist.
       1880 roll; page 405, #57, Jane Adair, Goingsnake Dist.
       1896 roll; page 721, #67, Adair, Virgil B. Goingsnake Dist.
       1896 roll; page 817, # 5, Adair, Jane, Goingsnake Dist.
       1896 roll; page 721, #71, Adair, Julius K, Goingsnake Dist.
       1894 roll; page 612, #65, Julius K. Adair, Goingsnake Dist.

Mr. Adair you are duly identified on the roll of 1880 and 1896. Your wife is identified on the same rolls, and your child, Julius K. Adair, is identified on the rolls of 1894 and 1896. You and your child will be enrolled as Cherokees by blood and your wife as a Cherokee by adoption.

Edward G. Rothenberger, being duly sworn by Commissioner Breckinridge as Stenographer to the Commission to the Five Civilized Tribes, he reported in full the testimony of the above named witness, Virgil B. Adair, and that the foregoing is a full, true and correct transcript of his notes.

                                                        Edward G. Rothenberger

Sworn to and subscribed before me this 31st day of July, 1900, at Bunch, I. T.

                                                        CR Breckinridge

JOR.
Cher. 835.

Department of the Interior.
Commission to the Five Civilized Tribes.
Tahlequah, I. T., October 13, 1902.

SUPPLEMENTAL TESTIMONY AND PROCEEDINGS in the matter of the application for the enrollment of TALITHA J. ADAIR as a citizen by intermarriage of the Cherokee Nation.

TALITHA J. ADAIR, being first duly sworn, and being examined, testified as follows:

BY COMMISSION: What is your name? A Talitha J. Adair.
Q How old are you? A Sixty.
Q What is your post office address? A Dutch Mills, Arkansas.
Q You are a white woman, are you? A Yes sir.
Q Have you heretofore made application to this Commission for enrollment as a citizen by intermarriage of the Cherokee Nation? A Yes sir, my husband did for me.
Q What is the name of your husband? A Virgil B. Adair.

Cherokee Intermarried White 1906
Volume I

Q Is he living? A Yes sir.
Q Is he a Cherokee by blood? A Yes sir.
Q Do you claim your rigt[sic] to enrollment by reason of your marriage to him? A Yes sr[sic].
Q When were you and he married? A In 1865.
Q Have you and he lived together continuously since that time? A Yes sir.
Q Were you living together on the 1st day of September, 1902? A Yes sir.
Q You have never been separated from him? A No sir.
Q Were you ever married before you married him? A No sir.
Q Was he ever married before he married you? A No sir.
Q He is your first husband and you are his first wife? A Yes sir.
Q Have you resided in the Cherokee Nation continuously since you and he were married? A Yes sir.
Q Has he also? A Yes sir.
Q Have you any children that application was made for? A Yes sir, one.
Q What is its name? A John K.
Q Is that child living? A Yes sir.

This testimony will be filed with and made a part of the record in the matter of the application for the enrollment of Talitha J. Adair as a citizen by intermarriage of the Cherokee Nation, Cherokee straight card filed No. 835.

Wm. Hutchinson, being first duly sworn, states that as stenographer to the Commission to the Five Civilized Tribes he correctly recorded the testimony and proceedings in this case, and that the foregoing is a true and complete transcript of the stenographic notes thereof.

Wm Hutchinson

Subscribed and sworn to before me this 21st day of October, 1902.

John O Rosson
Notary Public.

◇◇◇◇◇

LGD   Cherokee 835.

DEPARTMENT OF THE INTERIOR,
COMMISSIONER TO THE FIVE CIVILIZED TRIBES.

Muskogee, Indian Territory, January 3, 1907.

In the matter of the application of TALITHA J. ADAIR for enrollment as a citizen by intermarriage of the Cherokee Nation.

Cherokee Intermarried White 1906
Volume I

Virgil B. Adair, being first duly sworn by B. P. Rasmus, a notary, testified as follows:

Q What is your name? A Virgil B. Adair.
Q What is your age? A 64 years old.
Q What is your postoffice address? A Dutch Mills, Arkansas.
Q Are you a citizen of the Cherokee Nation? A Yes sir.
Q By blood? A Yes sir.
Q Do you know Talitha J. Adair? A Yes sir.
Q What relation is she to you? A She is my wife.
Q You appear here today in her interests? A Yes.
Q When were you married to her? A in 1864.
Q Where were you married to her? A In Georgia.
Q When did you remove to the Cherokee Nation? A In 1869.
Q When were you admitted to citizenship in the Cherokee Nation? A In 1869.
Q By act of the council? A No sir, by the court.
Q Were you ever married before you married Talitha Adair? A No sir.
Q Was she ever married before she married you? A No sir.
Q Have you lived together continuously as husband and wife ever since your marriage? [sic] Yes sir.
Q Have you a certificate of your marriage? A No sir.
Q Who married you? A A minister by the name of Bates.
Q Have you a license? A No sir.
Q Have you any documentary proof? A No sir.

The applicant is identified on the 1880 Cherokee roll, Goingsnake District, opposite No. 57. Her husband, through whom she claims her right to enrollment, is on said roll in said District, opposite No. 56. He is also identified upon the final roll of citizen by blood of the Cherokee Nation opposite No. 2275.

Q When was the first time you ever voted in the Cherokee Nation? A I cant[sic] tell you the date.
Q About when? A I suppose it was in that year, '69.
Q Have you had the privilege of voting since 1869? A Yes.
Q Have you held property in the Cherokee Nation since 1869? A Yes sir.

Witness excused.

Solon H. Roberts, being first duly sworn by B. P. Rasmus, a notary public, testified as follows:

Q What is your name? A Solon H. Roberts.
Q What is your age? A 63 years old.
Q What is your postoffice address? A Dutch Mills, Arkansas.
Q Are you a citizen of the Cherokee Nation? A Ye sir.
Q By blood? A No sir, by adoption.
Q Are you acquainted with Virgil B. Adair? A Yes.

Cherokee Intermarried White 1906
Volume I

Q Are you acquainted with his wife? A Yes sir.
Q How long have you known them? A Since 1869.
Q Have they lived together continuously as husband and wife? A Yes, considered so.
Q Has Virgil B. Adair been recognized as a citizen of the Cherokee Nation ever since you knew him? A Yes, he has been a voter.

Witness excused.

Daniel K. Wetsel, being first duly sworn by B. P. Rasmus, a notary public, testified as follows:

Q What is your name? A Daniel K. Wetsel.
Q What is your age? A 66 years old.
Q What is your postoffice address? A Maysville, Arkansas.
Q Are you a citizen of the Cherokee Nation? A Yes sir.
Q By blood? A No, by adoption.
Q Do you know Virgil B. Adair? A Yes sir.
Q Are you acquainted with his wife? A Yes sir.
Q Do you know when they were married? A In 1866 or 1867, I dont[sic] know positively.
Q Where were they married? A In Georgia.
Q Were you present when they were married? A Yes.
Q You saw them married? A Yes.
Q Have they lived together as husband and wife ever since they were married? A Yes.
Q Living together at the present time, are they? A Yes.

Witness excused.

Demie T. Stubblefield, beinf[sic] first duly sworn, on oath, states that as stenographer to the Commissioner to the Five Civilized Tribes she correctly recorded the proceedings in the above cause, and that the above and foregoing is a true and correct transcript of her stenographic notes thereof.

Demie T. Stubblefield

Subscribed and sworn to before me this, January 4, 1907.

Edward Merrick
Notary Public.

Cherokee Intermarried White 1906
Volume I

DEPARTMENT OF THE INTERIOR,
COMMISSIONER TO THE FIVE CIVILIZED TRIBES.

"Going Snake District.
Cherokees whose citizenship is doubtful."

" 4, VIRGIL B. ADAIR: Decided in favor of clmnt Apl. 17th. "

-------------------oOo------------------

This is to certify that the above and foregoing is a true and correct copy of words and figures found on page 12, of the "Docket of Doubtful Cases for Cherokee Citizenship tried in 1871" by the "Daniels Court" of the Cherokee Nation, in the possession of this office.

The docket referred to shows that the case preceding this one was decided on April 17, 1871, and that the case following the one referred to was decided on April 7, 1871.

Tams Bixby
Commissioner.

Dated at Muskogee, Indian Territory,
this JAN 11 1907

◇◇◇◇◇

E.C.M.
Cherokee 835

DEPARTMENT OF THE INTERIOR THE,
COMMISSIONER TO THE FIVE CIVILIZED TRIBES.

In the matter of the application for the enrollment of Talitha J. Adair as a citizen by intermarriage of the Cherokee Nation.

D E C I S I O N .

THE RECORDS OF THIS OFFICE SHOW: That at Bunch, Indian Territory, July 30, 1900, Virgil B. Adair appeared before the Commission to the Five Civilized Tribes and made application for the enrollment of his wife, Talitha J. Adair, as a citizen by intermarriage, and for the enrollment of himself and his son, Julius J, Adair, as citizens by blood of the Cherokee Nation. The application for the enrollment of the said Virgil B. Adair and his son, Julius K. Adair as citizens by blood of the Cherokee Nation had been heretofore disposed of, and their rights to enrollment will not be considered in this decision. Further proceedings in the matter of said application were had at Tahlequah, Indian Territory, October 13, 1902 and at Muskogee, Indian Territory, January 3, 1907.

Cherokee Intermarried White 1906
Volume I

THE EVIDENCE IN THIS CASE SHOWS: That the applicant herein, Talitha J. Adair, a white woman, married about 1864 one Virgil B. Adair, a Cherokee by blood, who was at that time a resident of the state of Georgia; that the said Virgil b. Adair and Talitha J. Adair removed about the year 1869 to the Cherokee Nation, and have since continuously resided therein as husband and wife; that the said Virgil B. Adair was admitted to citizenship in the Cherokee Nation by the order of the Supreme Court of the Cherokee Nation, commonly known as the "Daniels Court" April 17, 1870. Said Talitha J. Adair is identified on the Cherokee Authenticated Tribal roll of 1880 and the Cherokee Census Roll of 1896 as an intermarried citizen of the Cherokee Nation.

IT IS THEREFORE ORDERED AND ADJUDGED: That in accordance with the decision of the Supreme Court of the United States, dated November 5, 1906, in the case of Daniel Red Bird et al. vs. the United States, under the provisions of Section 21, of the Act of Congress approved June 28, 1898 (30th Stat., 495) Talitha J. Adair is entitled to enrollment as a citizen by intermarriage of the Cherokee Nation, and her application for enrollment as such is accordingly granted.

            Tams Bixby
              Commissioner.

Dated at Muskogee, Indian Territory,
this JAN 18 1907

◇◇◇◇◇

Cherokee
835.

            Muskogee, Indian Territory, December 22, 1906.

Talitha J. Adair,
  Dutch Mills, Arkansas.

Dear Madam:

  November 6, 1906, the United States Supreme Court held that white persons who intermarried with Cherokee citizens according to Cherokee law prior to November 1, 1875, are entitled to enrollment and allotments of land as citizens of the Cherokee Nation.

  You are advised that to properly determine your right to enrollment as a citizen by intermarriage of the Cherokee Nation, it will be necessary for you to appear before the Commissioner for the purpose of giving testimony as to the date of your marriage and whether or not your husband, by reason of your marriage to whom you claim the right to enrollment as a citizen by intermarriage of the Cherokee Nation, was a recognized Cherokee citizen at the time of your marriage to him.

  You are therefore directed to appear before the Commissioner at Muskogee, Indian Territory, at 9 o'clock A. M., on Thursday, January 3, 1907, and give testimony as above indicated.

Cherokee Intermarried White 1906
Volume I

Respectfully,

H.J.C.   Acting Commissioner.

Cherokee
835.

Muskogee, Indian Territory, January 18, 1907.

W. W. Hastings,
    Attorney for the Cherokee Nation,
        Muskogee, Indian Territory.

Dear Sir:

    There is enclosed herewith a copy of the decision of the Commissioner to the Five Civilized Tribes, dated January 18, 1907, granting the application for the enrollment of Talitha J. Adair, as a citizen by intermarriage of the Cherokee Nation.

Respectfully,

Encl. HJ-44.
  HJC   Commissioner.

Cherokee 835   W.W.HASTINGS. ATTORNEY.   OFFICE OF   H.M. VANCE. SECRETARY.

Attorney for the Cherokee Nation,
MUSKOGEE, I. T.

January 18, 1907.

The Commissioner to the Five Civilized Tribes,
    Muskogee, Indian Territory.

Sir:

    Receipt is acknowledged of the testimony and of your decision enrolling Talitha J. Adair as a citizen by intermarriage of the Cherokee Nation. Time for protesting said decision is waived and I consent that said person may be placed upon the schedule immediately.

Yours very truly,
W. W. Hastings
Attorney for Cherokee Nation.

Cherokee Intermarried White 1906
Volume I

Cherokee

835

Muskogee, Indian Territory, January 21, 1907.

Talitha J. Adair,
    Dutch Mills, Ark.

Dear Madam:

    There is enclosed herewith copy of the decision of the Commissioner to the Five Civilized Tribes, dated January 18, 1907, granting the application for your enrollment as a citizen by intermarriage of the Cherokee Nation.

    You will be advised when your name has been placed upon the schedule of citizens of the Cherokee Nation and approved by the Secretary of the Interior.

Respectfully,

Enc M - 3

m t m   Commissioner.

Cher I W 15
(Trans from Cher 1270)

◇◇◇◇◇

DEPARTMENT OF THE INTERIOR,

COMMISSIONER TO THE FIVE CIVILIZED TRIBES.

In the matter of the application for the enrollment of

CHARLES R. SAMUELS

as a citizen by intermarriage of the Cherokee Nation.

CHEROKEE 1270.

◇◇◇◇◇

Cherokee Intermarried White 1906
Volume I

DEPARTMENT OF THE INTERIOR.
COMMISSION TO THE FIVE CIVILIZED TRIBES.
MULDROW, I. T., AUGUST 13th, 1900.

IN THE MATTER OF THE APPLICATION OF Charles R. Samuels and two children, for enrollment as citizens of the Cherokee Nation, and he being sworn by Commissioner, C. R. Breckinridge, testified as follows:

Q What is your name? A Charles R. Samuels.
Q What is your age Mr. Samuels? A Fifty six.
Q What is your Postoffice? A Muldorw[sic].
Q What is your District? A Sequoyah.
Q For whom do you make application for enrollment at this time? A Myself and two children; I have four living, but two are of age.
Q You apply for yourself and two children? A Yes sir; I am an adopted citizen.
Q Is your wife dead? A Yes sir.
Q You apply for yourself as a citizen by adoption? A Yes sir.
Q Was your wife a Cherokee by blood? A Yes sir.
Q What was your wifes[sic] name? A Matilda Samuels.
Q What was her name before you married her? A Matilda Fence.
Q Was that her maiden name? A Yes sir.
Q When did she die? A She died in September, I think; it was nine years ago last September.
Q How old was your wife when she died? A She was about forty-one.
Q Was she on the roll of 1880? A Yes sir.
Q Have you a marriage liscence[sic]? A Yes sir.
Q Let me see it, please? (Applicant hands paper to Commissioner)
   A duly authenticated marriage liscence[sic], issued by Ellis Sanders, Clerk of Sequoyah District, the 4th day of May, 1870, authorizing the marriage according to Cherokee Law between the applicant and his wife, and the certificate of the Reverend S. Wainwright shows that this marriage was duly consumated[sic] on the 12th day of May, 1870.
Q Are you on the roll of 1880? A Yes sir.
Q Did you and your wife live together all the time from 1880 until the time she died, nine years ago? A Yes sir.
Q Did you live during all that time in the Cherokee Nation? A Yes sir.
Q Ant that is your home at the present time? A Yes sir
Q Have you remarried since your wife's death? A No sir.
Q Give me please the names of your children? Q[sic] Jesse C. Samuels.
Q How old is he? A Sixteen.
Q Your next child? A Lutetia Samuela[sic].
Q How old is she? A Thirteen.
Q That is all you apply for now? A Yes sir.
Q These are both living at this time? A Yes sir.
(Applicant identified on the roll of 1880, Page 722, #1259, Charles Samuels, Sequoyah District)
(On the roll of 1896, Page 1118, #160, as Charlie Samuels, Sequoyah District.)

Cherokee Intermarried White 1906
Volume I

(On the roll of 1896, Page 1098, #1301, Jesse C. Samuls[sic], Sequoyah District - applicant's son)

(On the roll of 1896, Page 1098, #1302, Lue T. Samuls[sic], Sequoyah District - Applicant's daughter)

(Applicant's deceased wife identified on the roll of 1880, Page 722, #1260, Matilda Samuels, Sequoyah District)

This applicant, Charles R. Samuels is duly identified on the rolls of 1880, and 1896, as an intermarried Cherokee citizen. His wife is identified on the roll of 1880, and is shown to have died nine years ago, he living with his wife continuously in the Cherokee Nation, and never remarrying, he will be enrolled now as a Cherokee by adoption.

His two children, Jesse C. and Lutetia are both identified on the roll of 1896, and they will be enrolled as Cherokees by blood.

R. R. Cravens, being sworn, states that as stenographer to the Commission to the Five Civilized Tribes, he reported the foregoing case, and that the above and foregoing is a true, full and correct transcript of his stenographic notes in said case.

R R Cravens

Sworn to and subscribed before
me this 13th day of August, 1900.

Clifton R. Breckinridge
COMMISSIONER.

◇◇◇◇◇

DEPARTMENT OF THE INTERIOR.
Commission to the Five Civilized Tribes.
Muskogee, Indian Territory, October 13th, 1902.

In the matter of the application Charles R. Samuels for the enrollment of himself as a citizen by intermarriage and his children, Jesse C. and Lutetia Samuels, as citizens by blood of the Cherokee Nation.

Supplemental to #127o.

CHARLES R. SAMUELS, being duly sworn, testified as follows:
Examination by the Commission.

Q. What is your name? A. Charles R. Samuels.
Q. How old are you? A. 58
Q. What is your post office? A. Muldrow
Q. Are you a white man? A. Yes, sir.
Q. Intermarried citizen? A. Yes, sir.
Q. You are on the eighty roll as an intermarried white man? A. Yes, sir.

Cherokee Intermarried White 1906
Volume I

Q. What was your wife's name at that time? A. Matilda Samuels.
Q. Is she dead? A. Yes, sir.
Q. When did she die? A. She died in '91.
Q. Did you live with her continuously from 1880 until 1891? A?[sic] Yes, sir.
Q. Never was separated from her? A. No, sir.
Q. Have you married since then? A. No, sir.
Q. You are a widower, then, now? A. Yes, sir.
Q. Have you been living in the Cherokee Nation ever since 1880? A. Yes, sir.
Q. Never been out? A. No, sir.
Q. How many children have you? A. I have got four living.
Q. How many living at home? A. Two.
Q. Two married? A. One of them.
Q. Where is the other one? A. Living with his aunt.
Q. The two younger children have lived in the Cherokee Nation ever since their birth? A. Yes, sir.

****

Jesse O. Carr, being first duly sworn, states that as stenographer to the Commission to the Five Civilized Tribes he reported the above entitled case and that the foregoing is a true and complete transcript of his stenographic notes thereof.

Jesse O. Carr

Subscribed and sworn to before me this 20th day of December, 1902.

BC Jones
Notary Public.

◇◇◇◇◇

Cherokee 1270.

DEPARTMENT OF THE INTERIOR,
COMMISSION TO THE FIVE CIVILIZED TRIBES.
Muskogee, Indian Territory, January 3, 1907.

In the Matter of the Application for the Enrollment of Charles R. Samuels as a citizen by intermarriage of the Cherokee Nation.

Charles R. Samuels being first duly sworn by B. P. Rasmus, testified as follows:

Q What is your name? A Charles R. Samuels
Q What is your age? A 62.
Q What is your post office address?
A Muldrow, Indian Territory.
Q Are you an applicant for enrollment as a citizen by intermarriage of the Cherokee Nation?
A Yes sir.

Cherokee Intermarried White 1906
Volume I

Q You have no Cherokee blood?   A No sir.
Q You claim the right to enrollment solely by virtue of your marriage to a citizen by blood of the Cherokee Nation, do you?
A Yes sir.
Q What is the name of the person through whom you claim the right to enrollment?
A Matilda Fence.
Q When were you married to her?
A '70, first day of May.
Q Where was she living at the time you married her?
A About eight miles Souteast[sic] of Muldrow, on the river, in the Cherokee Nation.
Q Were you a resident of the Cherokee Nation at that time?
A Yes sir.
Q Is your wife living at this time?
A No sir.
Q When did she die?
A About 14 years ago.
Q Did you and she continuously live together as husband and wife from the date of your marriage until the time of her death?
A Yes sir.
Q Have you married since her death?
A No sir.
Q Have you resided in the Cherokee Nation continuously since your marriage up until the present time?
A Yes sir.
Q Were you ever married prior to your marriage to your deceased wife?
A No sir.
Q Was she ever married prior to her marriage to you?
A No sir.
Q Did you marry her in accordance with the laws of the Cherokee Nation?
A Yes sir.
Q Have you a marriage license and certificate?
A Yes sir.

The applicant presents the original marriage license and certificate showing that on May 5, 1870, license was granted in accordance with the laws of the Cherokee Nation, authorizing the marriage of himself to Miss Matilda Fence, a Cherokee, and that said Charles R. Samuels and Matilda Fence were united in marriage in accordance with the terms of said license, May 12, 1870, by L. Wainwright, M. G. Said marriage license and certificate is filed herewith and made a part of the record in this case. The applicant, Charles R. Samuels, is identified on the Cherokee authenticated Tribal Roll of 1880, Sequoyah District, No. 1259.

The undersigned being first duly sworn states that as stenographer to the Commission to the Five Civilized Tribes, she correctly recorded the testimony taken in this case and that the foregoing is a full, true and correct transcript of her stenographic notes thereof.

Cherokee Intermarried White 1906
Volume I

Myrtle Hill

Subscribed and sworn to before me this the 4th day of January, 1907.

B.P. Rasmus
Notary Public.

◇◇◇◇◇

(The Marriage License and Certificate below, typed as given.)

(COPY)

Cherokee Nation I
                I   Charles R. Samuels a white man and citizen of the U.S.A.
Sequoyah Dist I   having already complid with the laws of the Cherokee
Nation Respecting intermarriage with white men to Any of the Judges of this Nation or any legal autherised Minister of the Gospel Greeting you are hereby autherised to Join Together in a holy state of Matrimoney by marriage Charles R. Samuels a white man to Miss Matilda Fence a Cherokee .

Given from under my hand this 5th day May A. D. 1870.

Ellis Sanders CLK. S.D.C.

I hereby certify that I have this day Soleminized the rights of mattrimony between the parties whose names are contained in the above license this May 12th 1870.

S. Weinwright M.G.

I, Homer J. Councilor, being first duly sworn state that as stenographer to the Commissioner to the Five Civilized Tribes I made the above and foregoing copy from the original thereof and that the same is a true and correct copy thereof.

Homer J. Councilor

Subscribed and sworn to before me this tenth day of January, 1907.

B.P. Rasmus
Notary Public.

◇◇◇◇◇

Cherokee Intermarried White 1906
Volume I

E.C.M.

E.C.M.
Cherokee 1270.

DEPARTMENT OF THE INTERIOR,

COMMISSIONER TO THE FIVE CIVILIZED TRIBES.

In the matter of the application for the enrollment of CHARLES R. SAMUELS as a citizen by intermarriage of the Cherokee Nation.

D E C I S I O N

THE RECORDS OF THIS OFFICE SHOW: That at Muldrow, Indian Territory, August 13, 1900, Charles R. Samuels appeared before the Commission to the Five Civilized Tribes, and made application for the enrollment of himself as a citizen by intermarriage, and for the enrollment of his children, Jesse C. and Lutetia Samuels, as citizens by blood, of the Cherokee Nation. The application for the enrollment of the said Jesse C. and Lutetia Samuels as citizens by blood of the Cherokee Nation has been heretofore disposed of, and their rights to enrollment will not be considered in this decision. Further proceedings in the matter of said application were had at Muskogee, Indian Territory, October 13, 1902, and January 3, 1907.

THE EVIDENCE IN THIS CASE SHOWS: That the applicant herein, Charles R. Samuels, a white man, was married in accordance with Cherokee law in May, 1870, to his wife, Matilda Samuels, nee Fence, deceased, who was at the time of said marriage a recognized citizen by blood of the Cherokee Nation, and whose name appears on the Cherokee authenticated tribal roll of 1880, opposite No. 1260; that from the time of said marriage until the death of the said Matilda Samuels in the year 1891, said Charles R. Samuels and said Matilda Samuels resided together as husband and wife, and since the death of said Matilda Samuels the said Charles R. Samuels has remained unmarried, and has continuously lived in the Cherokee Nation. Said Charles R. Samuels is identified on the Cherokee authenticated tribal roll of 1880, and the Cherokee census roll of 1896, as an intermarried citizen of the Cherokee Nation.

IT IS, THEREFORE, ORDERED AND ADJUDGED: That in accordance with the decision of the Supreme Court of the United States, dated November 5, 1906, in the case of Daniel Red Bird et al. vs. the United States, under the provisions of Section 21, of the Act of Congress approved June 28, 1898 (30 Stat., 495), Charles R. Samuels is entitled to enrollment as a citizen by intermarriage of the Cherokee Nation, and his application for enrollment as such is accordingly granted.

Tams Bixby
Commissioner.

Dated at Muskogee, Indian Territory,
this   JAN 18 1907

Cherokee Intermarried White 1906
Volume I

REFER IN REPLY TO THE FOLLOWING:
Cherokee
1270

DEPARTMENT OF THE INTERIOR,
COMMISSIONER TO THE FIVE CIVILIZED TRIBES.

Muskogee, Indian Territory, December 24, 1906.

Charles R. Samuels,
    Muldrow, Indian Territory.

Dear Sir:

    November 6, 1906, the United States Supreme Court held that white persons who intermarried with Cherokee citizens according to Cherokee law prior to November 1, 1875, are entitled to enrollment and allotments of land as citizens of the Cherokee Nation.

    You are advised that to properly determine your right to enrollment as a citizen by intermarriage of the Cherokee Nation, it will be necessary for you to appear before the Commissioner for the purpose of giving testimony as to the date of your marriage and whether or not your wife, by reason of your marriage to whom you claim the right to enrollment as a citizen of the Cherokee Nation, was a recognized citizen of the Cherokee Nation at the time of your marriage to her, and whether or not you were married to her in accordance with Cherokee laws.

    You are, therefore, directed to appear before the Commissioner at Muskogee, Indian Territory, at 9 o'clock A. M., on Thursday, January 3, 1907, and give testimony as above indicated.

                      Respectfully,
                        Wm O. Beall
LMC   Acting Commissioner.

Cherokee
1270.

                        Muskogee, Indian Territory, January 18, 1907.

W. W. Hastings,
    Attorney for the Cherokee Nation,
        Muskogee, Indian Territory.

Dear Sir:

    There is enclosed herewith a copy of the decision of the Commissioner to the Five Civilized Tribes, dated January 18, 1907, granting the application for the enrollment of Charles R. Samuels, as a citizen by intermarriage of the Cherokee Nation.

Cherokee Intermarried White 1906
Volume I

Respectfully,

Encl. HJ-42.
HJC.

Commissioner.

◇◇◇◇◇

Cherokee 1270   W.W. HASTINGS.   OFFICE OF   H.M. VANCE.
                  ATTORNEY.   SECRETARY.

Attorney for the Cherokee Nation,
MUSKOGEE, I. T.

January 18, 1907.

The Commissioner to the Five Civilized Tribes,
   Muskogee, Indian Territory.

Sir:

    Receipt is acknowledged of the testimony and of your decision enrolling Charles R. Samuels as a citizen by intermarriage of the Cherokee Nation. Time for protesting said decision is waived and I consent that said person may be placed upon the schedule immediately.

Yours very truly,
W. W. Hastings
Attorney for Cherokee Nation.

◇◇◇◇◇

Cherokee
   127o[sic]

Muskogee, Indian Territory, January 21, 1907.

Charles R. Samuels,
   Muldrow, Indian Territory.

Dear Sir:

    There is enclosed herewith copy of the decision of the Commissioner to the Five Civilized Tribes, dated January 18, 1907, granting the application for your enrollment as a citizen by intermarriage of the Cherokee Nation.

    You will be advised when your name has been placed upon the schedule of citizens of the Cherokee Nation and approved by the Secretary of the Interior.

Cherokee Intermarried White 1906
Volume I

Respectfully,

Enc M - 2

M T M   Commissioner.

◇◇◇◇◇

Cherokee
  I. W. 15

Muskogee, Indian Territory, April 6, 1907.

Charles R. Samuels,
    Muldrow, Indian Territory.

Dear Sir:

    Your marriage license and certificate, filed in connection with your application for enrollment as a citizen by intermarriage of the Cherokee Nation, is returned to you herewith, copies of the same being retained in this office.

Respectfully,

Encl. B-86   Acting Commissioner.

L. M. B

Cher I W 16
Trans from Cher 1317 3-13-07

◇◇◇◇◇

E.C.M.

DEPARTMENT OF THE INTERIOR,

COMMISSIONER TO THE FIVE CIVILIZED TRIBES.

In the matter of the application for the enrollment of

JAMES K. PEMBERTON

as a citizen by intermarriage of the Cherokee Nation.

Cherokee Intermarried White 1906
Volume I

CHEROKEE 1317.

DEPARTMENT OF THE INTERIOR,
COMMISSION TO THE FIVE CIVILIZED TRIBES,
MULDROW, I.T., AUGUST 13, 1900.

In the matter of the application of James K. Pemberton for enrollment of himself and wife as citizens of the Cherokee Nation, said Pemberton being sworn by Commissioner Needles, testified as follows:

Q What is your name? A James K. Pemberton.
Q Your age? A 52.
Q Your postoffice? A Redland.
Q Are you a Cherokee citizen by blood? A No sir, by adoption.
Q For whom do you apply for enrollment? A For myself and wife.
Q What district do you live in? A Sequoyah.
Q How long have you lived there? A Since '71 continuously.
Q Your father is a non-citizen? A Yes.
Q Your mother is also a non-citizen? A Yes.
Q Are you married? A Yes.
Q What is your wife's name? A Mary.
Q What was her name before you married her? A Hernam[sic].
Q When did you marry her? A In February '72.
Q Have you any evidence of your marriage A Yes, I have my license.
Q Is your wife living? A Yes.
Q What was her father's name? A Frank.
Q Was he a citizen by blood? A No sir.
Q What was her mother's name? A Baggs. I don't remember her first name?
A Is she living? A No sir.
Q Was she a citizen by blood? A Yes.
   Applicant's wife on '80 roll, page 714, number 1002 as Mary A. Pemberton.
   Applicant on '80 roll, page 714, number 1001 as James Pemberton.
   Applicant's wife on '96 roll, page 1089, number 1071.
   Applicant on '96 roll, page 1117, number 133.
Q Have you lived with your wife since your marriage all the time? A Yes.

 The name of James K. Pemberton and his wife, Mary, appear upon the autheticated[sic] roll of '80 as well as the census roll of '96, they both being fully identified according to page and number of the rolls as indicated in this testimony, and having made satisfactory proof of their residence, they will be duly listed for enrollment by this Commission as Cherokee citizens, he by intermarriage, and she by blood.

 The undersigned, being first duly sworn, states that as Stenographer to the Commission to the Five Civilized Tribes, he correctly recorded the testimony and proceedings in this case, and that the foregoing is a true and complete transcript of his stenographic notes thereof.

Cherokee Intermarried White 1906
Volume I

Brown McDonald

Subscribed and sworn to before me this 31st day of August, 1900, at Fort Gibson, I.T.

        Tams Bixby
          Commissioner.

Cher
Supp'l to # 1317

Department of the Interior,
Commission to the Five Civilized Tribes,
Muskogee, I. T., October 13, 1902.

In the matter of the application of JAMES K. PEMBERTON, for the enrollment of himself as a citizen by intermarriage, and his wife MARY A. PEMBERTON, as a citizen by blood, of the Cherokee Nation.

JAMES K. PEMBERTON, being duly sworn and examined by the Commission, testified as follows:

Q Your full name is James K. Pemberton ? A Yes sir.
Q How old are you ? A Fifty five.
Q What is your post office address ? A Redland.
Q You are a white man, are you ? A Yes sir.
Q Your name appears upon the roll of 1880 as an intermarried white ? A Yes sir.
Q What is the name of your wife ? A Mary A.
Q Was she your wife in 1880 ? A Yes sir.
Q Have you and your wife been living together in the Cherokee Nation since 1880 ?
A Yes sir.
Q Never been separated ? A No sir.
Q Never have lived outside the Cherokee Nation ? A No sir Not out of the District even.
Q You were living together on the first day of last September ? A Yes sir.
Q You have no children ? A No sir, none living with us; they are all married off. We have four children living though.

  E. C. Bagwell, on oath states that, as stenographer to the Commission to the Five Civilized Tribes, he correctly recorded the testimony and proceedings had in the above entitled cause, and that the foregoing is an accurate transcript of his stenographic notes thereof.

              EC Bagwell

Cherokee Intermarried White 1906
Volume I

Subscribed and sworn to before me this October 31, 1902.

BC Jones
Notary Public.

◇◇◇◇◇

Cherokee No. 1317.

DEPARTMENT OF THE INTERIOR.
COMMISSIONER TO THE FIVE CIVILIZED TRIBES.

Muskogee, Indian Territory, January 3, 1907.

In the matter of the application for the enrollment of James K. Pemberton as a citizen by intermarriage of the Cherokee Nation.

James K. Pemberton, being first duly sworn and examined, testifies as follows:

BY THE COMMISSIONER:

[sic] What is your name? A James K. Pemberton.
Q How old are you? A I am 58 years old.
Q What is your Post Office address? A Redland.
Q You claim to be a citizen by intermarriage to the Cherokee Nation? A Yes, sir.
Q Through whom do you claim your intermarriage rights? A Mary A. Hineman.
Q When were you married to Mary A. Hineman? A It was in '72 I think.
Q Have you got your licence[sic]? A Yes, sir.
Q Were you ever married before you married Mary A. Hineman? A No, sir.
Q Was she ever married before she married you? A I think not.
Q Have you lived together continuously as husband and wife since your marriage up to the present time? A Until she died.
Q When did she die? A Last February.
Q Have you married since her death? A No, sir.
Q Married under the Cherokee Law? A Yes, sir.
Q Have you got a marriage licence[sic]? A Yes, sir.
Q Have you got it with you? A Yes, sir.

Applicant offers in evidence marriage licence[sic] granted him on the 1st day of February, 1872 to marry Mary Ann Hyman, together with a cirtificate[sic] of said marriage dated February 4th, 1872 showing that applicant was married according to the Cherokee Law. The same will be filed with a record in this case and made a part thereof.

Cherokee Intermarried White 1906
Volume I

Applicant is identified on the 1880 Cherokee Roll opposite No. 1001. His wife through whom he claims his right to enrollment as an intermarriage[sic] citizen is identified on said roll opposite No. 1002. She is also identified on the final roll of citizens by blood opposite No. 3620.

WITNESS EXCUSED.

F. Elma Lane, upon oath, states that she reported the proceedings in the above entitled cause and that the foregoing is a true and correct transcript of her stenographic notes taken therein.

F. Elma Lane

Subscribed and sworn to before me this 3rd day of January, 1907.

Chas E Webster
Notary Public.

◇◇◇◇◇

(The Marriage License and Certificate below typed as given.)

(COPY)

Cherokee Nation I

             I   James Pemberton a white man and a citizen of the U.S.A.
Sequoyah District I   after haveing allready complied with the laws of the Cherokee Nation in regard to intermarriage with white To any of the Judges of this Nation or any legal autherized minister of the gosspel Greeting you are hereby commanded to Join together in a holy state of martimony by marriage Mr. James Pemberton a white man to Miss Mary H. Hynam a Cherokee lady.

Given from under my had in office This the 1st day February A D 1872.

John Funter Clk
of District Court.

This will certify that I Performed the marriage ceremony Between James Pemberton and Mary Ann Hynam on the 4th day of February 1872.

Franklin Falkner Judge
Sequoyah Dist Court.

Cherokee Intermarried White 1906
Volume I

Homer J. Councilor being first duly sworn states that as stenographer to the Commission to the Five Civilized Tribes he amade the above and foregoing copy from the original thereof and that the same is a true and correct copy thereof.

Homer J Councilor

Subscribed and sworn to before me this 10th day of January 1907.

B.P. Rasmus
Notary Public.

◇◇◇◇◇

E.C.M.
Cherokee 1317.

DEPARTMENT OF THE INTERIOR,
COMMISSIONER TO THE FIVE CIVILIZED TRIBES.

In the matter of the application for the enrollment of Jamed[sic] K. Pemberton as a citizen by intermarriage of the Cherokee Nation.

D E C I S I O N

THE RECORDS OF THIS OFFICE SHOW: That at Muldrow, Indian Territory, August 13, 1900, James K. Pemberton, appeared before the Commission to the Five Civilized Tribes and made application for the enrollment of himself as a citizen by intermarriage and for the enrollment of his wife, Mary A. Pemberton, as a citizen by blood of the Cherokee Nation. The application for the enrollment of said Mary A. Pemberton, as a citizen by blood of the Cherokee Nation will not be considered in this decision. Further proceedings in the matter of said application were had at Muskogee, Indian Territory, October 13, 1902, and January 3, 1907.

THE EVIDENCE IN THIS CASE SHOWS: That the applicant herein James K. Pemberton, a white man, was married in accordance with Cherokee law, February 4, 1872, to his wife Mary A. Pemberton, nee Hynam, deceased, who was at the time of said marriage a recognized citizen by blood of the Cherokee Nation, whose name appears upon the roll of citizens by blood of 1880, opposite number 1002, and upon the roll of 1896, opposite number 1071; that from the time of said marriage until the death of Mary A. Pemberton, which occurred in 1906, said James K. Pemberton and Mary A. Pemberton resided together as husband and wife and continuously lived in the Cherokee Nation. Said James K. Pemberton is identified upon the Cherokee authenticated roll of

Cherokee Intermarried White 1906
Volume I

1880, and the Cherokee Census roll of 1896, as an intermarried citizen of the Cherokee Nation.

IT IS THEREFORE ORDERED AND ADJUDGED: That in accordance with the decision of the Supreme Court of the United States, dated November 5, 1906, in the case of Daniel Red Bird et al., vs the United States under the provision of Section 21 of the Act of Congress approved June 28, 1898 (30 Stat., 495), James K. Pemberton is entitled to enrollment as a citizen by intermarriage of the Cherokee Nation, and his application for enrollment as such is accordingly granted.

Tams Bixby
Commissioner.

Dated at Muskogee, Indian Territory,
this   JAN 18 1907

◇◇◇◇◇

Cherokee
1317.

Muskogee, Indian Territory, December 24, 1906.

James K. Pemberton,
    Redland, Indian Territory.

Dear Sir:

November 6, 1906, the United States Supreme Court held that white persons who intermarried with Cherokee citizens according to Cherokee law prior to November 1, 1875, are entitled to enrollment and allotments of land as citizens of the Cherokee Nation.

You are advised that to properly determine your right to enrollment as a citizen by intermarriage of the Cherokee Nation, it will be necessary for you to appear before the Commissioner for the purpose of giving testimony as to the date of your marriage and whether or not your wife, by reason of your marriage to whom you claim the right to enrollment as a citizen of the Cherokee Nation, was a recognized citizen of the Cherokee Nation at the time of your marriage to her, and whether or not you were married to her in accordance with Cherokee laws.

You are, therefore, directed to appear before the Commissioner at Muskogee, Indian Territory, at 9 o'clock A. M., on Thursday, January 3, 1907, and give testimony as above indicated.

Respectfully,

LMC   Acting Commissioner.

◇◇◇◇◇

Cherokee Intermarried White 1906
Volume I

Cherokee
1317

Muskogee, Indian Territory, January 18, 1907.

W. W. Hastings,
    Attorney for the Cherokee Nation,
        Muskogee, Indian Territory.

Dear Sir:

    There is enclosed herewith a copy of the decision of the Commissioner to the Five Civilized Tribes, dated January 18, 1907, granting the application for the enrollment of James K. Pemberton as a citizen by intermarriage of the Cherokee Nation.

                  Respectfully,

Encl. HJ-43.
HJC   Commissioner.

Cherokee 1317.   W.W.HASTINGS. ATTORNEY.   OFFICE OF   H.M. VANCE. SECRETARY.

Attorney for the Cherokee Nation,
MUSKOGEE, I. T.

January 18, 1907.

The Commissioner to the Five Civilized Tribes,
    Muskogee, Indian Territory.

Sir:

    Receipt is acknowledged of the testimony and of your decision enrolling James K. Pemberton, as a citizen by intermarriage of the Cherokee Nation. Time for protesting said decision is waived and I consent that said person may be placed upon the schedule immediately.

                  Yours very truly,
                        W. W. Hastings
                        Attorney for Cherokee Nation.

Cherokee Intermarried White 1906
Volume I

Cherokee
1317

Muskogee, Indian Territory, January 21, 1907.

James K. Pemberton,
    Redland, Indian Territory.

Dear Sir:

    There is enclosed herewith a copy of the decision of the Commissioner to the Five Civilized Tribes, dated January 18, 1907, granting the application for your enrollment as a citizen by intermarriage of the Cherokee Nation.

    You will be advised when your name has been placed upon the schedule of citizens of the Cherokee Nation and approved by the Secretary of the Interior.

                  Respectfully,

Enc. M - 1   Commissioner.
MTM.

◇◇◇◇◇

Cherokee
I. W. 16

Muskogee, Indian Territory, April 6, 1907

James K. Pemberton,
    Redland, Indian Territory.

Dear Sir:

    Your marriage license and certificate, filed in connection with your application for enrollment as a citizen by intermarriage of the Cherokee Nation, is returned to you herewith, copies of the same being retained in this office.

                    Respectfully,

Encl. B-87   Acting Commissioner.

L M B

Cherokee Intermarried White 1906
Volume I

Cher I W 17
Trans from Cher 1684 3-13-07

C.E.W.

DEPARTMENT OF THE INTERIOR,

COMMISSIONER TO THE FIVE CIVILIZED TRIBES.

In the matter of the application for the enrollment of

THOMAS J. AYERS

as a citizen by intermarriage of the Cherokee Nation.

CHEROKEE 1684

Department of the Interior,
COmission[sic] to the Five Civilized Tribes,
Ft. Gibson, I.T., August 21, 1900.

In the matter of the application of Thomas J. Ayers for the enrollment of himself, wife and child and grand-child as Cherokee citizens; being sworn and examined by Commissioner Needles he testifies as follows:

Q What is your name? A Thomas J. Ayers.
Q What is your age? A Forty-eight
Q What is your post-office? A Fort Gibson.
Q Are you a recognized citizen of the Cherokee Nation? A Yes sir.
Q By blood or intermarriage? A Intermarriage.
Q I what district do you live? A Illinois.
Q How long have you lived in Illinois District? A I have lived here six years this time.
Q Where did you live before that? A I lived in Tahlequah District about fourteen years.
Q You have lived in the Cherokee Nation then continuously about twenty years? A Yes sir.
Q For whom do you apply for enrollment? A Myself and wife and daughter.
Q Your father and mother living? A Nos sir.
Q They were non-citizens? A Yes sir.
Q What is your wife's name? A Virginia.
Q What is her age? A Fifty-two.
Q When were you married to her? A In 1873.
Q Is her father living? A No sir.

Cherokee Intermarried White 1906
Volume I

Q Did they die before 1880? A Yes sir.
Q Wyat[sic] are the names of your children? A The one that's with me is Alice Ayers, fifteen years old.
Q This child is alive and living with you? A Yes sir.
1880 roll page 680 #14 Tom J. Ayers sequoyah[sic] District.
1880 roll page 680 #15 Virginia Ayers, Sequoyah District.
1896 roll page 925 #4 Thomas J. Ayers, Illinois District.
1896 roll page 836 #43 Virginia Ayers, Illinois District.
1896 roll page 836 #44 Alice Ayers Illinois District.
Q Are you and your wife Virginia living together ans[sic] have lived together ever since your first marriage? A Yes sir.

Examination by Cherokee Representative Hastings:
Q Where were you married? A I was married on Richard Griffin's place in 1873, by Rev. T. B. K. McSpadden.
Q Have you your marriage license? A No sir.
Q You never did get it? A No sir.
I called for a copy of the record; I supposed that was sufficient; I have that (Produces paper.)
Com'r Needles: Thomas J. Ayers presents a certificate signed T. J. Thornton Clerk, under the seal of Illinois District, certifying that marriage license was issued to him to marry Virginia Frazier, February 8th 1873, and that the marriage ceremony was performed by T. K. B.[sic] McSpadden.

Virginia Ayers, being sworn and examined by Commissioner Needles, testifies as follows, in the application for enrollment of grand-child:
Q What is your name? A Virginia Ayers.
Q What is your age? A Fifty-two.
Q What is your post-office? A Fort Gibson.
Q What is the name of the grand-child you desire to enroll? A Bessie Frazier.
Q Who was Bessie Frazier's mother? A She was Alice Cooper until she was married; Alice Frazier is her name.
Q What is your father's name? A William Frazier.
Q Was the child's father a citizen of the Cherokee Nation? A Yes sir.
Q Is he living? A Yes sir.
Q Is the mother living? A I couldn't tell you; I don't know that.
Q Why don't William Frazer come and *(illegible)* his own child?
A After this child was born he and the mother separated and he sued for divorce, and he married another woman, and she gave me the child, and I have guardian papers. (Presented papers.)
She wasn't able to take care of the child, and I took it, because it was a grand-child *(illegible....)*.
Q Was William Frazier ever married to Alice Frazier? A Yes sir.
Q When were they married? A The child is eight years old. I guess it was in 1891 or 1890.
Q Who married them? A Mr. J. Thornton married them.
Q Is he living? A No sir, he is dead

Cherokee Intermarried White 1906
Volume I

Q Was any certificate of marriage given? A If there was I never did see it; Mr. Thornton said he would *(illegible....)*.
Q Do you know whether it was *(illegible)* or not? A No sir, I don't know. The child's mother was a white girl and her *(illegible)* was a Cooper.
1880 roll examined for child's *(illegible....)* Sequoyah District.
1896 roll for child page *(illegible....)*

Marcus D. L. Dowell being sworn and examined by Commissioner Needles testifies as follows:

Q What is your name? A Marcus D. L. Dowell.
Q What is your age? A Fifty.
Q What is your post-office address? A Fort Gibson.
Q Are you a recognized citizen of the Cherokee Nation? A *(Illegible)*
Q Do you know William Frazier? A Yes sir.
Q Is he living? A I suppose he is; I *(illegible....)*.
Q Do you know his wife Alice? A Yes sir.
Q What was her maiden name? A Alice Cooper.
Q Do you know whether they were married or not? A Yes sir, they were married in my house, at Fort Gibson by J. T. Thornton then Clerk of Illinois District, Cherokee Nation.
Q When was that? A About 1890 or 1891.
Q Is William Frazier an Indian by blood? A *(Illegible....)*
Q What was his wife, a white woman? A Yes sir.
Q You know how long they lived together *(illegible....)* after they were married? A No sir, I do not.
Q Do you know whether they had any children or not? A Yes sir, I remember seeing them together when they had one child.
Q You know its name? A No sir.

Com'r Needles:

(The remainder is illegible)

◇◇◇◇◇

(The entire page is illegible)

◇◇◇◇◇

Cherokee Intermarried White 1906
Volume I

Cherokee *(illegible)*.

DEPARTMENT OF THE INTERIOR,
COMMISSION TO THE FIVE CIVILIZED TRIBES,
CHEROKEE LAND OFFICE.
Tahlequah, I. T., August 30, 1904.

In the matter of the application of Thomas J. Ayers, for the enrollment of himself as a citizen by intermarriage, and of his wife, Virginia, and daughter Alice Ayers, and granddaughter Bessie Frazier, as citizens by blood of the Cherokee Nation.

(The remainder is illegible.)

Cherokee No. 1684.

DEPARTMENT OF THE INTERIOR.
COMMISSIONER TO THE FIVE CIVILIZED TRIBES.

Muskogee, Indian Territory, January 3, 1907.

In the matter of the application for the enrollment of Thomas J. Ayres[sic] as a citizen by intermarriage of the Cherokee Nation.

Thomas J. Ayres, being first duly sworn and examined, testifies as follows:

BY THE COMMISSIONER:

Q What is your name? A Thomas J. Ayres.
Q How old are you? A 55.
Q What is your postoffice address? A Watova, Indian Territory.
Q Do you claim to be a citizen by intermarriage of the Cherokee Nation? A Yes, sir.
Q Through whom do you claim your intermarriage rights? A Virginia Frazier.
Q When were you married to Virginia Frazier? A In February, 1873.
Q Got a marriage licence[sic]? A No, sir, I haven't.
Q Did you get one? Yes, sir, I got one.
Q What became of it? A I lost it in some way.
Q Who issued your marriage licence[sic]? A Henry Efforts[sic].
Q Were you ever married before you married Virginia Frazier? A No, sir.
Q Was she ever married before she married you? A Yes, sir, I suppose she was. Her maiden name was Barker.
Q What was the name of her former husband? A Frazier.
Q Was he alive or dead at the time you married Virginia Frazier? A He was dead.
Q She had no living husband at the time you married her? A No, sir.

Cherokee Intermarried White 1906
Volume I

Q Did you live together continuously as husband and wife once you were married?
A Yes, sir.
Q Living together at the present time? A Yes, sir.
Q Where were you married? A It was eight miles east of Fort Gibson, on the old *(Illegible)* farm.
Q Have you lived in the Cherokee Nation ever since your marriage? A Yes, sir.

The applicant is identified on the 1880 roll opposite No. 14. His wife through whom he claims the right to enrollment is identified on said roll opposite No. *(illegible)*. She is also identified on the final roll of citizens by blood of the Cherokee Nation the Cherokee Nation opposite No. *(illegible)*.

Q It will be necessary for you to supply this office with evidence of your marriage to Virginia Frazier in accordance with the Cherokee Laws.
Q What District were you married in? A In Illinois District.

The applicant offer in evidence cirtificate[sic] of T. J. Thornton certified on the 13th day of December 1895, showing issuance of marriage licence[sic] to him, February 8th, 1873 to marry Virginia Frazier, and that he was married on said date.

Q When did you loose your original marriage licence[sic]? A I lost them right away after I married.
Q Did you make a search for them? A Yes, sir.
Q Never have been able to find them? A Never have been able to find them.

WITNESS EXCUSED.

F. Elma Lane, upon oath, states that she reported the proceedings in the above entitled cause and that the foregoing is a true and correct transcript of her stenographic notes taken therein.

F. Elma Lane

Subscribed and sworn to before me this 4th day of January, 1907.

Chas E. Webster
Notary Public.

COPY

Fort Gibson, I. T., December 13, 1890

In the matter of Mr. T. J. Ayers marriage License & c

This is to certify that a marriage license was issued to T. J. Ayers to marry Virginia Frazier by Hon. Henry Eiffent CLK of Illinois District C. N. February 8, 1873.

Cherokee Intermarried White 1906
Volume I

And marriage ceremony performed by T. K. B. McSpadden P. C. of Tahlequah Ck. Ind Mission.

The above is a true copy of the original on record in this office.

This D. C. 13, 1890

T. Jay Thornton
CLK I.D.C.N.

The undersigned being first duly sworn states that as stenographer to the Commissioner to the Five Civilized Tribes, she made the above copy and that the same is a true and correct copy of the original marriage record now on file in this office.

Lola M Champlin

Subscribed and sworn to before me this 10 day of January 1907.

Chas E Webster
notary public.

◇◇◇◇◇

C.E.W.   Cherokee 1684.

DEPARTMENT OF THE INTERIOR,

COMMISSIONER TO THE FIVE CIVILIZED TRIBES.

In the matter of the application for the enrollment of Thomas J. Ayers, as a citizen by intermarriage of the Cherokee Nation.

D E C I S I O N

THE RECORDS OF THIS OFFICE SHOW: That at Fort Gibson, Indian Territory, August 21, 1900, Thomas J. Ayers appeared before the Commission to the Five Civilized Tribes and made application for the enrollment of himself, as a citizen by intermarriage, and for the enrollment of his wife, Virginia Ayers, et al., as citizens by blood of the Cherokee Nation has been heretofore disposed of, and their rights to enrollment will not be considered in this decision. Further proceedings in the matter of said applicant were had at Muskogee, Indian Territory, October 21, 1902, at Tahlequah, Indian Territory, August 30, 1904, and at Muskogee, Indian Territory, January 3, 1907.

THE EVIDENCE IN THIS CASE SHOWS: That the applicant herein, Thomas J. Ayers, a white man, was married in accordance with Cherokee law in February 1873 to his wife, Virginia Ayers, nee Frazier, who was at the time of said marriage a recognized citizen by blood of the Cherokee Nation, and whose name appears upon the approved partial roll of citizens by blood, opposite number 4492; that since said marriage the said

Cherokee Intermarried White 1906
Volume I

Thomas J. Ayers and Virginia Ayers have resided together as husband and wife and have continuously lived in the Cherokee Nation. Said Thomas J. Ayers is identified on the Cherokee Authenticated tribal roll of 1880, and the Cherokee Census Roll of 1896, as an intermarried citizen of the Cherokee Nation.

IT IS, THEREFORE, ORDERED AND ADJUDGED: That in accordance with the decision of the Supreme Court of the United States, dated November 5, 1906, in the case of Daniel Red Bird et al., vs. the United States, under the provision of Section 21 of the Act of Congress approved June 28, 1898, (30 Stat. 495), Thomas J. Ayers is entitled to enrollment as a citizen by intermarriage of the Cherokee Nation, and his application for enrollment as such is accordingly granted.

Tams Bixby
Commissioner.

Dated at Muskogee, Indian Territory,
this   JAN 17 1907

◇◇◇◇◇

Cherokee
   1684.

Muskogee, Indian Territory, December 24, 1906.

Thomas J. Ayers,
    Watova, Indian Territory.

Dear Sir:

November 6, 1906, the United States Supreme Court held that white persons who intermarried with Cherokee citizens according to Cherokee law prior to November 1, 1875, are entitled to enrollment and allotments of land as citizens of the Cherokee Nation.

You are advised that to properly determine your right to enrollment as a citizen by intermarriage of the Cherokee Nation, it will be necessary for you to appear before the Commissioner for the purpose of giving testimony as to the date of your marriage and whether or not your wife, by reason of your marriage to whom you claim the right to enrollment as a citizen of the Cherokee Nation, was a recognized citizen of the Cherokee Nation at the time of your marriage to her, and whether or not you were married to her in accordance with Cherokee laws.

You are, therefore, directed to appear before the Commissioner at Muskogee, Indian Territory, at 9 o'clock A. M., on Thursday, January 3, 1907, and give testimony as above indicated.

Respectfully,

LMC   Acting Commissioner.

◇◇◇◇◇

Cherokee Intermarried White 1906
Volume I

Cherokee
1684.

Muskogee, Indian Territory, January 17, 1907.

W. W. Hastings,
    Attorney for the Cherokee Nation,
        Muskogee, Indian Territory.

Dear Sir:

    There is enclosed herewith a copy of the decision of the Commissioner to the Five Civilized Tribes, dated January 17, 1907, granting the application of Thomas J. Ayres for enrollment as a citizen by intermarriage of the Cherokee Nation.

                  Respectfully,

E. R. C.   Commissioner.

Enc. E. C. - I.

◇◇◇◇◇

Cherokee 1684   W.W. HASTINGS, ATTORNEY.   OFFICE OF   H.M. VANCE, SECRETARY.

Attorney for the Cherokee Nation,
MUSKOGEE, I. T.

                                                    January 18, 1907.

The Commissioner to the Five Civilized Tribes,
    Muskogee, Indian Territory.

Sir:

    Receipt is acknowledged of the testimony and of your decision enrolling Thomas J. Ayres, as a citizen by intermarriage of the Cherokee Nation. Time for protesting said decision is waived and I consent that said person may be placed upon the schedule immediately.

                    Yours very truly,
                            W. W. Hastings
                            Attorney for Cherokee Nation.

◇◇◇◇◇

Cherokee Intermarried White 1906
Volume I

Cherokee
1684

Muskogee, Indian Territory, January 21, 1907/

Thomas J. Ayers,
    Watova, Indian Territory.

Dear Sir:

    There is enclosed herewith copy of the decision of the Commissioner to the Five Civilized Tribes, dated January 17, 1907, granting the application for your enrollment as a citizen by intermarriage of the Cherokee Nation.

You will be advised when your name has been placed upon the schedule of citizens of the Cherokee Nation and approved by the Secretary of the Interior.

                        Respectfully,

Enc M - 17

M.T.M.   Commissioner.

◇◇◇◇◇

Cherokee
    I. W. 17.

Muskogee, Indian Territory, April 6, 1907

Thomas J. Ayers,
    Watova, Indian Territory.

Dear Sir:

Your marriage license and certificate, filed in connection with your application for enrollment as a citizen by intermarriage of the Cherokee Nation, is returned to you herewith, copies of the same being retained in this office.

                        Respectfully,

Encl. B-88   Acting Commissioner.

L M B

Cherokee Intermarried White 1906
Volume I

Cher I W 18
Trans from Cher 1736 3-13-07

C.E.W.

DEPARTMENT OF THE INTERIOR,

COMMISSIONER TO THE FIVE CIVILIZED TRIBES.

In the matter of the application for the enrollment of

CHARLES E. WILLEY

as a citizen by intermarriage of the Cherokee Nation.

CHEROKEE 1736

DEPARTMENT OF THE INTERIOR.
COMMISSION TO THE FIVE CIVILIZED TRIBES.
FT. GIBSON, I. T., AUGUST 21st, 1900.

IN THE MATTER OF THE APPLICATION OF Mary Willy[sic] and husband, for enrollment as citizens of the Cherokee Nation, and she being sworn by Commissioner, T. B. Needles, testified as follows:

Q What is your name? A Mary Willy.
Q What is your age? A Forty eight.
Q What is your Postoffice? A Ft. Gibson.
Q Are you a recognized citizen of the Cherokee Nation? A Yes sir.
Q By blood or intermarriage? A By blood.
Q What degree of blood do you claim? A I do not know; about one sixteenth.
Q What District do you live in? A Illinois.
Q How long have you lived in the Cherokee Nation continuously? A Ever since I was born.
Q For whom do you apply? Whom do you want to enroll? A Me and my husband.
Q Any children? A They are all grown and married.
Q Yourself and husband? A Yes sir.
Q What is your father's name? A Thomas Barnes.
Q Is he living? A No sir.
Q Was he a Cherokee citizen? A No sir; white man.
Q Are his father and mother white persons; non citizens? A Yes sir.
Q What is the name of your mother? A Mary Foreman.

Cherokee Intermarried White 1906
Volume I

Q Indian or white person? A Indian.
Q Is she living? A No sir.
Q When did she die? A Soon after the war.
Q What is your husband's name? A Charles E. Willy.
Q Is he a citizen by blood, or intermarriage? A Intermarriage.
Q When were you married? A About thirty years ago.
Q Have you any children living, under twenty one years of age? A No sir.
(Applicant identified on the roll of 1880, Page 602, #2158, Mary Willy, Illinois District)
(Applicant's husband identified on the roll of 1880, Page 602, #2157, Charles Willy, Illinois District)
(Applicant identified on the roll of 1896, Page 919, #2224, Mary Willy, Illinois District.)
(Applicant's husband identified on the roll of 1896, Page (919,)(937)(#219)(#2226,) Charlie Willie, Illinois District)
Q Your name is Minnie, is it not? A They used to call me Mary.

The name of Mary Willy, appearing on the authenticated roll of 1880, and the census roll of 1896, and the name of her husband, Charles E. Willy, appearing on the authenticated roll of 1880, and the census roll of 1896; they being fully identified, and having made satisfactory prroof[sic] as to their residence, they will both be listed for enrollment by this Commission, she (the applicant) as a citizen by blood, and her husband as a citizen by intermarriage.

R. R. Cravens, being sworn, states that as stenographer to the Commission to the Five Civilized Tribes, he reported the foregoing testimony and proceedings in full, and that same is a true, full and correct transcript of his stenographic notes in said case.

R R Cravens

Sworn to and subscribed before
me this 28th day of August, 1900.

TB Needles
COMMISSIONER.

◇◇◇◇◇

Cherokee 1736.

DEPARTMENT OF THE INTERIOR,
COMMISSION TO THE FIVE CIVILIZED TRIBES.
Muskogee, I. T., October 16, 1902.

In the matter of the application of Charley E. Willey for the enrollment of himself as a citizen by intermarriage, and for the enrollment of his wife, Mary Willey, as a citizen by blood, of the Cherokee Nation.

SUPPLEMENTAL PROCEEDINGS.

CHARLES E. WILLEY, being sworn, testified as follows:

Cherokee Intermarried White 1906
Volume I

By the Commission,

Q What is your name? A Charles E. Willey.
Q How old are you? A Fifty-two the twenty-first day of April.
Q What is your postoffice? A Fort Gibson.
Q Are you a white man? A Yes, sir.
Q Your name appears on the roll of 1880 as an adopted white citizen, does it? A Yes, sir.
Q What is your wife's name? A Minnie, or Mary; sometimes she signs it Mary Willey.
Q I see she is enrolled as Mary, do you want it Mary? A I would just as soon.
Q Is she a Cherokee by blood? A Yes, sir.
Q Is she the wife through whom you claim your citizenship? A Yes, sir.
Q You were married in 1880? A Yes, sir.
Q Have you been living together since 1880? A Yes, sir.
Q Living together at this time, are you? A Yes, sir.
Q Have you made your home in the Cherokee Nation ever since 1880? A Yes, sir, been at Fort Gibson.
Q Never lived anywhere else during the last twenty-two years? A Never been away from Fort Gibson.

Retta Chick, being first duly sworn, states that, as stenographer to the Commission to the Five Civilized Tribes, she recorded the testimony and proceedings in the matter of the forgoing application, and that the above is a true and complete transcript of her stenographic notes taken thereof.

Retta Chick

Subscribed and sworn to before me this 12th day of November, 1902.

BC Jones
Notary Public.

◇◇◇◇◇

Cherokee No. 1736.

DEPARTMENT OF THE INTERIOR.
COMMISSIONER TO THE FIVE TRIBES.

Muskogee, Indian Territory, January 3, 1907.

In the matter of the application for the enrollment of Charles E. Willey as a citizen by intermarriage of the Cherokee Nation.

Charles E. Willey, being first duly sworn and examined, testifies as follows:

Cherokee Intermarried White 1906
Volume I

BY THE COMMISSIONER:

Q What is your name? A Charles E. Willey.
Q How old are you? A 56.
Q What is your postoffice address? A Fort Gibson.
Q You claim to be an intermarried citizen of the Cherokee Nation? A Yes, sir.
Q Through whom do you claim your intermarriage rights? A Through my wife.
Q What is her name? A Minnie Barnes.
Q When were you married to Minnie Barnes? A The fall of &70.
Q Were you ever married before you married her? A No, sir.
Q Was she ever married before she married you? A No, sir.
Q Where were you married? A Up close to Tahlequah.
Q Cherokee Nation? A Yes, sir.
Q Married under the Cherokee ?aw[sic]?
Q Got a licence[sic]? A No, sir.
Q Did you get a licence[sic]? A Yes, sir.
Q Where is it? A William Tunnell was clerk of the Tahlequah District when I was married. Mr. Rubell married me.
Q You never got the licence[sic] back? A No, sir.
Q Was your wife sometims[sic] known as Mary Barnes? A Yes, sir.
Q What was the name of her father? A Thomas.
Q What was the name of her mother? A Polly.
Q Was that her name or a nickname.[sic] A I don't know.

An examination of the marriage records of the Tahlequal[sic] District from 1879 to 1872, on page 7 shows that Charles Willey, a white man was issued a licence[sic] on November 11th, 1870 to marry Miss. Mary Barnes, and that he was married by the Rev. Stephen Foreman.

Q You heard the record I just read? from the Tahlequal[sic] District. Is that absolutely correct? A It is with the exception that a mistake was made in the man that performed the ceremony.
Q You say you were married by Rev. Rubel[sic]. A Yes, sir. Mrs. Foreman was my wife's uncle and so we got Mr. Rubel to perform the ceremony, but Mr. Foreman was present.
Q Have you and Minnie Willey, your wife, lived together continuously as husband and wife since your marriage in 1870 up to the present time? A Yes, sir.
Q Still living together? A Yes, sir. Living at Fort Gibson.

The applicant is identified on the 1880 Cherokee Roll, Illinois District, opposite No. 2157. His wife through whom he claims his right to enrollment is identified on said roll in said district opposite No. 2158. She is also identified on the final roll of the citizens by blood of the Cherokee Nation, opposite No. 2604.

WITNESS EXCUSED.

Cherokee Intermarried White 1906
Volume I

F. Elma Lane, upon oath, states that she reported the proceedings in the above entitled cause and that the foregoing is a true and correct transcript of her stenographic notes taken therein.

F. Elma Lane

Subscribed and sworn to before me this 4th day of January, 1907.

Chas E Webster
Notary Public.

◇◇◇◇◇

C.E.W. Cherokee 1736

DEPARTMENT OF THE INTERIOR,

COMMISSIONER TO THE FIVE CIVILIZED TRIBES.

In the matter of the application for the enrollment of Charles E. Willey, as a citizen by intermarriage of the Cherokee Nation.

D E C I S I O N

THE RECORDS OF THIS OFFICE SHOW: That at Fort Gibson, Indian Territory, August 21, 1900, Mary Willey appeared before the Commission to the Five Civilized Tribes and made application for the enrollment of herself, as a citizen by blood, and for the enrollment of her husband, Charles E. Willey, as a citizen by intermarriage of the Cherokee Nation. The application for the enrollment of the said Mary Willey, as a citizen by blood of the Cherokee Nation has been heretofore disposed of and her rights to enrollment will not be considered in this decision.

THE EVIDENCE IN THIS CASE SHOWS: That the applicant herein, Charles E. Willey, a white man, was married in accordance with Cherokee law November 11, 1870, to his wife, Mary Willey, nee Barnes, who was at the time of said marriage a recognized citizen by blood of the Cherokee Nation, and whose name appears upon the approved partial roll of citizens by blood of the Cherokee Nation, opposite number 4604; that since said marriage the said Charles E. Willey and Mary Willey have resided together as husband and wife and have continuously lived in the Cherokee Nation. Said Charles E. Willey is identified on the Cherokee Authenticated tribal roll of 1880, and the Cherokee Census roll of 1896 as an intermarried citizen of the Cherokee Nation.

IT IS, THEREFORE, ORDERED AND ADJUDGED: That in accordance with the decision of the Supreme Court of the United States, dated November 5, 1906, in the case of Daniel Red Bird et al., vs the United States under the provisions of Section 21 of the Act of Congress approved June 28, 1898, (30 Stat. 495), Charles E. Willey is entitled to enrollment as a citizen by intermarriage of the Cherokee Nation, and his application for enrollment as such is accordingly granted.

Cherokee Intermarried White 1906
Volume I

Tams Bixby
Commissioner.

Dated at Muskogee, Indian Territory,
this   JAN 17 1907

◇◇◇◇◇

Cherokee
   1736.

Muskogee, Indian Territory, December 24, 1906.

Charles E. Willey,
      Fort Gibson, Indian Territory.

Dear Sir:

November 6, 1906, the United States Supreme Court held that white persons who intermarried with Cherokee citizens according to Cherokee law prior to November 1, 1875, are entitled to enrollment and allotments of land as citizens of the Cherokee Nation.

You are advised that to properly determine your right to enrollment as a citizen by intermarriage of the Cherokee Nation, it will be necessary for you to appear before the Commissioner for the purpose of giving testimony as to the date of your marriage and whether or not your wife, by reason of your marriage to whom you claim the right to enrollment as a citizen of the Cherokee Nation, was a recognized citizen of the Cherokee Nation at the time of your marriage to her, and whether or not you were married to her in accordance with Cherokee laws.

You are, therefore, directed to appear before the Commissioner at Muskogee, Indian Territory, at 9 o'clock A. M., on Thursday, January 3, 1907, and give testimony as above indicated.

                      Respectfully,

LMC   Acting Commissioner.

◇◇◇◇◇

Cherokee Intermarried White 1906
Volume I

Cherokee
1736.

Muskogee, Indian Territory, January 17, 1907.

W. W. Hastings,
   Attorney for the Cherokee Nation,
     Muskogee, Indian Territory.

Dear Sir:

There is enclosed herewith a copy of the decision of the Commissioner to the Five Civilized Tribes, dated January 17, 1907, granting the application of Charles E. Willey for enrollment as a citizen by intermarriage of the Cherokee Nation.

Respectfully,

E. R. C.   Commissioner.

Enc. E. C. - 2.

◇◇◇◇◇

Cherokee   W.W. HASTINGS,   OFFICE OF   H.M. VANCE,
1736   ATTORNEY.   SECRETARY.

Attorney for the Cherokee Nation,
MUSKOGEE, I. T.

January 18, 1907.

The Commissioner to the Five Civilized Tribes,
   Muskogee, Indian Territory.

Sir:

Receipt is acknowledged of the testimony and of your decision enrolling Charles E. Willey, as a citizen by intermarriage of the Cherokee Nation. Time for protesting said decision is waived and I consent that said person may be placed upon the schedule immediately.

Yours very truly,
W. W. Hastings
Attorney for Cherokee Nation.

◇◇◇◇◇

Cherokee Intermarried White 1906
Volume I

Cherokee
1736

Muskogee, Indian Territory, January 21, 1907.

Charles E. Willey,
    Fort Gibson, Indian Territory.

Dear Sir:

    There is enclosed herewith copy of the decision of the Commissioner to the Five Civilized Tribes, dated January 17, 1907, granting the application for your enrollment as a citizen by intermarriage of the Cherokee Nation.

    You will be advised when your name has been placed upon the schedule of citizens of the Cherokee Nation and approved by the Secretary of the Interior.

                  Respectfully,

Enc M - 16

M.T.M.   Commissioner.

Cher I W 19
Trans from Cher 1750   3-13-07

                                                                              E.C.M.

DEPARTMENT OF THE INTERIOR,

COMMISSIONER TO THE FIVE CIVILIZED TRIBES.

In the matter of the application for the enrollment of

EDWIN WREN

as a citizen by intermarriage of the Cherokee Nation.

CHEROKEE 1750.

Cherokee Intermarried White 1906
Volume I

DEPARTMENT OF THE INTERIOR,
COMMISSION TO THE FIVE CIVILIZED TRIBES,
FORT GIBSON, I. T., AUGUST 21, 1900.

In the matter of the application of Edwin Wren for enrollment of himself and children, as citizens of the Cherokee Nation, said Wren being duly sworn by Commissioner Breckinridge, testified as follows:

Q What is your name? A Edwin Wren.
Q How old are you? A 64.
Q What is your postoffice? A Bragg.
Q Your district? A Illinois.
Q Whom do you apply for enrollment for? A Myself and two children.
Q You apply for yourself as a Cherokee by blood? A No sir, by intermarriage.
Q Have you a certificate and license of marriage? A No sir, not with me.
Q When were you married? A '74.
Q You are on the roll of '80? A Yes.
Q What is the name of your father? A William A. Wren.
Q He was a white man? A Yes.
Q Is he dead? A Ye.
Q What is the name of your mother? A Margarett.
Q She was white too? A Yes.
Q Is she dead? A Yes.
Q When did your wife die? A 7 years ago.
Q Did you and she live together as husband and wife from the time of your marriage until her death? A Yes.
Q And lived continuously in the Cherokee Nation? A Yes.
Q That is your home at this time and has been ever since your wife's death? A Yes sir.
Q Have you ever remarried? A No sir.
Q Now give me names of your children? A George H., 17 years old.
    On '96 roll, page 914, number 2077.
Q Next child? A Charles R., 14 years old.
    On '96 roll, page 914, number 2078.
Q What was the name of their mother? A Her name was Kate.
Q You had never been married except with the wife you enrolled with in '80?
A No sir, never married but the one time.
Q She was a Cherokee by blood? A Yes.
    Applicant on '80 roll, page 602, number 2148, as Edward.
    On '96 roll, page 937, number 225.
    Applicant's wife on '80 roll page 602, number 2149.
Q These children are both living now? A Yes.
    The applicant is duly identified on the roll of '80 and roll of '96 as an adopted Cherokee. He has lived continuously to this time in the Cherokee Nation, has never removed, and will be enrolled now as a Cherokee by adoption. His children, George H., and Charles R., are identified on the roll of '96. Their mother is identified on the roll of '80 as a Cherokee by blood— she is dead. These children will now be enrolled as Cherokees by blood.

Cherokee Intermarried White 1906
Volume I

The undersigned, being first duly sworn, states that as stenographer to the Commission to the Five Civilized Tribes, he correctly recorded the testimony and proceedings in this case, and that the foregoing is a full, true and correct transcript of his stenographic notes thereof.

Brown McDonald

Subscribed and sworn to before me this 10th day of September, 1900.

TB Needles
Commissioner.

◇◇◇◇◇

Cher
Supp'l to # 1750

Department of the Interior,
Commission to the Five Civilized Tribes,
Muskogee, I. T., October 21, 1902.

In the matter of the application of EDWIN WREN, for the enrollment of himself as a citizen by intermarriage, and his children, GEORGE H. and CHARLES R. WREN, as citizens by blood, of the Cherokee Nation:

EDWIN WREN, being duly sworn and examined by the Commission, testified as follows:

Q What is your name ? A Edwin Wren.
Q What is your post office Mr. Wren ? A Edna, Kansas.
Q What is your age at this time ? A I am 66 years old
Q Are you the same Edwin Wren that made application to the Commission in August, 1900, for enrollment as an intermarried citizen of the Cherokee Nation ? A Yes sir.
Q What was your wife's name ? A Ada C.
Q Is your wife living ? A No sir.
Q When did she die Mr. Wren ? A She's been dead about 10 years.
Q She was a Cherokee was she ? A Yes sir.
Q When were you married to her ? A In 1874.
Q Were you ever married before you married this wife ? A No sir.
Q Did you and she live together from 1880 up to the day of her death ? A Yes sir.
Q Never were separated during her lifetime ? A No sir.
Q Have you married since the death of your wife ? A No sir.
Q You were still a widower and single on the first day of September, 1902 ? A Yes sir.
Q Are these children, George H. and Charles R. Wren, you children by your wife Ada C? A Yes sir.
Q Are they living now ? A Yes sir.
Q Have they lived all their lives in the Cherokee Nation ? A Yes sir.
Q Have you lived in the Cherokee Nation all the time since your marriage in 1879 up to the present time ? A Yes sir.

Cherokee Intermarried White 1906
Volume I

E. C. Bagwell, on oath states that, as stenographer to the Commission to the Five Civilized Tribes, he correctly recorded the testimony and proceedings had in the above entitled cause, and that the foregoing is an accurate transcript of his stenographic notes thereof.

EC Bagwell

Subscribed and sworn to before me this November 25, 1902.

BC Jones
Notary Public.

◇◇◇◇◇

Cherokee 1750

DEPARTMENT OF THE INTERIOR,
COMMISSIONER TO THE FIVE CIVILIZED TRIBES.
Muskogee, I. T., January 3, 1907.

In the matter of the application for the enrollment of Edwin Wren as a citizen by intermarriage of the Cherokee Nation.

Edwin Wren, being first sworn by Walter W. Chappell, a Notary Public for the Western District, testified as follows:

By the Commissioner:
Q What is your name? A Edwin Wren.
Q Your age? A Sixty-nine the 4th of March.
Q What is your postoffice address? A Edna, Kansas.
Q You claim to be a citizen by intermarriage of the Cherokee Natil[sic], do you? A Yes sir.
Q Through whom do you claim that right? A My wife, Kate Cummings.
Q Is she living? A No sir.
Q When did she die? A Been ded[sic] about 14 years.
Q What was her citizenship? A Cherokee by blood.
Q When were you married to Kate Cummings? A In 1874.
Q Where were you married to her? A I was married over here where Braggs Station is now. There was no town there then.
Q Marrid[sic] in the Cherokee Nation? A Yes sir.
Q Were you married under a Cherokee license? A Yes sir.
Q Have you a copy of that license with you? A Yes sir.
Q At the time of your marriage to Kate Cummings was she a citizen of the Cherokee nation[sic]? A Yes sir.
Q Had she ever been married prior to that time? A No sir
Q Had you? A No sir.
Q After your marriage where did you liv[sic]? A Lived here in this place, in Muskogee.

Cherokee Intermarried White 1906
Volume I

Q How long did you liv[sic] here? A Lived here 3 or 4 years I think-- about 4 years.
Q Then where did you move to? A Moved back over to Braggs.
Q Have you ever lived outside of the Indian Territory since your marriage in 1874?
A No sir.
Q You say your wife died about 14 years ago? A Yes sir.
Q About 1892? A Do you remember the year she died? A I don't know; I am a poor hand to remember dates.
Q Have you married since her death? A No sir.
Q Had you any children by Kate Wren? A Yes, four.
Q Are these children now living? A Two of them are living; two are dead.
Q What are the names of the living children? A George H. Wren and Charles R. Wren.

> The names of George H. and Charles R. Wren, appear upon Cherokee straight card No. 1750, as children of Edwin Wren and Kate Wren, deceased, and their names are included in an approved partial roll of Cherokees by blood of the Cherokee Nation, opposite Nos. 4646 and 4647 respectively.
>
> The name of the applicant, Edwin Wren, appears upon the authenticated Cherokee tribal roll, 1880 and Cherokee Census Card, roll of 1896, opposite Nos. 2148 and 225, Illinois District.
>
> The applicant offers in evidence an instrument certified by "Geo. O. Sanders, Clerk Illinois District Court", under dte[sic] of August 13, 1874, issued its certificate that Mr. Edwin Wren, a citizen of the United States having made application in due form of law regulating intermarriage with white men, was licensed to marry Miss Kate Cummings, a citizen of the Cherokee Nation. The license has been issued by said Geo. O. Sanders, authorizing the marriage of the above named parties, the same being filed herewith and made a part of the records in this case.
>
> An examination of the "Marriage Register for Illinois District, 1869- 1892", Book A. fails to sow[sic] that any record of the marriage license issued to said applicant was made by the Cherokee authorities.
>
> Further examination will be made for the record of the aforesaid license.

Frances R. Lane upon oath states that as stenographer to the Commissioner to the Five Civilized Tribes she reported the testimony in the above entitled cause and that the above and foregoing is an accurate transcript of her stenographic notes thereof.

Frances R Lane

Cherokee Intermarried White 1906
Volume I

Subscribed and sworn to before me this January 4, 1907.

Edward Merrick
Notary Public.

◇◇◇◇◇

(COPY)

Office District Clerk I
I
of Illinois District I

To any Regular Minister of an Evangelical Denomination or Judge of the Courts of the Cherokee Nation to whom these may come:-

Greeting- Mr. Edwin Wren a citizen of the United States having made application in due form of law "Regulating intermarriage with white men" for a license to marry Miss Kate Cummings a citizen of the Cherokee Nation.

The refore[sic] be it known that I by the authority in me vested by law, have this day granted the said Edwin Wren license to marry Miss Kate Cummings a citizen of the Cherokee Nation, and you are therefore authorized to solemnize the rites of matrimony between the above mentioned parties, according to the form practiced in your Church or Office, and to attach a Certificate of said marriage hereunto and to return the same to this office for record.

Given from under my hand this 13th of August 1874.

Geo. W. Somders[sic] Clk.

Illinois Dist. Court.

I, Homer J. Councilor, being first duly sworn state that as stenographer to the Commissioner to the Five Civilized Tribes, I made the above and foregoing copy from the original thereof and that the same is a correct copy thereof.

Homer J. Councilor

Subscribed and sworn to before me this 10th day of January 1907.

B.P. Rasmus
Notary public.

◇◇◇◇◇

Cherokee Intermarried White 1906
Volume I

E.C.M.
Cherokee 1750.

DEPARTMENT OF THE INTERIOR,

COMMISSIONER TO THE FIVE CIVILIZED TRIBES.

In the matter of the application for the enrollment of Edwin Wren as a citizen by intermarriage of the Cherokee Nation.

D E C I S I O N

THE RECORDS OF THIS OFFICE HSOW[sic]: That at Fort Gibson, Indian Territory, August 21, 1900, Edwin Wren appeared before the Commission to the Five Civilized Tribes and made application for the enrollment of himself as a citizen by intermarriage and for the enrollment of his children as citizens by blood of the Cherokee Nation. The application for the enrollment of the children of the said Edwin Wren as citizens by blood of the Cherokee Nation has heretofore been disposed of and their rights to enrollment will not be considered in this decision. The records further show that the name of Kate Wren, wife of said Edwin Wren, appears upon the Cherokee authenticated tribal roll of 1880, Illinois District, page 602, opposite number 2149, marked "dead". Further proceedings in the matter of said application were had at Muskogee, Indian Territory, October 21, 1902, and January 3, 1907.

THE EVIDENCE IN THIS CASE SHOWS: That the applicant herein, Edwin Wren, a white man, was married in accordance with Cherokee law in August 1874, to one, Kate Wren, nee Cummings, deceased, who was at the time of said marriage a recognized citizen by blood of the Cherokee Nation,; and from the time of said marriage until the death of Kate Wren, which occurred in 1892, said Edwin Wren and Kate Wren resided together as husband and wife and that since the death of Kate Wren the said Edwin Wren has remained unmarried and has since the date of his said marriage continuously lived in the Cherokee Nation. Said Edwin Wren is identified upon the Cherokee Authenticated roll of 1880, and the Cherokee Census roll of 1896, as an intermarried citizen of the Cherokee Nation.

IT IS THEREFORE ORDERED AND ADJUDGED: That in accordance with the decision of the Supreme Court of the United States, dated November 5, 1906, in the case of Daniel Red Bird et al., vs the United States, under the provisions of Section 21 of the Act of Congress approved June 28, 1898 (30 Stat., 495), Edwin Wren, is entitled to enrollment as a citizen by intermarriage of the Cherokee Nation, and his application for enrollment as such is accordingly granted.

Tams Bixby
Commissioner.

Dated at Muskogee, Indian Territory,
this   JAN 16 1907

Cherokee Intermarried White 1906
Volume I

Cherokee
1750

Muskogee, Indian Territory, December 24, 1906.

Edwin Wren,
    Edna, Kansas.

Dear Sir:

November 6, 1906, the United States Supreme Court held that white persons who intermarried with Cherokee citizens according to Cherokee law prior to November 1, 1875, are entitled to enrollment and allotments of land as citizens of the Cherokee Nation.

You are advised that to properly determine your right to enrollment as a citizen by intermarriage of the Cherokee Nation, it will be necessary for you to appear before the Commissioner for the purpose of giving testimony as to the date of your marriage and whether or not your wife, by reason of your marriage to whom you claim the right to enrollment as a citizen of the Cherokee Nation, was a recognized citizen of the Cherokee Nation at the time of your marriage to her, and whether or not you were married to her in accordance with Cherokee laws.

You are, therefore, directed to appear before the Commissioner at Muskogee, Indian Territory, at 9 o'clock A. M., on Thursday, January 3, 1907, and give testimony as above indicated.

                        Respectfully,

LMC   Acting Commissioner.

Cherokee 1750

                        Muskogee, Indian Territory, January 17, 1907.

W. W. Hastings,
    Attorney for the Cherokee Nation,
        Muskogee, Indian Territory.

Dear Sir:

There is enclosed herewith copy of the decision of the Commissioner to the Five Civilized Tribes, dated January 16, 1907, granting the application for the enrollment of Edwin Wren as a citizen by intermarriage of the Cherokee Nation.

Cherokee Intermarried White 1906
Volume I

Respectfully,

Commissioner.

Enc I-4

RPI

◇◇◇◇◇

Cherokee 1750.   W.W. HASTINGS,   OFFICE OF   H.M. VANCE.
                  ATTORNEY.   SECRETARY.

Attorney for the Cherokee Nation,
MUSKOGEE, I. T.

January 18, 1907.

The Commissioner to the Five Civilized Tribes,
　　Muskogee, Indian Territory.

Sir:

　　Receipt is acknowledged of the testimony and of your decision enrolling Edwin Wren as a citizen by intermarriage of the Cherokee Nation. Time for protesting said decision is waived and I consent that said person may be placed upon the schedule immediately.

　　　　　　　　　　Yours very truly,
　　　　　　　　　　W. W. Hastings
　　　　　　　　　　Attorney for Cherokee Nation.

◇◇◇◇◇

Cherokee 1750

Muskogee, Indian Territory, January 19, 1907.

Edwin Wren,
　　Edna, Kansas.

Dear Sir:

　　There is enclosed herewith copy of the decision of the Commissioner to the Five Civilized Tribes, dated January 16, 1907, granting the application for your enrollment as a citizen by intermarriage of the Cherokee Nation.

　　You will be advised when your name has been placed upon the schedule of citizens of the Cherokee Nation and approved by the Secretary of the Interior.

Cherokee Intermarried White 1906
Volume I

Respectfully,

Commissioner.

Enc I-3

RPI

◇◇◇◇◇◇

Cherokee
I W. 19

Muskogee, Indian Territory, April 6, 1907.

Edwin Wren,
    Edna, Kansas.

Dear Sir:

Your marriage license filed in connection with your application for enrollment as a citizen by intermarriage of the Cherokee Nation, is returned to you herewith, copies of the same being retained in this office.

Respectfully,

Encl. B- 93   Acting Commissioner.

L M B

Cher I W 30
Trans from Cher 1880 3-13-07

◇◇◇◇◇◇

E.C.M.

DEPARTMENT OF THE INTERIOR,

COMMISSIONER TO THE FIVE CIVILIZED TRIBES.

In the matter of the application for the enrollment of

PATRICK FOLEY

as a citizen by intermarriage of the Cherokee Nation.

Cherokee Intermarried White 1906
Volume I

CHEROKEE 1770.

◇◇◇◇◇

DEPARTMENT OF THE INTERIOR.
COMMISSION TO THE FIVE CIVILIZED TRIBES.
FT. GIBSON, I. T., AUGUST 22nd, 1900.

IN THE MATTER OF THE APPLICATION OF Patrick Foley, wife and children for enrollment as citizens of the Cherokee Nation, and he being sworn by Commissioner, T. B. Needles, testified as follows:

Q What is your name? A Patrick Foley.
Q What is your age? A Fifty six.
Q What is your Postoffice? A Starvilla.
Q Are you a recognized citizen of the Cherokee Nation? A Yes sir.
Q By blood or intermarriage? A By adoption.
Q What district do you live in? A Canadian.
Q How long have you lived there? A Twenty two or three years.
Q Continuously? A Yes sir.
Q For whom do you apply? A My wife.
Q Yourself? A Yes sir.
Q Any children? A Yes sir.
Q Yourself, wife and children? A Yes sir.
Q Is your father living? A No sir.
Q Was he a non citizen? A Yes sir.
Q Is your mother living? A Yes sir.
Q Are you married? A Yes sir.
Q What is your wifes[sic] name? A Addie Loony was her maiden name.
Q Is she an Indian by blood? A Yes sir.
Q Is she living? A Yes sir.
Q What is her mother's name? A Nellie Highland.
Q What was her mother's name in 1880? A Loony.
Q Is she living? A Yes sir.
Q Is she an Indian? A Yes sir.
Q What is the name of your wifes[sic] father.[sic] A William Loony.
Q Is he living? A No sir.
Q Was he a non citizen? A They claim he was an Indian.
Q When did he die? A About twenty seven or eight years ago.
Q Have you any certificate of marriage? A No sir.
Q When were you married? A About twenty five years ago.
Q What are the name of your children under twenty one? A Maggie Foley.
Q How old is Maggie? A Twenty one.
Q Is she living with you at home? A She is with my borther[sic] in law
Q What is the next one? A Laura.
Q How old is Laura? A Eighteen
Q Next one? A Clarence.

Cherokee Intermarried White 1906
Volume I

Q How old is Clarence? A Seventeen, I believe.
Q What is the next one? A Lizzie.
Q How old is Lizzie? A Sixteen I believe.
Q Next one? A Sarah.
Q How old is Sarah? A Thirteen.
Q What is the name of the next one? A Lawrence.
Q How old is Lawrence? A Eight.
Q Next is? A Roachman.
Q How old is he? A About five.
Q Seven children at home? A Yes sir.
Q Ar these children all living and living with you? A Yes sir, all except Maggie.
Q Have you another one? A Yes sir.
Q What is its name? A Cornelius.
Q How old is Cornelius? A Four months old the twenty seventh of this month.
Q This child is living and living with you: These children are all living and living at home with you, are they? A All except Maggie.
(Applicant identified on the roll of 1880, Page 17, #457, Pat Foley, Canadian District)
(1896 Roll, Page 87, #81, Patrick Foley, Canadian District)
(Applicant's wife identified on the roll of 1880, Page 17, #458, Addie Foley, Canadian District)
(1896 Roll, Page 23, #618, Adline Foley, Canadian District)
Identification of applicant's children:
(1896 Roll, Page 23, #621, Maggie Foley, Canadian District)
(1896 Roll, Page 17, #622, Laura Foley, Canadian District)
(1896 Roll, Page 23, #461, Maggie Foley, Canadian District)
(1896 Roll, Page 23, #623. Clarence Foley, Canadian District)
(1896 Roll, Page 23, #624, Lizzie Foley, Canadian District)
(1896 Roll, Page 23, #625, Sarah Foley, Canadian District)
(1896 Roll, Page 23, #626, Lawrence Foley, Canadian District)
(1896 Roll, Page 23, #627, Joseph B. Foley, Canadian District)

The name of Patrick Foley appears on the authenticated roll of 1880, as Pat Foley; the name of Patrick Foley appears on the census roll of 1896; the name of his wife Adline appears on the authenticated roll of 1880, as Addie Foley and on the census roll of 1896 as Adline Foley; and the names of his children, Maggie, Laura, Clarence, Lizzie, Sarah, Lawrence and Joseph B. Foley appear on the census roll of 1896 and authenticated roll of 1880 respectively, the name of Roachman, appearing on the census roll as Joseph B.; they all being fully identified according to the page and number of the rolls as indicated in the testimony, and having made satisfactory proof of residence; the said Patrick Foley will be listed for enrollment by this Commission as a citizen by intermarriage; and his wife and children, as named in the testimony will be duly listed for enrollment as citizens by blood. He avers that he has a child named Cornelius, four months old, whose name does not appear on the census roll of 1896, he having been born since said rolls were compiled. Said Cornelius will also be listed for enrollment by this Commission, upon the filing with this Commission satisfactory proof of his birth.

Cherokee Intermarried White 1906
Volume I

The undersigned, being first duly sworn, states that as stenographer to the Commission to the Five Civilized Tribes, he correctly recorded the testimony and proceedings in this case, and that the foregoing is a true and complete transcript of his stenographic notes thereof.

R R Cravens

Subscribed and sworn to before
me this 29th day of August, 1900.

TB Needles
COMMISSIONER.

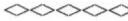

Cherokee 1770.

Department of the Interior,
Commission to the Five Civilized Tribes,
Muskogee, I. T., October 28, 1902.

In the matter of the application of Patrick Foley for the enrollment of himself as a citizen by intermarriage, and for the enrollment of his wife, Addie, and children, Maggie, Clarence, Lizzie, Sarah, Lawrence, Roachman, Cornelius Foley and Laura Starr, as citizens by blood of the Cherokee Nation; he being sworn and examined by the Commission, testified as follows:

Q What is your name? A Patrick Foley.
Q What is your postoffice? A Starvilla.
Q How old are you at this time? A I am going on fifty-seven.
Q You are an applicant are you for enrollment as an intermarried citizen of the Cherokee Nation A Yes sir.
Q What is your wife's name? A Addie Looney was her name before I married her, that was her maiden name.
Q When were you married to your wife, Addie? A It must have been about twenty-eight or nine years ago.
Q You married before 1880 were you? A Yes sir.
Q You are on the 1880 roll with her? A Yes sir, they recognized it so over at Fort Gibson when we enrolled.
Q Have you and your wife, Addie, lived together since 1880 as husband and wife up to the present time? A Yes sir, up until the night I left.
Q You and she have never been separated? A No sir.
Q You and she were living together as husband and wife on the first day of September, 1902, were you? A Yes sir, living together as man and wife ever since we married.
Q Have you and your wife lived in the Cherokee Nation from 1880 up until the present time? A Yes sir, I believe I stayed one year in McAlester I worked there.
Q You lived all the time in the Cherokee Nation except one year in McAlester?
A I think that was before '80, and been living here ever since '80 in Canadian District.
Q And you wife has also been here since '80? A Yes sir.

Cherokee Intermarried White 1906
Volume I

Q Maggie, Laura, Clarence, Lizzie, Sarah, Lawrence, Roachman and Cornelius are they all your children by your wife, Addie? A Yes sir, as far as I know, I recognize them all.
Q Are all these children living? A Yes sir, they are all living now.
Q Have they all lived in the Cherokee Nation all their lives? A Yes sir. The oldest I sent off to school when they were little, to Iowa, the two that are married off now.
Q Laura has married since the original application? A Yes sir.
Q What is her husband's name? A Henry Starr.

The undersigned, being duly sworn, states that as stenographer to the Commission to the Five Civilized Tribes he correctly recorded the testimony and proceedings in this case, and that the foregoing is a true and correct transcript of his stenographic notes thereof.

E.G. Rothenberger

Subscribed and sworn to before me this 29th day of November, 1902.

BC Jones
Notary Public.

◇◇◇◇◇

DEPARTMENT OF THE INTERIOR
COMMISSIONER TO THE FIVE CIVILIZED TRIBES
MUSKOGEE, IND. TER.
JAN. 3, 1907.

CHEROKEE.1770.

IN THE MATTER OF THE APPLICATION FOR THE
ENROLLMENT OF PATRICK FOLEY AS A CITIZEN
BY INTERMARRIAGE OF THE CHEROKEE NATION.

PATRICK FOLEY BEING FIRST DULY SWORN BY B. P. RASMUS A NOTARY PUBLIC, TESTIFIED AS FOLLOWS:

EXAMINATION BY THE COMMISSIONER:

Q What is your name? A Patrick Foley.
Q What is your age? A My age, it's about sixty, I will be sixty one years old the 16th day of July, I think that's correct.
Q What is your post office address? A Porum.
Q You are an applicant for enrollment as a citizen by intermarriage of the Cherokee Nation are you.[sic] A Yes sir.
Q You have no Cherokee blood.[sic] A No sir.
Q Your sole claim to the right to enrollment as a citizen of the Cherokee Nation is by virtue of your marriage to a citizen by blood of the Cherokee Nation? A Yes sir.

Cherokee Intermarried White 1906
Volume I

Q What is the name of the citizen thru whom you claim the right to enrollment.[sic]
A Adeline Looney, was her maiden name.
Q Is she living or dead.[sic] A She's living.
Q Was she a recognized citizen of the Cherokee Nation at the time you married her.[sic]
A Yes sir; at least they always was recognized as far as I know; there was no complaint.
Q She was living in the Cherokee Nation at that time was she.[sic] A No we were living here at Muskogee, you see, just across the line.
Q Were you married to her here in Muskogee? A Yes sir.
Q What is the date of your marriage to her.[sic] A I believe it was in April, the 21st --I forget now; it's on there.
Q What year? A In '75. In April.
Q In April 1875 you married your Cherokee wife thru whom you claim your right to enrollment as a citizen by intermarriage of the Cherokee Nation? A Yes sir.
Q Were you ever married prior to your marriage to her? A No sir.
Q Were you her first husband? A First husband.
Q Since your marriage to your wife in April 1875 have you and she lived together continuously as husband and wife? A Always.
Q And your permanent home since that time has been in the Cherokee Nation has it?
A I lived here one year after I married and went to McAester[sic] and lived a year, and we sent from McAlester down to where I'm living now near Porum and have lived there ever since.

> The applicant Patrick Foley is identified on the Cherokee Authenticated Tribal roll of 1880, Canadian District, No. 457; his wife Addie Foley is included in the Approved Partial Roll of citizens by blood of the Cherokee Nation opposite No. 4713.

Q Were you married to your wife in accordance with the law of the Cherokee Nation?
A Yes sir, but it was a Ministr[sic] married me; it was at the Presbyterian Church; Presbyterian Minister.
Q Did you obtain a license at that time? A Yes sir
Q In what district was that license issued? A Fort Gibson.
Q Illinois District? A Illinois District.

> The applicant presents a copy of marriage license and certificate signed by C. J. Harris Assistant Executive Secretary of the Cherokee Nation, showing that on April 21, 1875 license was issued by George O. Sanders, Clerk Illinois District Cherokee Nation, authorizing the marriage of Patrick Foley a citizen of the United States to Miss Adeline Looney a Cherokee Nation[sic]; said parties were united in marriage in accordance with the terms of said license, April 29, 1875 by John Elliott a Minister of the Gospel.

ooOoo

Clara Mitchell Wood, being first duly sworn upon her oath states that as stenographer to the Commissioner to the Five Civilized Tribes she reported the above and proceedings and that this is a correct transcript of his stenographic note.

Cherokee Intermarried White 1906
Volume I

Clara Mitchell Wood

Subscribed and sworn to before me this 3rd day of January 19[sic] 1907.

B.P. Rasmus
Notary Public.

◇◇◇◇◇

Patrick Foley to Miss Adeline Looney.
Clerks Office)
Illinois Dist)

To any Ordained Minister of an Evangelical Denomination, or Judge of the Courts of the Cherokee Nation, to whom these may come; Greeting:

Patrick Folley[sic], a citizen of the United States, having made application in conformity with the laws of the Cherokee Nation "Regulating intermarriage with white men" for a license to marry Miss Adaline Looney, a Cherokee lady, and a citizen of the Cherokee Nation, you are therefore authorized to solemnize the rites of matrimony between the above named parties, according to the usual ceremony practiced in your church or office and to return the same to this office for record.

Given from under my hand in office this
21st. day of April 1875.

Geo. O. Sanders, Clerk
Illinois Dist. C. N.

At Muskogee, On the 29th. day of April 1875, I united Patrick Foley and Adaline Looney in marriage according to the laws of the Presbyterian Church

Signed   John Elliott
             Minister of the Gospel

A true copy of the original on file.

Geo. Sanders.
Clerk.

Executive Dept.
Cherokee Nation.
Tahlequah, Ind. Tery.
June 15, 1905

This is to certify that the foregoing is a correct copy taken from the "Record of Marriage, Illinois District, Cherokee Nation" page 39, which Record is on file in this Office by authority of law and I am custodian of same.

C.J. Harris
Ass't. Executive Sec'y of the
Cherokee Nation.

Cherokee Intermarried White 1906
Volume I

The undersigned being duly sworn states that as stenographer to the Commissioner to the Five Civilized Tribes, she made the above copy, and that the same is a true and correct copy of the instrument now on file in this office.

Mary Tabor Mallory

Subscribed and sworn to before me the 15 day of January 1907

Chas E Webster
Notary Public.

◇◇◇◇◇

E.C.M. Cherokee 1770.

DEPARTMENT OF THE INTERIOR,

COMMISSIONER TO THE FIVE CIVILIZED TRIBES.

In the matter of the application for the enrollment of PATRICK FOLEY as a citizen by intermarriage of the Cherokee Nation.

D E C I S I O N

THE RECORDS OF THIS OFFICE SHOW: That at Fort Gibson, Indian Territory, August 22, 1900, Patrick Foley appeared before the Commission to the Five Civilized Tribes, and made application for the enrollment of himself as a citizen by intermarriage, and for the enrollment of his wife, Addie Foley, et al., as citizens by blood of the Cherokee Nation. The application for the enrollment of the said Addie Foley et al. as citizens by blood of the Cherokee Nation has been heretofore disposed of, and their rights to enrollment will not be considered in this decision. Further proceedings in the matter of said application were had at Muskogee, Indian Territory, October 28, 1902, and January 3, 1907.

THE EVIDENCE IN THIS CASE SHOWS: That the applicant herein, Patrick Foley, a white man, was married, in accordance with Cherokee law, April 29, 1875, to his wife, Addie Foley, nee Looney, who was at the time of said marriage a recognized citizen by blood of the Cherokee Nation, and whose name appears on the approved partial roll of citizens by blood of the Cherokee Nation, opposite No. 4713; that since said marriage the said Patrick Foley and the said Addie Foley have resided together as husband and wife, and have continuously lived in the Cherokee Nation. The said Patrick Foley is identified on the Cherokee authenticated tribal roll of 1880, and the Cherokee census roll of 1896, as an intermarried citizen of the Cherokee Nation.

IT IS, THEREFORE, ORDERED AND ADJUDGED: That in accordance with the decision of the Supreme Court of the United States, dated November 5, 1906, in the case of Daniel Red Bird et al. vs. the United States, under the provisions of Section 21, of the

Cherokee Intermarried White 1906
Volume I

Act of Congress approved June 28, 1898 (30 Stat., 495), Patrick Foley is entitled to enrollment as a citizen by intermarriage of the Cherokee Nation, and his application for enrollment as such is accordingly granted.

            Tams Bixby
            Commissioner.

Dated at Muskogee, Indian Territory,
this   JAN 17 1907

◇◇◇◇◇

Cherokee
1770

          Muskogee, Indian Territory, December 27, 1906.

Patrick Foley,
  Porum, Indian Territory.

Dear Sir:

  November 6, 1906, the United States Supreme Court held that white persons who intermarried with Cherokee citizens according to Cherokee law prior to November 1, 1875, are entitled to enrollment and allotments of land as citizens of the Cherokee Nation.

  You are advised that to properly determine your right to enrollment as a citizen by intermarriage of the Cherokee Nation, it will be necessary for you to appear before the Commissioner for the purpose of giving testimony as to the date of your marriage and whether or not your wife, by reason of your marriage to whom you claim the right to enrollment as a citizen of the Cherokee Nation, was a recognized citizen of the Cherokee Nation at the time of your marriage to her, and whether or not you were married to her in accordance with Cherokee laws.

  You are, therefore, directed to appear before the Commissioner at Muskogee, Indian Territory, at 9 o'clock A. M., on Thursday, January 3, 1907, and give testimony as above indicated.

          Respectfully,

JMH   Acting Commissioner.

◇◇◇◇◇

Cherokee Intermarried White 1906
Volume I

Cherokee
1770

Muskogee, Indian Territory, January 17, 1907.

W. W. Hastings,
    Attorney for the Cherokee Nation,
        Muskogee, Indian Territory.

Dear Sir:

There is enclosed herewith a copy of the decision of the Commissioner to the Five Civilized Tribes, dated January 17, 1907, granting the application for the enrollment of Patrick Foley as a citizen by intermarriage of the Cherokee Nation.

Respectfully,

Encl. Hp36   Commissioner.
JMH

◇◇◇◇◇

Cherokee 1770   W.W.HASTINGS.   OFFICE OF   H.M. VANCE.
                      ATTORNEY.   SECRETARY.

Attorney for the Cherokee Nation,
MUSKOGEE, I. T.

January 18, 1907.

The Commissioner to the Five Civilized Tribes,
    Muskogee, Indian Territory.

Sir:

Receipt is acknowledged of the testimony and of your decision enrolling , as a citizen by intermarriage of the Cherokee Nation. Time for protesting said decision is waived and I consent that said person may be placed upon the schedule immediately.

Yours very truly,
W. W. Hastings
Attorney for Cherokee Nation.

◇◇◇◇◇

Cherokee Intermarried White 1906
Volume I

Cherokee
1770

Muskogee, Indian Territory, January 19, 1907.

Patrick Foley,
    Porum, Indian Territory.

Dear Sir:

    There is enclosed herewith a copy of the decision of the Commissioner to the Five Civilized Tribes, dated January 17, 1907, granting the application for your enrollment as a citizen by intermarriage of the Cherokee Nation.

    You will be advised when your name has been placed upon the schedule of citizens of the Cherokee Nation and approved by the Secretary of the Interior.

                Respectfully,

Encl.H-88   Commissioner.
JMH

◇◇◇◇◇

Cherokee
    I. W. 20

                Muskogee, Indian Territory, April 6, 1907

Patrick Foley,
    Porum, Indian Territory.

Dear Sir:

    Your marriage license and certificate filed in connection with your application for enrollment as a citizen by intermarriage of the Cherokee Nation, is returned to you herewith, copies of the same being retained in this office.

                Respectfully,

L M B   Acting Commissioner.

Encl. B-94

Cherokee Intermarried White 1906
Volume I

Cher IW 21
Trans from Cher 1800 3-13-07

C.E.W.

DEPARTMENT OF THE INTERIOR,

COMMISSIONER TO THE FIVE CIVILIZED TRIBES.

In the matter of the application for the enrollment of

WILLIAM WINTON

as a citizen by intermarriage of the Cherokee Nation.

CHEROKEE 1800

Department of the Interior,
Commission to the Five Civilized Tribes,
Ft. Gibson, I.T. August 22, 1900.

In the matter of the application of William Winton for the enrollment of himself as a Cherokee citizen being sworn and examined by Commissioner Breckinridge he testifies as follows:

Q What is your full name? A William Winton.
Q What is your age? A Fifty-two.
Q What is your post-office? A Wagoner.
Q What is your district? A Cooweescoowee.
Q For whom do you apply for enrollment? A Myself alone.
Q You apply as a Cherokee by blood? A No sir.
Q Intermarriage? A Intermarriage.
Q Have you a marriage license? A None at all.
Q When did you marry? A About seventy. as well as I can remember.
Q Are you on any of the rolls of the Cherokee Nation? A Yes sir, on all of them I expect.
Q Have you ever remarried since your wife's death? A No sir.
Q What is the name of your father? A James Winton.
Q He was a white man? A Yes sir.
Q Is he dead? A Yes sir.
Q What is the name of your mother? A Minerva Winton.
Q She was a white woman? A Yes sir.

Cherokee Intermarried White 1906
Volume I

Q She is dead? A Yes sir.
Q Have you lived in the Cherokee Nation from 1880 until this time? A Yes sir, except about three months I went to Wagoner to school a little boy, but I left my effects here. 1880 roll page 486 #1880 Wm. Winton, Goingsnake District.
(Page 330) 1896 roll page (33) #1092 William Winton Cooweescoowee District.
Q When did your wife die? A About eight or nine years back.
Q What was your wife's name? A Martha.

    Com'r Breckinridge: The applicant is duly identified on the roll of 1880 and 1896 as a Cherokee by adoption; his Cherokee wife died some eight years ago, and he testifies that he has n of remarried; he will be listed now for enrollment as a Cherokee by adoption.

    M.D. Green, being first duly sworn, states that as stenographer to the Commission to the Five Civilized Tribes he correctly recorded the testimony and proceedings in this case and that the foregoing is a true and complete transcript of his stenographic notes thereof.

                                                                MD Green

Subscribed and sworn to before me this 29 day of August 1900.

                                      C R Breckinridge
                                                                             Commissioner.

Statement of Applicant Taken Under Oath.

CHEROKEE BY BLOOD AND ADOPTION.

<u>52</u>   Date   August 22nd 1900.
Name   William Winton   Wagoner I.T.
District   Goingsnake   Year   1880   Page   486   No.   1880
Citizen by blood   No   Mother's citizenship   U.S. ⎰ Jas. Winton - dead
Intermarried citizen   Yes   Parents ⎱ Minerva " - dead
Married under what law...Date of marriage   1870
License ....Certificate..
Wife's name..
District...Year...............Page..............No. ....
Citizen by blood..........................Mother's citizenship...
Intermarried citizen...
Married under what law..Date of marriage...............
License ....Certificate..
       Names of Children:
....Dist...............Year...........Page........No..........Age.........
....Dist...............Year...........Page........No..........Age.........
....Dist...............Year...........Page........No..........Age.........
....Dist...............Year...........Page........No..........Age.........
....Dist...............Year...........Page........No..........Age.........

On 1880 Roll as Wm Winton.   #1800

Cherokee Intermarried White 1906
Volume I

Cherokee 1800.

DEPARTMENT OF THE INTERIOR, COMMISSION TO THE FIVE CIVILIZED TRIBES.
Muskogee, I. T., October 13, 1902.

In the matter of the application of William Winton for the enrollment of himself as a citizen by intermarriage of the Cherokee Nation.

SUPPLEMENTAL PROCEEDINGS.

WILLIAM WINTON, being sworn, testified as follows:

By the Commission,

Q What's your name? A William Winton.
Q What's your age at this time? A Fifty-four, as well as I can tell you.
Q Postoffice? A Wagoner.
Q What is your Cherokee wife's name? A Martha Elizabeth Crittenden.
Q Is she living? A She is not living.
Q How long has she been dead? A Ten years I think. We have a record of it but one of the children's got it. Ten years this coming January.
Q Are you the same William Winton that applied to the Commission for enrollment as an intermarried citizen in August 1900? A Same William Winton.
Q When were you married to your wife, Martha E? A About '72 or '3, as well as I can recollect.
Q Under the Cherokee license? A Under the Cherokee license.
Q Did you live with your wife, Martha E., from 1880 up until her death? A Lived with that woman alone.
Q You and she were never separated during her lifetime? A Never was separated at all.
Q Have you married since her death? A Never have married again.
Q You are a widower and single on the first day of September, 1902? A Yes, sir.
Q Have you lived in the Indian Territory all the time since 1880 up to the present time? A Always have had no other place for home only the Cherokee Nation.

Retta Chick, being first duly sworn, states that, as stenographer to the Commission to the Five Civilized Tribes, she recorded the testimony and proceedings in the matter of the foregoing application, and that the above is a true and complete transcript of her stenographic notes thereof.

Retta Chick

Subscribed and sworn to before me this 27th day of October, 1902.

BC Jones
Notary Public.

Cherokee Intermarried White 1906
Volume I

Cherokee 1800

DEPARTMENT OF THE INTERIOR,
COMMISSIONER TO THE FIVE CIVILIZED TRIBES.
Muskogee, I. T., January 3, 1907.

In the matter of the application for the enrollment of William Winton as a citizen by intermarriage of the Cherokee Nation.

William Winton, being first duly sworn by Walter W. Chappelle, a Notary Public for the Western District, testified as follows:

By the Commissioner:
Q What is your name? A William Winton.
Q Your age? A I don't know my age; about 54 to 56.
Q What is your postoffice address? A It is Peggs, I. T., now.
Q Do you claim to be a citizen by intermariage[sic] of the Cherokee Nation? A Yes sir.
Q Through whom do you claim that right. A Martha Elizabeth Crittenden.
Q Is she living A No, she is dead.
Q When did she die? A I don't remember; something like 14 or 15 years ago.
Q What is her citizenship? A She was a Cherokee by blood.
Q Were[sic] was she born? A She was born in Polk County, Ark.
Q What was her age at the time of her death? A About 30 years of age.
Q When were you and Martha Elizabeth Crittenden married? A We was married twice.
Q When were you married the first time? A About 1867 I think. I have no record of it.
Q Where were you married? A Polk County, Ark.
Q Married in accordance with the laws of Arkansas? A Yes sir.
Q Married under a license issued by that state? A Yes sir.
Q What was the citizenship of your wife? A Cherokee.
Q Was she living in the Cherokee nation[sic] at that time? A No, in Arkansas
Q How long has she been living there. A Born and raised there. I suppose she was 18 years old when we was married.
Q What were the names of your wife's parents? A Mose Crittenden was her father and her mother's name was Edith Crittenden
Q What was their citizenship at the time of your wife's birth? A They was Cherokees, both of them.
Q Had they ever lived in the Cherokee Nation? A Yes, they had both lived in the Cherokee Nation; married in the Cherokee Nation.
Q When did they move to Arkansas? A I don't know; in the early day before my birth or my wife's birth.
Q Isn't it a fact that they became citizens of the state of Arkansas? A No, they came back here and drawed their annuities.
Q When they returned here were they admitted or re-admitted as citizens of the Cherokee Nation the Cherokee Nation? A Her father was. Her mother died back in Arkansas.

Cherokee Intermarried White 1906
Volume I

Q What time did your wife's father return to the Cherokee Nation? A I have forgotten. About 1867-8, somewhere along there
Q And your wife's father was re-admitted to citizenship in the Cherokee nation[sic] on his return in 1866-7-8? A Yes sir.
Q How long did you and your wife reside in Arkansas after your first marriage? A We were married and came away in December.
Q What year? A I dis-remember, but it was sixty something-- about 1868 or '70, along there.
Q When you left Arkansas where did you move to? A The Cherokee Nation, Going Snake District.
Q Were you and your wife re-admitted to citizenship in the Cherokee nation[sic] on your return here--was you wife re-admitted? A Yes sir.
Q In what District? A His[sic] father was admitted and his family, by the council.
Q You say your wife's father's family were re-admitted by the Cherokee council when they returned to the Cherokee Nation? A That's correct.
Q Have you a copy of that act of readmission? A No sir.
Q Have you made any efort[sic] to secure a copy of that act? A None at all.
Q Now, after you moved to the Cherokee Nation you were again married, were you?
A Yes, re-married acording[sic] to the laws of the Cherokee Nation.
Q In what year were you married the second time? A It was somewhere between 1870 and 1873-- '72 or 3. I have lost our license; my wife has been dead several years.
Q Were you married under authority of Cherokee license? A Yes sir.
Q Have you a certified copy of that license? A Not with me.
Q Where was that license procured? A It was procurd[sic] in Going Snake District.
Q From what authority, do you remember? A The Clerk issud[sic] the license, John Thornton, was the clerk.
Q And who performed the marriage ceremony? A His father, Glover Thornton
Q What was his official capacity? A District Judge.
Q Of Going Snake District? A Yes sir.
Q Had either you or your wife been married prior to your marriage in Arkansas?
A No sir.
Q After you second marriage to your wife did you live together continuously until her death? A Yes sir.
Q Where did you reside during that time? A Going Snake District, until her death.
Q Have you remarried since her death? A Never.
Q Did you have any children by her? A Yes sir.
Q Are they living at the present time? A Only four of them.
Q Have they made application for enrollment? A Yes, and their names are on the roll.
Q What are the names of the living children?
A Mansfield Winton, Fagan Winton and Alice Wyley.
Q Was Alive[sic] Wyley married prior to Sept 1, 1902? A Yes sir.
Q And the next one? A Bettie King.
Q Was she married prior to Sept. 1, 1902? A Yes sir.
Q What is the year that license was issued? A I can't tell you; think in 60 something or '70.

Cherokee Intermarried White 1906
Volume I

Q Mr. Winton, you have no documentary evidence whatever showing your marriage to your deceased wife, have you? A No, I have not; you will fine me and my family on two or three rolls.

This office has no record of marriage licenses issued by the Cherokee nation[sic] in Going Snake District prior to the year 1877.

Q Do you suppose you can obtain a certified copy of the license issued to you by the Cherokee Nation? A No, I don't know who has the records. I have been informed the records was all in Washington, and nobody could get even a copy but I can bring my wife's sister or step-mother or brother who can swear to my being married. As to getting a copy, I wouldn't know how to proceed since they have gone into the hands of the Commission.
Q If these records are in existence they are probably at Tahlequah, and you can correspond with the Cherokee officials at Tahlequah and see whether or not you can secure a copy of this marriage license, and also secure a copy of the Act of Council admitting your wife's father and his family to citizenship in the Cherokee Nation. If you should be unable to secure a certified copy of the license issued by the Cherokee authorities, can you produce witnesses to prove that such a license was issued?
A No, I don't know that I can. Both the judge and clerk are dead, and if they wasn't put on record I couldn't get them.
Q What procedure did you follow in obtaining this Cherokee license? A My father-in-law told me, - he said, we are all admitted Cherokees, but you, being a white man, the law requires you to take out a license and be married and you will then be a citizen.
Q What did you realy[sic] do? A The law required us to pay $5 for this license. I applied to the clerk for this license, and then we took that to the judge and the judge would perform the ceremony and enter it on record. That was the way the law was at that time, thirty years ago.
Q Did you secure any signers as to your character? A No, I didn't; it didn't require it then. The signed law had not come in yet. It just required that we go and notify the clerk that we wanted a license to be an intermarried white man in the Cherokee nation[sic], and then we took an oath that we would not seek protection under any other government than the Cherokee Nation--any protection of law other than the Cherokee Nation; they gave them $5 and tell they[sic] they wanted to be an intermarried white man, and he gave you a license and administered this oath, and we went to the judge to be married, and he sent us a little slip like that. It is so far back we didn't have much law.
Q Can you produce any witnesses as to the marriage ceremony being performed?'
A I believe Joe Thornton was there that day. There was several there but he is all the one I can recollect; the Judges' son he was, a young fellow.

The applicant, william[sic] Winton is identified on the Authenticated Cherokee roll of 1880, Going Snake District, and on Cherokee census roll of 1896, Cooweescoowee District, opposite Nos. 1880 and 1092, respectively, as an intermarried white.

Cherokee Intermarried White 1906
Volume I

Frances R. Lane being first duly sworn states that as stenographer to the Commissioner to the Five Civilized Tribes she correctly reported the testimony in the above entitled cause and that the foregoing is an accurate transcript of her stenographic notes thereof.

Frances R Lane

Subscribed and sworn to before me this January 4, 1907.

Edward Merrick
Notary Public.

◇◇◇◇◇

C. F. B.   Cherokee 1800.

DEPARTMENT OF THE INTERIOR,
COMMISSION TO THE FIVE CIVILIZED TRIBES.
Muskogee, Indian Territory, January 7, 1907.

Supplemental proceedings in the Matter of the Application for the Enrollment of William Winton as a citizen by intermarriage of the Cherokee Nation the Cherokee Nation.

APPEARANCES: Applicant appears in person.

         Cherokee Nation represented by
         W. W. Hastings, Attorney.

William Winton being first duly sworn by John E. Tidwell, Notary Public, testified as follows:

ON BEHALF OF COMMISSIONER:

Q What is your name?   A William Winton.
Q What is your age?
A I don't know my age exactly. I think I am about 55 or 56.
Q What is your post office address?
A Peggs, Indian Territory.
Q Are you an applicant for enrollment as a citizen by intermarriage of the Cherokee Nation?
A Yes sir.
Q You have no Cherokee blood?
A No sir, full blood white man.
Q Your only claim to the right to enrollment as a citizen of the Cherokee Nation is by virtue of your marriage to a citizen by blood?
A Yes sir.
Q What is the name of that citizen?
A Martha Elizabeth Crittendon[sic].

Cherokee Intermarried White 1906
Volume I

Q Is she living or dead?
A She is dead.
Q When did she die?
A About twelve or thirteen years ago.
Q When did you marry her?
A It seems to me that I was re-married here in the Cherokee Nation in '72 or '73. I have no record of it here.
Q Were you married to her more than once?
A Yes sir.
Q Where were you married to her the first time?
A In Polk County, Arkansas.
Q What year?   A About '67.
Q Was she a resident of the State of Arkansas when you married her?
A At that time she was.
Q How long did you and she live in Arkansas after your marriage?
A We married in May and came away the following December.
Q On coming to the Cherokee Nation, was your wife recognized as a citizen of the Cherokee Nation?
A Yes sir.
Q t wasn't necessary for her to go before the authorities and be re-admitted?
A Why, her father went before the authorities and was re-admitted and put all his family on, my wife included.
Q What year was that?
A It must have been about 1870, as well as I can remember.
Q Were you ever married before you married her?
A No sir.
Q Was she ever married before she married you?
A No sir.
Q Did you and she live together as husband and wife until her death?
A Always; yes sir.
Q After your wife was re-admitted to citizenship in the Cherokee Nation, which you say you think was about the year 1870, were you and she re-married according to the laws of the Cherokee Nation?
A Yes sir; so far as we know. We bought license and went before the Judge and were re-married.
Q In what district?
A Going Snake District.
     In what year
A About '72 or '73. I lost the license after my wife died.
Q Who married you?   A Glover Thornton.
Q Was he a minister?   A He was the district judge.
Q You have lived in the Cherokee Nation continuously since you and your wife came here from Arkansas?
A Continuously; never lived anywhere else.

       The applicant, William Winton, is identified on the Cherokee authenticated tribal roll of 1880, Going Snake District, at No. 1880.

Cherokee Intermarried White 1906
Volume I

Q Are there any persons living who witnessed your marriage when you were married in accordance with the laws of the Cherokee Nation?
A Yes sir.
Q What are their names?
A Mr. Joe Thornton.
Q Was he present at the marriage ceremony?
A Yes sir; his father was the judge and his brother was the clerk.

Joseph Thornton being first duly sworn by John E. Tidwell, Notary Public, testified as follows:

ON BEHALF OF COMMISSIONER.

Q What is your name?
A Joseph Thornton.
Q What is your age?
A About 56; we lost our records in the time of the war.
Q What is your post office address?
A Wauhilla.
Q Are you a citizen by blood of the Cherokee Nation?
A Yes sir.
Q Do you know a man in the Cherokee Nation by the name of William Winton?
A Yes sir.
Q Was he at one time married to a citizen by blood of the Cherokee Nation?
A Yes sir.
Q What was the name of his citizen wife?
A Crittendon.
Q That was her maiden name?
A Yes sir.
Q Was he ever married except to her, to your knowledge?
A Not that I know of.
Q Was she ever married to your knowledge, except to him?
A No sir.
Q Do you know when they were married?
A Why, I remember the marriage but I can't tell you what year.
Q About what year was it?
A I can't tell you that.
Q How long after the war was it
A I can't tell you that for certain either.
Q Do you remember the district in which they were living at the time they were married?
A Going Snake District.
Q Who was Judge?
A Glover Thornton.
Q Was he related to you?
A He was my father.
Q Who was clerk at the time?
A John Thornton.
Q Was he your brother?
A Yes sir.

Cherokee Intermarried White 1906
Volume I

Q Were you present and did you witness the marriage of William Winton?
A Yes; I think I was there at the time.
Q But you haven't a very distinct recollection of it?
A No sir.
Q Has William Winton since his marriage been recognize as a citizen by intermarriage of the Cherokee Nation by the people who have known him?
A Why, I never did hear any dispute.
Q He has always exercised the rights and enjoyed the privileges of that class of citizens?
A Yes sir.

William B. Beck being first duly sworn by John E. Tidwell, Notary Public, testified as follows:

ON BEHALF OF COMMISSIONER.

Q What is your name?   A William B. Beck.
Q What is your age?   A 58.
Q What is your post office address?
A Fawn.
Q Are you a citizen by blood of the Cherokee Nation?
A No sir.
Q You appear here for the purpose of giving testimony relative to the right to enrollment of William Winton as a citizen by intermarriage of the Cherokee Nation?
A Yes sir.
Q How long have you known him?
A Since about '60. Ever since he was a boy.
Q Has he been married?
A Yes sir.
Q What was his wife's name?
A Crittendon.
Q She as a recognized citizen of the Cherokee Nation at the time they were married?
A Yes sir; they were re-admitted in '69. He made a mistake in saying they were admitted in '70.
Q Did he first marry this woman in Arkansas?
A Yes sir.
Q Do you know of your own personal knowledge that his wife was re-admitted to citizenship after coming here in '69?
A Yes sir; I can't swear it was in '69 but I think it was; either '69 or '70.
Q Did he marry after coming to the Cherokee Nation and his wife was re-admitted to citizenship, - did he marry her again?
A I suppose so; I didn't see this but I told him I had gone and re-married and he had better do as I had done. We were living some 12 or 15 miles from the Judge and he went. That was in '71. I remember the time he went.
Q You did not witness the marriage?
A No sir; I did not.
Q Was it your understanding that he went and complied with the Cherokee law?
A Yes sir.

Cherokee Intermarried White 1906
Volume I

Q Since his marriage at that time, he has enjoyed all the privileges of a citizen by intermarriage?
A Yes, to the best of my knowledge. I haven't been with him all the time but he has been in the Cherokee Nation. I am satisfied he has.

ON BEHALF OF CHEROKEE NATION.

Q Was this his first marriage?
A First I ever knew of.
Q Was his wife ever previously married
A No, she never was.
Q The first marriage for each of them?
A Yes sir.
Q Is she living?
A No, she is dead.
Q Has he since re-married?
A Not that I know of.

The undersigned being first duly sworn states that as stenographer to the Commission to the Five Civilized Tribes, she recorded the testimony taken in this case and that the foregoing is a full, true and correct transcript of her stenographic notes thereof.

Myrtle Hill

Subscribed and sworn to before me this the 8th day of January, 1907.

John E. Tidwell
Notary Public.

◇◇◇◇◇

C.E.W.   Cherokee 1800.

DEPARTMENT OF THE INTERIOR,

COMMISSIONER TO THE FIVE CIVILIZED TRIBES.

In the matter of the application for the enrollment of William Winton, as a citizen by intermarriage of the Cherokee Nation.

D E C I S I O N

THE RECORDS OF THIS OFFICE SHOW: That at Fort Gibson, Indian Territory, August 22, 1900, William Winton appeared before the Commission to the Five Civilized Tribes, and made application for the enrollment of himself, as a citizen by intermarriage

Cherokee Intermarried White 1906
Volume I

of the Cherokee Nation. Further proceedings in the matter of said application were had at Muskogee, Indian Territory, October 13, 1904, January 3, 1907, and January 7, 1907.

THE EVIDENCE IN THIS CASE SHOWS: That the applicant herein, William Winton, a white man, was married prior to November 1, 1875, in accordance with Cherokee law to his wife, Martha Elizabeth Winton, nee Crittenden, since deceased, who was at the time of said marriage a recognized citizen by blood of the Cherokee Nation, and who is identified on the Cherokee authenticated tribal roll of 1880, Going Snake District, page 286 number 1880, as a native Cherokee; that after said marriage the said William Winton and Martha Elizabeth Winton lived together as husband and wife until her death, which occurred about the year 1894, and that since her death said William Winton has not married and that he has continuously lived in the Cherokee Nation since his marriage to the said Martha Elizabeth Winton. Said William Winton is identified on the Cherokee authenticated tribal roll of 1880, and the Cherokee census roll of 1896 as an intermarried citizen of the Cherokee Nation.

IT IS, THEREFORE, ORDERED AND ADJUDGED: That in accordance with the decision of the Supreme Court of the United States, dated November 5, 1906, in the cases of Daniel Red Bird et al. vs. the United States, Nos 125, 126, 127 and 128, the said applicant William Winton is entitled, under the provision of Section 21 of the Act of Congress approved June 28, 1898 (30 Stat., 495) to enrollment, as a citizen by intermarriage of the Cherokee Nation, and his application for enrollment as such is accordingly granted.

Tams Bixby
Commissioner.

Dated at Muskogee, Indian Territory,
this JAN 19 1907

◇◇◇◇◇

Cherokee
1800.

Muskogee, Indian Territory, December 24, 1906.

William Winton,
Wagoner, Indian Territory.

Dear Sir:

November 6, 1906, the United States Supreme Court held that white persons who intermarried with Cherokee citizens according to Cherokee law prior to November 1, 1875, are entitled to enrollment and allotments of land as citizens of the Cherokee Nation.

You are advised that to properly determine your right to enrollment as a citizen by intermarriage of the Cherokee Nation, it will be necessary for you to appear before the Commissioner for the purpose of giving testimony as to the date of your marriage and whether or not your wife, by reason of your marriage to whom you claim the right to

Cherokee Intermarried White 1906
Volume I

enrollment as a citizen of the Cherokee Nation, was a recognized citizen of the Cherokee Nation at the time of your marriage to her, and whether or not you were married to her in accordance with Cherokee laws.

You are, therefore, directed to appear before the Commissioner at Muskogee, Indian Territory, at 9 o'clock A. M., on Thursday, January 3, 1907, and give testimony as above indicated.

Respectfully,

LMC   Acting Commissioner.

◇◇◇◇◇

Cherokee
   1800.

Muskogee, Indian Territory, January 19, 1907.

W. W. Hastings,
     Attorney for the Cherokee Nation,
          Muskogee, Indian Territory.

Dear Sir:

There is enclosed herewith a copy of the decision of the Commissioner to the Five Civilized Tribes, dated January 18, 1907, granting the application for the enrollment of William Winton, as a citizen by intermarriage of the Cherokee Nation.

Respectfully,

Commissioner.

Incl. C-24
LMC

◇◇◇◇◇

Cherokee Intermarried White 1906
Volume I

Cherokee 1800

W.W. HASTINGS.
ATTORNEY.

OFFICE OF

H.M. VANCE.
SECRETARY.

Attorney for the Cherokee Nation,
MUSKOGEE, I. T.

January 19, 1907.

The Commissioner to the Five Civilized Tribes,
    Muskogee, Indian Territory.

Sir:

    Receipt is acknowledged of the testimony and of your decision enrolling William Winton, as a citizen by intermarriage of the Cherokee Nation. Time for protesting said decision is waived and I consent that said person may be placed upon the schedule immediately.

                    Respectfully,
                    W. W. Hastings
                    Attorney for Cherokee Nation.

◇◇◇◇◇

Cherokee
1800

                    Muskogee, Indian Territory, January 21, 1907.

William Winton,
    Peggs, Indian Territory.

Dear Sir:

    There is enclosed herewith copy of the decision of the Commissioner to the Five Civilized Tribes, dated January 19, 1907, granting the application for your enrollment as a citizen by intermarriage of the Cherokee Nation.

    You will be advised when your name has been placed upon the schedule of citizens of the Cherokee Nation and approved by the Secretary of the Interior.

                    Respectfully,

Enc M -14

M.T.M.   Commissioner.

Cherokee Intermarried White 1906
Volume I

Cher IW 22
Trans from Cher 1823 3-13-07

◇◇◇◇◇

C.E.W.

DEPARTMENT OF THE INTERIOR,

COMMISSIONER TO THE FIVE CIVILIZED TRIBES.

In the matter of the application for the enrollment of

ROLAND M. LEWIS

as a citizen by intermarriage of the Cherokee Nation.

CHEROKEE 1823

◇◇◇◇◇

Department of the Interior,
Commission to the Five Civilized Tribes,
Fort Gibson, I.T., August 22, 1900.

In the matter of the application of Amanda Lewis for the enrollment of herself as a Cherokee by blood and her husband as a Cherokee by intermarriage: being sworn an examined by Commissioner Breckenridge[sic], she testified as follows:

Q What is your full name? A Amanda Lewis.
Q What is your age? A 58.
Q What is your post office? A Bragg.
Q What is your district? A Illinois.
Q For whom do you make application for enrollment, yourself? A Yes sir, and my husband.
Q And how many children? A Well, can I register for them that are of age? A They must register for themselves. A I haven't got any to register.
Q Do you apply for yourself as a Cherokee by blood? A Yes, sir.
Q Is your husband a Cherokee by blood? A No, sir, he is a white man.
Q How long have you lived in the Cherokee Nation? A All my life.
Q How long have you lived in Illinois district? A 30 years.
Q What is the name of your father? A His name was Phillip Inlow.
Q Was he a Cherokee or a white man? A He was a white man.
Q Is he dead or alive? A He is dead.
Q The name of your mother, please? A Elizabeth Inlow.
Q Is she a white woman or a Cherokee? A She was a Cherokee.

Cherokee Intermarried White 1906
Volume I

Q Is she living or dead? A She is dead.
Q How long has she been dead? A About 35 years.
Q How long as your father been dead? A He died in 1880; no, he just lived two years longer that[sic] she did.
Q Please give me the name of your husband? A Rowland[sic] M. Lewis.
Q How old is he? A He is 67 years old.
Q When where[sic] you married to him? A In 1866 Im[sic] think.
Q He is on the roll of 1880 as your husband? A Yes, sir.
Q He has lived with you in the Cherokee Nation ever since you were married?
A Yes, sir.
Q What is the name of your father? A His father was named Joseph Lewis.
Q He was a white man, was he? A Yes, sir.
Q Is he dead? A Yes, sir.
Q His mother, what was her name? A Mary Lewis was his mother's name.
Q A white woman? A Yes, sir.
Q Is she dead? A Yes, sir.
(Amanda Lewis on 1880 roll, page 548, No. 1021, Illinois district. Rowland M. Lewis on 1880 roll, page 548, No. 1020, Robin Lewis, Illinois district. Amanda Lewis on 1896 roll, page 874, No. (1036), #1030 Amanda M[sic]. Lewis, Illinois district. Rowland M. Lewis on 1896 roll, page 931, No. 112, Rollen Lewis, Illinois district._

The applicant is duly identified on the rolls of 1880 and 1896 as a native Cherokee, and she will be listed now for enrollment as a Cherokee by blood. Her husband is identified on the rolls of 1880 and 1896 as her husband, and as a Cherokee by adoption, and he will be listed now for enrollment as a Cherokee by adoption.

-----o-----

Bruce C. Jones, being duly sworn, says that as stenographer to the Commission to the Five Civilized Tribes he reported correctly the proceedings and testimony in the above case and the foregoing is a true and complete translation of his stenographic notes.

Bruce C Jones

Sworn to and subscribed before me this the 30th day of August, 1900.

TB Needles
Commissioner.

Cherokee Intermarried White 1906
Volume I

DEPARTMENT OF THE INTERIOR.
Commission to the Five Civilized Tribes.
Muskogee, Indian Territory, October 20th, 1902.

In the matter of the application of Rowland M. Lewis for the enrollment of himself as a citizen by intermarriage and his wife, Amanda Lewis, as a citizen by blood of the Cherokee Nation.

Supplemental to #1823.

ROWLAND M. LEWIS, being duly sworn, testified as follows:
Examination by the Commission.

Q. Your name is what? A. Rowland M. Lewis.
Q. How old are you? A. In my 70th year.
Q. What is your post office? A. Braggs.
Q. Are you a white man? A. Yes, sir.
Q. Is your name on the roll of 1880 as an adopted white citizen? A. Yes, sir.
Q. What is your wife's name? A. Amanda.
Q. Is she a Cherokee by blood? A. Yes, sir.
Q. Is she the wife through whom you claim citizenship? A. Yes, sir.
Q. She was your wife in 1880, was she? A. Yes, sir.
Q. Have you and your wife Amanda been living together ever since you were married? A. We were married in '66.
Q. Living tobether[sic] ever since? A. Yes, sir.
Q. Never been separated? A. No, sir.
Q. Living together now? A. Yes, sir.
Q. Your home has been in the Cherokee Nation all the time? A. Yes, sir.

IIIIIIIIIIIIIIIIIIIIIIIIIIIII

Jesse O. Carr, being first duly sworn, states that as stenographer to the Commission to the Five Civilized Tribes he reported the above entitled case and that the foregoing is a true and complete transcript of his stenographic notes thereof.

Jesse O. Carr

Subscribed and sworn to before me this 10th day of January, 1903.

Samuel Foreman
Notary Public.

Cherokee Intermarried White 1906
Volume I

Cherokee 1823.

DEPARTMENT OF THE INTERIOR?[sic]
COMMISSIONER TO THE FIVE CIVILIZED TRIBES.
Muskogee, I. T., January 3, 1907.

In the matter of the application for the enrollment of Roland W[sic]. Lewis as a citizen by intermarriage of the Cherokee Nation.

Roland M. Lewis being first duly sworn by Walter W. Chappelle, a Notary Public for the Western District of Indian Territory, testified as follows:

By the Commissioner:
Q What is your name? A Roland M?[sic] Lewis.
Q What is your age? A Going on 74 years.
Q What is your postoffice address? A Braggs
Q In the Cherokee Nation? A Yes sir.
Q You claim to be a citizen by intermarriage of the Cherokee nation[sic]? A Yes sir.
Q Through whom do you claim that right? A My wife.
Q What is her name? A Her maiden name was Amanda Inlow
Q Is she living? A Yes sir.
Q What is her citizenship? A Cherokee by blood.
Q Where was she born? A That might be too hard for me, but I think in Flint District.
Q Was she born in the Cherokee nation[sic]? A Yes sir.
Q Has she lived there all her life? A Yes sir.
Q When were you and she married? A The 5th day of Sept., 1866
Q Where? A In the Choctaw Nation.
Q Were you married under a license? A No, not at that time; was afterwards.
Q When were you married to her the second time? A I aint[sic] positive but I think in 1868 or 1869.
Q Where were you married to her the second time? A Canadian District.
Q What Nation? A Cherokee.
Q Married under Cherokee license? A Yes sir.
Q Have you a copy of that license with you? A No, I only have the certificate of marriage. The judge told me he would have it filed at Tahlequah. I don't know whether you can read this or not, its[sic] so long ago.
Q Was this Cherokee license issued by the Cherokee authorities in the Cherokee nation?
A By the authorities in Illinois District. I lived in Illinois District but I had to go over in Canadian District to get married.
Q That was about the year 1868-9? A Yes, just after the first council convened; after the adjournment of the first council after the war; quite a number of them was married over under the new order.
Q Had either you or your present wife been married prior to your marriage there in the Choctaw Nation? A No sir.
Q How long did you live in the Choctaw Nation after you were married? A We were married in 1866. I think we came to Fort Gibson in the fall of 1867.

Cherokee Intermarried White 1906
Volume I

Q Where have you lived ever since that time? A Right around Braggs station in the Cherokee Nation.
Q Have you and your wife lived together continuously since your marriage in 1866?
A Yes sir, only what time she has been with her daughter at Wagoner.
Q You are living together at the present time? A Yes sir.

> The records of this office show that Amanda A. Lewis, nee Inlow, wife of the applicant, is included in the approved partial roll of Cherokees by blood of the Cherokee Nation, opposite No. 4836.
>
> The applicant is identified on the authenticated Cherokee tribal roll of 1880 and on Cherokee Census roll of 1896, opposite Nos. 1020 and 112, Illinois District, as an intermarried white.
>
> An examination of the record of marriage certificates issued by the authorities of Illinois and Canadian Districts, Cherokee Nation, fails to show the record of any marriage license issued by the Cherokee nation[sic] to the aplicant[sic], Roland M. Lewis.
>
> The applicant offers in evidence a certificate of J. Hildebrand, Judge of the District Court of Canadian District, under date of December 9, 1867, wherein said Judge certifies that he "joined in the holy bonds of matrimony Roland Lewis (citizen of the United States) to A. M. Inlow, citizen of this (Cherokee) Nation, they having complied with the requirements of the laws of this nation".
> And same is filed herewith and made a part of the records in this case.

Frances R. Lane upon oath states that as stenographer to the Commissioner to the Five Civilized Tribes, she reported the testimony in the above entitled cause and that the foregoing is an accurate transcript of her stenographic notes therein.

Frances R Lane

Subscribed and sworn to before me this 4th day of January, 1907.

Edward Merrick
Notary Public.

Cherokee Intermarried White 1906
Volume I

COPY

This is to certify that J. M. Hildebrand Judge of the Dist Court of Canadian District have this day joined in the Holy Bonds of matrimony Rowland Lewis a citizen of the United States to A. M. Inlow, a citizen of this Nation, they having complied with the requirements of the laws of this Nation.
Dec oth[sic] 1867, J. M. Hildebrand

Judge I.C.C.D.

The undersigned being duly sworn states that as stenographer to the Commissioner to the Five Civilized Tribes, she made the foregoing copy and that the same is a true and correct copy of the original marriage certificate now on file in this office.

Lola M Champlin

Subscribed and sworn to before me this 10 day of January 1907.

Chas E Webster
Notary Public.

◇◇◇◇◇

C.E.W.	Cherokee 1823

DEPARTMENT OF THE INTERIOR,

COMMISSIONER TO THE FIVE CIVILIZED TRIBES.

In the matter of the application for the enrollment of Rowland M. Lewis, as a citizen by intermarriage of the Cherokee Nation.

D E C I S I O N.

THE RECORDS OF THIS OFFICE SHOW: That at Fort Gibson, Indian Territory, August 22, 1900, Amanda Lewis appeared before the Commission to the Five Civilized Tribes and made application for the enrollment of herself, as a citizen by blood, and for the enrollment of her husband, Rowland M. Lewis, as a citizen by intermarriage of the Cherokee Nation. The application for the enrollment of the said Amanda Lewis, as a citizen by blood of the Cherokee Nation has been heretofore disposed of and her rights to enrollment will not be considered in this decision. Further proceedings in the matter of said application were had at Muskogee, Indian Territory, October 20, 1902, and January 3, 1907.

THE EVIDENCE IN THIS CASE SHOWS: That the applicant herein, Rowland M. Lewis, a white man, was married in accordance with Cherokee law December 9, 1867, to his wife Amanda Lewis, nee Inlow, who was at the time of said marriage a recognized citizen by blood of the Cherokee Nation, and whose name appears upon the approved

Cherokee Intermarried White 1906
Volume I

partial roll of citizens by blood of the Cherokee Nation, opposite number 4836; that since said marriage the said Roland[sic] M. Lewis and Amanda Lewis have resided together as husband and wife and have continuously lived in the Cherokee Nation. Said Roland M. Lewis is identified on the Cherokee Authenticated Tribal roll of 1880, and the Cherokee Census Roll of 1896 as an intermarried citizen of the Cherokee Nation.

IT IS THEREFORE ORDERED AND ADJUDGED: That in accordance with the decision of the Supreme Court of the United States, dated November 5, 1906, in the case of Daniel Red Bird et al., vs. the United States, under the provision of Section 21 of the Act of Congress approved June 28, 1898, (30 Stat. 495), Rowland M. Lewis is entitled to enrollment as a citizen of the Cherokee Nation, and his application for enrollment as such is accordingly granted.

Tams Bixby
Commissioner.

Dated at Muskogee, Indian Territory,
this   JAN 16 1907

◇◇◇◇◇

Cherokee
1823

Muskogee, Indian Territory, December 27, 1906.

Rowland M. Lewis,
    Braggs, Indian Territory.

Dear Sir:

November 6, 1906, the United States Supreme Court held that white persons who intermarried with Cherokee citizens according to Cherokee law prior to November 1, 1875, are entitled to enrollment and allotments of land as citizens of the Cherokee Nation.

You are advised that to properly determine your right to enrollment as a citizen by intermarriage of the Cherokee Nation, it will be necessary for you to appear before the Commissioner for the purpose of giving testimony as to the date of your marriage and whether or not your wife, by reason of your marriage to whom you claim the right to enrollment as a citizen of the Cherokee Nation, was a recognized citizen of the Cherokee Nation at the time of your marriage to her, and whether or not you were married to her in accordance with Cherokee laws.

You are, therefore, directed to appear before the Commissioner at Muskogee, Indian Territory, at 9 o'clock A. M., on Thursday, January 3, 1907, and give testimony as above indicated.

Respectfully,

JMH   Acting Commissioner.

◇◇◇◇◇

Cherokee Intermarried White 1906
Volume I

Cherokee
1823

Muskogee, Indian Territory, January 17, 1907.

W. W. Hastings,
    Attorney for the Cherokee Nation,
    Muskogee, Indian Territory.

Dear Sir:

    There is enclosed herewith a copy of the decision of the Commissioner to the Five Civilized Tribes, dated January 17, 1907, granting the application for the enrollment of Rowland M. Lewis as a citizen by intermarriage of the Cherokee Nation.

Respectfully,

Encl. .H-42
JMH.
                              Commissioner.

◇◇◇◇◇

W.W. HASTINGS.   OFFICE OF   H.M. VANCE.   Cherokee 1823
ATTORNEY.   SECRETARY.

Attorney for the Cherokee Nation,
MUSKOGEE, I. T.

January 18, 1907.

The Commissioner
    to The Five Civilized Tribes,
        Muskogee, Indian Territory.

Sir:

    Receipt is acknowledged of the testimony and of your decision enrolling Rowland M. Lewis as a citizen by intermarriage of the Cherokee Nation. Time for protesting said decision is waived and I consent that said person may be placed upon the schedule immediately.

                              W. W. Hastings
                              Attorney for Cherokee Nation.

◇◇◇◇◇

Cherokee Intermarried White 1906
Volume I

Cherokee 1823

Muskogee, Indian Territory, January 19, 1907.

Rowland M. Lewis,
    Braggs, Indian Territory.

Dear Sir:

    There is enclosed herewith copy of the decision of the Commissioner to the Five Civilized Tribes, dated January 16, 1907, granting the application for your enrollment as a citizen by intermarriage of the Cherokee Nation.

    You will be advised when your name has been placed upon the schedule of citizens of the Cherokee Nation and approved by the Secretary of the Interior.

                      Respectfully,

Enc I-20   Commissioner.

RPI

◇◇◇◇◇

Cherokee
I. W. 22

Muskogee, Indian Territory, April 6, 1907.

Rowland M. Lewis,
    Braggs, Indian Territory.

Dear Sir:

    Your certificate of marriage, filed in connection with your application for enrollment as a citizen by intermarriage of the Cherokee Nation, is returned to you herewith, copies of the same being retained in this office.

                        Respectfully,

Encl. B- 92   Acting Commissioner.

L M B

Cherokee Intermarried White 1906
Volume I

Cher IW 23
Trans from Cher 1868 3-13-07

E.C.M.

DEPARTMENT OF THE INTERIOR,

COMMISSIONER TO THE FIVE CIVILIZED TRIBES.

In the matter of the application for the enrollment of

ANNIE E. CROSSLAND

as a citizen by intermarriage of the Cherokee Nation.

CHEROKEE 1868.

DEPARTMENT OF THE INTERIOR,
COMMISSION TO THE FIVE CIVILIZED TRIBES,
FORT GIBSON, IT., AUGUST 23, 1900.

In the matter of the application of Annie E. Crossland for enrollment of herself and two children, as citizens of the Cherokee Nation, said Crossland being sworn by Commissioner Breckinridge, testified as follows:

Q What is your name? A Annie E. Crossland.
Q Your age? A 52.
Q Your postoffice? A Menard.
Q Your district? A Illinois
Q For whom do you make application for enrollment? A Myself and two children?[sic]
Q Do you apply for yourself as a Cherokee by blood? A No sir.
Q When were you married? A '68.
Q Has your name been Crossland ever since '68? A Yes.
Q Are you on the roll of '80? A Yes.
Q Lived in the Cherokee Nation ever since '68? A Yes.
Q What is the name of your father? A Anderson Fowler.
Q Cherokee or white man? A White man.
Q Is he living? A Dead.
Q When did he die? A When I was a child.
Q What is the name of your mother? A Laura Schrimsher, before she was married.
Q White woman? A Yes.
Q Dead or alive? A Dead.

Cherokee Intermarried White 1906
Volume I

Q Been dead over 25 years? A Yes.
Q What is the name of your children? A Richard F., 24 years old.
    On '80 roll, page 514, number 348, as R. F. Crossland.
    On '96 roll, page 851, number 483.
[sic]   Is he on the roll of '80? A Yes.
Q Living in the Cherokee Nation all the time? A Yes.
Q What is the next child? A Samuel, 18 years old.
    On '96 roll, page 851, number 485.
    Applicant on '80 roll, page 514, number 345, as A. E. Crossland.
    On '96 roll, page 926, number 35, as Anni Crossland.
Q Is your husband dead? A Yes.
Q What was his name? A Samuel.
Q When did he die? A '82.
    The applicant is duly identified on the rolls of '80 and '96. She has lived in the Cherokee Nation ever since her enrollment in '80. She has never remarried since the death of her husband, and she will now be listed as a Cherokee by adoption.
Her child, Richard F. Crossland, though 24 years of age, is permitted to be applied for by his mother on account of his being an invalid. He is indentified[sic] on the rolls of '80 and '96. The child, Samuel, is identified on the roll of '96, and both of these will now be listed as Cherokees by blood.

    The undersigned, being first duly sworn, states that as stenographer to the Commission to the Five Civilized Tribes, he correctly recorded the testimony and proceedings in this case, and that the foregoing is a true and complete transcript of his stenographic notes thereof.

                                    Brown McDonald

Subscribed and sworn to before me this 11th day of September, 1900.

                    CR Breckinridge   Commissioner.
                    ◇◇◇◇◇

DEPARTMENT OF THE INTERIOR.
Commission to the Five Civilized Tribes.
Muskogee, Indian Territory, October 14th, 1902.

    In the matter of the application of Annie E. Crossland for the enrollment of herself as a citizen by intermarriage and her children, Richard F. and Samuel Crossland, as citizens by blood of the Cherokee Nation.

Supplemental to #1868.

ANNIE E. CROSSLAND, being duly sworn, testified as follows:
                Examination by the Commission.

Cherokee Intermarried White 1906
Volume I

Q. Your full name is Annie E. Crossland? A. Yes, sir.
Q. How old are you? A. I am 54.
Q. What is your post office? A. Manard and Fort Gibson to[sic].
Q. You are a white woman? A. Yes, sir.
Q. You are on the roll of 1880 as an intermarried citizen? A. Yes, sir.
Q. What was your husband's name in 1880? A. Samuel Crossland.
Q. Is he dead? A. Yes, sir.
Q. When did he die? A. He died in '82.
Q. You lived with him from 1880 to 1882? A. Yes, sir; from '66 to '82.
Q. Have you been living in the Cherokee Nation since 1880? A. Yes, sir.
Q. Never been out? A. Not to live.
Q. You have two children? A. Yes, sir.
Q. Richard and Samuel? A. Richard is dead.
Q. Samuel is living? A. Yes, sir.
Q. Living with you? A. Yes, sir.

I I I I I I I I I I I I I I I I I I I I I I I I I I I

Jesse O. Carr, being first duly sworn, states that as stenographer to the Commission to the Five Civilized Tribes he reported the above entitled case and that the foregoing is a true and complete transcript of his stenographic notes thereof.

Jesse O Carr

Subscribed and sworn to before me this 3rd day of January, 1903.

John O Rosson
Notary Public.

◇◇◇◇◇

Cherokee No. 1868.

DEPARTMENT OF THE INTERIOR.
COMMISSIONER TO THE FIVE CIVILIZED TRIBES.

Muskogee, Indian Territory, January 3, 1907.

In the matter of the application for the enrollment of Annie E. Crossland as a citizen by intermarriage of the Cherokee Nation.

Annie E. Crossland, being first duly sworn and examined, testifies as follows:

BY THE COMMISSIONER:

Cherokee Intermarried White 1906
Volume I

Q What is your name? A Annie E. Crossland.
Q How old are you? A I can't exactly tell you, I don't know my age. I am away long in the 50's, about 58.
Q What is your postoffice address? A Manard.
Q You claim to be a citizen by intermarriage of the Cherokee Nation. A Yes, sir.
Q Through whom do you claim your intermarriage rights? A Samuel Crossland.
Q When were you married to Samuel Crossland? A 1868.
Q Where were you married to him? A Five miles below Manard.
Q In the Cherokee Nation? A Yes, sir.
Q Under the Cherokee Law? A Yes, sir.
Q Did you get a cirtificeate[sic].[sic] A No, sir, they didn't give cirtificates[sic].
Q Was your husband a citizen of the Cherokee Nation when you married him?
A Yes, sir.
Q Where was he born.[sic] A Cherokee Nation.
Q Always lived in the Cherokee Nation? A Always lived in the Cherokee Nation.
Q Had you ever been married before you married Samuel Crossland? A No, sir.
Q Had he ever been married before he married you? A No, sir.
Q Is Samuel Crossland living at this time? A No, sir.
Q When did he die? A 1882.
Q Did you live with Samuel Crossland from the date of your marriage in 1868 up until 1882? A Yes, sir.
Q Have you ever been married since his decease? A No, sir.
Q Have you any children? A I have one living.
Q What is its name? A Samuel.
Q Child of Samuel Crossland? A Yes, sir.
Q Is there any one here to-day that knows of your marriage to Samuel Crossland?
A Yes, sir, Mrs. Scott.

The applicant is identified on the 1880 Cherokee Roll, Illinois District opposite No. 345.
WITNESS EXCUSED.

Nannie Scott, being first duly sworn and examined, testifies as follows:

BY THE COMMISSIONER:

Q What is your name? A Nannie Scott.
Q How old are you? A 48.
Q What is your postoffice addriss[sic]? A Fort Gibson.
Q Are you a citizen of the Cherokee Nation? A Yes, sir.
Q Citizen by blood? A Yrs, sir.
Q Are you acquainted with Annie E. Crossland? A Yes, sir.
Q Do you know her husband, Samuel Crossland? A He is my uncle.
Q Do you know when Samuel Crossland and Annie E. Crossland were married? A Yes, sir, I was at the wedding.
Q When were they married? A I can't tell you the year. I was there and remember all about it.

Cherokee Intermarried White 1906
Volume I

Q How long was it after the Civil War? A I couldn't tell you that.
Q Did they live together from the date of their marriage as husband and wife up to the time of his death in 1882? A Yes, sir.
Q Was he always recognized as a citizen of the Cherokee Nation during his life-time? A Yes, sir.

WITNESS EXCUSED.

F. Elma Lane, upon oath, states that she reported the proceedings in the above entitled cause and that the foregoing is a true and correct transcript of her stenographic notes taken therein.

F. Elma Lane

Subscribed and sworn to before me this 4th day of January, 1907.

Chas E Webster
Notary Public.

◇◇◇◇◇

E.C.M. Cherokee 1868.

DEPARTMENT OF THE INTERIOR,

COMMISSIONER TO THE FIVE CIVILIZED TRIBES.

In the matter of the application for the enrollment of ANNIE E. CROSSLAND as a citizen by intermarriage of the Cherokee Nation.

D E C I S I O N

THE RECORDS OF THIS OFFICE SHOW: That at Fort Gibson, Indian Territory, August 23, 1900, application was received by the Commission to the Five Civilized Tribes for the enrollment of Annie E. Crossland as a citizen by intermarriage of the Cherokee Nation. Further proceedings in the matter of said application were had at Muskogee, Indian Territory, October 14, 1902, and January 3, 1907.

THE EVIDENCE IN THIS CASE SHOWS: That the applicant herein, Annie E. Crossland, a white woman, married in the year 1868 one Samuel Crossland, who was at the time of said marriage a recognized citizen by blood of the Cherokee Nation, and who is identified on the Cherokee authenticated tribal roll of 1880, opposite No. 344, as a native Cherokee. It is further shown that from the time of said marriage the said Samuel Crossland and Annie E. Crossland resided together as husband and wife, and ontinuously lived in the Cherokee Nation until the time of the death of the said Samuel Crossland in the year 1892[sic]; that after the death of said Samuel Crossland the said Annie E. Crossland remained unmarried, and continued a resident of the Cherokee Nation up to

Cherokee Intermarried White 1906
Volume I

and including September 1, 1902. Said applicant is identified on the Cherokee authenticated tribal roll of 1880, and the Cherokee census roll of 1896, as an intermarried citizen of the Cherokee Nation.

IT IS, THEREFORE, ORDERED AND ADJUDGED: That in accordance with the decision of the Supreme Court of the United States, dated November 5, 1906, in the cases of Daniel Red Bird et al. vs. the United States, Nos. 125, 126, 127 and 128, the said applicant, Annie E. Crossland, is entitled, under the provisions of Section 21, of the Act of Congress approved June 28, 1898 (30 Stats., 495), to enrollment as a citizen by intermarriage of the Cherokee Nation, and her application for enrollment as such is accordingly granted.

Tams Bixby
Commissioner.

Dated at Muskogee, Indian Territory,
this   JAN 19 1907

◇◇◇◇◇

Cherokee
1868

Muskogee, Indian Territory, December 27, 1906.

Annie E. Crossland,
    Manard, Indian Territory.

Dear Madam:

November 6, 1906, the United States Supreme Court held that white persons who intermarried with Cherokee citizens according to Cherokee law prior to November 1, 1875, are entitled to enrollment and allotments of land as citizens of the Cherokee Nation.

You are advised that to properly determine your right to enrollment as a citizen by intermarriage of the Cherokee Nation, it will be necessary for you to appear before the Commissioner for the purpose of giving testimony as to the date of your marriage and whether or not your husband, by reason of your marriage to whom you claim the right to enrollment as a citizen by intermarriage of the Cherokee Nation, was a recognized Cherokee citizen at the time of your marriage to him.

You are, therefore, directed to appear before the Commissioner at Muskogee, Indian Territory, at 9 o'clock A. M., on Thursday, January 3, 1907, and give testimony as above indicated.

Respectfully,

JMH   Acting Commissioner.

◇◇◇◇◇

Cherokee Intermarried White 1906
Volume I

Cherokee
1868

Muskogee, Indian Territory, January 19, 1907.

W. W. Hastings,
    Attorney for the Cherokee Nation,
        Muskogee, Indian Territory.

Dear Sir:

There is enclosed herewith a copy of the decision of the Commissioner to the Five Civilized Tribes, dated January 19, 1907, granting the application for the enrollment of Annie E. Crossland, as a citizen by intermarriage of the Cherokee Nation.

        Respectfully,

                Commissioner.

Incl. C-20
LMC

◇◇◇◇◇

Cherokee 1868   W.W. HASTINGS, ATTORNEY.   OFFICE OF   H.M. VANCE, SECRETARY.

Attorney for the Cherokee Nation,
MUSKOGEE, I. T.

        January 19, 1907.

The Commissioner to the Five Civilized Tribes,
    Muskogee, Indian Territory.
Sir:

Receipt is acknowledged of the testimony and of your decision enrolling Annie E. Crossland as a citizen by intermarriage of the Cherokee Nation. Time for protesting said decision is waived and I consent that said person may be placed upon the schedule immediately.

        Respectfully,
        W. W. Hastings
        Attorney for Cherokee Nation.

◇◇◇◇◇

Cherokee Intermarried White 1906
Volume I

Cherokee
1868

Muskogee, Indian Territory, January 21, 1907.

Annie E. Crossland,
    Manard, Indian Territory.

Dear Madam:

    There is enclosed herewith copy of the decision of the Commissioner to the Five Civilized Tribes, dated January 19, 1907, granting the application for your enrollment as a citizen by intermarriage of the Cherokee Nation.

You will be advised when your name has been placed upon the schedule of citizens of the Cherokee Nation and approved by the Secretary of the Interior.

                Respectfully,

Enc M - 13

M.T.M.   Commissioner.

Cher IW 24
Trans from Cher 1941 3-13-07

⋄⋄⋄⋄⋄⋄

                                                           C.E.W.

DEPARTMENT OF THE INTERIOR,

COMMISSIONER TO THE FIVE CIVILIZED TRIBES.

In the matter of the application for the enrollment of

FRANK N. SMITH

as a citizen by intermarriage of the Cherokee Nation.

CHEROKEE 1941

⋄⋄⋄⋄⋄⋄

Cherokee Intermarried White 1906
Volume I

Department of the Interior,
Commission to the Five Civilized Tribes,
Fort Gibson, I.T., August 24, 1900.

In the matter of the application of Frank N. Smith for the enrollment of himself as a Cherokee by intermarriage and his four children as Cherokees by blood; being sworn and examined by Commissioner Needles, he testified as follows:

Q What is your name? A Frank N. Smith.
Q How old are you? A 54.
Q What is your post office address? A Fort Gibson.
Q What district do you live in? A Illinois.
Q How long have you been a resident of the Cherokee Nation? A Well, sir, I was born and raised in the Nation, I was married in 1870.
Q Are you a recognized citizen of the Cherokee Nation? A Yes, sir.
Q By blood or adoption? A By adoption.
Q You say you have lived in the Nation since 1870? A I was married at that time, I was born and raised here/
Q For whom do you apply? A For myself and four children.
Q And your wife? A No, sir.
Q Your father and mother non citizens? A Yes, sir.
Q What was the name of your wife? A She was a Fields, Ella Fields.
Q Is she living? A No, sir.
Q What was her name in 1880, Fields? A No, sir, Smith.
Q Were you married to her in 1880? A Yes, sir, I was married in 1870.
Q What was the name of your children? A The oldest one at home with me is 20 years old, Richard.
Q What is the name of the next one? A May Belle, 14.
Q What is the next one? A Willie, 12 years old.
Q What is the name of the next one? A Elizabeth.
Q Is your son's name William? A No, sir, Willie
Q How old is Elizabeth? A 10 years old.
Q What is the next one? A That is all.
Q Are these four children alive and living with you? A Yes, sir.
Q You say your wife is dead? A Yes, sir, she died in 1891.
(1880 roll, page 581, No. 1690, Frank N. Smith, Illinois district.
Ella Smith on 1880 roll, page 581, No. 1691, Illinois district.
Richard Smith on 1880 roll, page 581, No. 1694, Richard Smith, Illinois district.
Frank N. Smith on 1896 roll, page 935, No. 191, Illinois district.
Richard Smith on 1896 roll, page 906, No. 1885, Richard M. Smith, Illinois district.
May Belle Smith on 1896 roll, page 906, No. 1886, Mabel Smith, Illinois district.
Willie Smith on 1896 roll, page 906, No. 1887, Willie E. Smith, Illinois district.
Elizabeth Smith on 1896 toll, page 906, No. 1888, Lizzie Smith, Illinois district.)
Q Are these children all alive and living with you? A Yes, sir.

The name of Frank N. Smith appears upon the authenticated roll of 1880, as well as the census roll of 1896. The name of his wife, Ella, also appears upon the authenticated

Cherokee Intermarried White 1906
Volume I

roll of 1880, she now being deceased. The name of her son Richard appears upon the authenticated roll of 1880, and their other children, May Belle, Willie and Elizabeth, their names appear upon the census roll of 1896, and they being duly identified as the children of Ella Smith, and Frank N. Smith, and having made satisfactory proof as to their residence, the said Frank N. Smith will be duly listed for enrollment by this commission as a Cherokee citizen, and his said children as Cherokee citizens by blood.

-----o-----

Bruce C. Jones. being duly sworn, says that as stenographer to the Commission to the Five Civilized Tribes he correctly recorded the proceedings and testimony in the above case, and the foregoing is a true and complete transcript of his stenographic notes thereof.

Bruce C. Jones

Sworn to and subscribed before me this the 3rd day of September, 1900.

TB Needles
Commissioner.

◇◇◇◇◇

DEPARTMENT OF THE INTERIOR.
Commission to the Five Civilized Tribes.
Muskogee, Indian Territory, October 20th, 1902.

In the matter of the application of Frank N. Smith for the enrollment of himself as a citizen by intermarriage and for the enrollment of his children, Richard, May B., Willie E. and Elizabeth Smith, as citizens by blood of the Cherokee Nation.

Supplemental to #1941.

FRANK N. SMITH, being duly sworn, testified as follows:
Examination by the Commission.

Q. Your name is Frank N. Smith, if it? A. Yes, sir.
Q. How old are you? A. 55 or 6.
Q. What is your post office? A. Fort Gibson.
Q. Are you a white man? A. Yes, sir.
Q. Does your name appear upon the roll of 1880 as an adopted white citizen?
A. Yes, sir.
Q. What is your wife's name? A. Ella Fields.
Q. Is she a Cherokee by blood? A. Yes, sir.
Q. Was she your wife in 1880? A. Yes, sir.
Q. Is she the only wife you ever had? A. Yes, sir.
Q. You are the only husband she ever had? A. Yes, sir.

Cherokee Intermarried White 1906
Volume I

Q. Is she living or dead? A. She is dead.
Q. When did she die? A. She has been dead 11 years.
Q. Had you been living together ever since 1880 up to the time she died? A. Yes, sir.
Q. Never separated during that time? A. No, sir.
Q. Have you married since her death? A. No, sir.
Q. Have you been residing in the Cherokee Nation since 1880? A. Yes, sir.
Q. Never lived anywhere else? A. No, sir.
Q. How many children have you? A. Six.
Q. All living? A. Yes, sir.
Q. Is Richard living? A. Yes, sir.
Q. May B.? A. Yes, sir.
Q. Willie E.? A. Yes, sir.
Q. And Elizabeth? A. Yes, sir.
Q. Those four children are living at home with you, are they? A. Yes, sir.

++++++++++++++++++++++++++++++++

Jesse O. Carr, being first duly sworn, states that as stenographer to the Commission to the Five Civilized Tribes he reported the above entitled case and that the foregoing is a true and complete transcript of his stenographic notes thereof.

Jesse O. Carr

Subscribed and sworn to before me this 10th day of January, 1903.

Samuel Foreman
Notary Public.

◇◇◇◇◇

Cherokee-1941

Department of the Interior
Commission to the Five Civilized Tribes.
Muskogee, I.T. February 24, 1906.

In the matter of the application for the enrollment of Frank N. Smith, as a citizen by intermarriage of the Cherokee Nation.

Frank N. Smith, having been first duly sworn, testified as follows:

Examination by the Commission:

Q What is your name? A Frank N. Smith.
Q What is your age? A 58.
Q What is your postoffice address? A Fort Gibson, I.T.
Q You claim no rights as a citizen by blood? A By intermarriage.
Q What is your wife's name? A Ella Smith.

Cherokee Intermarried White 1906
Volume I

Q What was her maiden name? A Fields.
Q She a Cherokee by blood? A Yes sir.
Q Is she your first wife? A Yes sir.
Q You her first husband/ A Yes sir.
Q When did she die? A She died in 1891.
Q Have you married since then? A No sir
Q Did you have a tribal license when you married her? A Yes sir.
Q Have you lived in the Cherokee Nation ever since your marriage to Ella Smith? A Yes sir.
Q No where else? A No sir.;[sic] never lived out of the Nation.

(Witness excused).

Josie Davies, having been first duly sworn, on oath states: That as stenographer to the Commission to the Five Civilized Tribes she reported all proceedings had in the above entitled cause on the 24th day of February, 1905, and that the above and foregoing is a full, true, and complete transcript of her stenographic notes thereof.

Josie Davies

Subscribed and sworn to before me this 25th day of February, 1905.

Myron White
Notary Public.

DEPARTMENT OF THE INTERIOR
COMMISSIONER TO THE FIVE CIVILIZED TRIBES
MUSKOGEE, IND. TER. JAN. 3 1907.
CHEROKEE 1941.

IN THE MATTER OF THE APPLICATION FOR THE
ENROLLMENT OF FRANK N. SMITH AS A CITIZEN
BY INTERMARRIAGE OF THE CHEROKEE NATION.

FRANK N. SMITH BEING FIRST DULY SWORN BY JOHN E. TIDWELL, NOTARY PUBLIC, TESTIFIED AS FOLLOWS:

EXAMINATION BY THE COMMISSIONER:

Q What is your name.[sic] A Frank N. Smith.
Q What is your age.[sic] About sixty years.
Q What is your post office address? A Fort Gibson.
Q Are you an appliant[sic] for enrollment as a citizen by intermarriage of the Cherokee Nation? A Yes sir.
Q You have no Cherokee blood? A No sir.

Cherokee Intermarried White 1906
Volume I

Q The only claim you have to the right to enrollment as a citizen of the Cherokee Nation is by virtue of a marriage to a Cherokee citizen by blood. A Yes sir.
Q What is the name of the Cherokee citizen thru who you claim the right to enrollment. A Ella Fields before she married.
Q Is she living or dead.[sic] A She's dead.
Q When did she die.[sic] A She died the 6th of November 1891.
Q When did you marry her.[sic] A I married her in accordance with Cherokee laws. April 1870.
Q Was she living in the Cherokee Nation at the time you married her.[sic] A Yes sir.
Q And was a recognized citizen of the Cherokee Nation was she.[sic] A Yes sir.
Q Were you living in the Cherokee Nation at that time? A Yes sir.
Q From the time you married her did you and she continuousl[sic] live in the Cherokee Nation and reside together as husband and wife until the time of her death.[sic] A Yes sir.
Q Since her death have you married? A No sir.
Q But since her death you have resided continuously in the Cherokee Nation have you up till the present time? A Yes sir.
Q In what district was she living at the time you married her? A Illinois District.
Q Did you marry her in accordance with Cherokee laws.[sic] A Yes sir.
Q You secured a license did you, in due form.[sic] A Yes sir.
Q Have you a copy of the license with you.[sic] A No sir; in 1886 I had my house burned; I had a certificate[sic] and I had my license but it was burned up.
Q But you married her in Illinois District in 1870.[sic] A Yes sir.

Book A of the original record of marriage certificates Illinois District, Cherokee Nation in the possession of this office shows that on April 22, 1970 license was issued in accordance with the law of the Cherokee Nation authorizing the marriage of Frank Smith to Ella Fields and that said parties were united in marriage in accordance with the terms of said license, April 22 1870 by Albert Barns, Clerk of the District Court.

The applicant, Frank N. Smith is identified on the Cherokee authenticated tribal roll of 1880, Illinois District, No. 1690.

ooOoo

Clara Mitchell Wood being first duly sworn upon her oath states that as stenographer for the Commissioner to the Five Civilized Tribes she reported the above and foregoing proceedings and that this is a correct transcript of her stenographic notes.

Clara Mitchell Wood

Subscribed and sworn to before me this 3rd day of January 1907.

B.P. Rasmus
Notary Public.

Cherokee Intermarried White 1906
Volume I

C.E.W. Cherokee 1941

DEPARTMENT OF THE INTERIOR,

COMMISSIONER TO THE FIVE CIVILIZED TRIBES.

In the matter of the application for the enrollment of Frank N. Smith as a citizen by intermarriage of the Cherokee Nation.

D E C I S I O N

THE RECORDS OF THIS OFFICE SHOW: That at Fort Gibson, Indian Territory, August 24, 1900, application was received by the Commission to the Five Civilized Tribes, for the enrollment of Frank N. Smith, as a citizen by intermarriage of the Cherokee Nation. Further proceedings in the matter of said application were had at Muskogee, Indian Territory, October 20, 1902, February 24, 1905, and January 3, 1907.

THE EVIDENCE IN THIS CASE SHOWS: That the applicant herein, Frank N. Smith, a white man, was married, in accordance with Cherokee law April 22, 1870, to one Ella Smith, nee Fields, since deceased, who was, at the time of said marriage, a recognized citizen by blood of the Cherokee Nation, who is identified on the Cherokee authenticated tribal roll of 1880, Illinois District, No. 1691, as a native Cherokee; that from the time of said marriage the said Frank N. and Ella Smith lived together continuously as husband and wife until the death of said Ella Smith, which occurred November 6, 1891; that since the death of said Ella Smith, the said Frank N. Smith has not married, and that he has continuously resided in the Cherokee Nation since April 22, 1870. Said applicant is identified on the Cherokee authenticated tribal roll of 1880, and the Cherokee census roll of 1896, as an intermarried citizen of the Cherokee Nation.

IT IS, THEREFORE, ORDERED AND ADJUDGED: That in accordance with the decision of the Supreme Court of the United States, dated November 5, 1906, in the case of Daniel Red Bird et al., vs. the United States, Nos. 125, 126, 127 and 128, the said applicant, Frank N. Smith is entitled, under the provisions of Section twenty-one of the Act of Congress approved June 28, 1898 (30 Stat. 495), to enrollment as a citizen by intermarriage of the Cherokee Nation, and his application for enrollment as such is accordingly granted.

Tams Bixby
Commissioner.

Dated at Muskogee, Indian Territory,
this   JAN 19 1907

Cherokee Intermarried White 1906
Volume I

Cherokee
1941.

Muskogee, Indian Territory, December 24, 1906.

Frank N. Smith,
Fort Gibson, Indian Territory.

Dear Sir:

November 6, 1906, the United States Supreme Court held that white persons who intermarried with Cherokee citizens according to Cherokee law prior to November 1, 1875, are entitled to enrollment and allotments of land as citizens of the Cherokee Nation.

You are advised that to properly determine your right to enrollment as a citizen by intermarriage of the Cherokee Nation, it will be necessary for you to appear before the Commissioner for the purpose of giving testimony as to the date of your marriage and whether or not your wife, by reason of your marriage to whom you claim the right to enrollment as a citizen of the Cherokee Nation, was a recognized citizen of the Cherokee Nation at the time of your marriage to her, and whether or not you were married to her in accordance with Cherokee laws.

You are, therefore, directed to appear before the Commissioner at Muskogee, Indian Territory, at 9 o'clock A. M., on Thursday, January 3, 1907, and give testimony as above indicated.

Respectfully,

LMC   Acting Commissioner.

◇◇◇◇◇

Cherokee
1941

Muskogee, Indian Territory, January 21, 1907.

Frank N. Smith,
Fort Gibson, Indian Territory.

Dear Sir:

There is enclosed herewith copy of the decision of the Commissioner to the Five Civilized Tribes, dated January 19, 1907, granting the application for your enrollment as a citizen by intermarriage of the Cherokee Nation.

You will be advised when your name has been placed upon the schedule of citizens of the Cherokee Nation and approved by the Secretary of the Interior.

Cherokee Intermarried White 1906
Volume I

Respectfully,

E.R.C.   Commissioner.
Enc. E.C.1

◇◇◇◇◇

Cherokee
1941

Muskogee, Indian Territory, January 19, 1907.

W. W. Hastings,
     Attorney for the Cherokee Nation,
          Muskogee, Indian Territory.

Dear Sir:

There is enclosed herewith a copy of the decision of the Commissioner to the Five Civilized Tribes dated January 19, 1907, granting the application for the enrollment of Frank N. Smith, as a citizen by intermarriage of the Cherokee Nation.

Respectfully,

Commissioner.

Incl.C-27
  LMC

◇◇◇◇◇

Cherokee 1941.   W.W. HASTINGS.   OFFICE OF   H.M. VANCE.
                     ATTORNEY.   SECRETARY.

Attorney for the Cherokee Nation,
MUSKOGEE, I. T.

January 19, 1907.

The Commissioner to the Five Civilized Tribes,
     Muskogee, Indian Territory.

Sir:

     Receipt is acknowledged of the testimony and of your decision enrolling Frank N. Smith as a citizen by intermarriage of the Cherokee Nation. Time for protesting said decision is waived and I consent that said person may be placed upon the schedule immediately.

Respectfully,
W. W. Hastings
Attorney for Cherokee Nation.

Cherokee Intermarried White 1906
Volume I

Cher IW 25
Trans from Cher 2038 3-13-07

E.C.M.

DEPARTMENT OF THE INTERIOR,

COMMISSIONER TO THE FIVE CIVILIZED TRIBES.

In the matter of the application for the enrollment of

Nancy H. McALLISTER

as a citizen by intermarriage of the Cherokee Nation.

CHEROKEE 2038.

Department of the Interior the,
Commission to the Fve[sic] Civilized Tribes,
Ft. Gibson, I.T., August 27, 1900.

In the matter of the application of John W. McAlester[sic] for the enrollment of himself, wife and child as Cherokee citizens; being sworn and examined by Commissioner Needles he testifies as follows:

Q What is your name? A John W. McAlester.
Q What is your age? A Fifty-four this fall.
Q What is your post-office address? A Chouteau.
Q Are you a recognized citizen of the Cherokee Nation by blood? A Yes sir.
Q What degree of blood do you claim? A One-eighth.
Q For whom do you apply? A For myself, wife and one child.
Q What district do you live in? A Cooweescoowee.
Q How long have you resided in the Cherokee Nation? A Ever since the spring of 1869.
Q What is the name of your father? A Peter McAlester.
Q Is he living? A No sir.
Q Did he died before 1880? A I don't recollect.
Q What is the name of your mother? A Rebecca.
Q Is she living? A No sir.
Q Was she a citizen by blood? A Yes sir.
Q What is the name of your wife? A Nancy.
Q Is she a non-citizen or an Indian? A She is a white woman.
Q When did you marry her? A Twenty-nine years ago last spring.

224

Cherokee Intermarried White 1906
Volume I

Q Are her father and mother living? A No sir, they are both dead
Q What are the names of your children under twenty-one years old?
A John W. Jr., seventeen years old.
Q Is he alive and living with you? A Yes sir.
1880 roll page 782 #1384 John Wesley McAllister, Tahlequah Dis't.
1880 roll page 787 #1385 Nancy H. McAllister, Tahlequah District.
1896 roll page 1207 #2059 John W. McAlester Tahlequah District.
1896 roll page 1285 #172 Nancy H. McAlister[sic] Tahlequah District.
1896 roll page 1207 #2060 John W. McAlester, Indian Territory Jr., Tahlequah District

Com'r Needles: The name of John W. McAlester Sr. appearing upon the authenticated roll of 1880 as wel[sic] as the census roll of 1896, and the name of his wife Nancy appearing upon the authenticated roll of 1880 as Nancy H. McAllister, and also upon the census roll of 1896, and the name of his son, John W. Jr. appearing upon the census roll of 1896, they being fully identified according to page and number of the said rolls as indicated in the testimony, and having made satisfactory proof as to their residence, the said John W. McAlester Sr. and his son John W. Jr. will be duly listed for enrollment by this Commission as Cherokee citizens by blood; the name of his wife, Nancy will be duly listed for enrollment as a Cherokee citizen by intermarriage.

M.D. Green, being first duly sworn, states that as stenographer to the Commission to the Five Civilized Tribes he correctly recorded the testimony and proceedings in this case and that the foregoing is a true and complete transcript of his stenographic notes thereof.

MD Green

Subscribed and sworn to before me this 4 day of Sept 1900.

TB Needles
Commissioner.

◇◇◇◇◇

R.

DEPARTMENT OF THE INTERIOR.
Commission to the Five Civilized Tribes.
Muskogee, Indian Territory, October 4th, 1902.

In the matter of the application of John W. McAllister for the enrollment of himself as a citizen by blood of the Cherokee Nation; for the enrollment of his wife, Nancy H. McAllister, as a citizen by intermarriage of the Cherokee Nation, and for the enrollment of his son, John W. McAllister, Jr, and his grandson, Joe William McAllister, as citizens by blood.

Cherokee Intermarried White 1906
Volume I

Supplemental to #2038.

Applicant appears in person.
Cherokee Nation by J. C. Starr.

JOHN W. McALLISTER, being duly sworn, testified as follows:
Examination by the Commission.
Q. What is your name? A. John Wesley McAllister.
Q. What is your age at this time? A. 55.
Q. What is your wife's name? A. Nancy; Nancy H.
Q. Is your wife a citizen by blood of the Cherokee Nation? A. No, sir.
Q. She claims by intermarriage, does she? A. Yes, sir.
Q. You are a citizen by blood, are you, Mr. McAllister? A. Yes, sir.
Q. When were you and your wife married? A. '71.
Q. In 1871? A. Yes, sir.
Q. Were you ever married prior to your marriage to this wife? A. No, sir.
Q. Was she ever married prior to her marriage to you? A. Yes, sir.
Q. How many time has she been married? A. Once.
Q. Was that husband living or dead when you married her? A. Dead.
Q. You are her second husband, she is your first wife? A. Yes, sir.
Q. Now, have you and your wife Nancy H. lived together as husband and wife since your marriage? A. Yes, sir.
Q. Never have been separated during that time? A. No, sir.
Q. She has never married any other man since her marriage to you? A. No, sir.
Q. You were living together as husband and wife on the first of September, 1902? A. Yes, sir.
Q. Have you lived in the Cherokee Nation since 1880? A. Yes, sir.
Q. Your wife has lived here all the time since 1880? A. Yes, sir.
Q. Is John W. Jr. and Joe William your children by your wife Nancy H.[sic]?
A. Yes, sir. That Joe William is a grandson of mine. He is the son of that junior, whatever you call it.
Q. He is the son of John W. Jr.? A. Yes, sir.
Q. The two children are living at this time? A. Yes, sir.
Q. Have they always lived in the Cherokee Nation since their berth[sic] until the present time? A. Yes, sir.

Jesse O. Carr, being first duly sworn, states that as stenographer to the Commission to the Five Civilized Tribes he reported the above entitled case and that the foregoing is a true and complete transcript of his stenographic notes thereof.

Jesse O. Carr

Subscribed and sworn to before me this 31st day of October, 1902.
BC Jones
Notary Public.

Cherokee Intermarried White 1906
Volume I

C.F.B. Cherokee 2038.

DEPARTMENT OF THE INTERIOR,
COMMISSIONER TO THE FIVE CIVILIZED TRIBES.
MUSKOGEE, I. T., JANUARY 3, 1907.

In the matter of the application for the enrollment of Nancy H. McAllister as a citizen by intermarriage of the Cherokee Nation.

APPEARANCES: Applicant appears in person.

Nancy H. MCALLISTER, being first duly sworn by John E. Tidwell, Notary Public, testified as follows:

ON BEHALF OF THE COMMISSIONER:

Q What is your name? A Nancy H. McAllister.
Q What is your age? A 59 years old, in November.
Q What is your post office address? A Chouteau.
Q Are you an applicant for enrollment as a citizen by intermarriage of the Cherokee Nation? A Yes sir.
Q You have no Cherokee blood? A No sir, none at all.
Q You claim solely by right of intermarriage? A Yes sir.
Q What is the name of your husband through whom you claim the right to enrollment as a citizen by intermarriage of the Cherokee Nation? A John W. McAllister.
Q When were you married to him? A Married in May, 1871.
Q Was he ever married prior to his marriage to you? A No sir.
Q Was he your first husband? A No sir. My first husband died when I was nothing much but a child.
Q Then you were married prior to your marriage to John W. McAllister, but your former husband was dead at the time you married John W. McAllister? A Yes sir.
Q Where was he living at the time you were married? A Down close to Maysville.
Q In the Cherokee Nation? A Yes sir.
Q Did you and he continuously live in the Cherokee Nation after your marriage?
  A Yes sir, lived here, and raised a family right here.
Q And have always lived here, up to the present time? A Yes sir.
Q Your husband, John W. McAllister, is living at the present time, is he? A Yes sir.
Q Since you marriage to your husband, John W. McAllister, you and he have continuously lived together as husband and wife, have you? A Yes sir.
Q Have you a certificate of marriage? A No sir, we didn't get none them days, nearly 36 years ago, you know.
Q You never had any certificate of marriage? A No sir, the preacher married us, that is all.

The applicant, Nancy H. McAllister, is identified on the authenticated Cherokee tribal roll of 1880, Tahlequah District, No. 1385. Her husband, John W. McAllister,

Cherokee Intermarried White 1906
Volume I

in[sic] included in the approved partial roll of citizens by blood of the Cherokee Nation, opposite No. 5305.

The undersigned, being first duly sworn, states that as stenographer to the Commissioner to the Five Civilized Tribes, she correctly reported the above and foregoing testimony, and that the same is a full, true and correct transcript of her stenographic notes thereof.

Sarah Waters

Subscribed and sworn to before me this 4th day of Jan. 1907.

John E. Tidwell
Notary Public.

◇◇◇◇◇

E.C.M.

E.C.M.
Cherokee 2038.

DEPARTMENT OF THE INTERIOR,

COMMISSIONER TO THE FIVE CIVILIZED TRIBES.

In the matter of the application for the enrollment of NANCY H. MCALLISTER, as a citizen by intermarriage of the Cherokee Nation.

D E C I S I O N

THE RECORDS OF THIS OFFICE SHOW: That at Fort Gibson, Indian Territory, August 27, 1900, John W. McAllister appeared before the Commission to the Five Civilized Tribes, and made application for the enrollment of himself et al. as citizens by blood, and for the enrollment of his wife, Nancy H. McAllister, as a citizen by intermarriage, of the Cherokee Nation. the[sic] application for the enrollment of John W. McAllister et al. as citizens by blood of the Cherokee Nation has been heretofore disposed of and their rights to enrollment will not be considered in this decision. Further proceedings in the matter of said application were had at Muskogee, Indian Territory, October 4, 1902, and January 3, 1907.

THE EVIDENCE IN THIS CASE SHOWS: That the applicant herein, Nancy H. McAllister, a white woman, married in the year 1871 one John W. McAllister, who was at the time of said marriage a recognized citizen by blood of the Cherokee Nation, and whose name appears on the approved partial roll of citizens by blood of the Cherokee Nation, opposite No. 5305; that from the time of said marriage the said John W. and Nancy McAllister resided together as husband and wife continuously, and lived in the Cherokee Nation up to and including September 1, 1902. Said Nancy H. McAllister is identified on the Cherokee authenticated tribal roll of 1880, and the Cherokee census roll of 1896, as an intermarried citizen of the Cherokee Nation.

Cherokee Intermarried White 1906
Volume I

IT IS, THEREFORE, ORDERED AND ADJUDGED: That in accordance with the decision of the Supreme Court of the United States, dated November 5, 1906, in the case of Daniel Red Bird et al. vs. the United States, under the provisions of Section 21, of the Act of Congress approved June 28, 1898 (30 Stat., 495), Nancy H. McAllister is entitled to enrollment as a citizen by intermarriage of the Cherokee Nation, and her application for enrollment as such is accordingly granted.

             Tams Bixby
              Commissioner.

Dated at Muskogee, Indian Territory,
this   JAN 18 1907

◇◇◇◇◇

          Choteau, Ind. Tery. Aug. 22d 1902

Hon. Dawes Commission:

  I herewith return certificate of John W. McAlister child as formerly prepared & also the affidavit of John W. Jr. & John W. McAlister Sr. as to the correct way to spell their name   It has always been spelled McAlister & is on the rolls that way and if it is now spelled McAlester it is wrong & we want it changed to McAlister, the right way.
Our family history & record demands it for the benefit of our future posterity- I wrote the above at their request and herewith enclose their affidavits of approval- I know of my own knowledge & from business relations with them that the true way to spell the name is McAlister and it should be thus.

             Resply

           (Signed) I. P. Bledsoe.

We requested I. P. Bledsoe to write the above and know that to be the only true way to spell our name and we hereby request the Commission to make the necessary correction on the roll.

Attest
                    his
Belle Bledsoe,   John W. X McAlister Sr.
                  mark
Ellen Saby   John W. X McAlister Jr.
                 his mark
SEAL
Subscribed & sworn to before me Aug. 22d 1901.
Choteau, I. T.   (Signed) I.P. Bledsoe Notary Public

The undersigned, being first duly sworn, states that as stenographer to the Commissioner to the Five Civilized Tribes, she made the above copy, and that the same is a full, true and correct copy of the original instrument now on file in this office.

Cherokee Intermarried White 1906
Volume I

Mattie M. Pace

Subscribed and sworn to before me this 5th day of April, 1907

Walter W Chappelle
Notary Public.

◇◇◇◇◇

Cherokee
2038.

Muskogee, Indian Territory, December 24, 1906.

Nancy H. McAllister,
    Chouteau, Indian Territory.

Dear Madam:

    November 6, 1906, the United States Supreme Court held that white persons who intermarried with Cherokee citizens according to Cherokee law prior to November 1, 1875, are entitled to enrollment and allotments of land as citizens of the Cherokee Nation.

    You are advised that to properly determine your right to enrollment as a citizen by intermarriage of the Cherokee Nation, it will be necessary for you to appear before the Commissioner for the purpose of giving testimony as to the date of your marriage and whether or not your husband, by reason of your marriage to whom you claim the right to enrollment as a citizen by intermarriage of the Cherokee Nation, was a recognized Cherokee citizen at the time of your marriage to him.

    You are, therefore, directed to appear before the Commissioner at Muskogee, Indian Territory, at 9 o'clock A. M., on Thursday, January 3, 1907, and give testimony as above indicated.

Respectfully,

LMC   Acting Commissioner.

◇◇◇◇◇

Cherokee Intermarried White 1906
Volume I

Cherokee
2038.

Muskogee, Indian Territory, January 18, 1907.

W. W. Hastings,
    Attorney for the Cherokee Nation,
        Muskogee, Indian Territory.

Dear Sir:

There is enclosed herewith a copy of the decision of the Commissioner to the Five Civilized Tribes, dated January 18, 1907, granting the application for the enrollment of Nancy H. McAllister, as a citizen by intermarriage of the Cherokee Nation.

Respectfully,

Encl. HJ-41.
HJC   Commissioner.

◇◇◇◇◇

Cherokee
2038

Muskogee, Indian Territory, January 21, 1907.

Nancy H. McAllister
    Choteau, Indian Territory.

Dear Madam:

There is enclosed herewith a copy of the decision of the Commissioner to the Five Civilized Tribes, dated January 18, 1907, granting the application for your enrollment as a citizen by intermarriage of the Cherokee Nation.

You will be advised when your name has been placed upon the schedule of citizens of the Cherokee Nation and approved by the Secretary of the Interior.

Respectfully,

E.R.C.   Commissioner.
Enc. E.C.-2

◇◇◇◇◇

Cherokee Intermarried White 1906
Volume I

Cherokee 2038   W.W. HASTINGS,   OFFICE OF   H.M. VANCE,
                 ATTORNEY.   SECRETARY.

Attorney for the Cherokee Nation,
MUSKOGEE, I. T.

January 18, 1907.

The Commissioner to the Five Civilized Tribes,
Muskogee, Indian Territory.

Sir:

Receipt is acknowledged of the testimony and of your decision enrolling Nancy H. McAllister as a citizen by intermarriage of the Cherokee Nation. Time for protesting said decision is waived and I consent that said person may be placed upon the schedule immediately.

Yours very truly,
W. W. Hastings
Attorney for Cherokee Nation.

Cher IW 26
Trans from Cher 2094   3-13-07

Cherokee 2094.

DEPARTMENT OF THE INTERIOR,
COMMISSION TO THE FIVE CIVILIZED TRIBES.
Muskogee, I. T., October 11, 1902.

In the matter of the application of Walter G. Fields for the enrollment of Walter G. Fields for the enrollment of himself and his two minor children, Louvenia and Joseph A Fields, as citizens by blood, and for the enrollment of his wife, Ella E. Fields, as a citizen by intermarriage of the Cherokee Nation.

SUPPLEMENTAL PROCEEDINGS.

WALTER G. FIELDS, being sworn, testified as follows:

By the Commission,

Q What is your name, please? A Are you speaking to me?
Q Yes, sir. A Walter G. Fields.
Q What's your postoffice, Mr. Fields? A Bennett, Indian Territory.

Cherokee Intermarried White 1906
Volume I

Q Are you a citizen by blood of the Cherokee Nation? A Yes, sir.
Q What's your wife's name? A Ella E. Fields.
Q Is she an applicant for enrollment as an intermarried citizen? A Yes, sir.
Q How old is she at this time, Mr. Fields? A Forty-nine years old.
Q When were you and your wife married? A Thirty years ago last April.
Q Thirty years ago? A Yes, sir.
Q Married before 1880? A Yes, sir, married in 1872. Her name is on the rolls since '75.
Q Is her name on the 1880 roll with you, as husband and wife? A Yes, sir.
Q Have you and Ella lived together all the time since 1880? A Yes, sir.
Q Never been separated since then? A No, sir.
Q Living together as husband and wife on the first day of September, 1902? A Yes, sir.
Q And she has never married any other man since 1880? A No, sir.
Q Have you and your wife, Ella E., lived in the Cherokee Nation all the time since 1880 up to the present time? A Yes, sir.
Q These children, Louvenia and Joseph A., are your children by your wife, Ella E.?
A Yes, sir.
Q Are they living in the Cherokee Nation? A Yes, sir.
Q Been living in the Cherokee Nation all their lives? A Yes, sir, were raised here.

Retta Chick, being first duly sworn, states that, as stenographer to the Commission to the Five Civilized Tribes, she recorded the testimony and proceedings in the matter of the foregoing application, and that the above is a true and complete transcript of her stenographic notes thereof.

Retta Chick

Subscribed and sworn to before me this 22nd day of October, 1902.

BC Jones
Notary Public.

◇◇◇◇◇

Cherokee 2094.

DEPARTMENT OF THE INTERIOR,
COMMISSIONER TO THE FIVE CIVILIZED TRIBES.
Muskogee, I. T., January 2, 1907.

In the matter of the application for the enrollment of Ella M[sic]. Fields as a citizen by intermarriage of the Cherokee Nation.

Walter G. Fields being first duly sworn by Frances R. Lane, a Notary Public for the Western District of Indian Territory, testified as follows:

By the Commissioner.
Q What is your name? A Walter G. Fields
Q How old are you? A Fiffty-nine.
Q Waht[sic] is your postoffice address? A Warner, I. T.

Cherokee Intermarried White 1906
Volume I

Q Do you Know Ella E. Fields? A Yes sir, she is my wife.
Q When were you married to her? A The 8th day of April, 1872.
Q Where were you married? A At Sumner county[sic], Kansas.
Q Did you get a license? A Yes sir.
Q Have you got a copy of the license? A No sir.
Q Did you get a certificate of marriage? A No, the license was returned to the Probate Judge. I left there within a few days after we was married.
Q Where did you go? A Come back home.
Q To the Cherokee Nation? A Ye sir.
Q Have you lived in the Cherokee continuously, as husband and wife, from the time you were married in 1872 up to and including the present time? A Yes sir.
Q Have you always lived together since you were married? A Yes sir
Q Were you ever married before you married her? A No sir.
Q Was she ever married before you married her? A No sir.
Q Who married you? A Parson Collier.
Q Can't you get a certificate from him of your marriage? A I don't know. I have never heard of that man for 25 years. He moved away from the neighborhood and I don't know where he went to.
Q Could you write to the Probate Judge of Sumner county[sic], Kansas and have him send a certificate showing that the license was returned there? A I believe I could
Q That would be the best evidence.
Witness excused.

Ella E. Fields, being first duly sworn by Frances R. Lane, testified as follows:
By the Commissioner:
Q What is your name? A Ella E. Fields.
Q How old are you? A Fifty-three.
Q What is your postoffice address? A Warner.
Q You claim to be an intermarried citizen of the Cherokee Nation? A Yes sir.
Q Through whom do you claim the right as an intermarried citizen A Walter G. Fields.
Q When were you married to him? A The 8th day of April, 1872.
Q Have you lived continuously as husband and wife in the Cherokee Nation since the date of your marriage in 1872 up to and including the present time? A Yes sir.
Q Was your husband a citizen of the Cherokee Nation at the time you married him?
A Yes sir.

The applicant is identified on the 1880 Cherokee roll, opposite No. 479. Her husband, through whom she claims her right to enrollment, is identified on said roll opposite No. 748. and is also identified on the final roll of citizens by blood of the Cherokee Nation opposite No. 5431.

Frances R. Lane upon oath states that as stenographee[sic] to the Commissioner to the Five Civilized Tribes she repprted[sic] the testimony in the above entitled cause and that the foregoing is an accurate transcript of her stenographic notes thereof.

Cherokee Intermarried White 1906
Volume I

Frances R Lane

Subscribed and sworn to before me this January 4, 1907.

Edward Merrick
Notary Public.

◇◇◇◇◇

E.C.M.   Cherokee 2094.

DEPARTMENT OF THE INTERIOR,

COMMISSIONER TO THE FIVE CIVILIZED TRIBES.

In the matter of the application for the enrollment of ELLA E. FIELDS as a citizen by intermarriage of the Cherokee Nation.

D E C I S I O N

THE RECORDS OF THIS OFFICE SHOW: That at Fort Gibson, Indian Territory, August 27, 1900, Walter G. Fields appeared before the Commission to the Five Civilized Tribes and made application for the enrollment of himself et al. as citizens by blood, and for the enrollment of his wife, Ella E. Fields, as a citizen by intermarriage, of the Cherokee Nation. The application for the enrollment of said Walter G. Fields et al. as citizens by blood of the Cherokee Nation has been heretofore disposed of, and their rights to enrollment will not be considered in this decision. Further proceedings in the matter of said application were had at Muskogee, Indian Territory, October 11, 1902, and January 2, 19.

THE EVIDENCE IN THIS CASE SHOWS: That the applicant herein, Ella E. Fields, a white woman, married April 8, 1872, one Walter G. Fields, who was at the time of said marriage a resident of the State of Kansas, and a recognized citizen by blood of the Cherokee Nation; that shortly after said marriage the said Walter G. Fields and the said Ella E. Fields removed to the Cherokee Nation. The name of the said Walter G. Fields appears on the approved partial roll of citizens by blood of the Cherokee Nation, opposite No. 5431. The evidence further shows that from the time of their said marriage the said Walter G. Fields and the said Ella E. Fields resided together as husband and wife continuously and lived in the Cherokee Nation up to and including September 1, 1902. Said Ella E. Fields is identified on the Cherokee authenticated tribal roll of 1880, and the Cherokee census roll of 1896, as an intermarried citizen of the Cherokee Nation.

IT IS, THEREFORE, ORDERED AND ADJUDGED: That in accordance with the decision of the Supreme Court of the United States, dated November 5, 1906, in the case of Daniel Red Bird et al. vs. the United States, under the provisions of the Act of Congress approved June 28, 1898 (30 Stat., 495), Ella E. Fields is entitled to enrollment

Cherokee Intermarried White 1906
Volume I

as a citizen by intermarriage of the Cherokee Nation, and her application for enrollment as such is accordingly granted.

Tams Bixby
Commissioner.

Dated at Muskogee, Indian Territory,
this   JAN 17 1907

◇◇◇◇◇

Cherokee
2094

Muskogee, Indian Territory, January 17, 1907.

W. W. Hastings,
    Attorney for the Cherokee Nation,
        Muskogee, Indian Territory.

Dear Sir:

There is enclosed herewith a copy of the decision of the Commissioner to the Five Civilized Tribes, dated January 17, 1907, granting the application for the enrollment of Ella E. Fields as a citizen by intermarriage of the Cherokee Nation.

Respectfully,

Encl. H-40   Commissioner.
JMH

◇◇◇◇◇

Cherokee 2094.   W.W. HASTINGS, ATTORNEY.   OFFICE OF   H.M. VANCE, SECRETARY.

Attorney for the Cherokee Nation,
MUSKOGEE, I. T.

January 18, 1907.

The Commissioner to the Five Civilized Tribes,
    Muskogee, Indian Territory.

Sir:

Receipt is acknowledged of the testimony and of your decision enrolling Ella E. Fields as a citizen by intermarriage of the Cherokee Nation. Time for protesting said decision is waived and I consent that said person may be placed upon the schedule immediately.

Yours very truly,
W. W. Hastings
Attorney for Cherokee Nation.

Cherokee Intermarried White 1906
Volume I

◇◇◇◇◇

Cherokee
2094

Muskogee, Indian Territory, January 19, 1907.

Ella E. Fields,
    Bennett, Indian Territory.

Dear Madam:

There is enclosed herewith a copy of the decision of the Commissioner to the Five Civilized Tribes, dated January 16, 1907, granting your application for enrollment as a citizen by intermarriage of the Cherokee Nation.

You will be advised when your name has been placed upon the schedule of citizens of the Cherokee Nation and approved by the Secretary of the Interior.

                Respectfully,

Enc I-1   Commissioner.

RPI

Cher IW 27
Trans from Cher 2425 3-13-07

◇◇◇◇◇

                                              C.E.W.

DEPARTMENT OF THE INTERIOR,

COMMISSIONER TO THE FIVE CIVILIZED TRIBES.

In the matter of the application for the enrollment of

CLEMENT HAYDEN

as a citizen by intermarriage of the Cherokee Nation.

CHEROKEE 2425

Cherokee Intermarried White 1906
Volume I

Department of the Interior,
Commission to the Five Civilized Tribes,
Pryor Creek, I. T., Sept. 10, 1900.

In the matter of the application of Clement Hayden for the enrollment of himself, wife and children as Cherokee citizens; beig[sic] sworn and examined by Commissioner Breckinridge he testified as follows:

Q What is your full name? A Clement Hayden.
Q How old are you? A Fifty-four.
Q What is your post-office? A Chouteau.
Q In what district do y Alice? A Cooweescoowee.
Q Who do you want to have put on the roll? A Myself and wife and children.
Q Do you apply for yourself as a Cherokee by blood? A No sir, as an adopted citizen.
Q Do you apply for your wife as a Cherokee by blood? A Yes sir
Q Have you your marriage license? A Yes sir.
Q When were you married? A 1869.
Q You on the roll of 1880? A Yes sir.
Q Have you lived in the Cherokee Nation ever since 1880? A Yes sir.
Q Is you wife living at this time? A Yes sir.
Q You and she have lived together ever since you were married? A Yes sir.
Q Give me the name of your father? A Clement Hayden.
Q White man? A Yes sir.
Q Is he dead or alive? A Dead.
Q Your mother's name? A Lucy.
Q She a white woman? A Yes sir.
Q She dead or alive? A She is dead.
Q Give me your wife's given name? A Rebecca Carolina.
Q How old is she? A Fifty.
Q Is she on the roll of 1880 as your wife? A Yes sir.
Q And on the roll of 1896 as your wife? A Yes sir.
Q She is living at this time? A Yes sir.
Q She has continued to live with you since 1880 in the Cherokee Nation? A Yes sir.
Q Give me the names of your children? A Ida M., sixteen; Lona, fourteen; Lela, twelve; Essie, eight.
Q No middle name for these children except the first one? A No sir.
Q They are all living at this time? A Yes sir.
Applicant: We have an orphan child with us, - my wife's niece, that we have raised, - I would like to enroll her.
Q What is her name? A Edna Lindsey. Ten years old.
Q What was her mother's name? A Dolly Lindsey.
Q When did she die? A Three years ago.
Q How old was she when she died? A I don't know. her exact age, about twenty-six years old.
Q Was her mother a Cherokee or a white woman? A Cherokee.

Cherokee Intermarried White 1906
Volume I

Q What was her mother's maiden name? A Bennett.
Q She is on the roll of 1880 is she? A Yes sir.
Q She is on the roll of 1896 as a Lindsey? A Yes sir.
Q Give me the name of the father? A R. P. Lindsey.
Q Cherokee or a white man? A White man.
Q How long has he been dead? A He has been dead since 1894.
Q When were they married? A I couldn't give you the year, that[sic] had been six or seven years.
Q They were married along about 1886? A I think so, yes sir.
Q Give me the name of your wife's father? A J. M. Bryan.
Q Cherokee or a white man? A White man.
Q Dead or alive? A Dead.
Q How long has he been dead? A About two years.
Q Name of her mother? A Rebecca C.
Q Cherokee or a white woman? A Cherokee.
Q Dead or alive? A Dead.
Q How long has she been dead? A Fourteen or fifteen years.
1880 roll page 116 #1396 Clem Hayden Cooweescoowee District;
1880 roll page 116 #1397 Carry Hayden, Cooweescoowee District.
1880 roll page 67 #215 Dolly Bennett Cooweescoowee District;
1896 roll page 307 #440 Clem Hayden Cooweescoowee Dist, adopted white
1896 roll page 172 #2092 Carrie Hayden, Cooweescoowee Dist, native Cherokee;
1896 roll page 172 #2095 Ida Hayden, Cooweescoowee District;
1896 roll page 172 #2097 Lela Hayden, Cooweescoowee District;
1896 roll page 172 #2098 Essie Hayden, Cooweescoowee District;
1896 roll page 196 #2752 Edna Lindsey Cooweescoowee District.
1896 roll page 196 #2751 Rebecca C. or Dollie Lindsey, Cooweescoowee

Com'r Breckinridge: The applicant applies for the enrollment of himself his wife and four children, and for one orphan child, brought up by him and his wife; the applicant is identified on the rolls of 1880 and 1896 as a Cherokee by adoption; he has continued to live with his Cherokee wife ever since his enrollment in 1880, and both of them have continued to live in the Cherokee Nation, and he will be listed now for enrollment as a Cherokee by adoption; his wife is identified on the rolls of 1880 and 1896 as a native Cherokee; their four children are identified on the roll of 1896, with them; They are all living at this time; the applicant's wife and the se[sic] four children will now be listed for enrollment as Cherokees by blood; the orphan child, Edna Lindsey, Indian Territory ten years of age, is identified on the roll of 1896 as a native Cherokee; the child's mother is identified on both the rolls of 1880 and 1896, and this child will now be listed for enrollment as a Cherokee by blood.

M.D. Green, being first duly sworn, states that as stenographer to the Commission to the Five Civilized Tribes he correctly recorded the testimony and proceedings in this case and that the foregoing is a true and complete transcript of his stenographic notes thereof.

MD Green

Cherokee Intermarried White 1906
Volume I

Subscribed and sworn to before me this 11 day of September 1900.

CR Breckinridge
Commissioner.

DEPARTMENT OF THE INTERIOR.
Commission to the Five Civilized Tribes.
Muskogee, Indian Territory, October 9th, 1902.

In the matter of the application of Clement Hayden for the enrollment of himself as a citizen by intermarriage of the Cherokee Nation and for the enrollment of his wife, Rebecca C. Hayden, and his children, Ida M., Lona, Lela and Essie Hayden, and his ward, Edna Lindsey, Indian Territory as citizens by blood of the Cherokee Nation.

Supplemental to #2425.

CLEMENT HAYDEN, being duly sworn, testified as follows:
Examination by the Commission.
Q. State your full name? A. Clement Hayden.
Q. How old are you? A. 56.
Q. What is your post office? A. Choteau.
Q. Are you a white man? A. Yes, sir.
Q. Claiming as a citizen by intermarriage? A. Yes, sir.
Q. What is the name of the wife through whom you claim citizenship? A. Rebecca C.
Q. Is she a Cherokee by blood? A. Yes, sir.
Q. Have you and your wife been living together in the Cherokee Nation since 188o[sic]? A. Yes, sir.
Q. This is the wife you were married to in 1880? A. I was married before 1880.
Q. Never been separated? A. No, sir.
Q. And were living together on the first day of last September? A. Yes, sir.
Q. How many children have you? A. Five.
Q. Are they all living? A. Yes, sir. One of them, the older one, is married. She is enrolled, probably, by herself.
Q. Who is Edna Lindsey? A. She is a little orphan girl living with us. We are raising her.
Q. What is her mother's name? A. Rebecca C. was her mother's name. Rebecca C. Lindsey.
Q. Rebecca C. is your wife's name? A. Yes, sir. Rebecca C. Lindsey was a niece of mine.
Q. Was she a Cherokee by blood? A. Yes, sir.
Q. When did she die? A. She has been dead 3 or 4 years. I couldn't give you the exact dates.
Q. Is Edna Lindsey an orphan? A. Yes, sir.

Cherokee Intermarried White 1906
Volume I

Q. How long have you had the custody of the child? A. Almost all her life. Ever sine her mother died. We raised her mother.
Q. This child was born in the Cherokee Nation? A. Yes, sir.
Q. Live in the Cherokee Nation all her live? A. Yes, sir.
Q. With you? A. Yes, sir.

Jesse O. Carr, being first duly sworn, states that as stenographer to the Commission to the Five Civilized Tribes he reported the above entitled case and that the foregoing is a true and complete transcript of his stenographic notes thereof.

Jesse O. Carr

Subscribed and sworn to before me this 10th day of December, 1902.

(Name Illegible)
Notary Public.

◇◇◇◇◇

Cherokee 2425.

DEPARTMENT OF THE INTERIOR,
COMMISSIONER TO THE FIVE CIVILIZED TRIBES.
Muskogee, I. T. January 3, 1907.

In the matter of the application for the enrollment of Clement Hayden for enrollment as a citizen by intermarriage of the Cherokee Nation.

Clement Hayden being first duly sworn by Walter W. Chappell, a Notary Public for the Western District, testified as follows:

By the Commissioner:
Q What is your name? A Clement Hayden.
Q Your age? A Sixty years.
Q Your postoffice address? A Choteau, I. T.
Q You claim to be a citizen of the Cherokee Nation by intermarriage? A Yes sir.
Q Through whom do you claim that right? A My wife, her maiden name was Rebecca C. Bryan
Q Is she living? A Yes sir.
Q What is her citizenship? A Cherokee by blood.
Q When were you married to her? A March, 1869.
Q Where were you married to her? A In Cooweescowee[sic] District.
Q Under a Cherokee license? A Yes sir.
Q Issued by what authority? A Authorities of the Cherokee Nation.
Q What District? A Cooweescowee[sic] District.
Q Have you a certified copy of that marriage license? A Yes sir.

Cherokee Intermarried White 1906
Volume I

Applicant offers in evidence certificate of Daniel R. Hicks, Clerk pro tem of the District Court of Cooweescowee[sic] District, under date of March 3, 1869, to the effect that "Clement Hayden, a citizen of the United States, has on this day presented his application for marriage license as is required by an act of the National Council, dated Oct. 15, 1855, and that a license has been issued by said Daniel R. Hicks to the said Clement Hayden, authorizing his marriage to Miss Rebecca C. Bryan, a citizen by blood of the Cherokee Nation", the same being filed herewith and made a part of the records in this case.

Q At the time of your marriage to your present wife, had either one of you been married before? A No sir.

Q Where have you lived ever since your marriage? A Continuously in the Cherokee Nation.

Q Have you lived together ever since your marriage? A Yes sir.

On page 8, Book A., Record of Marriage Licenses, Cooweescowee[sic] District, now in the custody of this office, is found the following:
"June 26, 1871 issued license of marriage to Clement Hayden, citizen of the United States to marry Mary Rebeca[sic] Carloline[sic] Bryan, a citizen of the C. N. Issued by J. B. Mayes, District Clerk, married by Judge Redbird Sixkiller June 28, 1871."

Q Mr. Hayden, how do you account for the difference in the dates appearing in the certificate of Daniel R. Hicks, which you have offered in evidence, and the date appearing upon the marriage records of the Cherokee Nation, Cooweescoowee District, wherein you are licensed to marry Rebecca C. Bryan?
A The copy I have offered in evidence is the license issued by Daniel R. Hicks. The question was raised as to the validity of the first marriage, as to whether this John A. Richards was authorized or not--the question was raised as to whether he was a licensed minister or not, and I procured a second license issued by J. B. Mayes, and the ceremony was performed by Judge Sixkiller.

Q There was some question then, as to whether or not the marriage performed under the first license granted by the Cherokee Nation was valid, and in order to cure any defect in the first marriage, you procured a second license and was married by the judge of the District? A Yes sir.

The applicant, Clement Hayden, is identified on the authenticated tribal Cherokee roll of 1880, and on the Cherokee census roll of 1896, Cooweescoowee District, opposite Nos. 1396 and 440, respectively.

The records of this office show that Rebecca C. Hayden, nee Bryan, wife of the applicant, is included in a partial approved roll of the citizens by blood of the Cherokee Nation opposite No. 6201.

Frances R. Lane upon oath states that as stenographer to the Commissioner to the Five Civilized Tribes she reported the testimony in the above entitled cause and that the foregoing is an accurate transcript of her stenographic notes thereof.

Cherokee Intermarried White 1906
Volume I

Frances R Lane

Subscribed and sworn to before me this January 4, 1907.

Edward Merrick
Notary Public.

◇◇◇◇◇

(The Marriage License below typed as given.)

COPY

Cherokee Nation

Cooweeskoowe District

To who whom it may concern

Know ye that Clement Hayden a citizen of the United States, have this day presented a recommendation, such as is required by an Act of the National Council, entitled an act to legalize intermarriage with white man dated Oct 15th 1855.

    Therefore I Daniel R. Hecks Clerk pro-tem, of the District Court of the aforesaid District by virtue of the authority in me vested by law Grant these my letters of licence to the said Clement Hayden to Mary in the manner as prescribed by law Miss Rebecca C. Bryan of said District and Nation, the marriage ceremony to be performed by any Judge of the Cherokee Nation or Minister of the Gospel who shall certify on the face of this license that he did perform such marriage ceremony between said parties and return the same to my office. Given from under my hand in office this 3rd day of March A. D. 1869.

Daniel R. Hecks
Clerk pro-tem
Dist Ck Cooskee Dist
C. N.

  I hereby certify that I have this day performed the marriage ceremony uniting Clement Hayden and Rebecca C. Bryan
in the holy bonds of matrimony
Grand Saline Cherokee Nation
  March 7th 1869

(Signed John A. Richards

  The undersigned being first duly sworn states that as stenographer to the Commissioner to the Five Civilized Tribes she made the above and foregoing copy of the same is a true and correct copy of the marriage license and certificate now on file in this office.

Lola M. Champlin

Cherokee Intermarried White 1906
Volume I

Subscribed and sworn to before me this 10 day of January 1907

Chas E Webster
notary public.

◇◇◇◇◇

C.E.W.   Cherokee 2425.

DEPARTMENT OF THE INTERIOR,

COMMISSIONER TO THE FIVE CIVILIZED TRIBES.

In the matter of the application for the enrollment of Clement Hayden, as a citizen by intermarriage of the Cherokee Nation.

D E C I S I O N

THE RECORDS OF THIS OFFICE SHOW: That at Pryor Creek, Indian Territory, September 10, 1900, Clement Hayden appeared before the Commission to the Five Civilized Tribes, and made application for the enrollment of himself, as a citizen by intermarriage, and for the enrollment of his wife, Rebecca C. Hayden, et al., as citizens by blood of the Cherokee Nation. The application for the enrollment of Rebeca C. Hayden, et al., as citizens by blood of the Cherokee Nation has been heretofore disposed of and their rights to enrollment will not be considered in this decision. Further proceedings in the matter of said application were had at Muskogee, Indian Territory, October 9, 1902, and January 3, 1907.

THE EVIDENCE IN THIS CASE SHOWS: That the applicant herein, Clement Hayden, a white man, was married in accordance with Cherokee law June 28, 1871 to his wife, Rebecca C. Hayden, nee Bryan, who was at the time of said marriage a recognized citizen by blood of the Cherokee Nation, and whose name appears upon the approved partial roll of citizens by blood of the Cherokee Nation, opposite number 6201; that since said marriage the said Clement Hayden and Rebecca C. Hayden have resided together as husband and wife and have continuously lived in the Cherokee Nation. Said Clement Hayden is identified on the Cherokee authenticated tribal roll of 1880, and the Cherokee census roll of 1896 as an intermarried citizen of the Cherokee Nation.

IT IS, THEREFORE, ORDERED AND ADJUDGED: That in accordance with the decision of the Supreme Court of the United States, dated November 5, 1906, in the case of Daniel Red Bird et al., vs. the United States, under the provisions of Section 21 of the Act of Congress approved June 28, 1898, (30 Stat., 495), Clement Hayden is entitled to enrollment as a citizen by intermarriage of the Cherokee Nation, and his application for enrollment as such is accordingly granted.

Tams Bixby
Commissioner.

Cherokee Intermarried White 1906
Volume I

Dated at Muskogee, Indian Territory,
this   JAN 16 1907

◇◇◇◇◇

Cherokee
2425

Muskogee, Indian Territory, December 24, 1906.

Clement Hayden,
    Choteau, Indian Territory.

Dear Sir:

    November 6, 1906, the United States Supreme Court held that white persons who intermarried with Cherokee citizens according to Cherokee law prior to November 1, 1875, are entitled to enrollment and allotments of land as citizens of the Cherokee Nation.

    You are advised that to properly determine your right to enrollment as a citizen by intermarriage of the Cherokee Nation, it will be necessary for you to appear before the Commissioner for the purpose of giving testimony as to the date of your marriage and whether or not your wife, by reason of your marriage to whom you claim the right to enrollment as a citizen of the Cherokee Nation, was a recognized citizen of the Cherokee Nation at the time of your marriage to her, and whether or not you were married to her in accordance with Cherokee laws.

    You are, therefore, directed to appear before the Commissioner at Muskogee, Indian Territory, at 9 o'clock A. M., on Thursday, January 3, 1907, and give testimony as above indicated.

                          Respectfully,

JMH   Acting Commissioner.

◇◇◇◇◇

Cherokee 2425

Muskogee, Indian Territory, January 17, 1907.

W. W. Hastings,
    Attorney for the Cherokee Nation,
        Muskogee, Indian Territory.

Dear Sir:

    There is enclosed herewith copy of the decision of the Commissioner to the Five Civilized Tribes, dated January 18, 1907, granting the application for the enrollment of Clement Hayden as a citizen by intermarriage of the Cherokee Nation.

Cherokee Intermarried White 1906
Volume I

Respectfully,

Commissioner.

Enc I-2

RPI

◇◇◇◇◇

Cherokee 2425.   W.W. HASTINGS,   OFFICE OF   H.M. VANCE,
      ATTORNEY.   SECRETARY.

Attorney for the Cherokee Nation,
MUSKOGEE, I. T.

January 18, 1907.

The Commissioner to the Five Civilized Tribes,
  Muskogee, Indian Territory.

Sir:

  Receipt is acknowledged of the testimony and of your decision enrolling Clement Hayden as a citizen by intermarriage of the Cherokee Nation. Time for protesting said decision is waived and I consent that said person may be placed upon the schedule immediately.

      Yours very truly,
      W. W. Hastings
      Attorney for Cherokee Nation.

◇◇◇◇◇

Cherokee
2425

Muskogee, Indian Territory, January 19, 1907.

Clement Hayden,
  Choteau, Indian Territory.

Dear Sir:

  There is enclosed herewith a copy of the decision of the Commissioner to the Five Civilized Tribes, dated January 18, 1907, granting your application as a citizen by intermarriage of the Cherokee Nation.

  You will be advised when your name has been placed upon the schedule of citizens of the Cherokee Nation and approved by the Secretary of the Interior.

Cherokee Intermarried White 1906
Volume I

Respectfully,

Encl. H-85 Commissioner.
JMH

◇◇◇◇◇

Cherokee
I. W. 27

Muskogee, Indian Territory, April 6 1907

Clement Hayden,
    Choteau, Indian Territory.

Dear Sir:

    Your marriage license and certificate, filed in connection with your application for enrollment as a citizen by intermarriage of the Cherokee Nation, is returned to you herewith, copies of the same being retained in this office.

Respectfully,

Encl. B-90 Acting Commissioner.

L M B

Cher IW 28
Trans from Cher 2978 3-13-07

◇◇◇◇◇

C.E.W.

DEPARTMENT OF THE INTERIOR,

COMMISSIONER TO THE FIVE CIVILIZED TRIBES.

In the matter of the application for the enrollment of

JESSE A. THOMAS

as a citizen by intermarriage of the Cherokee Nation.

CHEROKEE 2978

Cherokee Intermarried White 1906
Volume I

◇◇◇◇◇

DEPARTMENT OF THE INTERIOR.

COMMISSION TO THE FIVE CIVILIZED TRIBES.

Vinita, I.T. September 18th, 1900.

IN THE MATTER OF THE APPLICATION OF JOHNANNA THOMAS FOR THE ENROLLMENT OF HERSELF, HER HUSBAND, CHILDREN AS CHEROKEE CITIZENS.

The said Johnanna Thomas, being sworn and examined by Commissioner C. R. Breckinridge, testified as follows:

Q Give me your name, please.
A Johnanna Thomas.
Q Any middle name? A That is all.
Q Are you----How old are you? A Forty-six.
Q What is your postoffice? A Vinita.
Q What district do you liv in? A Cooweescoowee.
Q Who is it you want to hve[sic] put on the roll? A Myself and family.
Q Have you a husband you want to enroll? A Yes, sir.
Q How many children? A I have seven.
Q These are all alive are they, these seven? A Yes, sir.
Q Seven living children under twenty one years of age and unmarried? A Yes, sir.
Q Where is your husband? A He is here some place.
Q Well, he must put in his appearance. Where is he? What is his name?
A Jesse Thomas.

JESSE THOMAS, being called and sworn by the Commissioner testified as follows:
Q What is your full name? A Jesse A. Thomas.
Q How old are you? A Forty eight years old.
Q What is your postoffice? A Vinita.
Q What district do you live in? A Cooweescoowee.
Q Are you the husband of this lady here? A Yes, sir.
Q Stand by her please, in case I want to ask you some further questions.

(Examination of Mrs. Thomas continued)
Q Now, Madam, you apply for yourself as a Cherokee by blood? A Yes, sir.
Q What proportion of Cherokee blood do you claim? A One-sixteenth.
Q Your husband is a white man, is he? A Yes, sir.
Q How long have you lived in the Cherokee Nation? A All my life.
Q When were you married to your husband here? A In 1874.
Q You are on the roll of 1880 then as a Thomas? A Yes, sir.
Q From what district? A Cooweescoowee.
Q Give me your father's name, please. A John Williams.

Cherokee Intermarried White 1906
Volume I

Q Cherokee or white man? A White man.
Q Is he dead or alive? A Dead.
Q How long has he been dead? A About forty-five years.
Q Your mother's given name? A Jane Williams.
Q Dead or alive? A She is dead.
Q Cherokee? A Yes, sir.
Q When did she die? A In 1893.
Q Now, give me, please, the names of your children.
A Henry R., eighteen years old; Napoleon F., fifteen years old; Jessie Anna, fourteen years old; John L., twelve years old; Thura, ten years old; Ellis, eight years old; Elizabeth, two years old.
Q These children are all living now are they? A Yes, sir.
1880 Roll, page 186, No. 2889, Jessee[sic] Thomas, Native Cherokee, Cooweescoowee District.
1880 Roll, page 186, No. 2889, Johanna Thomas, Cooweescoowee District.
1896 Roll, page 268, No. 4766, Johanna Thomas, Cooweescoowee District.
1896 Roll, page 326, No. 1012, Jesse Thomas, Cooweescoowee District.
1896 Roll, Page 268, No. 4768, Henry R. Thomas, Cooweescoowee District.
1896 Roll, page 268, No. 4769, Frank N. Thomas, Cooweescoowee District.
1896 Roll, page 268, No. 4770, Jessanna Thomas, Cooweescoowee District.
1896 Roll, page 268, No. 4771, Lawrence Thomas, Cooweescoowee District.
1896 Roll, page 268, No. 4772, Thura Thomas, Cooweescoowee District.
1896 Roll, page 268, No. 4773, Ellis Thomas, Cooweescoowee District.
Q These children are all living now are they? A Yes, sir.
Q Your husband has lived with you ever since 1880, has he? A Yes, sir.

THE COMMISSIONER: The applicant applies for the enrollment of her self, her husband and seven children, all minors. Her husband appears with her in the application. She is identified on the rolls of 1880 and 1896 as a native Cherokee; she has lived in the Cherokee Nation all her life and she will be listed now for enrollment as a Cherokee by blood. Her husband is identified with her on the rolls of 1880 and 1896?[sic] He has lived with his wife from 1880 to this time, and he will be listed now for enrollment as a Cherokee by adoption. Of their seven children, the first six are enumerated in the testimony, and are identified with their parents on the roll of 1896. They are all living at this time, and will be listed now for enrollment as Cherokee citizens by blood, and when the Commission is supplied with a proper certificate of the birth of the youngest child Elizabeth, it also will be listed for enrollment as a Cherokee by blood.

The undersigned, being sworn, states that as stenographer to the Commission to the Five Civilized Tribes he correctly recorded the testimony and other proceedings in this application, and that the foregoing is a correct and complete transcript of his stenographic notes thereof.

Wm S. Meeshean

Cherokee Intermarried White 1906
Volume I

Subscribed and sworn to before me this 28th day of September A. D. 1900L[sic]

                                              TB Needles
                                              Commissioner.

Cherokee 2978.

Department of the Interior,
Commission to the Five Civilized Tribes,
Muskogee, I. T., October 4, 1902.

    In the matter of the application of Jesse A. Thomas for the enrollment of himself as a citizen by intermarriage, and for the enrollment of his wife, Johnanna, and children, Henry R., Napoleon F., Jessie A., John L., Thura, Ellis and Elizabeth Thomas, as citizens by blood of the Cherokee Nation.
    James S. davenport, being sworn and examined by the Commission, testified as follows:
Q What is your name? A James S. Davenport, age 38, postoffice Vinita.
Q Are you acquainted with Jesse A. Thomas who is an applicant before this Commission for enrollment as an intermarried citizen of the Cherokee Nation? A Yes sir.
Q Are you acquainted with his wife, Johnanna? A Yes sir.
Q Is she a citizen by blood? A Yes sir,
Q How long have you known Jesse A., A Since the fall of 1890.
Q Has Jesse A. and his wife, Johnanna Thomas, lived together as husband and wife since 1890 up until the present time? A I suppose they have. I got acquainted with Mr. Thomas when he visited his relatives here.
Q They never have been separated since 1893 to your knowledge? A No sir, they have got children.
Q Were they living together as husband and wife on the first day of September, 1902? A Yes sir.

    The undersigned, being duly sworn, states that as stenographer to the Commission to the Five Civilized Tribes he correctly recorded the testimony and proceedings in this case, and that the foregoing is a true and correct transcript of his stenographic notes thereof.

                                            E.G. Rothenberger

Subscribed and sworn to before me this 22nd day of October, 1902.

                                            BC Jones
                                            Notary Public.

Cherokee Intermarried White 1906
Volume I

Cherokee 2978.

Department of the Interior,
Commission to the Five Civilized Tribes,
Muskogee, I. T., October 14, 1902.

In the matter of the application of Jesse A. Thomas for the enrollment of himself as a citizen by intermarriage, and for the enrollment of his wife, Johnanna, and children, Henry R., Napoleon F., Jessie A., John L., Thura, Ellis and Elizabeth Thomas, as citizens by blood of the Cherokee Nation; he being sworn and examined by the Commission, testified as follows:

Q What is your name? A Jesse A. Thomas.
Q How old are you? A Fifty years old.
Q What is your postoffice? A Vinita.
Q You are a white man are you? A White man.
Q Is your name on the roll of 1880? A Yes sir.
Q What was your wife's name at that time? A Johnanna Thomas in '80.
Q Have you and your wife lived in the Cherokee nation since 1880? A Yes sir.
Q You never have been separated? A No sir.
Q You never made your home outside of the Cherokee Nation? A No sir.
Q You and your wife then were living together on the first day of last September? A Yes sir.
Q How many children did you apply for? A Seven.
Q Are they all living? A Yes sir.

The undersigned, being duly sworn, states that as stenographer to the Commission to the Five Civilized Tribes he correctly recorded the testimony and proceedings in this case, and that the foregoing is a true and correct transcript of his stenographic notes thereof.

E.G. Rothenberger

Subscribed and sworn to before me this 10th day of November, 1902.

BC Jones
Notary Public.

Cherokee Intermarried White 1906
Volume I

Cherokee 2978.

DEPARTMENT OF THE INTERIOR,
COMMISSIONER TO THE FIVE CIVILIZED TRIBES.
Muskogee, I. T., January 2, 1907.

In the matter of the application for the enrollment of Jesse Thomas as a citizen by intermarriage of the Cherokee Nation.

Jesse Thomas being first duly sworn by Frances R. Lane, a Notary Public for the Western District, Indian Territory, testified as follows:

By the Commissioner:
Q What is your name? A Jesse Thomas.
Q How old are you? A 55 the 18th of May.
Q What is your postoffice address? A Vinita, I. T.
Q You claim to be an intermarried citizen of the Cherokee Nation? A Yes sir.
Q Through whom do you claim your right as such? A Johnanna Williams.
Q When were you married to Joanna Williams? A The 6th day of September, 1874.
Q Did you get married under a license? A Yes sir.
Q Have you got a copy of that license? A I have got the license in my pocket.
    The applicant offers in evidence license issued to him By J. E. Harlin on Sept. 5, 1874, together with the certificate of his marriage to Johnanna Williams on September 6, 1874, signed by T. J. McGhee on September 6, 1874.
Q Were you ever married before you married before you married Johnanna Williams? A No sir.
Q Was she ever married before she was married to you? A No sir.
Q Have you lived together continuously as husband and wife in the Cherokee Nation, since your marriage in 1874? A Yes sir.
Q Was your wife a citizen of the Cherokee nation[sic] at the time you married her? A Yes sir.

The applicant is identified on the 1880 Cherokee roll opposite No. 2889. His wife, through whom he claims the right to enrollment is identified on said roll opposite No. 2890. She is also identified on the final roll of citizens by blood of the Cherokee nation[sic] opposite No. 7406.

Q Are you and your wife living together at the present time? A She is dead; she died about 6 months ago.
Q She lived with you up to the time of her death? A Yes sir.
                                    Witness excused.

Frances R. Lane upon oath states that as stenographer to the Commissioner to the Five Civilized Tribes she reported the testimony in the above entitled cause and that the above and foregoing is an accurate transcript of her shorthand notes therein.

                                                        Frances R Lane

Cherokee Intermarried White 1906
Volume I

Subscribed and sworn to before me this January 4, 1906.

Edward Merrick
Notary Public.

◇◇◇◇◇

(The Marriage License and Certificate below typed as given.)

COPY

Cherokee Nation

Delaware District

To any lawfull Judge or regulor minister of the Gospel of the Cherokee Nation

GREETING

In the name of the Cherokee Nation you are hereby aurthorized and impowered to solemoneze the Rites of matrimony between J. A. Thomas a citizen of the U States and Miss Johnana William a citizen of the Cherokee Nation and the said J. A Thomas having fully conformed to the Act entitled an act to provide for the licensey of citizens of the U States to enter marry with citizens of the Cherokee Nation

Approved Oct 15, 1855

Here in fail not. Done in my office officially this 5 day of September A D 1874

J. E. Harlin

Clerk

Delaware Dist

C. N.

I do hereby certify that the within licens was issued and return executed and recorded in conformity with act entitled and act to provide for liceny white men to entermarry with citizens of the Cherokee Nation.

In testimony whereof I have hereunto set my hand and the seal of Delaware Dist this the 6 day of September A. D. 1874

J. E. Harlin   Clerk

(Seal)   Delaware Dist. C. N.

Cherokee Intermarried White 1906
Volume I

I hereby certify that the marriage of ceremony was duely performed by me with the parties named in the within licens this Sept 6th 1874

F. J. McShee   Judge

D.C.D.D.C.N.

The undersigned being first duly sworn states that as stenographer to the Commissioner to the Five Civilized Tribes, she made the above and foregoing copy and that the same is a true and correct copy of the original marriage license and certificate now on file in this office.

Lola M. Champlin

Subscribed and sworn to before me this 10 day of January 1907

Chas E Webster
notary public.

◇◇◇◇◇

C.E.W.   Cherokee 2978

DEPARTMENT OF THE INTERIOR,

COMMISSIONER TO THE FIVE CIVILIZED TRIBES.

In the matter of the application for the enrollment of Jesse A. Thomas as a citizen by intermarriage of the Cherokee Nation.

D E C I S I O N

THE RECORDS OF THIS OFFICE SHOW: That at Vinita, Indian Territory, September 18, 1900, Johnanna Thomas appeared before the Commission to the Five Civilized Tribes, and made application for the enrollment of herself and children, as citizens by blood, and for the enrollment of her husband, Jesse A. Thomas, as a citizen by intermarriage of the Cherokee Nation. The application for the enrollment of the said Johnanna Thomas, et al., as citizens by blood of the Cherokee Nation has been heretofore disposed of and their rights to enrollment will not be considered in this decision. Further proceedings in the matter of said application were had at Muskogee, Indian Territory, October 4, 1902, October 14, 1902 and January 2, 1907.

THE EVIDENCE IN THIS CASE SHOWS: That the applicant herein, Jesse A. Thomas, a white man, was married in accordance with Cherokee law September 6, 1874 to his wife Johnanna Thomas, nee Williams, who was at the time of said marriage a recognized citizen by blood of the Cherokee Nation, and whose name appears upon the approved partial roll of citizens by blood of the Cherokee Nation, opposite number 7406; that since said marriage the said Jesse A. Thomas and Johnanna Thomas have resided

Cherokee Intermarried White 1906
Volume I

together as husband and wife and have continuously lived in the Cherokee Nation. Said Jesse A. Thomas is identified on the Cherokee Authenticated tribal roll of 1880, and the Cherokee Census Roll of 1896 as an intermarried citizen of the Cherokee Nation.

IT IS THEREFORE ORDERED AND ADJUDGED: That in accordance with the decision of the Supreme Court of the United States, dated November 5, 1906, in the case of Daniel Red Bird et al., vs. the United States, under the provisions of Section 21 of the Act of Congress approved June 28, 1898, (30 Stat. 495), Jesse A. Thomas is entitled to enrollment as a citizen by intermarriage of the Cherokee Nation, and his application for enrollment as such is accordingly granted.

            Tams Bixby
            Commissioner.

Dated at Muskogee, Indian Territory,
this JAN 17 1907

◇◇◇◇◇

Cherokee
2976

          Muskogee, Indian Territory, December 24, 1906.

Jesse A. Thomas,
  Vinita, Indian Territory.

Dear Sir:

November 6, 1906, the United States Supreme Court held that white persons who intermarried with Cherokee citizens according to Cherokee law prior to November 1, 1875, are entitled to enrollment and allotments of land as citizens of the Cherokee Nation.

You are advised that to properly determine your right to enrollment as a citizen by intermarriage of the Cherokee Nation, it will be necessary for you to appear before the Commissioner for the purpose of giving testimony as to the date of your marriage and whether or not your wife, by reason of your marriage to whom you claim the right to enrollment as a citizen of the Cherokee Nation, was a recognized citizen of the Cherokee Nation at the time of your marriage to her, and whether or not you were married to her in accordance with Cherokee laws.

You are, therefore, directed to appear before the Commissioner at Muskogee, Indian Territory, at 9 o'clock A. M., on Thursday, January 3, 1907, and give testimony as above indicated.

            Respectfully,

JMH   Acting Commissioner.

◇◇◇◇◇

Cherokee Intermarried White 1906
Volume I

Cherokee
2978.

Muskogee, Indian Territory, January 17, 1907.

W. W. Hastings,
Attorney for the Cherokee Nation,
Muskogee, Indian Territory.

Dear Sir:

There is enclosed herewith a copy of the decision of the Commissioner to the Five Civilized Tribes, dated January 17, 1907, granting the application of Jesse A. Thomas for enrollment as a citizen by intermarriage of the Cherokee Nation.

Respectfully,

E. R. C.   Commissioner.

Enc. E. C. - 36

◇◇◇◇◇

Cherokee 2978   W.W.HASTINGS.   OFFICE OF   H.M. VANCE.
                 ATTORNEY.   SECRETARY.

Attorney for the Cherokee Nation,
MUSKOGEE, I. T.

January 18, 1907.

The Commissioner to the Five Civilized Tribes,
Muskogee, Indian Territory.

Sir:

Receipt is acknowledged of the testimony and of your decision enrolling Jesse H[sic]. Thomas, as a citizen by intermarriage of the Cherokee Nation. Time for protesting said decision is waived and I consent that said person may be placed upon the schedule immediately.

Yours very truly,
W. W. Hastings
Attorney for Cherokee Nation.

◇◇◇◇◇

Cherokee Intermarried White 1906
Volume I

Cherokee
2978

Muskogee, Indian Territory, January 19, 1907/

Jesse A. Thomas,
    Vinita, Indian Territory.

Dear Sir:

    There is enclosed herewith a copy of the decision of the Commissioner to the Five Civilized Tribes, dated January 17, 1907, granting the application for your enrollment as a citizen by intermarriage of the Cherokee Nation.

    You will be advised when your name has been placed upon the schedule of citizens of the Cherokee Nation and approved by the Secretary of the Interior.

    Respectfully,

Encl. H-80   Commissioner.
JMH

◇◇◇◇◇

Cherokee
I. W. 28

Muskogee, Indian Territory, April 6, 1907.

Jesse A. Thomas,
    Vinita, Indian Territory.

Dear Sir:

    Your marriage license and certificate, filed in connection with your application for enrollment as a citizen by intermarriage of the Cherokee Nation, is returned to you herewith, copies of the same being retained in this office.

    Respectfully,

L M B   Acting Commissioner

Encl. B-91

Cherokee Intermarried White 1906
Volume I

Cher IW 29
Trans from Cher 2981 3-13-07

C.E.W.

DEPARTMENT OF THE INTERIOR,

COMMISSIONER TO THE FIVE CIVILIZED TRIBES.

In the matter of the application for the enrollment of

MARTHA A. MILLER

as a citizen by intermarriage of the Cherokee Nation.

CHEROKEE 2981

Department of the Interior,
Commission to the Five Civilized Tribes,
Vinita, I.T., September 18, 1900.

In the matter of the application of Andrew J. Miller for the enrollment of himself and children as Cherokees by blood and his wife as a Cherokee by intermarriage: being sworn and examined by Commissioner Needles, he testifies as follows:

Q What is your name? A Andrew J. Miller.
Q How old are you? A About 55 years old.
Q What is your post office address? A Fairland.
Q What district do you live in? A Delaware.
Q Are you a recognized citizen of the Cherokee Nation? A Yes, sir.
Q By blood? A Yes, sir.
Q What degree of blood do you claim? A Half breed.
Q Who do you apply for for enrollment? A Myself and wife and children.
Q Your name appear upon the authenticated roll of 1880? A Yes, sir.
Q What is the name of your wife? A Martha A. Miller.
Q Is she a Cherokee citizen by blood? A No, sir.
Q She is a white person? A Yes, sir.
Q When did you marry her? A In 1874 I think.
Q Her name then appears upon the authenticated roll of 1880, does it? A I think so.
Q Her father and mother were white people, were they? Q[sic] Yes, sir.
Q What are the names of your children? A The oldest one is Aggie, but she is 21.

Cherokee Intermarried White 1906
Volume I

Q I want the names of those under 21. A Mahana Miller, 18 years old; Robert L. Miller, 13 years old; Mamie J. Miller, 11 years old; Sallie E., 9 years old; Andrew J., 7 years old; Myrtle T., 5 years old; Pearly, about 2 years old.
Q Have you got another one yet? A Yes, sir, Dawes, born July 14, 1900.
Q That is eight, isn't it? A Yes, sir.
Q Are these children all alive and living with you at home? A Yes, sir.
(Andrew J. Miller on 1880 roll, page 290, No. 1793, Andrew Miller, Delaware district. Martha A. Miller on 1880 roll, page 290, No. 1794, Martha Ann Miller, Delaware district. Andrew J. Miller on 1896 roll, page 507, No. 2157, Andrew J. Miller, Delaware district. Martha A. Miller on 1896 roll, page 581, No. 362, Delaware district. Mahana Miller on 1896 roll, page 507, No. 2161, Delaware district. Robert L. Miller on 1896 roll, page 507, No. 2162, Robert Lee Miller, Delaware district. Mamie J. Miller on 1896 roll, page 507, No. 2163, Mamie Miller, Delaware district. Sallie E. Miller on 1896 roll, page 507, No. 2164, Sarah Miller, Delaware district. Andrew J. Miller on 1896 roll, page 507, No. 2165, William A. Miller, Delaware district. Myrtle T. Miller on 1896 roll, page 507, No. 2166, Mertie T. Miller, Delaware district.)
Q Have you got proof of birth as to these two younger children? A I haven't got that with me.
Q Are these children all alive and living with you? A Yes, sir.
Q You live in the Indian Territory with your wife? A Yes, sir.

The name of Andrew J. Miller appears upon the authenticated roll of 1880 as Andrew Miller, and the name of his wife appears upon the authenticated roll of 1880 as Martha Ann Miller. Their names appear upon the census roll of 1896 as Andrew J. and Martha A. Miller. The names of their children, Mahana, Robert L., Mamie J., Sallie E., Andrew J., and Myrtle T., appear upon the census roll of 1896. He avers that he has two younger children named Pearly and Dawes, born after the census roll of 1896 was compiled. Satisfactory proof having been made to his residence, and they all being duly identified according to page and number of the roll as indicated in the testimony, said Andrew J. Miller and his said children will be duly listed for enrollment as Cherokee citizens by blood, and his wife, Martha A., as a Cherokee citizen by intermarriage. In order to complete the enrollment of his two children, Pearly and Dawes, it will be necessary for him to file satisfactory proof of their birth.

-----o-----

Bruce C. Jones, being duly sworn, says that as stenographer to the Commission to the Five Civilized Tribes he correctly recorded the proceedings and testimony in the above case, and the foregoing is a true and complete transcript of his stenographic notes thereof.

Bruce C Jones

Sworn to and subscribed before me this the 19th of September, 1900.

TB Needles
Commissioner.

Cherokee Intermarried White 1906
Volume I

Cherokee No 2981.

DEPARTMENT OF THE INTERIOR.
COMMISSIONER TO THE FIVE CIVILIZED TRIBES.

Muskogee, Indian Territory, January 3, 1907.

In the matter of the application for the enrollment of Martha A. Miller as a citizen by intermarriage of the Cherokee Nation.

Martha A. Miller, being first duly sworn and examined, testifies as follows:

BY THE COMMISSIONER:

Q What is your name? A Martha A. Miller.
Q How old are you? A I am 49 years old.
Q What is your postoffice address? A Fairland.
Q You claim to be a citizen by intermarriage of the Cherokee Nation? A Yes, sir.
Q Through whom do you claim your intermarriage rights? A Andrew J. Miller.
Q When were you married to Andrew J. Miller? A In September, 1873.
Q Where were you married? A We was married south of Fairland about five miles.
Q Cherokee Nation? A Yes, sir.
Q Have you got a marriage cirtificate[sic]? A No, sir.
Q Were you ever married before you married Andrew J. Miller? A No, sir.
Q Has he ever been married before he married you? A No, sir.
Q Have you lived together continuously since your marriage as husband and wife? A Yes, sir.
Q Living together now? A No, sir, he is dead.
Q When did he die? A He died last July, the 17th.
Q Have you married since his death? A No, sir.
Q Was Andrew J. Miller a citizen of the Cherokee Nation when you married him? A Yes, sir.
Q Either one of you ever been out of the Cherokee Nation since 1873 to establish a home? A No, sir.
Q Is there anybody here to-day who knows of your marriage to Andrew J. Miller in 1873? A My mother.

The applicant is identified on the 1880 Cherokee Roll opposite No. 1784. Her husband through whom she claims her rights to enrollment is identified on said roll opposite No. 1793. He is also identified on the final roll of Cherokees by blood opposite No. 23732.

WITNESS EXCUSED.

Cherokee Intermarried White 1906
Volume I

Jemima McCrary, being first duly sworn and examined, testifies as follows:

BY THE COMMISSIONER:

[sic] What is your name? A Jemima McCrary.
Q How old are you? [sic] I will soon be 70 years old.
Q What is your post office address? A Vinita.
Q Are you acquainted with Martha A. Miller? A Yes, sir. She is my daughter.
X[sic] Were you present when she was married to A. J. Miller? A Yes, sir.
Q When were they married: A They was married in '73.
Q Had Martha A. Miller ever been married prior to her marriage to a. J. Miller? A No, sir.
Q Had he ever been married prior to his marriage to her? A No, sir.
Q Have they lived together continuously as husband and wife from the date of their marriage up to the death of A. J. Miller? A Yes, sir.

WITNESS EXCUSED.

F. Elma Lane, upon oath, states that she reported the proceedings in the above entitled cause and that the foregoing is a true and correct transcript of her stenographic notes taken therein.

F. Elma Lane

Subscribed and sworn to before me this 4th day of January, 1907.

Chas E Webster
Notary Public.

◇◇◇◇◇

Cher
Supp'l to # 2981

Department of the Interior,
Commission to the Five Civilized Tribes,
Muskogee, I. T., October 10, 1902.

In the matter of the application of ANDREW J. MILLER, for the enrollment of himself and his children, MAHANA, ROBERT L., MAMIE J., SALLIE E., ANDREW J. JR., PEARL, DAWES and MYRTLE T. MILLER, as citizens by blood, and his wife, MARTHA A. MILLER, as a citizen by intermarriage of the Cherokee Nation:

MARTHA A. MILLER, called as a witness, being duly sworn and examined by the Commission, testified as follows:

Q What is your name ? A Martha A. Miller.
Q How old are you ? A I was born in 1858. I guess I am about forty five.
Q What is your post office address ? A Fairland.

Cherokee Intermarried White 1906
Volume I

Q You are a white woman ? A Yes sir.
Q Your name appears upon the 1880 roll as an intermarried white ? A Yes sir.
Q Was Andrew J. Miller your husband in 1880 ? A Yes sir.
Q Is he living ? A Yes sir.
Q Have you and your husband been living together in the Cherokee Nation since 1880 ? A Yes sir.
Q You have never been separated ? A No sir.
Q You never made your home outside the Cherokee Nation ? A No sir.
Q Were you and he living together on the first day of last September ? A Yes sir.
Q How many children have you living at home with you ? A I have eight.
Q Have any of your children died within the last two years ? A No sir.

E. C. Bagwell, on oath states that, as stenographer to the Commission to the Five Civilized Tribes, he correctly recorded the testimony and proceedings had in the above entitled cause, and that the foregoing is an accurate transcript of his stenographic notes thereof.

E.C. Bagwell

Subscribed and sworn to before me this October 25, 1902.

BC Jones
Notary Public.

◇◇◇◇◇

(The testimony from January 3, 1907, above, is given again.)

◇◇◇◇◇

C.E.W.   Cherokee 2981

DEPARTMENT OF THE INTERIOR,

COMMISSIONER TO THE FIVE CIVILIZED TRIBES.

In the matter of the application for the enrollment of Martha A. Miller, as citizen by intermarriage of the Cherokee Nation.

D E C I S I O N

THE RECORDS OF THIS OFFICE SHOW: That at Vinita, Indian Territory, September 18, 1900, Andrew J. Miller appeared before the Commission to the Five Civilized Tribes, and made application for the enrollment of his wife, Martha A. Miller, as a citizen by intermarriage, and for the enrollment of himself, et al., as citizens by blood

Cherokee Intermarried White 1906
Volume I

of the Cherokee Nation. The application for the enrollment of the said Andrew J. Miller, et al., as citizens by blood of the Cherokee Nation has been heretofore disposed of and their rights to enrollment will not be considered in this decision.

THE EVIDENCE IN THIS CASE SHOWS: That the applicant herein, Martha A. Miller, a white woman, was married in September 1872 to Andrew J. Miller, who was at the time of said marriage a recognized citizen by blood of the Cherokee Nation, and whose name appears upon the approved partial roll of citizens by blood of the Cherokee Nation, opposite number 23732; that from the time of said marriage the said Andrew J. Miller and Martha A. Miller resided together as husband and wife and have continuously lived in the Cherokee Nation up to and including July 17, 1906. Said Martha A. Miller is identified on the Cherokee Authenticated Tribal roll of 1880, and the Cherokee Census Roll of 1896 as an intermarried citizen of the Cherokee Nation.

IT IS THEREFORE ORDERED AND ADJUDGED: That in accordance with the decision of the Supreme Court of the United States, dated November 5, 1906, in the case of Daniel Red Bird et al., vs. the United States, under the provision of Section 21 of the Act of Congress approved June 28, 1898, (30 Stat., 495), Martha A. Miller is entitled to enrollment as a citizen by intermarriage of the Cherokee Nation, and her application for enrollment as such is accordingly granted.

Tams Bixby
Commissioner.

Dated at Muskogee, Indian Territory,
this   JAN 17 1907

◇◇◇◇◇

Cherokee
2981

Muskogee, Indian Territory, December 24, 1906.

Martha A. Miller,
Fairland, Indian Territory.

Dear Madam:

November 6, 1906, the United States Supreme Court held that white persons who intermarried with Cherokee citizens according to Cherokee law prior to November 1, 1875, are entitled to enrollment and allotments of land as citizens of the Cherokee Nation.

You are advised that to properly determine your right to enrollment as a citizen by intermarriage of the Cherokee Nation, it will be necessary for you to appear before the Commissioner for the purpose of giving testimony as to the date of your marriage and whether or not your husband, by reason of your marriage to whom you claim the right to

Cherokee Intermarried White 1906
Volume I

enrollment as a citizen by intermarriage of the Cherokee Nation, was a recognized Cherokee citizen at the time of your marriage to him.

You are, therefore, directed to appear before the Commissioner at Muskogee, Indian Territory, at 9 o'clock A. M., on Thursday, January 3, 1907, and give testimony as above indicated.

Respectfully,

JMH

Acting Commissioner.

◇◇◇◇◇

Cherokee
2981

Muskogee, Indian Territory, January 17, 1907.

W. W. Hastings,
    Attorney for the Cherokee Nation,
        Muskogee, Indian Territory.

Dear Sir:

There is enclosed herewith a copy of the decision of the Commissioner to the Five Civilized Tribes, dated January 18, 1907, granting the application for the enrollment of Martha A. Miller as a citizen by intermarriage of the Cherokee Nation.

Respectfully,

Encl. H-34
JMH

Commissioner.

◇◇◇◇◇

Cherokee
2981

Muskogee, Indian Territory, January 19, 1907.

Martha A. Miller,
    Fairland, Indian Territory.

Dear Madam:

There is enclosed herewith a copy of the decision of the Commissioner to the Five Civilized Tribes, dated January 17, 1907, granting the application for your enrollment as a citizen by intermarriage of the Cherokee Nation.

Cherokee Intermarried White 1906
Volume I

You will be advised when your name has been placed upon the schedule of citizens of the Cherokee Nation and approved by the Secretary of the Interior.

Respectfully,

Encl. H-87
JMH

Commissioner.

◇◇◇◇◇

Cherokee 2981

W.W. HASTINGS.
ATTORNEY.

OFFICE OF

H.M. VANCE.
SECRETARY.

Attorney for the Cherokee Nation,
MUSKOGEE, I. T.

January 18, 1907.

The Commissioner to the Five Civilized Tribes,
    Muskogee, Indian Territory.

Sir:

    Receipt is acknowledged of the testimony and of your decision enrolling Martha A. Miller as a citizen by intermarriage of the Cherokee Nation. Time for protesting said decision is waived and I consent that said person may be placed upon the schedule immediately.

Yours very truly,
W. W. Hastings
Attorney for Cherokee Nation.

Cher IW 30
Trans from Cher 3321 3-13-07

◇◇◇◇◇

C.E.W.

DEPARTMENT OF THE INTERIOR,

COMMISSIONER TO THE FIVE CIVILIZED TRIBES.

In the matter of the application for the enrollment of

JAMES O. HALL

as a citizen by intermarriage of the Cherokee Nation.

Cherokee Intermarried White 1906
Volume I

CHEROKEE 3321

DEPARTMENT OF THE INTERIOR,
COMMISSION TO THE FIVE CIVILIZED TRIBES,
VINITA, I.T., SEPT., 22, 1900.

In the matter of the application of James O. Hall for the enrollment of himself, wife and one child as citizens of the Cherokee Nation, said Hall being duly sworn by Commissioner Needles, testified as follows:

Q What is your name? A James O. Hall.
Q What is your age? A 54.
Q What is your postoffice address? A Vinita.
Q What district do you live in? A Cooweescoowee.
Q Are you a recognized citizen of the Cherokee Nation? A Yes.
Q By blood or intermarriage? A Intermarriage.
Q What is the name of your wife? A Mary E. Davis, before I married her.
Q Is she a Cherokee by blood? A Yes.
Q What is her age? A 53.
Q When were you married to her? A '71.
Q Have you certificate of marriage? A Yes.
    Applicant presents a satisfactory certificate of marriage showing that he was married to one Miss Mary E. Davis, a citizen of the Cherokee Nation, on the 21st day of January, 1871.
Q What is the name of her father? A Martin Davis.
Q Is he living? A No sir.
Q What is the name of her mother? A Julia.
Q Is she living? A No sir.
Q What are the names of your children? A Janie P., 19 years old.
    On '96 roll, page 177, number 2252.
    Applicant on '80 roll, page 264, number 1185.
    Applicant's wife on '80 roll, page 264, number 1186.
    Applicant on '96 roll, page 309, number 528.
    Applicant's wife on '96 roll, page 177, number 2250.
Q You have all been continuous residents of the Cherokee Nation since your marriage?
A Yes.

The name of James O. Hall and his wife, Mary E. appears upon the authenticated roll of '80 and census roll of '96. The name of his daughter, Janie P. appears upon the '96 roll. They will all be duly identified according to page and number of the rolls as indicated i the testimony, and having made satisfactory proof of residence, said James O. Hall, his wife and child, named herein, will be listed for enrollment by this Commission, the former by intermarriage, and the two latter, by blood.

Cherokee Intermarried White 1906
Volume I

The undersigned, being first duly sworn, states that as stenographer to the Commission to the Five Civilized Tribes, he correctly recorded the testimony and proceedings in this case, and that the foregoing is a true and complete transcript of his stenographic notes thereof.

(Name Illegible)

Subscribed and sworn to before me this 28th day of Sept., 1900.

TB Needles
Commissioner.

◇◇◇◇◇

Cherokee 3321.

Department of the Interior,
Commission to the Five Civilized Tribes,
Muskogee, I. T., September 27, 1902.

In the matter of the application of James O. Hall for the enrollment of himself as a citizen by intermarriage, and for the enrollment of his wife, Mary E., and child Janie P., as citizens by blood of the Cherokee Nation.

L. B. Bell, being sworn and examined by the Commission, testified as follows:
Q Give your full name, age and residence? A L. B. Bell, 63, Vinita.
Q Are you a recognized citizen of the Cherokee Nation by blood? A Yes sir.
Q Are you acquainted with the applicant, James O. Hall? A Yes; he is a white man and married a Cherokee citizen.
Q What is his wife's name? A Mary.
Q What was her maiden name? A Davis.
Q How long have they been married? A I suppose they have been married since about '67; they married in the State of Georgia and my first acquaintance with Him was in '69 when they came out; it might have been '68.
Q You have been acquainted with James O. Hall since about '69? A Since about that; I have known him 32 or 3 years and maybe a little longer.
Q And he and his wife, Mary, lived together as husband and wife since you have known them? A Ever since they come here. They have lived neighbors to me, the last 12 years we have lived neighbors.
Q Have they lived together as husband and wife since you have known them? A Yes sir.
Q Were living together on the first day of September, 1902? A Yes sir.
Q He never has married any other woman since he come from Georgia? A No sir.
Q They have lived here in the Cherokee Nation since 1880, haven't they? A Yes sir.
Q Is his wife, Mary and his daughter Jennie[sic] P., alive? A Yes sir, both alive yesterday, although one of them is pretty sick, the girl.

Cherokee Intermarried White 1906
Volume I

The undersigned, being duly sworn, states that as stenographer to the Commission he correctly recorded the testimony and proceedings in this case, and that the foregoing is a true and correct transcript of his stenographic notes thereof.

E.G. Rothenberger

Subscribed and sworn to before me this 14th day of October, 1902.

BC Jones
Notary Public

◇◇◇◇◇

Cher
Supp'l to # 3321

Department of the Interior,
Commission to the Five Civilized Tribes,
Muskogee, I. T., October 11, 1902.

In the matter of the application of JAMES O. HALL, for the enrollment of himself as a citizen by intermarriage, his wife, MARY E. HALL, and his daughter, JANIE P. HALL, as citizens by blood, of the Cherokee Nation.

JAMES O. HALL, called as a witness, being duly sworn and examined by the Commission, testified as follows:

Q What is your name ? A James O. Hall.
Q What is your age at this time ? A Fifty six.
Q Your post office ? A Vinita.
Q Are your the same James O. Hall for whom application was made to this Commission for enrollment as an intermarried citizen in 1901 ? A Yes sir.
Q What is your wife's name ? A Mary E. Hall.
Q Is she living at this time ? A Yes sir.
Q Is she a citizen by blood of the Cherokee Nation ? A Yes sir.
Q When were you married to your wife Mary E. Hall ? A In 1869.
Q Are you and her both on the 1880 roll together as husband and wife ? A Yes sir.
Q Have you and your wife Mary E., lived together ever since 1880 as husband and wife? A Yes sir.
Q Have you never been separated ? A No sir.
Q Were you living together as husband and wife on September 1, 1902 ? A Yes sir.
Q Is this child Janie P., your child by your wife Mary E ? A Yes sir.
Q Is the child living now ? A Yes sir.
Q Has she lived in the Cherokee Nation all her life ? A Yes sir.
Q Have you and your wife Mary E. Hall lived in the Cherokee Nation all the time since 1880 up to the present time ? A Yes sir.

Cherokee Intermarried White 1906
Volume I

E. C. Bagwell, on oath states that, as stenographer to the Commission to the Five Civilized Tribes, he correctly recorded the testimony and proceedings had in the above entitled cause, and that the foregoing is an accurate transcript of his stenographic notes thereof.

E.C. Bagwell

Subscribed and sworn to before me this October 25, 1902.

B.C. Jones
Notary Public.

◇◇◇◇◇

Cherokee 3321.

DEPARTMENT OF THE INTERIOR,
COMMISSION TO THE FIVE CIVILIZED TRIBES.
Muskogee, Indian Territory, January 4, 1907.

In the Matter of the Application for the Enrollment of James O. Hall as a citizen by intermarriage of the Cherokee Nation.

APPEARANCES:
Applicant appears in person.

Cherokee Nation represented by H. M. Vance, in behalf of W. W. Hastings, Attorney.

James O. Hall being first duly sworn by B. P. Rasmus, Notary Public, testified as follows:

ON BEHALF OF COMMISSIONER.

Q What is your name?   A James O. Hall.
Q What is your age?   A 60 years old.
Q What is your post office address?
A Vinita.
Q Are you an applicant for enrollment as a citizen by intermarriage of the Cherokee Nation?   A Yes sir.
Q You have no Cherokee blood?
A No.
Q Your only claim to the right to enrollment as a citizen of the Cherokee Nation is by virtue of your marriage to a citizen by blood of the Cherokee Nation?
A Yes sir.
Q What is the name of the citizen through whom you claim the right to enrollment?
A Mary E. Davis.
Q Living or dead?
A Living.
Q When did you marry her?   A In '69.

Cherokee Intermarried White 1906
Volume I

Q Was she a recognized citizen of the Cherokee Nation at the time you married her?
A No sir; not at that time. I married in Georgia and we moved here and she was admitted.
Q After you came to the Cherokee Nation with your wife and she had been admitted by the tribal authorities, did you marry her again in accordance with the laws of the Cherokee Nation? A Yes sir; in '71.
Q You secured a license? A Yes.
Q In what district was that license issued?
A Cooweescoowee.
Q In what year did you marry her in the Cherokee Nation?
A In the Spring of '71.

The applicant presents a certified copy of marriage license issued by J. G. Mayes, district clerk of Cooweescoowee district, January 7, 1871, showing that on that date license of marriage was issued to James O. Hall, citizen of the United States, to marry Miss Mary E. Davis, citizen of the Cherokee Nation. Said certified copy also shows the following statement: "Married I suppose by George Cochran, January 21, 1871." This will be filed with and made a part of the record in this case.

Q Do you remember who married you?
A Yes sir.
Q What was his name?
A George Cochran.
Q This statement then in this certified copy of marriage license is true?
A Yes sir.
Q And you were married on the 21st of January, 1871?
A Yes sir.
Q Who was George Cochran?
A A Cherokee minister.
Q He was not an official of the Cherokee Nation?
A No sir.
Q Were you ever married prior to your marriage to Mary E. Davis?
A No sir.
Q Was she ever married before she married you?
A No sir.
Q Since you and she were married in 1871, have you continuously lived together as husband and wife?
A Yes sir.
Q And resided continuously in the Cherokee Nation?
A Yes sir.

The applicant James O. Hall is identified on the Cherokee Authenticated Tribal Roll of 1880, Delaware District, 1185. The name of his wife, Mary E. hall, is included in the approved partial roll of citizens by blood of the Cherokee Nation opposite No. 8160.

Cherokee Intermarried White 1906
Volume I

The undersigned being first duly sworn states that as stenographer to the Commission to the Five Civilized Tribes, she correctly recorded the testimony taken in the this case and that the foregoing is a full, true and correct transcript of her stenographic notes thereof.

Myrtle Hill

Subscribed and sworn to before me this the 5th day of January, 1907.

John E. Tidwell
Notary Public.

◇◇◇◇◇

Jany 7 1871 Issued licence[sic] of marriage to James O. Hall citizen of the U. S. to marry Miss Mary E. Davis citizen of the C N

Issued by J. B. Mayes Dist Clerk   Married I suppose by Geo Cochran Jany 21 1871

The undersigned being first duly sworn states that as stenographer to the Commissioner to the Five Civilized Tribes, she made the above copy and that the same is a true and correct copy of the marriage record now on file in this office.

Lola M Champlin

Subscribed and sworn to before me this 10 day of January 1907.

Chas E Webster
notary public.

◇◇◇◇◇

C.E.W.   Cherokee 3321

DEPARTMENT OF THE INTERIOR,

COMMISSIONER TO THE FIVE CIVILIZED TRIBES.

In the matter of the application for the enrollment of James O. Hall, as a citizen by intermarriage of the Cherokee Nation.

D E C I S I O N

THE RECORDS OF THIS OFFICE SHOW: That at Vinita, Indian Territory, September 22, 1900, James O. Hall appeared before the Commission to the Five Civilized Tribes and made application for the enrollment of himself as a citizen by intermarriage, and for the enrollment of his wife, Mary E. Hall, et al., as citizens by blood of the Cherokee Nation, has been heretofore disposed of and their rights to enrollment

Cherokee Intermarried White 1906
Volume I

will not be considered in this decision. Further proceedings in the matter of said application were had at Muskogee, Indian Territory, September 27, 1902, October 11, 1902, and January 4, 1907.

THE EVIDENCE IN THIS CASE SHOWS: That the applicant herein, James O. Hall, a white man, was married in accordance with Cherokee law January 21, 1871, to his wife, Mary E. Hall, nee Davis, who was at the time of said marriage a recognized citizen by blood of the Cherokee Nation, and whose name appears upon the approved partial roll of citizens by blood of the Cherokee Nation, opposite number 8160; that since said marriage the said James O. Hall and Mary E. Hall have resided together as husband and wife and have continuously lived in the Cherokee Nation. Said James O. Hall is identified on the Cherokee Authenticated tribal roll of 1880, and the Cherokee Census Roll of 1896 as an intermarried citizen of the Cherokee Nation.

IT IS, THEREFORE, ORDERED AND ADJUDGED: That in accordance with the decision of the Supreme Court of the United States, dated November 5, 1906, in the case of Daniel Red Bird et al., vs. the United States under the provision of Section 21 of the Act of Congress approved June 28, 1898, (30 Stat. 495), James O. Hall is entitled to enrollment as a citizen by intermarriage of the Cherokee Nation, and his application for enrollment as such is accordingly granted.

              Tams Bixby
                Commissioner.

Dated at Muskogee, Indian Territory,
this JAN 18 1907

◇◇◇◇◇

Cherokee
3321.

            Muskogee, Indian Territory, December 27, 1906.

James O. Hall,
  Vinita, Indian Territory.

Dear Sir:

  November 6, 1906, the United States Supreme Court held that white persons who intermarried with Cherokee citizens according to Cherokee law prior to November 1, 1875, are entitled to enrollment and allotments of land as citizens of the Cherokee Nation.

  You are advised that to properly determine your right to enrollment as a citizen by intermarriage of the Cherokee Nation, it will be necessary for you to appear before the Commissioner for the purpose of giving testimony as to the date of your marriage and whether or not your wife, by reason of your marriage to whom you claim the right to enrollment as a citizen of the Cherokee Nation, was a recognized citizen of the Cherokee

Cherokee Intermarried White 1906
Volume I

Nation at the time of your marriage to her, and whether or not you were married to her in accordance with Cherokee laws.

You are therefore directed to appear before the Commissioner at Muskogee, Indian Territory, at 9 o'clock A. M., on Friday, January 4, 1907, and give testimony as above indicated.

Respectfully,

H.J.C.   Acting Commissioner.

◇◇◇◇◇

Cherokee
3321

Muskogee, Indian Territory, January 18, 1907.

W. W. Hastings,
    Attorney for the Cherokee Nation,
        Muskogee, Indian Territory.

Dear Sir:

    There is enclosed herewith a copy of the decision of the Commissioner to the Five Civilized Tribes, dated January 18, 1907, granting the application for the enrollment of James O. Hall, as a citizen by intermarriage of the Cherokee Nation.

Respectfully,

Encl. HJ-23.   Commissioner.
HJC

◇◇◇◇◇

Cherokee 3321   W.W.HASTINGS.   OFFICE OF   H.M. VANCE.
                        ATTORNEY.   SECRETARY.

Attorney for the Cherokee Nation,
MUSKOGEE, I. T.

January 18, 1907.

The Commissioner to the Five Civilized Tribes,
    Muskogee, Indian Territory.

Sir:

    Receipt is acknowledged of the testimony and of your decision enrolling James O. Hall as a citizen by intermarriage of the Cherokee Nation. Time for protesting said decision is waived and I consent that said person may be placed upon the schedule immediately.

Cherokee Intermarried White 1906
Volume I

                Yours very truly,
                    W. W. Hastings
                    Attorney for Cherokee Nation.

◇◇◇◇◇

Cherokee
3321

                Muskogee, Indian Territory, January 21, 1907.

James O. Hall,
    Vinita, Indian Territory.

Dear Sir:

    There is enclosed herewith a copy of the decision of the Commissioner to the Five Civilized Tribes, dated January 18, 1907, granting the application for your enrollment as a citizen by intermarriage of the Cherokee Nation.

    You will be advised when your name has been placed upon the schedule of citizens of the Cherokee Nation and approved by the Secretary of the Interior.

                Respectfully,

E.R.C.   Commissioner.
Enc. E.C. 3.

◇◇◇◇◇

Cherokee
   I. W. 30

                Muskogee, Indian Territory, April 6, 1907

James O. Hall,
    Vinita, Indian Territory.

Dear Sir:

    The certified copy of the record of your marriage, filed by you in connection with your application for enrollment as a citizen by intermarriage of the Cherokee Nation, is returned to you herewith, copies of the same being retained in this office.

                Respectfully,

L M B   Acting Commissioner.
Encl. B-89

Cherokee Intermarried White 1906
Volume I

Cher IW 31
Trans from Cher 3475 3-13-07

DEPARTMENT OF THE INTERIOR.
COMMISSION TO THE FIVE CIVILIZED TRIBES.
VINITA, I. T., SEPTEMBER 25th, 1900.

IN THE MATTER OF THE APPLICATION OF William L. Trott, wife and children for enrollment as citizens of the Cherokee Nation, and he being sworn by Commissioner, C. R. Breckinridge, testified as follows:

Q What is your full name? A William L. Trott.
Q How old are you? A Fifty six.
Q What is your Postoffice? A Vinita.
Q What district do you live in? A Cooweescoowee.
Q For whom do you apply? A Myself, wife and two children, and two orphans that live with me. My brother's children.
Q Do you apply for yourself as a Cherokee by blood? A Yes sir.
Q What proportion of Cherokee blood do you claim? A About one thirty second.
Q Is your wife a Cherokee? A A white woman.
Q How long have you lived in the Cherokee Nation? A Since 1857, except a little time during the war.
Q What district were you in in 1880? A In Cooweescoowee.
Q In 1896, what district? A Cooweescoowee.
Q Give me your wifes[sic] name? A Louisa J.
Q How old is she? A She is fifty.
Q When did you marry her? A In 1869.
Q She is with you on the rolls of 1880, and 1896, is she? A Yes sir.
Q She has lived with you ever since your marriage, has she? A Yes sir.
Q Give me the names of your children please? A Dot Fay.
Q How old is she? A Sixteen.
Q Is that the only one under age? A Yes sir.
  (1880 Roll, Page 330, #2756, W. L. Trott, Delaware District.)
  (1880 Roll, page 330, #2757, J. L. Trott, Delaware District)
  (1896 Roll, Page 270, #4831, Wm. L. Trott, Cooweescoowee D'st)
  (1896 Roll, Page 327, #1043.1/2, Lou J. Trott, Cooweescoowee)
  (1896 Roll, Page 270, #4833, Dot F. Trott, Cooweescoowee)

The applicant applies for the enrollment of himself wife and child: He is identified on the rolls of 1880 and 1896, as a native Cherokee; he has lived in the Cherokee Nation since 1857, and he will be listed now for enrollment as a Cherokee by blood.

His wife is identified with him on the roll of 1880 and 1896, and she will ne[sic] enrolled now as a Cherokee by adoption.

The child, Dot Fay is identified with her parents on the roll of 1896; she is living now, and she will be listed for enrollment as a Cherokee by blood.

Cherokee Intermarried White 1906
Volume I

The undersigned, being sworn, states that as stenographer to the Commission to the Five Civilized Tribes, he correctly recorded the testimony and proceedings in this case, and that the foregoing is a true and complete transcript of his stenographic notes thereof.

R.R. Cravens

Subscribed and sworn to before me,
this 26th day of September, 1900.

TB Needles
COMMISSIONER.

◇◇◇◇◇

R.

DEPARTMENT OF THE INTERIOR.
Commission to the Five Civilized Tribes.
Muskogee, Indian Territory, September 29th, 1902.

In the matter of the application of William L. Trott for the enrollment of himself as a citizen by blood of the Cherokee Nation; for the enrollment of his wife Louisa J. Trott as a citizen by intermarriage of the Cherokee and for the enrollment of his child Dor F. Trott as a citizen by blood of the Cherokee Nation.

Supplemental to #3475.

Appearances:

James S. Davenport for Applicant.
J. C. Starr for Cherokee Nation.

JAMES S. DAVENPORT, being duly sworn, testified as follows:
Examination by the Commission.
Q. Name, age and post office? A. James S. Davenport, 38, Vinita, I. T.
Q. Are you acquainted with Louisa J. Trott? A. Yes, sir.
Q. Are you acquainted with her husband? A. Yes, sir.
Q. What is his name? A. William L. Trott.
Q. How long have you known her? A. I have known her since 1891.
Q. Was she married to William L. Trott at that time? A. Yes, sir
Q. Have she and William L. Trott continued to live together as husband and wife since that time? A. Yes, sir.
Q. Lived all the time in the Cherokee Nation? A. Yes, sir.
Q. Never been separated during that time? A. No, sir.
Q. They were living together on the first day of September, 1902, were they?
A. Yes, sir.

Cherokee Intermarried White 1906
Volume I

Jesse O. Carr, being first duly sworn, states that as stenographer to the Commission to the Five Civilized Tribes he reported the above entitled case and that the foregoing is a true and complete transcript of his stenographic notes thereof.

Jesse O. Carr

Subscribed and sworn to before me this 8th day of October, 1902.

BC Jones
Notary Public.

◇◇◇◇◇

Cher-3475.

DEPARTMENT OF THE INTERIOR.
Commission to the Five Civilized Tribes.
Muskogee, I.T., October 29, 1902.

In the matter of the application of William L. Trott for the enrollment of himself and his daughter Dot F., as citizens by blood of the Cherokee nation[sic], and for the enrollment of his wife Louisa J., as a citizen by intermarriage.

William L. Trott, being first duly sworn and examined, testified as follows:

Q What is your name? A William L. Trott.
Q How old are you at this time? A Fifty-eight.
Q What is your postoffice address? A Vinita, I. T.
Q Are you a citizen by blood of the Cherokee nation[sic]? A Yes sir.
Q What is your wife's name? A Lpuisa[sic] J. Trott.
Q Is she a white woman? A Yes sir.
Q And an applicant for enrollment as a citizen by intermarriage of the Cherokee nation? A Yes sir.
Q When were you married to your wife Louisa J. Trott? A In 1869; about that time.
Q Had you ever been married prior to your marriage to your wife? A Yes.
Q How many time? A Once.
Q What was your first wife's name? A Malinda Stone.
Q Was she living or dead when you married Louisa J.? A Dead.
Q Had your wife ever been married prior to her marriage to you? A No.
Q You are her first husband? and she is your second wife? A Yes sir.
Q Have you and your wife Louisa J. lived together since your marriage up to the present time? A Yes sir.
Q Never separated? A No sir.
Q You were living together as husband and wife on the 1st day of September, 1902? A Yes sir.
Q You and Louis J. have lived in the Cherokee nation since 1880 up to the present time? A Yes sir.

Cherokee Intermarried White 1906
Volume I

Q You have never lived out of the Indian Territory? A No.
Q Is this child Dot F. your child by your wife Louisa J.? A Yes sir.
Q Is she living now? A Yes sir.
Q Lived all her life in the Cherokee nation? A Yes sir.

----o---

Frances R. Lane upon oath states that as stenographer to the Commission to the Five Civilized Tribes she correctly recorded the testimony taken in the above case, and that the foregoing is an accurate transcript of her stenographic notes thereof.

Frances R. Lane

Subscribed and sworn to before me this November 7th, 1902.

BC Jones
Notary Public.

◇◇◇◇◇

Cherokee No. 3475.

DEPARTMENT OF THE INTERIOR.
COMMISSIONER TO THE FIVE CIVILIZED TRIBES.

Muskogee, Indian Territory, January 4th, 1907.

In the matter of the application for the enrollment of Louisa J. Trott as a citizen by intermarriage of the Cherokee Nation.

Louisa J. Trott, being first duly sworn by B. P. Rasmus, testifies as follows:

BY THE COMMISSIONER:

Q What is your name? A Louisa J. Trott.
Q How old are you? A 56.
Q What is your post office address? A Vinita.
Q You are an applicant for enrollment as a citizen by intermarriage of the Cherokee Nation, are you? A Yes, sir.
Q You have no Cherokee blood? A No, sir.
Q You only claim the right of enrollment as a citizen of the Nation by virtue of your marriage to a citizen by blood of the Nation do you? A Yes, sir.
Q What is the name of the citizen through whom you claim the right to enrollment?
[sic] W. L. Trott.

Cherokee Intermarried White 1906
Volume I

Q Is he living? A Yes, sir.
Q When were you married to him? A 1869, 4th day of February.
Q Was he your first husband? A Yes, sir.
Q And you were his first wife, were you? A No, sir, he was married before.
Q Was his former wife living or dead at the time of your marriage? A Dead, he[sic] died for[sic] or five months after they were married.
Q Was W. J[sic]. Trott recognized as a citizen of the Cherokee Nation at the time you married him? A Yes, sir.
Q He was living in the Cherokee Nation, was he? A Yes, sir.
Q Since your marriage to him have you and he continuously lived together as husband and wife and lived in the Cherokee Nation? A Yes, sir.
Q You have never been out of the Nation for any length of time since your marriage? A No, sir.

The applicant Louisa J. Trott is identified on the Cherokee Authenticated Tribal Roll of 1880, Delaware District, No. 2759. The name of her husband, W. L. Trott is included in the approved partial roll of citizens by blood of the Cherokee Nation, opposite No. 8480.

Q Have you any evidence of a documentary character showing the marriage of yourself to W. L. Trott.[sic] A No, sir.
Q You have no marriage licence[sic] or cirtificate[sic] to present at this time? A No, sir, not at this time; we have a cirtificate[sic] but we haven't got it, we lost it this morning.
Q You had a cirtificate[sic], but lost it this morning? A Yes, sir.
Q You will make an attempt to get that cirtificate[sic] and send it to this office will you? A Yes, sir.

WITNESS EXCUSED.

R. Elma Lane, upon oath, states that she reported the proceedings in the above entitled cause and that the foregoing is a true and correct transcript of her stenographic notes thereof.

R. Elma Lane

Subscribed and sworn to before me this 5th day of January, 1907.

Chas E Webster
Notary Public.

Cherokee Intermarried White 1906
Volume I

C.E.W. Cherokee 3475.

DEPARTMENT OF THE INTERIOR,

COMMISSIONER TO THE FIVE CIVILIZED TRIBES.

In the matter of the application for the enrollment of Louisa J. Trott, as a citizen by intermarriage of the Cherokee Nation.

D E C I S I O N

THE RECORDS OF THIS OFFICE SHOW: That at Vinita, Indian Territory, September 25, 1900, William L. Trott appeared before the Commission to the Five Civilized Tribes and made application for the enrollment of his wife, Louisa J. Trott, as a citizen by intermarriage, and for the enrollment of himself, et al., as citizens by blood of the Cherokee Nation has been heretofore disposed of and their rights to enrollment will not be considered in this decision. Further proceedings in the matter of said application were had at Muskogee, Indian Territory, September 29, 1902, October 29, 1902, and January 4, 1907.

THE EVIDENCE IN THIS CASE SHOWS: That the applicant herein, Louisa J. Trott, a white woman, was married February 4, 1869 to one William L. Trott, who was at the time of said marriage a recognized citizen by blood of the Cherokee Nation, and whose name appears upon the approved partial roll of citizens by blood of the Cherokee Nation, opposite number 8480; that since said marriage the said William L. Trott and Louisa J. Trott have resided together as husband and wife and have continously[sic] lived in the Cherokee Nation up to and including September 1, 1902. Said Louisa J. Trott is identified on the Cherokee Authenticated tribal roll of 1880, and the Cherokee Census Roll of 1896 as an intermarried citizen of the Cherokee Nation.

IT IS, THEREFORE, ORDERED AND ADJUDGED: That in accordance with the decision of the Supreme Court of the United States, dated November 5, 1906, in the case of Daniel Red Bird et al., vs the United States under the provision of Section 21 of the Act of Congress approved June 28, 1898, (30 Stat. 495), Louisa J. Trott is entitled to enrollment as a citizen by intermarriage of the Cherokee Nation, and her application for enrollment as such is accordingly granted.

Tams Bixby
Commissioner.

Dated at Muskogee, Indian Territory,
this   JAN 17 1907

Cherokee Intermarried White 1906
Volume I

DEPARTMENT OF THE INTERIOR.
COMMISSIONER TO THE FIVE CIVILIZED TRIBES.

CHIEF CLERK,
    CHEROKEE LAND OFFICE.

DEAR SIR:

    The records of this office show   Louisa J Trott

listed on Cherokee card No. 3475 to be prima facie entitled to enrollment as intermarried of the Cherokee Nation for the following reason, viz: is on schedule for Departmental Approval

                            Respectfully,

                                              Commissioner.

Dated   Feby 8th 1907

                  ◇◇◇◇◇

Cherokee
  3475.

                        Muskogee, Indian Territory, December 27, 1906.

Louisa J. Trott,
    Vinita, Indian Territory.

Dear Madam:

    November 6, 1906, the United States Supreme Court held that white persons who intermarried with Cherokee citizens according to Cherokee law prior to November 1, 1875, are entitled to enrollment and allotments of land as citizens of the Cherokee Nation.

    You are advised that to properly determine your right to enrollment as a citizen by intermarriage of the Cherokee Nation, it will be necessary for you to appear before the Commissioner for the purpose of giving testimony as to the date of your marriage and whether or not your husband, by reason of your marriage to whom you claim the right to enrollment as a citizen by intermarriage of the Cherokee Nation, was a recognized Cherokee citizen at the time of your marriage to him.

Cherokee Intermarried White 1906
Volume I

You are therefore directed to appear before the Commissioner at Muskogee, Indian Territory, at 9 o'clock A. M., on Friday, January 4, 1907, and give testimony as above indicated.

Respectfully,

H.J.C.   Acting Commissioner.

Cherokee
3475

Muskogee, Indian Territory, January 17, 1907.

W. W. Hastings,
    Attorney for the Cherokee Nation,
        Muskogee, Indian Territory.

Dear Sir:

    There is enclosed herewith a copy of the decision of the Commissioner to the Five Civilized Tribes, dated January 17, 1907, granting the application for the enrollment of Louisa J. Trott as a citizen by intermarriage of the Cherokee Nation.

Respectfully,

Encl. H-35   Commissioner.
JMH

Cherokee 3475   W.W.HASTINGS.   OFFICE OF   H.M. VANCE.
                         ATTORNEY.   SECRETARY.

Attorney for the Cherokee Nation,
MUSKOGEE, I. T.

January 18, 1907.

The Commissioner to the Five Civilized Tribes,
    Muskogee, Indian Territory.

Sir:

    Receipt is acknowledged of the testimony and of your decision enrolling Louisa J. Trott as a citizen by intermarriage of the Cherokee Nation. Time for protesting said decision is waived and I consent that said person may be placed upon the schedule immediately.

Yours very truly,
W. W. Hastings
Attorney for Cherokee Nation.

Cherokee Intermarried White 1906
Volume I

◇◇◇◇◇

Cherokee
3475

Muskogee, Indian Territory, January 21, 1907.

Louisa J. Trott,
    Vinita, Indian Territory.

Dear Madam:

    There is enclosed herewith copy of the decision of the Commissioner to the Five Civilized Tribes, dated January 17, 1907, granting the application for your enrollment as a citizen by intermarriage of the Cherokee Nation.

    You will be advised when your name has been placed upon the schedule of citizens of the Cherokee Nation and approved by the Secretary of the Interior.

Respectfully,

Enc M - 15
M.T.M.
                          Commissioner.

Cher IW 32
Trans from Cher 3529 3-13-07

◇◇◇◇◇

CFB

DEPARTMENT OF THE INTERIOR,

COMMISSIONER TO THE FIVE CIVILIZED TRIBES.

In the matter of the application for the enrollment of

JENNIE WILLIAMS

as a citizen by intermarriage of the Cherokee Nation.

CHEROKEE 3529.

◇◇◇◇◇

Cherokee Intermarried White 1906
Volume I

Department of the Interior,
Commission to the Five Civilized Tribes,
Vinita, I.T., September 26, 1900.

In the matter of the application of Jennie Williams for the enrollment of herself and children as Cherokee citizens; being sworn and examined by Commissioner Breckinridge she testified as follows:

Q Give me your name? A Jennie Williams.
Q How old are you? A I guess about 52.
Q What is your post-office? A Miles.
Q What district do you live in? A Cooweescoowee Now.
Q Who is it you want to have put on the roll? A Myself, and four children I believe.
Q You apply as a Cherokee by blood? A No sir.
Q What are you? A White I reckon. The doubted me and put me on the white roll.
Q How long have you lived in the Cherokee Nation? A Born and raised here.
Q Lived here all your life[sic] A Yes sir.
Q What is the name of your father? A J.M. Bryan.
Q Cherokee or white man? A White man I reckon.
Q Dead or alive? A Dead.
Q Name of your mother? A I don't know.
Q When were you married? A 1870.
Q Were you married to Williams in 1870? A Yes sir.
Q That the only time you have ever been married? A Yes sir.
Q What district did you live in in 1880? A Goingsnake.
Q What district in 1896? A Cooweescoowee I believe.
Q Give me the names of these children? A Addie May.
Q How old is that child? A 15
Q What is the name of the next child? A Lottie.
Q How old is that child? A She will be 14 in January.
Q What is the name of the next child? A Davis Della.
Q How old is she? A She is about nine years old. That's all I got; the others are over age.
Q These children are all living now? A Yes sir.
Q What is the name of their father? A David Williams.
Q Cherokee, was he? A Yes sir.
Q He is dead? A Yes sir.
Q When did he die? A I believe it was 1889
Q You have got one child nine years old? A She may be ten; he got killed in December and she was born after he got killed.
1880 roll page 494 #2059 Jennie William[sic], Goingsnake Dist, as a native Cherokee; 31 years old.
1880 roll for husband, page 494 #2058 Dave Williams, Goingsnake District, native Cherokee/[sic]
1896 roll page 831 #---- Jennie Williams, Goingsnake District, intermarried white.
1896 roll page 805 #2365 Addie Williams, Goingsnake Dist;

Cherokee Intermarried White 1906
Volume I

1896 roll page 805 #2366 Lotta Williams, Goinganske[sic] Dist;
1896 roll page 805 #2367 as David Williams, Goingsnake   "
Q You have never married since your husband's death? A No sir.

    Com'r Breckinridge: The applicant applies for the enrollment of herself and three children; she is identified with her Cherokee husband on the roll of 1880; he died some years ago and she has not married since his death; she has lived in the Cherokee Nation all her life and she will be listed now for enrollment as a Cherokee by adoption.
    Her three children enumerated in the testimony are identified with her on the roll of 1896; they are all living at this time and they will be listed now for enrollment as Cherokees by blood.

    M.D. Green, being first duly sworn, states that as stenographer to the Commission to the Five Civilized Tribes he correctly recorded the testimony and proceedings in this case and that the foregoing is a true and complete transcript of his stenographic notes thereof.

                        MD Green

Subscribed and sworn to before me this 28 day of September 1900.

                        TB Needles
                        Commissioner.

◇◇◇◇◇

                        Cherokee 3529.

DEPARTMENT OF THE INTERIOR,
COMMISSION TO THE FIVE CIVILIZED TRIBES.
Muskogee, I. T., October 13, 1902.

    In the matter of the application of Jennie Williams, for the enrollment of herself as a citizen by intermarriage, and for the enrollment of her children, Addie M., Lottie and Davis[sic] D[sic]. Williams as citizens by blood of the Cherokee Nation.

    Jennie Williams, being first duly sworn and examined by the Commission, testified as follows:

Q What is your name? A J. E. Williams.
Q Jennie? A Yes sir.
Q How old are you? A About 52 I think.
Q What is your postoffice? A Miles.
Q You are a white woman are you? A Yes sir.
Q You are on the roll of 1880? A Yes sir.
Q As an intermarried white? A Yes sir.
Q What was the name of your husband at that time? A David Williams.
Q Is he dead? A Yes sir.
Q When did he die? A He has been dead about 10 or 11 years I guess.

Cherokee Intermarried White 1906
Volume I

Q Did you live with him in the Cherokee Nation from the time you were married . . . . . ?
A All my live, ever since I was married; never was out of it.
Q You never was separated? A No sir.
Q Have you married since his death? A No sir.
Q Still his widow? A Yes sir.
Q Have you lived in the Cherokee Nation ever since his death? A Yes sir.
Q How many children have you? A I have got five at home and one grand-child.
Q What is the name of your grand-child? A Ben Williams.
Q Is it enrolled? A Yes sir.
Q How many children have you under age? A I have got three.
Q Are they all living at home with you? A I have got three under age all living at home, the others enrolled themselves.
Q Who enrolled your grand-child? A Its mother.

R. Palmer, being first duly sworn, states that as stenographer to the Commission, to the Five Civilized Tribes, he correctly recorded the testimony and proceedings in the above case and that the foregoing is a true and complete transcript of his stenographic notes thereof.

R. Palmer

Subscribed and sworn to before me this 22nd day of December, 1902.

BC Jones
Notary Public.

◇◇◇◇◇

Cher
3529

Department of the Interior,
Commission to the Five Civilized Tribes,
Vinita, I. T., January 15, 1903.

In the matter of the application of JENNIE WILLIAMS, for the enrollment of herself as a citizen by intermarriage, and her children, ADDIE M., LOTTIE and DAVIE S. WILLIAMS, as citizens by blood, of the Cherokee Nation:

JENNIE E. WILLIAMS, being first duly sworn, and examined, testified as follows:

Examined by the Commission:

Q What is your name ? A J. E. Williams.
Q What does the "J" stand for ? A Jennie.
Q Jennie E. Williams ? A Yes sir.
Q That is your correct name is it ? A Yes sir.

Cherokee Intermarried White 1906
Volume I

Q How old are you ? A I am fifty three.
Q What is your post office address ? A Miles.
Q You are a white woman are you ? A Yes sir.
Q Claiming as a citizen by intermarriage of the Cherokee Nation ? A Yes sir.
Q You submitted some testimony in your case at Muskogee didn't you last October ?
A Yes sir.
Q What are your children's names ?
A One is named Addie May.
Q Addie M ? A Yes sir.
Q The next one ? A Lottie.
Q And the next one ? A Davie Stella.
Q It isn't Davis ? A No sir, its[sic] Davie.
Q Who made application for her enrollment ? A I did.
Q How did you give this child's name ?
A I gave it Davie Stella; I don't know how they got that.
Q That is the name it has gone by all its life ?
A Yes sir, we call her Davie.
Q This child appears on the roll of 1896 as David, that's wrong is it ? A Her father's name is David, her real name is David, but we call her Davie.
Q Well, what is her correct name ? A Davie Stella; it would not be right to call her David, we call it Davie.
Q That's the name you gave her, Davie Stella ? A Yes sir.
Q Its[sic] a girl is it ? A Yes sir.
Q You wish the child enrolled then as Davie S. Williams ?
A Davie S. Williams, she isn't known b any other name but Davie.

I, E. C. Bagwell, a stenographer to the Commission to the Five Civilized Tribes, on oath states that the foregoing is an accurate transcript of the stenographic notes of the testimony and proceedings had in the above entitled cause, as the same were reported by Jesse O. Carr, stenographer, and by him read to me.

EC Bagwell

Subscribed and sworn to before me this February 20, 1903.

Samuel Foreman
Notary Public.

Cherokee Intermarried White 1906
Volume I

C.D.B.   Cherokee 3529.

DEPARTMENT OF THE INTERIOR
COMMISSIONER TO THE FIVE CIVILIZED TRIBES.
MUSKOGEE, IND. TER., JANUARY 4, 1907.

In the matter of the application of JENNIE WILLIAMS for enrollment as a citizen by intermarriage of the Cherokee Nation.

APPEARANCES: Applicant appears in person;

Cherokee Nation represented by H. M. Vance, on behalf of W. W. Hastings, Attorney.

On Behalf of Commissioner:

Q. What is your name? A. Jennie Williams.
Q. What is your age? A. Fifty-six this last October.
Q. What is your postoffice address? A. Vinita.
Q. Are you an applicant for enrollment as a citizen by intermarriage of the Cherokee Nation? A. Yes sir.
Q. You have no Cherokee blood? A. No sir, not that I know of.
Q. Your only claim to enrollment as a citizen of the Cherokee Nation is by virtue of your marriage to a citizen of that Nation? A. Yes sir.
Q. What is the name of the citizen through whom you claim the right to enrollment? A. David Williams.
Q. Is he living or dead? A. He is dead.
Q. When did he die? A. I believe he died in 1889-1888 or 1889.
Q. When did you marry him? A. I was married to him on the fourteenth of February, 1870.
Q. Was he a recognized citizen of the Cherokee Nation at the time you married him? A. Yes sir, and all his people.
Q. Living in the Cherokee Nation? A. Yes sir.
Q. Was he your first husband? A. Yes sir.
Q. Were you his first wife? A. Yes sir.
Q. From the time of your marriage to him in accordance with Cherokee laws. 1870 did you and he continuously live together as husband and wife until his death? A. Yes sir.
Q. Since his death have you remarried? A. No sir.
Q. Has your residence been continuously in the Cherokee Nation from 1870 until the present time? A. Yes sir, never lived out.
Q. Were you married by a Minister? A. Yes sir, by a Minister of the Gospel.
Q. Did he give you a Certificate of marriage? A. No sir.
Q. Have you any documentary evidence of your marriage?
A. No sir; I have several witnesses.

Cherokee Intermarried White 1906
Volume I

Jennie Williams, the applicant, is identified on the Cherokee Tribal Roll of 1880, Going Snake District, No. 2059.

The undersigned, being first duly sworn, states that as stenographer to the Commissioner to the Five Civilized Tribes she correctly recorded the testimony taken in this case, and that the above and foregoing is a full, true and correct transcript of her stenographic notes thereof.

Lucy M Bowman

Subscribed and sworn to before me this 5th day of January, 1907.

John E Tidwell
Notary Public.

◇◇◇◇◇

C.F.B.   Cherokee 3529.

DEPARTMENT OF THE INTERIOR,
COMMISSIONER TO THE FIVE CIVILIZED TRIBES.

In the matter of the application for the enrollment of Jennie Williams as a citizen by intermarriage of the Cherokee Nation.

D E C I S I O N

THE RECORDS OF THIS OFFICE SHOW: That at Vinita, Indian Territory, September 26, 1900, Jennie Williams appeared before the Commission to the Five Civilized Tribes, and made application for the enrollment of herself as a citizen by intermarriage, and for the enrollment of her children, Addie M., et al., as citizens by blood of the Cherokee Nation, has heretofore been disposed of and their rights to enrollment will not be considered in this decision. Further proceedings in the matter of said application were had at Muskogee, Indian Territory, October 13, 1902, at Vinita, Indian Territory, January 15, 1903, and at Muskogee, Indian Territory, January 4, 1907.

THE EVIDENCE IN THIS CASE SHOWS: That the applicant herein, Jennie Williams, a white woman, married in the year of 1870, one David Williams, who was at the time of said marriage a recognized citizen by blood of the Cherokee Nation, and whose name appears upon the Cherokee Authenticated tribal roll of 1880, Going Snake District, Page 494, opposite number 2058; that the said David and Jennie Williams resided together continuously as husband and wife from the time of their marriage until the death of the said David Williams, which occurred in the year 1888 or 1889; that since the death of the said David Williams, said Jennie Williams has not married, and that her residence has been continuously in the Cherokee Nation since her marriage to David Williams in 1870. Said applicant is identified on the Cherokee authenticated tribal roll of

Cherokee Intermarried White 1906
Volume I

1880 and the Cherokee census roll of 1896, as an intermarried citizen of the Cherokee Nation.

IT IS, THEREFORE, ORDERED AND ADJUDGED: That in accordance with the decision of the Supreme Court of the United States, dated November 5, 1906, in the case of Daniel Red Bird et al., vs. the United States under the provision of Section 21 of the Act of Congress approved June 28, 1898, (30 Stat., 495), Jennie Williams is entitled to enrollment as a citizen by intermarriage of the Cherokee Nation, and her application for enrollment as such is accordingly granted.

Tams Bixby
Commissioner.

Dated at Muskogee, Indian Territory,
this   JAN 17 1907

◇◇◇◇◇

Cherokee
3529.

Muskogee, Indian Territory, December 27, 1906.

Jennie Williams,
  Miles, Indian Territory.

Dear Madam:

November 6, 1906, the United States Supreme Court held that white persons who intermarried with Cherokee citizens according to Cherokee law prior to November 1, 1875, are entitled to enrollment and allotments of land as citizens of the Cherokee Nation.

You are advised that to properly determine your right to enrollment as a citizen by intermarriage of the Cherokee Nation, it will be necessary for you to appear before the Commissioner for the purpose of giving testimony as to the date of your marriage and whether or not your husband, by reason of your marriage to whom you claim the right to enrollment as a citizen by intermarriage of the Cherokee Nation, was a recognized Cherokee citizen at the time of your marriage to him.

You are therefore directed to appear before the Commissioner at Muskogee, Indian Territory, at 9 o'clock A. M., on Friday, January 4, 1907, and give testimony as above indicated.

Respectfully,

H.J.C.   Acting Commissioner.

◇◇◇◇◇

Cherokee Intermarried White 1906
Volume I

Cherokee
3529

Muskogee, Indian Territory, January 17, 1907.

W. W. Hastings,
    Attorney for the Cherokee Nation,
        Muskogee, Indian Territory.

Dear Sir:

    There is enclosed herewith a copy of the decision of the Commissioner to the Five Civilized Tribes, dated January 17, 1907, granting the application for the enrollment of Jennie Williams as a citizen by intermarriage of the Cherokee Nation.

                Respectfully,

E.R.C.   Commissioner.

Enc. E.C.
    -40

◇◇◇◇◇

Cherokee 3529   W.W. HASTINGS, ATTORNEY.   OFFICE OF   H.M. VANCE, SECRETARY.

Attorney for the Cherokee Nation,
MUSKOGEE, I. T.

                                                   January 18, 1907.

The Commissioner to the Five Civilized Tribes,
    Muskogee, Indian Territory.

Sir:

    Receipt is acknowledged of the testimony and of your decision enrolling Jennie Williams as a citizen by intermarriage of the Cherokee Nation. Time for protesting said decision is waived and I consent that said person may be placed upon the schedule immediately.

                Yours very truly,
                W. W. Hastings
                Attorney for Cherokee Nation.

◇◇◇◇◇

Cherokee Intermarried White 1906
Volume I

Cherokee
3529

Muskogee, Indian Territory, January 19, 1907.

Jennie Williams,
Vinita, Indian Territory.

Dear Madam:

There is enclosed herewith a copy of the decision of the Commissioner to the Five Civilized Tribes, dated January 17, 1907, granting your application for enrollment as a citizen by intermarriage of the Cherokee Nation.

You will be advised when your name has been placed upon a schedule of citizens of the Cherokee Nation and approved by the Secretary of the Interior.

Respectfully,

Encl. H-81
JMH

Commissioner.

Cher IW 33
Trans from Cher 3782 3-13-07

◇◇◇◇◇

C.F.B.

DEPARTMENT OF THE INTERIOR,

COMMISSIONER TO THE FIVE CIVILIZED TRIBES.

In the matter of the application for the enrollment of

HENRY DONNELLY

as a citizen by intermarriage of the Cherokee Nation.

CHEROKEE 3782.

◇◇◇◇◇

Cherokee Intermarried White 1906
Volume I

Department of the Interior,
Commission to the Five Civilized Tribes,
Vinita, I.T., September 29, 1900.

In the matter of the application of Henry Donnelly for the enrollment of himself as a Cherokee by intermarriage and his wife and children as Cherokees by blood; being sworn and examined by Commissioner Needles, he testified as follows:

Q What is your name? A Henry Donnelly.
Q How old are you? A 60.
Q What is your post office address? A Vinita.
Q What district do you live in? A Cooweescoowee.
Q Are you a recognized citizen of the Cherokee Nation? A Yes, sir.
Q By blood or intermarriage? A By intermarriage.
Q What is the name of your wife? A Emma J.
Q When did you marry her? A In 1869.
Q She is a white person? A No, sir, a Cherokee.
Q What was her name before you married her? A Daniels.
Q What is her father's name? A John Daniels.
Q He living? A No, sir.
Q Her mother's name? A Martha.
Q She living? A No, sir.
Q What is the names of your children? A James, 29 years old.
Q He must apply for himself; have you got any children under 21?
A I have got three.
Q What are their name? A Emma, 17 years old.
Q What is the name of the next one? A Paul, 14 years old.
Q The next one? A Ada, 10 years old.
(Henry Donnelly on 1880 roll, page 95, No. 938, Henry Donley[sic], Cooweescoowee district. Emma J. Donnelly on 1880 roll, page 95, No. 939, Emma Donley, Cooweescoowee district. Henry Donnelly on 1896 roll, page 301, No. 297, Cooweescoowee district. Emma Donnelly on 1896 roll, page 147, No. 1435, Cooweescoowee district. Paul Donnelly on 1896 roll, page 147, No. 1440, Cooweescoowee district. Ada Donnelly on 1896 roll, page 147, No. 1441, Cooweescoowee district.)
Q These children all alive and living with you at this time? A Yes, sir.

The name of Henry Donnelly and his wife, Emma J., are found upon the census roll of 1880, as well as the census roll of 1896, and the names of his children are found upon the census roll of 1896. They are all duly identified according to the page and number of the roll as indicated in the testimony, and having made satisfactory proof as to their residence, said Henry Donnelly, his wife, Emma J., and his children as enumerated in the testimony will be duly listed for enrollment by this Commission as Cherokee citizens by blood.

-------o-------

Bruce C. Jones, being duly sworn, says that as stenographer to the Commission to the Five Civilized Tribes he correctly recorded the proceedings and testimony in the

Cherokee Intermarried White 1906
Volume I

above case, and the foregoing is a true and complete transcript of his stenographic notes thereof.

Bruce C Jones

Sworn to and subscribed before me this the 2nd of October, 1900.

TB Needles
Commissioner.

◇◇◇◇◇

R.

DEPARTMENT OF THE INTERIOR.
Commission to the Five Civilized Tribes.
Muskogee, Indian Territory, October 6th, 1902.

In the matter of the application of Henry Donnelly for the enrollment of himself as a citizen by intermarriage of the Cherokee Nation and for the enrollment of his wife, Emma J. Donnelly, and his children, Emma, Paul and Ada Donnelly, as citizens by blood of the Cherokee Nation.

Supplemental to #3782.

Applicant appears in person.
Cherokee Nation by J. C. Starr.

HENRY DONNELLY, being duly sworn, testified as follows:
Examination by the Commission.
Q. Give us your full name? A. Henry Donnelly.
Q. How old are you? A. 65.
Q. What is your post office? A. Vinita.
Q. Are you the same Henry Donnelly who made application to this Commission September 29th, 1906, for enrollment as an intermarried citizen? A. Yes, sir.
Q. What is the name of your wife? A. Emma J.
Q. When were you married to her? A. '69, I think.
Q. Have you been living with her in the Cherokee Nation ever since that time? A. Yes, sir.
Q. Continuously? A. Yes, sir.
Q. Never made your home any where else? A. No, sir.
Q. Were you ever married before you married Emma J.? A. No, sir.
Q. Was she ever married before she married you? A. No, sir.
Q. How many children have you? A. Seven.
Q. Only three of them that is under age? A. Four. Under age?

Cherokee Intermarried White 1906
Volume I

Q. Yes, sir. A. Yes, sir; we got three.
Q. Emma, Paul and Ada? A. Yes, sir.
Q. Are they living with you now? A. Yes, sir.
Q. In the Cherokee Nation? A. Yes, sir.
Q. You are a white man? A. Yes, sir.

++++++++++++++++++++++++++++++++

Jesse O. Carr, being first duly sworn, states that as stenographer to the Commission to the Five Civilized Tribes he reported the above entitled case and that the foregoing is a true and complete transcript of his stenographic notes thereof.

Jesse O. Carr

Subscribed and sworn to before me this 5th day of November, 1902.

BC Jones
Notary Public.

◇◇◇◇◇

DEPARTMENT OF THE INTERIOR.
COMMISSION TO THE FIVE CIVILIZED TRIBES.
AUXILIARY CHEROKEE LAND OFFICE

Muskogee, Indian Territory, April 6, 1905.

In the matter of the allotment of land to Emma Donnelly Cherokee citizen roll No. 12498, Field Card No. 3782, applied for by Henry Donnelly.

Henry Donnelly, citizen father, being sworn, testified as follows:

Examination by the Commission:
Q What is your name? A Henry Donnelly.
Q What is your post office address? A Vinita, Indian Territory.
Q Are you a citizen of the Cherokee Nation? A Yes sir.
Q Is your object in appearing here today to select an allotment for Emma Donnelly? A Yes sir.
Q What relation are you to Emma Donnelly? A Her father.
Q Has she executed this power of attorney which you file here for that purpose? A Yes sir.
Q Why is it that Emma Donnelly cannot appear herein person? A Well she could.
Q Is she living at home? A Yes sir.
Q Is the land which you desire to select for Emma Donnelly under improvement? A It is fenced.
Q Sufficient land to make her complete allotment? A No sir, not the fractions.
Q Has anyone ever applied at either Vinita or Tahlequah for an allotment for Emma Donnelly? A No sir.

Cherokee Intermarried White 1906
Volume I

Q Is this land located west of the Grand and Arkansas rivers? A Yes sir.
Q In what district? A Coo-wee-wcoo-wee.

Witness offers power of attorney executed by Emma Donnelly to Henry Donnelly, dated April 4, 1905, authorizing him to select an allotment for her in the Cherokee Nation.

WITNESS EXCUSED.

Blanch Asjtpm[sic] upon oath states that as stenographer to the Commission to the Five Civilized Tribes she accurately recorded the testimohy[sic] in the above entitled cause and that the foregoing is a correct transcript of her stenographic notes thereof.

Blanch Ashton

Sworn and subscribed to before me this 6th day of April, 1905.

W S Hawkins
Notary Public.

◇◇◇◇◇

(Below was originally a handwritten letter as given on the microfilm. The transcribed copy immediately followed and is given below and typed as given.)

COPY

Brushy Creek C. N.
Sept. 27, 1869

To Hon. T. I. McClerk,
    Clerk, Dist Court

    Mr. H. Donelly a citizen of the United States wishing to comply with the laws of the Cherokee Nation and become a citizen of the same by marriage we the undersigned citizens of the Cherokee Nation having been acquainted with him for one year or more can safely recommend him to be of good morral character and to make a good citizen

    Thos. Daniel   Wm. A. Daniel
    John M. Daniel   H. L. Hill
    M. D. Daniel   D. Freeman
    T. . B. McGhee

Cherokee Intermarried White 1906
Volume I

To the Judge or any ordained Minister of the Gospel, you are hereby authorized to solemnize the rights of Matrimony-----------Miss Emma Daniel-------------------Donelly, according----------------------or custom of your---------------------------
Given from --------------------------in office Oct 2 1869.

Signed T. Z. B. McGhee

Clk D.C. C.N.

I do certify that I joined in marriage Mr. H. Donlly on the one part and Miss Emmy Daniels on the other part. Don according to the laws or rules of all church on this 5th day of Oct 1869.

Signed. A. J. Farthing M. G.

Lola M. Champlin being first duly sworn states that as stenographer to the Commissioner to the Five Civilized Tribes, she made the above and foregoing copy and that the same is a true and correct copy of the original marriage certificate now on file in this office.

Lola M. Champlin

Subscribed and sworn to before me this 20" day of December 1906.

B.P. Rasmus
notary public.

◇◇◇◇◇

Cherokee 3782

DEPARTMENT OF THE INTERIOR,
COMMISSIONER TO THE FIVE CIVILIZED TRIBES.
MUSKOGEE, IND. TER., December 20, 1906.

In the matter of the application of Henry Donnelly for enrollment as a citizen by intermarriage of the Cherokee Nation.

HENRY DONNELLY being first sworn by B.P. Rasmus, a Notary Public, testified as follows:

ON BEHALF OF THE COMMISSIONER:

Q. What is your name? A. Henry Donnelly.
Q. How old are you? A. Sixty-nine.
Q. What is your postoffice? A. Vinita.
Q. You are a white man? A. Yes sir.
Q. You claim enrollment as a citizen by intermarriage of the Cherokee Nation?
A. Yes sir.

Cherokee Intermarried White 1906
Volume I

Q. What is the name of your wife? A. Emma J. Daniels.
Q. Is she a Cherokee by blood? A. Yes sir
Q. Is she living? A. Yes sir.
Q. You and she living together now? A. Yes sir.
Q. When were you married? A. I think it was in '69, the fall of '69, I don't know exactly, '69 or '70.
Q. Who married you? A. Farthing.
Q. Was he a Minister? A. Yes sir
Q. Did you secure a Cherokee license to marry your wife? A. Yes sir.
Q. Who issued it? A. Well, I don't know whether it was Woodall or McGhee, one of the two was Clerk at that time, I don't remember which, it has been so long now.
Q. Clerk of what? A. Delaware District.
Q. Cherokee Nation? A. Yes sir.
Q. Is this the license that you present? (Shows paper)
A. I think so-- Yes sir.

There is offered in evidence a petition dated September 27, 1869, to the Clerk of the District Court as to the moral character of H. Donelly[sic], and a license signed by T. B. (?) McGhee "Clk. D.C. & D. C.N. ", authorizing the marriage of Miss Emma Daniel and *(space)* Donelly. The license is torn and that part apparently containing the name of the man in the license is missing.
There is endorsed on the back of the petition and license a certificate signed by A. J. Farthing, a Minister of the Gospel, certifying that he joined in matrimony Mr. H. Donlly[sic] and Miss Emmy[sic] Danils[sic], according to the laws of the Cherokee Nation, on the fifth day of October, 1869. The license bears date of October 2, 1869

Q. Was your wife a recognized Cherokee citizen by blood at the time you married her?
A. Yes sir.
Q. Has she lived in the Cherokee Nation all her life? A. Yes sir-- Well, not all of her life, during the was her folks went out.
Q. Have you and she lived together continuously from the time you married up until the present date? A. Yes sir.

The applicant and his wife are identified on the Cherokee authenticated tribal roll of 1880, at Numbers 938 and 939, Cooweescoowee District.

Lucy M. Bowman, being first duly sworn, states that as stenographer to the Commissioner to the Five Civilized Tribes she correctly recorded the testimony in this case and that the above and foregoing is a full, true and correct transcript of her stenographic notes thereof.

Lucy M. Bowman

Subscribed and sworn to before me this 20th day of December, 1906.

B.P. Rasmus
Notary Public.

Cherokee Intermarried White 1906
Volume I

◇◇◇◇◇

Cherokee 3782

DEPARTMENT OF THE INTERIOR,

COMMISSIONER TO THE FIVE CIVILIZED TRIBES.

In the matter of the application for the enrollment of Henry Donnelly as a citizen by intermarriage of the Cherokee Nation.

D E C I S I O N

THE RECORDS OF THIS OFFICE SHOW: That at Vinita, Indian Territory, September 29, 1900, Henry Donnelly appeared before the Commission to the Five Civilized Tribes, and made application for the enrollment of himself as a citizen by intermarriage, and for the enrollment of his wife, Emma J. and their minor children, Emma, Paul and Ada Donnelly as citizens by blood of the Cherokee Nation. The application for the enrollment of the said Emma J., Emma, Paul and Ada Donnelly has been heretofore disposed of, and their rights to enrollment will not be considered in this decision. Further proceedings in the matter of said application were had before the Commission to the Five Civilized Tribes at Muskogee, Indian Territory, October 6, 1902, and April 6, 1905, and before the Commissioner to the Five Civilized Tribes December 20, 1906.

THE EVIDENCE IN THIS CASE SHOWS: That the applicant herein, Henry Donnelly, a white man, was married in accordance with the Cherokee law October 5, 1869, to his wife, Emma J. Donnelly, who was at the time of said marriage, a recognized citizen by blood of the Cherokee Nation, and that since said marriage the said Henry and Emma J. Donnelly have resided together as husband and wife and have continuously lived in the Cherokee Nation. Said Henry Donnelly is identified on the Cherokee authenticated tribal roll of 1880 and the Cherokee census roll of 1896, as an intermarried citizen of the Cherokee Nation.

IT IS, THEREFORE, ORDERED AND ADJUDGED: That in accordance with the decision of the Supreme Court of the United States, dated November 5, 1906, in the case of Daniel Red Bird et al., vs. the United States, under the provision of Section twenty-one of the Act of Congress approved June 28, 1898 (30 Stat. 495), Henry Donnelly is entitled to enrollment as a citizen by intermarriage of the Cherokee Nation, and his application for enrollment as such is accordingly granted.

Tams Bixby
Commissioner.

Dated at Muskogee, Indian Territory,
this   JAN 10 1907

◇◇◇◇◇

Cherokee Intermarried White 1906
Volume I

W. C. ROGERS, Principal Chief
D. M. FAULKNER, Assistant Chief
W. W. HASTINGS, National Attorney
J. H. COVEL, Interpreter

A. B. CUNNINGHAM, Executive Secretary
C. J. HARRIS, Assistant Secretary
W. H. WALKER, Assistant Secretary

CHEROKEE NATION
TAHLEQUAH, INDIAN TERRITORY
December 20, 1906.

J.O. Rosson,
Muskogee, Indian Territory.

Sir:-

    Referring to our conversation over the phone this morning, I enclose herewith certified copy of what the record shows in the matter of the Marriage of Henry Dondly[sic] and Emma Daniel. I am satisfied this is the record desired, while the name is spelled different, in those days many of the Cherokee officials used Mr. Roosevelts[sic] method of spelling.

    You will see from the certificate of the record that it does not show that the license was ever returned, it appears that the record was made and blank spece[sic] left to fill in when the license was returned.

Yours very truly,

A.B. Cunningham

◇◇◇◇◇

W. C. ROGERS, Principal Chief
D. M. FAULKNER, Assistant Chief
W. W. HASTINGS, National Attorney
J. H. COVEL, Interpreter

A. B. CUNNINGHAM, Executive Secretary
C. J. HARRIS, Assistant Secretary
W. H. WALKER, Assistant Secretary

CHEROKEE NATION
TAHLEQUAH, INDIAN TERRITORY

"No. 18.
    This is to certify that Henry Dondly, a white man was licensed to marry Emma Daniel, a female Cherokee, on the 21st, day of Oct. 1868, and that the license was was[sic] executed and returned _____ 18___ being in accordance with the Act passed by the National Council bearing date Oct. 15, 1865, in regard to whitemen marrying in this nation.

T.J. McGhee, Clk.
D.C.D.D.C.N."

    I hereby certify that the above is a true copy of the original record relating to the marriage of Henry Dondly and Emma Daniel, said record being numbered 18, Book "S" Marriage records of Deleware[sic] District Cherokee Nation.

Cherokee Intermarried White 1906
Volume I

Said Marriage record now being a part of the records of this office and in my custody.

          A.B. Cunningham
          Executive Secretary.

◇◇◇◇◇

Cherokee
3782.

         Muskogee, Indian Territory, January 10, 1907.

W. W. Hastings,
  Attorney for the Cherokee Nation,
    Muskogee, Indian Territory.

Dear Sir:

  There is enclosed herewith a copy of the decision of the Commissioner to the Five Civilized Tribes, dated January 10, 1907, granting the application for the enrollment of Henry Donnelly, as a citizen by intermarriage of the Cherokee Nation.

  You are advised that you will be given fifteen days from date hereof within which to file such protest as you may desire to make against the action of the Commissioner the applicant. If you fail to file protest within the time allowed, this decision will be considered final.

         Respectfully,

Encl. H.J.-40
H.J.C.   Commissioner.

◇◇◇◇◇

| Cherokee | W.W. HASTINGS. | OFFICE OF | H.M. VANCE. |
| 2782[sic] | ATTORNEY. | | SECRETARY. |

Attorney for the Cherokee Nation,
Muskogee, I. T.

              January 18, 1907.

The Commissioner to the Five Civilized Tribes,
  Muskogee, Indian Territory.

Sir:

  Receipt is acknowledged of the testimony and of your decision enrolling Henry Donnelly, as a citizen by intermarriage of the Cherokee Nation. Time for protesting said decision is waived and I consent that said person may be placed upon the schedule immediately.

Cherokee Intermarried White 1906
Volume I

Yours very truly,
W. W. Hastings
Attorney for Cherokee Nation.

Cherokee
3782

Muskogee, Indian Territory, January 21, 1907.

Henry Donnelly,
Vinita, Indian Territory.

Dear Sir:

There is enclosed herewith a copy of the decision of the Commissioner to the Five Civilized Tribes, dated January 10, 1907, granting the application for your enrollment as a citizen by intermarriage of the Cherokee Nation.

You will be advised when your name has been placed upon the schedule of citizens of the Cherokee Nation and approved by the Secretary of the Interior.

Respectfully,

E.R.C.   Commissioner.
Enc. E.C.4.

Cher IW 34
Trans from Cher 3829 3-13-07

C.E.W.

DEPARTMENT OF THE INTERIOR,

COMMISSIONER TO THE FIVE CIVILIZED TRIBES.

In the matter of the application for the enrollment of

MARY S. TITTLE

as a citizen by intermarriage of the Cherokee Nation.

Cherokee Intermarried White 1906
Volume I

CHEROKEE 3829.

DEPARTMENT OF THE INTERIOR.

COMMISSION TO THE FIVE CIVILIZED TRIBES.

Vinita, I.T. October 1st, 1900/

IN THE MATTER OF THE APPLICATION OF ROBERT W TITTLE FOR THE ENROLLMENT OF HIMSELF, HIS WIFE AND CHILDREN, AS CHEROKEE CITIZENS.

The said Robert W. Tittle, being sworn and examined by Commissioner C. R. Breckinridge, testified as follows:
Q Give me your full name, please. A Robert W. Tittle.
Q How old are you? A Fifty-one.
Q What is your postoffice? A Vinita.
Q In what district do you live? A Delaware.
Q Who is it you want to have put on the roll, yourself? A Myself.
Q Your wife? A My wife.
Q And how many children? A Four children.
Q Do you apply for yourself as a Cherokee by blood? A Yes, sir.
Q Is your wife a Cherokee by blood? A No sir.
Q How long have you been in the Cherokee Nation? A Well, sir I have been here ever since the 3rd year after the rebellion.
Q You have been living here all the time since then? A Yes, sir.
Q What district have you been in since 1880? A I have been in the Delaware district all the time.
Q What is your wife's name? A Mary S.
Q How old is she? A Forty-nine.
Q When did you marry her? A In 1872.
Q Have you lived together ever since you were married? A Yes, sir.
Q Give me the names of your four children. A Otis W.
Q How old is Otis? A Eighteen.
Q The next child? A Hugh Thomas E. Tittle.
Q How old is that child? A Fifteen.
Q The next ones? A They are twins, Mary and Robert.
Q How old are they? A They are 10 years old, or about eleven.
Q These are all? A Yes, sir.
Q All living at this time, are they? A Yes, sir.
Q What was your father's name? A Daniel.
Q Is he dead or living? A He is dead.
Q How long has he been dead? A About twenty-five years.
Q What is your mother's name? A Rosanna.
Q Is she dead or alive? A She is dead.

Cherokee Intermarried White 1906
Volume I

Q How long has she been dead? A She has been dead something near three or four months.
1880 Roll, page 325, No. 2616, Robert Tittle, Delaware District. Native.
1880 Roll, page 325, No. 2617, Mary S. Tittle, Delaware District.
1896 Roll, page 544, No. 3178, Robert W. Tittle, Deo laware[sic] District
1896 Roll, page 590, No. 541, Mary S. Tittle, Delaware District.
1896 Roll, page 544, No. 3181, Otis Wooden Tittle, Delaware District.
1896 Roll, page 544, No. 3182, Hugh T. E. Tittle, Delaware District.
1896 Roll, page 544, No. 3183, Mary Ellis (Alice) Tittle, Delaware District.
1896 Roll, page 544, No. 3184, Robert Wooden Tittle, Delaware District.
Q Mary Alice Tittle, is it? A Yes, sir.

THE COMMISSIONER: The applicant applies for the enrollment of himself, his wife and four children. He and his wife are both identified on the rolls of 1880 and 1896 as husband and wife, he as a native Cherokee, she as a Cherokee by adoption. They have lived together ever since their enrollment in 1880, and lived continuously in the Cherokee Nation, and they will be listed now for enrollment, he as a Cherokee by blood and she as a Cherokee by adoption.

The four children named in the testimony are all identified with their parents on the roll of 1896; they are living at this time and will be listed now for enrollment as Cherokees by blood.

---------o---------

The undersigned, being sworn, states that as stenographer to the Commission to the Five Civilized Tribes he correctly recorded the testimony and other proceedings in this application for enrollment and that the foregoing is a correct and complete transcript of his stenographic notes thereof.

(Name Illegible)

Subscribed and sworn to before me this 18th day of October A.D. 1900.

CR Breckinridge

Commissioner.

◇◇◇◇◇

Cher
Supp'l to # 3829

Department of the Interior,
Commission to the Five Civilized Tribes,
Muskogee, I. T., October 22, 1902.

In the matter of the application of ROBERT W. TITTLE, for the enrollment of himself, and his children, OTIS W., HUGH T. E., MARY A., AND ROBERT W. J. TITTLE, as citizens by blood, and his wife, MARY S. TITTLE, as a citizen by intermarriage, of the Cherokee Nation.

Cherokee Intermarried White 1906
Volume I

MARY S. TITTLE, being duly sworn and examined by the Commission, testified as follows:

Q Your name is Mary S. Tittle ? A Yes sir.
Q How old are you ? A Fifty.
Q What is your post office ? A Vinita.
Q You are a white woman ? A Yes sir.
Q Your name is on the roll of 1880 as an adopted white citizen ? A Yes sir.
Q What is the name of your husband ? A Robert W. Tittle.
Q Is he a Cherokee by blood ? A Yes sir.
Q Was he your husband in 1880 ? A Yes sir.
Q He is the husband through whom you claim your citizenship ? A Yes sir.
Q Have you and your husband Robert W. Tittle been living together ever since 1880 ? A Yes sir.
Q Are you living together now ? A Yes sir, since 1982.
Q Has the Cherokee Nation been your home during all that time ? A Yes sir.
Q You and your husband have never lived anywhere else have you ? A No sir.
Q How many children have you ? A Eight.
Q Are four of them under age and living at home with you ? A Yes sir.
Q Have there been any deaths in your family for the past two years ? A Yes sir, my son Deck.
Q How old was he ? A Twenty seven.
Q That's the only one ? A Yes sir, since then.

E. C. Bagwell, on oath states that, as stenographer to the Commission to the Five Civilized Tribes, he correctly recorded the testimony and proceedings had in the above entitled cause, and that the foregoing is an accurate transcript of his stenographic notes thereof.

                      EC Bagwell

Subscribed and sworn to before me this November 29, 1902.

                      BC Jones
                      Notary Public.

Cherokee Intermarried White 1906
Volume I

DEPARTMENT OF THE INTERIOR
COMMISSIONER TO THE FIVE CIVILIZED TRIBES
MUSKOGEE, IND. TER.
JAN. 4, 1907

ooOoo

IN THE MATTER OF THE APPLICATION FOR THE
ENROLLMENT OF MARY S. TITTLE AS A CITIZEN
BY INTERMARRIAGE OF THE CHEROKEE NATION.

CENSUS CARD NO. 3829.

ROBERT W. TITTLE BEING FIRST DULY SWORN TESTIFIED AS FOLLOWS:

EXAMINATION BY THE COMMISSIONER:

Q What is your name? A Robert W. Tittle.
Q What is your age? A Fifty seven years old.
Q What is your post office address? A Vinita.
Q Are you acquainted with Mary S. Tittle? A Yes sir.
Q What relation is she to you? A She's my wife.
Q When were you and Mary S. Tittle married? A Married the 17th day of March 1872.
Q Where.[sic] A We was married in Delaware District on Spavinaw seven miles of Maysville.
Q Was you ever married before you married her? A No sir.
Q Was she ever married before she married you? A Yes sir.
Q Was her husband living or dead? A Dead.
Q Have you lived together as husband and wife continuously since 1872. up to and including the present time? A Yes sir.
Q Have you got any documentary evidence of your marriage to Mary S. Tittle?
A No sir, at the time a man wasn't married under the Cherokee laws.
Q Is there anyone here today who knows of your marriage to Mary S. Tittle.[sic]
A Yes sir.
Q Will you have them come in here and testify? A Yes sir.

ooOoo

JOHN PARKS BEING FIRST DULY SWORN TESTIFIED AS FOLLOWS:

EXAMINATION BY THE COMMISSIONER:

Q What is your name? A John Parks.
Q How old are you Mr. Parks.[sic] A Fifty four years old.
Q How old are you Mr. Parks. A Fifty four years old.[sic]
Q What is your post office address? A Vinita.
Q Are you a citizen of the Cherokee Nation? A Yes sir.

Cherokee Intermarried White 1906
Volume I

Q Do you know Robert W. Tittle and Mary S. Tittle.[sic] A Yes.
Q How long have you known them.[sic] A I've known Bob ever since I've been in the country and I knew his wife before she married.
Q Do you know when they were married? A Along in the spring of Seventy two.
Q Were you present at the marriage? A No sir.
Q You have known them ever since then? A Yes sir.
Q You know they have been recognized as husband and wife in the community in which they lived.[sic] A Yes sir.

The applicant is identified on the 1880 Cherokee Roll Delaware District opposite No. 2617; her husband thru whom she claims her right to enrollment is identified on said roll, said district opposite No. 2616; is also identified upon the final roll of citizens by blood of the Cherokee Nation opposite No. 9246.

ooOoo

Clara Mitchell Wood, being first duly sworn upon her oath states that as stenographer for the Commissioner to the Five Civilized Tribes she reported the above and foregoing proceedings and that this is a correct transcript of her stenographic notes.

Clara Mitchell Wood

Subscribed and sworn to before me this 8th day of January 1907.

B.P. Rasmus
Notary Public.

DEPARTMENT OF THE INTERIOR
COMMISSIONER TO THE FIVE CIVILIZED TRIBES
MUSKOGEE, IND. TER.
JAN. 4, 1907

ooOoo

ADDITIONAL TESTIMONY IN THE MATTER OF THE APPLICATION FOR ENROLLMENT AS A CITIZEN BY INTERMARRIAGE OF THE CHEROKEE NATION OF MARY S. TITTLE.

CENSUS CARD NO. 3829.

ANN ELIZA CHANDLER BEING FIRST DULY SWORN TESTIFIED AS FOLLOWS:

EXAMINATION BY THE COMMISSIONER:

Q What is your name? A Ann Eliza Chandler.

Cherokee Intermarried White 1906
Volume I

Q How old are you? A I'm fifty nine.
Q What is your post office address? A Vinita.
Q Are you a citizen of the Cherokee Nation? A Yes sir.
Q Do you know Robert W. Tittle and Mary S. Tittle? A Yes sir.
Q How long have you known them? A I've known Robert Tittle all my life.
Q How long have you known his wife.[sic] A I've known her ever since they was married.
Q Were you present at the marriage? A No, sir I was at the infair tho; I didn't go to the wedding.
Q When were they married? A They were married in '72 I think.
Q Do you know they have held themselves out in the community in which they lived, as husband and wife ever since 1872[sic] A Yes sir.
Q You know they were married about that time? A Yes sir.

ooOoo

Clara Mitchell Wood being first duly sworn upon her oath states that as stenographer for the Commissioner to the Five Civilized Tribes she reported the above and foregoing proceedings and that this is a correct transcript of her stenographic notes.

Clara Mitchell Wood

Subscribed and sworn to before me this 8th day of January 1907.

B.P. Rasmus
Notary Public.

C.E.W.   Cherokee 3829.

DEPARTMENT OF THE INTERIOR,

COMMISSIONER TO THE FIVE CIVILIZED TRIBES.

In the matter of the application for the enrollment of Mary S. Tittle, as a citizen by intermarriage of the Cherokee Nation.

D E C I S I O N

THE RECORDS OF THIS OFFICE SHOW: That at Vinita, Indian Territory, October 1, 1900, Robert W. Tittle appeared before the Commission to the Five Civilized Tribes, and made application for the enrollment of his wife, Mary S. Tittle, as a citizen by intermarriage, and for the enrollment of himself, et al., as citizens by blood of the Cherokee Nation has been heretofore disposed of, and their rights to enrollment will not be considered in this decision. Further proceedings in the matter of said application were had at Muskogee, Indian Territory, October 22, 1902, and January 4, 1907.

Cherokee Intermarried White 1906
Volume I

THE EVIDENCE IN THIS CASE SHOWS: That the applicant herein, Mary S. Tittle, a white woman, married March 17, 1872, one Robert W. Tittle, who was at the time of said marriage a recognized citizen by blood of the Cherokee Nation, and whose name appears upon the approved partial roll of citizens by blood, opposite number 9246; that from the time of said marriage the said Robert W. Tittle and Mary S. Tittle have resided together as husband and wife and have continuously lived in the Cherokee Nation. Said Mary s. Tittle is identified on the Cherokee Authenticated tribal roll of 1880, and the Cherokee Census Roll of 1896 as an intermarried citizen of the Cherokee Nation.

IT IS, THEREFORE, ORDERED AND ADJUDGED: That in accordance with the decision of the Supreme Court of the United States, dated November 5, 1906, in the case of Daniel Red Bird et al., vs. the United States, under the provision of Section 21 of the Act of Congress approved June 28, 1898, (30 Stat. 495), Mary S. Tittle is entitled to enrollment as a citizen by intermarriage of the Cherokee Nation, and her application for enrollment as such is accordingly granted.

Tams Bixby
Commissioner.

Dated at Muskogee, Indian Territory,
this   JAN 16 1907

◇◇◇◇◇

Cherokee
3829.

Muskogee, Indian Territory, December 27, 1906.

Mary S. Tittle,
    Vinita, Indian Territory.

Dear Madam:

November 6, 1906, the United States Supreme Court held that white persons who intermarried with Cherokee citizens according to Cherokee law prior to November 1, 1875, are entitled to enrollment and allotments of land as citizens of the Cherokee Nation.

You are advised that to properly determine your right to enrollment as a citizen by intermarriage of the Cherokee Nation, it will be necessary for you to appear before the Commissioner for the purpose of giving testimony as to the date of your marriage and whether or not your husband, by reason of your marriage to whom you claim the right to enrollment as a citizen by intermarriage of the Cherokee Nation, was a recognized Cherokee citizen at the time of your marriage to him.

Cherokee Intermarried White 1906
Volume I

You are therefore directed to appear before the Commissioner at Muskogee, Indian Territory, at 9 o'clock A. M., on Friday, January 4, 1907, and give testimony as above indicated.

Respectfully,

H.J.C.   Acting Commissioner.

◇◇◇◇◇

Cherokee
3829

Muskogee, Indian Territory, January 19, 1907.

Mary S. Tittle,
    Vinita, Indian Territory.

Dear Madam:

There is enclosed herewith a copy of the decision of the Commissioner to the Five Civilized Tribes, dated January 16, 1907, granting your application for enrollment as a citizen by intermarriage of the Cherokee Nation.

You will be advised when your name has been placed upon the schedule of citizens of the Cherokee Nation and approved by the Secretary of the Interior.

Respectfully,

Encl. H-77   Commissioner.
JMH

◇◇◇◇◇

(The above letter, dated January 19, 1907, to Mary S. Tittle, given again.)

◇◇◇◇◇

Cherokee Intermarried White 1906
Volume I

Cherokee 3829 W.W.HASTINGS. OFFICE OF H.M. VANCE.
ATTORNEY. SECRETARY.

Attorney for the Cherokee Nation,
MUSKOGEE, I. T.

January 18, 1907.

The Commissioner to the Five Civilized Tribes,
Muskogee, Indian Territory.

Sir:

Receipt is acknowledged of the testimony and of your decision enrolling Mary S. Tittle as a citizen by intermarriage of the Cherokee Nation. Time for protesting said decision is waived and I consent that said person may be placed upon the schedule immediately.

Yours very truly,
W. W. Hastings
Attorney for Cherokee Nation.

◇◇◇◇◇

Cherokee 3829

Muskogee, Indian Territory, January 17, 1907

W. W. Hastings,
Attorney for the Cherokee Nation,
Muskogee, Indian Territory.

Dear Sir:

There is enclosed herewith copy of the decision of the Commissioner to the Five Civilized Tribes, dated January 16, 1907, granting the application for the enrollment of Mary S. Tittle as a citizen by intermarriage of the Cherokee Nation.

Respectfully,

Encl. I-11 Commissioner.
RPI

◇◇◇◇◇

(The above letter, dated January 17, 1907, to W. W. Hastings, given again.)

Cherokee Intermarried White 1906
Volume I

Cher IW 35
Trans from Cher 3844 3-13-07

C.E.W.

DEPARTMENT OF THE INTERIOR,

COMMISSIONER TO THE FIVE CIVILIZED TRIBES.

In the matter of the application for the enrollment of

LUCINDA J. CRAIG

as a citizen by intermarriage of the Cherokee Nation.

CHEROKEE 3844.

Department of the Interior,
Commission to the Five Civilized Tribes,
Vinita, I. T., October 1st, 1900.

In the matter of the application of Granville Craig for the enrollment of him self[sic] and wife as Cherokee citizens; being sworn and examined by Commissioner Needles he testified as follows:

Q What is your name? A Granville Craig/[sic]
Q What is your age? A 51 years.
Q What is your post-office address? A Bluejacket.
Q What district do you live in? A Cooweescoowee.
Q Are you a recognized citizen of the Cherokee Nation by blood? A Yes sir.
Q What degree of blood do you claim? A 1/16
Q For whom do you apply for enrollment? A Myself and wife.
Q What is your wife's name? A Lucinda Jane.
Q Is she a citizen by blood? A No sir.
Q What was her name when you married her? A Beans[sic].
Q When did you marry her? A In 1867.
Q Is she living? A Yes sir.
Q How long have you and her lived in the Cherokee Nation? A Since 1869, I was admitted to citizenship in 1869.
Q Are you a citizen by blood? A I am a citizen by blood.
Q They have got you on the 1880 roll here as an adopted citizen? A They had it that way on the 1896 roll, and Judge Clingan changed it.

Cherokee Intermarried White 1906
Volume I

1880 roll page 238 #594 Granville Craig, Delaware District;
1880 roll page 238 #595 as Jane Craig, Delaware District.
1896 roll page 131 #968 Granville Craig, Cooweescoowee District.
1896 roll page 298 #172 Jane Craig, Cooweescoowee District.

Com'r Needles: The name of Granville Craig appears upon the authenticated roll of 1880 as well as that of his wife Lucinda Jane; he as an intermarried white and she as a Cherokee by blood he avers that this is an error, and he should be enrolled as a Cherokee by blood and his wife as a citizen by intermarriage, and they will consequently be so enrolled.

M.D. Green, being first duly sworn states that as stenographer to the Commission to the Five Civilized Tribes he correctly recorded the testimony and proceedings in this case and that the foregoing is a true and complete transcript of his stenographic notes thereof.

MD Green

Subscribed and sworn to before me this 1st October 1900.

CR Breckinridge
Commissioner.

◇◇◇◇◇

Cher 3844

Department of the Interior,
Commission to the Five Civilized Tribes,
Muskogee, I. T., October 2, 1902.

In the matter of the application of GRANVILLE CRAIG, for the enrollment of himself as a citizen by blood, and his wife Lucinda J. Craig, as a citizen by intermarriage, of the Cherokee Nation:

GRANVILLE CRAIG, called as a witness, being duly sworn and examined by the Commission, testified as follows:

Q What is your name ? A Granville Craig.
Q What is your age at this time ? A 52.
Q Your post office address ? A Welch, I. T.
Q Are you a citizen by blood of the Cherokee Nation ? A Yes sir.
Q Are you acquainted with Lucinda J. Craig ? A Yes sir.
Q Is she your wife ? A Yes sir.
Q She is the same Lucinda J. Craig for whom application was made to this Commission on October 1, 1900, for enrollment as an intermarried citizen of the Cherokee Nation ? A Yes sir.
Q She is a white woman ? A Yes sir.
Q When were you and she married ? A In 1867.

Cherokee Intermarried White 1906
Volume I

Q Were you ever married prior to your marriage to this wife ? A No sir.
Q Was she ever married prior to her marriage to you ? A No sir.
Q She is your first wife ? A Yes sir.
Q You are her first husband ? A Yes sir.
Q Have you and she been living together as husband and wife continuously since your marriage ? A Yes sir, all the time.
Q Were you living together in the Cherokee Nation on September 1, 1902 ? A Yes sir.
Q How long has your wife lived in the Cherokee Nation ? A Since 1869.
Q Have you lived the same length of time in the Cherokee Nation ? A Yes sir.

E. C. Bagwell, on oath states that, as stenographer to the Commission to the Five Civilized Tribes, he correctly recorded the testimony and proceedings had in the above entitled cause, and that the foregoing is an accurate transcript of his stenographic notes thereof.

EC Bagwell

Subscribed and sworn to before me this October 11, 1902.

BC Jones
Notary Public.

◇◇◇◇◇

DEPARTMENT OF THE INTERIOR
COMMISSIONER TO THE FIVE CIVILIZED TRIBES
MUSKOGEE, IND. TER.
JAN. 4, 1907.

IN THE MATTER OF THE APPLICATION FOR THE
ENROLLMENT OF LUCINDA J. CRAIG AS A
CITIZEN BY INTERMARRIAGE OF THE CHEROKEE
NATION.

CENSUS CARD NO. 3844.

LUCINDA J. CRAIG BEING FIRST DULY SWORN TESTIFIED AS FOLLOWS:

EXAMINATION BY THE COMMISSIONER:

Q What is your name? A Lucinda J. Craig.
Q How old are you.[sic] A Fifty six
Q What is your post office address? A Welch.
Q Do you claim to be a citizen by intermarriage of the Cherokee Nation? A Yes sir.
Q Thru whom do you claim your intermarried rights. A Thru my husband.
Q What is his name? Granville Craig.
Q When were you and Granville Craig married? A 1867.

Cherokee Intermarried White 1906
Volume I

Q Where? A Johnson County Missouri.
Q Have you got any documentary evidence of your marriage? A We didn't have to have that. We didn't have to have any license of our marriage but our marriage was recorded.
Q Have you got any certificate of that record? A No sir.
Q You have lived together continuously since your marriage in 1867 up to the present time? A Yes sir.
Q Have you got a copy of that act admitting you in 1869? A I haven't got it with me; of course you can look on the roll and see we was admitted; we are on every roll from '69 up until now.
Q Is there anyone here today who knows of your marriage to Mr Craig in 1867.[sic]
A Yes sir.
Q Can you get them to come in here and testify.[sic] A Yes.

ooOoo

W. L. TROTT BEING FIRST DULY SWORN TESTIFIED AS FOLLOWS:

EXAMINATION BY THE COMMISSIONER:

Q What is your name? A W. L. Trott.
Q How old are you? A Sixty two.
Q What is your post office address? A Vinita.
Q Are you a citizen of the Cherokee Nation? A Yes sir.
Q Are you acquainted with Granville Craig and Lucinda J. Craig? A Yes sir.
Q How long have you known them? A O[sic] I've known them twenty five or thirty years I guess.
Q Do you know when they were married? A I do not for certain
Q Have they held themselves out as husband and wife ever since you have known them? A Yes sir.
Q Do you know whether Granville Craig is a citizen by blood of the Cherokee Nation or not.[sic] A Yes sir.
Q When was he admitted; do you know? A I think he was admitted in, somewhere along about seventy.
Q You wasn't present at their marriage? A No sir.
Q Have you lived in the same community with them? A Yes sir.

ooOoo

LOUISA J. TROTT BEING FIRST DULY SWORN TESTIFIED AS FOLLOWS:

EXAMINATION BY THE COMMISSIONER:

Q What is your name? A Louisa J. Trott.
Q How old are you? A Fifty six years old.
Q What is your post office address? A Vinita.
Q Are you a citizen of the Cherokee Nation? A Yes sir.
Q Are you acquainted with Granville Craig and Lucinda J. Craig[sic] A Yes sir.

Cherokee Intermarried White 1906
Volume I

Q How long have you known them? A I've known them thirty years any way; thirty two or three years.
Q Do you know when they were married? A No sir I dont[sic] know when they were married. They have been married quite a long while.
Q They have been recognized and held themselves out to the community in their neighborhood as husband and wife for the past thirty years. A Yes sir.
Q Where have they been living since you have known them.[sic] A Been living up on Cabin Creek above Vinita.
Q Is that in the Cherokee Nation? A Yes sir about eighteen miles northwest.
Q Is Granville Craig a citizen by blood of the Cherokee Nation. A Yes sir.
[sic] Do you know when he was admitted to citizenship? A No sir I dont[sic] know' he has been on the rolls and drawing money for a long time.

The applicant is identified on the 1880 Roll, Delaware District opposite No. 595; her husband through whom she claims her right to enrollment is identified on said roll, said district opposite No. 594; he is also identified on the final roll of citizens by blood of the Cherokee Nation opposite No. 9273.

Clara Mitchell Wood being first duly sworn upon her oath states that as stenographer for the Commissioner to the Five Civilized Tribes she reported the above and foregoing proceedings and that this is a correct transcript of her stenographic notes.

Clara Mitchell Wood

Subscribed and sworn to before me this 8th day of January 1907

B.P. Rasmus
Notary Public.

◇◇◇◇◇

AFFIDAVIT.

STATE OF MISSOURI } ss
COUNTY OF JOHNSON

On this the 17th day of January A.D. 1907, before me J. Ransom Grinstead, a Notary Public within and for Johnson County, Missouri, personally appeared John Q. McDonald, aged 61 years, and Carrie McDonald aged 49 years, both residents of Warrensburg, Johnson County, Missouri; who first being duly sworn according to law, upon their oaths say, that they were well acquainted with Granville C. Craig and Miss Jane Means A.D. 1867, who were also residents of said Johnson County, Missouri.

The affiants further state that the said Granville C. Craig and Miss Jane Means were married October 27th A.D. 1867, at the residence of William Draper in Jefferson

Cherokee Intermarried White 1906
Volume I

Township, Johnson County, Missouri, by Rev. S. F. Goodwin the officiating officer, and that the affiants were present and witnesses to said marriage.

The affiants further state that the said Rev. S. F. Goodwin, was a minister of the Baptist Church, and that he died at his home in Johnson County, Missouri, many years ago.

The affiants further state that the said Granville C. Craig and Jane Craig now reside at Blue Jackett, Indian Territory.

John Q. McDonald
Carrie McDonald

Subscribed and sworn to before me this the 17th day of January A.D. 1907.

J. Ransom Grinstead
Notary Public within and for

My Commission Expires March 28-1908. Johnson County, Missouri.

STATE OF MISSOURI } ss
COUNTY OF JOHNSON }

I, James L. Robinson, Recorder of Deeds of Johnson County, Missouri, hereby certify that no marriage licenses were issued in Johnson County, Missouri A.D. 1867, and I find no record of the marriage Garland C. Craig and Jane Means in my office.

Witness my hand and seal at my office in Warrensburg, Mo. this the 17th day of January A.D. 1907.

Jas L Robinson
Recorder of Deeds of
Johnson County, Missouri.

◇◇◇◇◇

C.E.W.   Cherokee 3844.

DEPARTMENT OF THE INTERIOR,

COMMISSIONER TO THE FIVE CIVILIZED TRIBES.

In the matter of the application for the enrollment of Lucinda J. Craig, as a citizen by intermarriage of the Cherokee Nation.

D E C I S I O N

THE RECORDS OF THIS OFFICE SHOW: That at Vinita, Indian Territory, October 1, 1900, Granville Craig appeared before the Commission to the Five Civilized

Cherokee Intermarried White 1906
Volume I

Tribes, and made application for the enrollment of his wife, Lucinda J. Craig, as a citizen by intermarriage, and for the enrollment of himself, as a citizen by blood of the Cherokee Nation. The application for the enrollment of the said Granville Craig, as a citizen by blood of the Cherokee Nation has been heretofore disposed of and his rights to enrollment will not be considered in this decision. Further proceedings in the matter of said application were had at Muskogee, Indian Territory, October 2, 1902, and January 4, 1907.

THE EVIDENCE IN THIS CASE SHOWS: That the applicant herein, Lucinda J. Craig, a white woman, married one Granville Craig in the State of Missouri in the year 1867, and removed to the Cherokee Nation in 1869; that said Granville Craig was admitted to citizenship as a citizen by blood of the Cherokee Nation in 1869, and whose name appears upon the approved partial roll of citizens by blood of the Cherokee Nation, opposite number 9273; that since said admission he and his said wife have resided together as husband and wife and have continuously lived in the Cherokee Nation. Said Lucinda J. Craig is identified on the Cherokee Authenticated tribal roll of 1880, and the Cherokee Census Roll of 1896 as an intermarried citizen of the Cherokee Nation.

IT IS, THEREFORE, ORDERED AND ADJUDGED: That in accordance with the decision of the Supreme Court of the United States, dated November 5, 1906, in the case of Daniel Red Bird et al., vs the United States under the provision of Section 21 of the Act of Congress approved June 28, 1898, (30 Stat. 495), Lucinda J. Craig is entitled to enrollment as a citizen by intermarriage of the Cherokee Nation, and her application for enrollment as such is accordingly granted.

Tams Bixby
Commissioner.

Dated at Muskogee, Indian Territory,
this   JAN 16 1907

◇◇◇◇◇

Cherokee 3844

Muskogee, Indian Territory, January 17, 1907.

W. W. Hastings,
    Attorney for the Cherokee Nation,
        Muskogee, Indian Territory.

Dear Sir:

There is enclosed herewith copy of the decision of the Commissioner to the Five Civilized Tribes, dated January 16, 1907, granting the application for the enrollment of Lucinda J. Craig as a citizen by intermarriage of the Cherokee Nation.

Cherokee Intermarried White 1906
Volume I

Respectfully,

Commissioner.

Encl. I-13
RPI

◇◇◇◇◇

Cherokee 3844.   W.W. HASTINGS,   OFFICE OF   H.M. VANCE,
                   ATTORNEY.   SECRETARY.

Attorney for the Cherokee Nation,
MUSKOGEE, I. T.

January 18, 1907.

The Commissioner to the Five Civilized Tribes,
Muskogee, Indian Territory.

Sir:

  Receipt is acknowledged of the testimony and of your decision enrolling Lucinda J. Craig as a citizen by intermarriage of the Cherokee Nation. Time for protesting said decision is waived and I consent that said person may be placed upon the schedule immediately.

Yours very truly,
W. W. Hastings
Attorney for Cherokee Nation.

◇◇◇◇◇

Cherokee
3844

Muskogee, Indian Territory, January 19, 1907.

Lucinda J. Craig,
  Welch, Indian Territory.

Dear Madam:

  There is enclosed herewith a copy of the decision of the Commissioner to the Five Civilized Tribes, dated January 17, 1907, granting the application for your enrollment as a citizen by intermarriage of the Cherokee Nation.

  You will be advised when your name has been placed upon the schedule of citizens of the Cherokee Nation and approved by the Secretary of the Interior.

Respectfully,

Commissioner.

Encl. H-83
JMH

Cherokee Intermarried White 1906
Volume I

Cherokee
3844.

Muskogee, Indian Territory, December 27, 1906.

Lucinda J. Craig,
    Welch, Indian Territory..

Dear Madam:

November 6, 1906, the United States Supreme Court held that white persons who intermarried with Cherokee citizens according to Cherokee law prior to November 1, 1875, are entitled to enrollment and allotments of land as citizens of the Cherokee Nation.

You are advised that to properly determine your right to enrollment as a citizen by intermarriage of the Cherokee Nation, it will be necessary for you to appear before the Commissioner for the purpose of giving testimony as to the date of your marriage and whether or not your husband, by reason of your marriage to whom you claim the right to enrollment as a citizen by intermarriage of the Cherokee Nation, was a recognized Cherokee citizen at the time of your marriage to him.

You are therefore directed to appear before the Commissioner at Muskogee, Indian Territory, at 9 o'clock A. M., on Friday, January 4, 1907, and give testimony as above indicated.

                Respectfully,

H.J.C.   Acting Commissioner.

Index

ADAIR
  Ann B 115
  J T 117,118,119
  James W 16,76,93,117,118
  James Ward 93
  Jane 124
  John 115,118
  John K 125
  Julius J 128
  Julius K 123,124,128
  Mildred T 117,118,119
  Sam 16
  Samuel 16
  Talitha 126
  Talitha J 123,124,125,126,128, 129,130,131
  Talitha Jane 123
  V B 124
  Virgil B 123,124,126,127,128,129
  Warren 16
ALLISON
  Amos 114
  Delaney 114
  Edgar G 115,116
  Edgar J 115
  Garfield E 115
  John R 114,115,116,117,119, 120,121,122
  John Rufus 117,118
  Mildred T 115,116,118,119
  Narcena 115
  Narcenia 115
  Narcenie 116
  Rufus 115
  Rufus B 118
  W L 115
ASHTON, Blanch 296
ASJTPM, Blanch 296
AYERS
  Alice 150,152
  Mr T J 153
  T J 153
  Thomas J 149,150,152,154,155,157
  Tom J 150
  Virginia 149,150,152,154,155
AYRES, Thomas J 152,156
BAGGS 141

BAGWELL
  E B 142
  E C 116,168,262,269,287,305,314
BARKER, Virginia 152
BARNES
  Mary 161,162
  Minnie 161
  Polly 161
  Thomas 158,161
BARNS, Albert 220
BATES 126
BEALL, Wm O 10,78,138
BEAN
  Jack 98
  Mark 98,99,100,101,102,103
  Ruth 98
  V T 98
  Victoria T 97,98,99,100,101,102, 103,104,105,106
BEANS, Lucinda Jane 312
BECK, William B 194
BELL, L B 267
BENNETT, Dolly 239
BIGBEY
  Charles 109
  David 107,109
  David E 107
  Ed 108
  Edward C 107
  Minnie 107,108
  Minnie C 107
  Rachel 107
  Rebecca M 106,107,108,109,110, 111,112,113
  Sammy 108
  Samuel A 107
  Sarah 108
  Sarah C 107
  Thomas 107,109
  Thomas M 111
  Thomas W 107,108,109,110,111
  Walter 108
BIGBY, Thomas W 109
BIXBY, Tams ....8,18,29,38,50,60,69, 78,82,86,95,104,111,120,128,129,137,142 ,146,155,163,171,182,196,205,213,221, 229,236,244,255,263,272,280,290,299,

Index

309,318
BLEDSOE
   Belle 229
   I P 229
BLUEBIRD, Sarah 86
BLUEBIRD, Sarah 81,84,85
BOGBEY, Rebecca M 110
BOWMAN, Lucy M 37,289,298
BOZEMAN, Mr 6
BRANSON, Eula Jeanes 48
BRECKENRIDE, Com'r 42
BRECKENRIDGE
   C R 13,21,32
   Commissioner. 12,13,14,41,72,107,199
BRECKINRIDGE
   C R .... 23,35,44,56,73,81,90,108, 124,132,186,209,240,248,275,303,304 ,313
   Clifton F 133
   Clifton R 13,14,23,34,42
   Commissioner 55,123,166,284
   Com'r 186,239,285
BRYAN
   J M 239,284
   Mary Rebeca Carloline 242
   Rebecca C 239,241,242,243,244
CARR, Jesse O 5,15,24,45,134,201, 210,218,226,241,277,295
CHAMPLIN, Lola M 59,154,204, 243,254,271,297
CHANDLER, Ann Eliza 307
CHAPPELL
   W W 15
   Walter W 6,48,117,118,168,241
   Warren W 17
CHAPPELLE, Walter W 188,202,230
CHICK, Retta 160,187,233
CHRISTIE
   Emma 73
   Jane 72,73,74,75,76,77
   Jennie 75
   Jinnie 76
   John 72
   John F M ... 72,73,74,75,76,77,78,79,80
   Nancy 73
   Nancy Emma 72
CLINGAN, Judge 312

CLOUD
   James 93
   James M 88,89,90,91,92,93,94, 95,96,97
   M C 89
   Martha 93
   Martha C 89,90,91,93,94
   William M 89,90
COCHRAN
   Geo 271
   George 270
COLLIER, Parson 234
CONNER
   Francis M 34
   Solon 34
COOPER 151
   Alice 150
   Lice 151
COUNCILOR, Homer J 136,145,170
CRAIG
   Garland C 317
   Granville 312,313,314,315, 316,317,318
   Granville C 316,317
   Jane 313,317
   Lucinda J 312,313,314,315,317, 318,319,320
   Lucinda Jane 312,313
   Mr 315
CRAVENS, R R 23,33,55,82,133,159, 177,276
CRITTENDEN
   Edith 188
   Martha Elizabeth 187,188,196
   Mose 188
CRITTENDON 194
   Martha Elizabeth 191
CROSSLAND
   Anni 209
   Annie E 208,209,210,211,212, 213,214,215
   A E 209
   R F 209
   Richard 210
   Richard F 209
   Samuel 209,210,211,212
CRUTSINGER

Index

Maragret 44
Margaret 44
CUMMINGS, Kate 168,169,170
CUNNINGHAM, A B 300,301
DANIEL
   Emma 297,298,300
   John M 296
   M D 296
   Thos 296
   Wm A 296
DANIELS
   Emma J 293,298
   Emmy 297
   John 293
   Martha 293
DANILS, Emmy 298
DANNENBERG, Mattie J 102
DAVENPORT
   James D 250
   James S 276
DAVIES, Josie 219
DAVIS
   Julia 266
   Martin 266
   Mary 267
   Mary E 266,269,270,271,272
DAWES, Hon 229
DONDLY, Henry 300
DONELLY
   H 298
   Mr H 296
DONLEY, Emma 293
DONLLY, Mr H 297,298
DONNELLY
   Ada 293,294,295,299
   Emma 293,294,295,296,299
   Emma J 293,294,299
   Henry 292,293,294,295,296,
   297,299,301,302
   James 293
   Paul 293,294,295,299
DOWELL, Marcus D L 151
DRAPER, William 316
DUMAS
   Jackson D 43
   Lucinda 43
   Lucinda Caroline 43

Roxie 48
DUNCAN, W A 76
EFFORTS, Henry 152
EIFFENT, Hon Henry 153
ELLIOTT
   Anna E 1,3,4,5,7,8
   Annie E 2,3
   A E 2
   G W 2,10
   George 1,7
   George W 1,2,3,4,5,6,7,8,9,10,11
   John 179,180
   Mamie 1,3
   Mary 1,3,4,5
EPEERS, Arch 81
FALKNER, Franklin 144
FARTHING, A J 27,297,298
FENCE, Matilda 132,135,136,137
FIELDS
   Ella 216,217,219,220,221
   Ella E 232,233,234,235,236,237
   Ella M 233
   Joseph A 232,233
   Louvena 233
   Louvenia 232
   Mr 233
   Walter G 232,233,234,235
FOLEY
   Addie 176,177,178,179,181
   Adline 176
   Clarence 175,176,177,178
   Cornelius 176,177,178
   Joseph B 176
   Laura 175,176,178
   Lawrence 176,177,178
   Lizzie 176,177,178
   Maggie 175,176,177,178
   Pat 176
   Patrick 174,175,176,177,178,179,
   180,181,182,183,184
   Roachman 176,177,178
   Sarah 176,177,178
FOLLEY, Patrick 180
FOREMAN
   Mary 158
   Mrs 161
   Rev Stephen 161

Index

Samuel 201,218,287
FOWLER, Anderson 208
FRAZIER
   Alice 150
   Bessie 150,152
   Virginia................... 150,152,153,154
   William 150,151
FREEMAN
   Clyde 41,42
   D 296
   D W 41,43,48
   Daniel W 44,45,46,47,48,49
   Daniel Webster 44
   R S 41,43
   Roxanna 42,44
   Roxie 45
   Roxie L 43,44,45,46,47,49,50,51,52
   Roxie Levania................................. 41
   Roxie S 40,51
   William Clyde 41,42,43,44,45,46,49
FUNTER, John 144
GOODWIN, Rev S F 317
GREEN, M D 1,4,56,64,90,186,
225,239,285,313
GRIFFIN, Richard 150
GRINSTEAD, J Ransom 316,317
HALL
   James O 265,266,267,268,269,
270,271,272,273,274
   Janie P 266,267,268
   Jennie P 267
   Mary 267
   Mary E 266,267,268,271,272
HAMPTON
   Alberten 15,16
   Albertin 12,13,14,15,17,18,19,20
   A B 16
   Bert 18
   Burt 14
   Dewitt 13,14
   Edgar 13,14
   Elizabeth 13
   Gracie 13,14
   J E 12,15
   Jane E 14,15,16,17
   Jane Elizabeth 12,16
   Mary 13,14

Pearl 13,14
HANNA, Gertrude 118
HARLIN, J E 252,253
HARRIS, C J 179,180
HASTINGS
   Representative 150
   W W 10,11,19,30,34,35,39,45,51,
56,57,60,61,70,71,74,79,87,96,105,
112,113,121,130,138,139,147,156,164
,172,173,183,191,197,198,206,214,
223,231,232,236,245,246,256,264,265
,269,273,274,282,288,291,301,302,
311,318,319
HAWKINS, W S 296
HAYDEN
   Carrie 239
   Carry 239
   Clem 239
   Clement 237,238,240,241,242,
243,244,245,246,247
   Edna 239
   Essie 238,239,240
   Ida 239
   Ida M 238,240
   Lela 238,239,240
   Lona 238,240
   Lucy 238
   Rebecca C 240,242,244
   Rebecca Carolina 238
HECKS, Daniel R 243
HERNAM
   Frank 141
   Mary 141
HICKS, Daniel R 242
HIGHLAND, Nellie 175
HILDEBRAND
   J 203
   J M 204
HILL
   H L 296
   Myrtle 136,195,271
HINEMAN, Mary A 143
HUTCHINSON, Wm 25,66,74,84,92,
100,101,109,125
HYMAN, Mary Ann 143
HYNAM
   Mary A 145

Mary Ann 144
Mary H 144
INLOW
   Amanda 202,204
   Amanda A 203
   Elizabeth 199
   A M 204
   Phillip 199
ISUDE, Lucas 27
JAMES
   Clara Bell 33
   Clara D 33
   Clara Dell 33,35
   Claud 33
   Claud Frank 33
   Cornelia Jane 33
   Jesse Lamar 33
   Lula Bell 33
   Mrs 32
   P J 32,33
   Solon 32,33,34,35,36,37,38,39,40
   Tennesee A 32
   Tennessee 33
   Tennessee A 33,35,36,37,38
JONES
   B C 5,24,35,46,57,65,101,109,
   116,134,143,160,168,178,187,226,233
   ,250,251,262,268,269,277,278,286,
   295,305,314
   Bruce C ... 73,108,200,217,259,293,294
   John B 84
   John D 81
KENNEY, George 53
KERR
   Anna 7
   Anna E 6,7,8
   Annie E 2
   Frederick A 2
   Laurena 2
KING, Bettie 189
KINNEY, Mary J 57,58,59
LANE
   F Elma 17,85,144,153,162,212,261
   Frances R 26,27,46,67,94,102,
   103,109,110,169,191,203,233,234,235
   ,242,243,252,278
   R Elma 279

Tanasse 36
Tennessee A 32,37
LESSLEY, Geo H 58
LESTER, Letitia 83
LEWIS
   Amanda 199,200,201,204,205
   Amanda A 203
   Amanda M 200
   Joseph 200
   Mary 200
   Robin 200
   Roland 203
   Roland M 199,203,205
   Roland W 202
   Rollen 200
   Rowland 204
   Rowland M 200,201,204,205,
   206,207
LINCOLN, A T 64
LINDSEY
   Dollie 239
   Dolly 238
   Edna 238,239,240
   R P 239
   Rebecca C 239,240
LOONEY
   Adaline 180
   Addie 177,181
   Adeline 179,180
LOONY
   Addie 175
   Nellie 175
   William 175
MALLORY
   Mamie Tabor 68,77
   Mary Tabor 27,48,181
MAYES
   J B 242,271
   J G 270
MCALESTER
   John W 224,225
   John W, Jr 225
   John W, Sr 225
   Nancy 224,225
   Peter 224
   Rebecca 224
MCALESTER 229

Index

MCALISTER
  John W.. 229
  John W, Jr... 229
  John W, Sr... 229
  Nancy H.. 225
MCALLISTER
  Joe William.................................225,226
  John W....................................225,227,228
  John W, Jr..................................225,226
  John Wesley 225,226
  Nancy 226
  Nancy H 224,225,226,227,228,229
MCALLISTER, Nancy H......230,231,232
MCCLERK, T I.. 296
MCCRARY, Jemima......................... 261
MCCRAW, J M.. 48
MCCROW, J M.. 48
MCDONALD
  Brown....13,14,42,98,115,142,167,209
  Carrie... 316
  John Q 316
MCDONALD
  Carrie... 317
  John Q 317
MCGHEE
  T G 27
  T J 26,57,67,68,300
MCGHEE
  (Clerk) 298
  T B (?) 298
  T J 252
  T Z B 296,297
MCKENNON, Commissioner................. 1
MCSHEE, T J.. 58
MCSHEE, F J.. 254
MCSPADDEN
  Rev T B K.. 150
  T K B 150,154
MEANS, Jane..................................316,317
MEESHEAN, Wm S 249
MERRICK, Edward..........7,27,68,94,103,
110,127,170,191,203,235,243,253
MILLER
  Aggie... 258
  Andrew 259
  Andrew J 258,259,260,261,262,263
  Andrew J, Jr....................................... 261

Dawes..................................259,261
A J 261
Mahana...259,261
Mamie.. 259
Mamie J 259,261
Martha A 258,259,260,261,
262,263,264,265
Martha Ann... 259
Mertie T... 259
Myrtle T..259,261
Pearl... 261
Pearly... 259
Robert L...259,261
Robert Lee 259
Sallie E 259,261
Sarah.. 259
William A 259
NEEDLE, T B 259
NEEDLES
  Commissioner.....................98,151,312
  Com'r 64,150,151,225,313
  T B........... 4,55,64,90,99,115,158,159,
167,177,200,217,225,250,267,276,285
,294
NEELY, James 57
PACE, Mattie M................................... 230
PALMER, R 286
PARKS, John... 306
PEMBERTON
  Jamed K.. 145
  James 141,144
  James K 140,141,142,143,145,
146,147,148
  Mary 141
  Mary A 141,142,145
PERRY
  F C... 68
  Florence C 64,67,68
  James 63
  Susan Jane 63
RALLS, J G 42
RASMUS
  B P 37,47,57,58,126,127,134,
136,145,170,178,180,220,269,297,298
,308,316
  R P 307
RED BIRD, Daniel........8,18,28,38,49,59,

69,77,86,94,104,111,120,129,137,146,155,162,171,181,196,205,213,221,229,235,244,255,263,272,280,290,299,309,318
RICHARDS, John A 242,243
RIDER, Jane 110
RINNEY, Mary J 58
ROBERTS, Solon H 126
ROBINSON
   James L 317
   Jas L 317
ROOSEVELT, Mr 300
ROSENWINKEL, G 44
ROSS, Chief John 6
ROSSON
   J O 300
   John O 125
   John O 15,25,66,74,84,92,100,210
ROTHENBERGER
   E G 34,57,65,178,250,251,268
   Edward G 124
RUBEL, Rev 161
RUBELL, Mr 161
RUBLE
   (Thomas B) 93
   Thomas B 93
SABY, Ellen 229
SAGER
   Amelia 21,22
   Amelia A 22,23,24,25,28
   August 27
   Augusta 21,23
   Augusta C 26
   Augustus C 20,23,24,25,26,28,29,30,31
   A C 21,22
   James 22
   James F 22,23
   Lewis H 22,23
   Louis 22
   Myrtle 22
   Ollie M 22
   Ollie Myrtle 22,23
   Robert Newton 22
SAMUELS
   Charles 132
   Charles R 131,132,133,134,135,136,137,138,139,140

Jesse C 132,133,137
Lue T 133
Lutetia 132,133,137
Matilda 132,133,134,137
SANDERS
   Ellis 132,136
   Geo 180
   Geo O 169,180
   George O 179
SCHRIMSHER, Laura 208
SCOTT
   Mrs 211
   Nannie 211
SHELLY, Mary 25,28
SIXKILLER
   Judge 242
   Judge Redbird 242
SMITH
   Elizabeth 216,217,218
   Ella 216,217,218,219,221
   Emmet B 63,64,65
   Emmett B 69
   Emmitt 64
   Florence 65
   Florence C 63,64,66,69
   Floy Lena 82
   Floyd L 82
   Frank 220
   Frank N 215,216,217,218,219,220,221,222,223
   Grover C 82
   Grover Cleaveland 82
   Jno D 82
   John D 81,83,84,85,86,87,88
   L B 63,64,68
   Lee B 62,63,64,65,66,67,69,70,71
   Leslie 85
   Lizzie 216
   Lucy L 82
   Mabel 216
   May B 217,218
   May Belle 216,217
   Rebeca E 82
   Rebecca Ethel 82
   Richard 216,217,218
   Richard M 216
   Sarah 82,83,84,85,86

Index

Walter D 82
William 216
Willie 216,217
Willie E 216,217,218
SOLON, James 35
SOMDERS, Geo W 170
SPEARS, Arch 84
STARR
  Henry 178
  J C 4,24,226,276,294
  James 76
  Jane 77
  Jennie 76
  Jinnie 76
  Laura 177
STONE, Malinda 277
STUBBLEFIELD, Demie T 127
THOMAS
  Elizabeth 16,249,250,251
  Ellis 249,250,251
  Frank N 249
  Henry R 249,250,251
  Henry T 249
  J A 253
  J E 12
  Jane 16
  Jessanna 249
  Jesse 248,249,252
  Jesse A .. 247,250,251,254,255,256,257
  Jesse H 256
  Jessee 249
  Jessie A 250,251
  Jessie Anna 249
  Johanna 249
  John L 249,250,251
  Johnanna 248,250,251,254
  Lawrence 249
  Napoleon F 249,250,251
  Tholiver 12
  Thura 249,250,251
THORNTON
  Amos 7
  Glover 189,192,193
  J T 151
  Joe 190,193
  John 189,193
  Joseph 193

Mr 151
Mr J 150
T J 150
T Jay 154
TIDWELL, John E 35,76,119,191,
193,194,195,219,227,228,271,289
TITTEL, Amelia A 26
TITTLE
  Amelia A 21,26,28
  Bob 307
  D M 21
  Daniel 303
  Hugh T E 304
  Hugh Thomas E 303
  Mary 303
  Mary A 304
  Mary Alice 304
  Mary Ellis (Alice) 304
  Mary S 302,303,304,305,306,307,
308,309,310,311
  Mela Arline 27
  Otis W 303,304
  Otis Wooden 304
  Robert 303,304,308
  Robert W 303,304,305,306,307,
308,309
  Robert W J 304
  Robert Wooden 304
  Rosa 21
  Rosanna 303
TROTT
  Dot F 275,276,277,278
  Dot Fay 275
  J L 275
  Lou J 275
  Louisa J 275,276,277,278,279,
280,281,282,283,315
  W J 279
  W L 275,278,279,315
  William L 275,276,277,280
  Wm L 275
TUNNELL, William 161
VANCE, H M 35,74,269,288
VON WEISE, Chas 90
WAINWRIGHT
  L 135
  Reverend S 132

Index

WARD
  Charles 89
  Martha 93
  Martha C 92,94
  Thomas 93
WATERS, Sarah 76,119,228
WEBSTER, Chas E 28,49,59,68,
77,85,144,153,154,162,181,204,212,244,
254,261,271,279
WEINWRIGHT, S 136
WETSEL, Daniel K 127
WHITE, Myron 219
WILLEY
  Charles 161
  Charles E 158,160,161,162,163,
  164,165
  Charley E 159
  Mary 159,160,162
  Minnie 160,161
WILLIAM, Jennie 284
WILLIAMS
  Addie 284
  Addie M 285,286,289
  Addie May 284,287
  Ben 286
  Carrie 53
  Dave 284
  David 284,285,287,288,289
  Davie 287
  Davie S 286,287
  Davie Stella 287
  Davis 287
  Davis D 285
  Davis Della 284
  J E 285,286
  Jane 249
  Jennie 283,284,285,286,288,
  289,290,291,292
  Jennie E 286
  Johana 253
  John 248
  Johnanna 252,254
  Lotta 285
  Lottie 284,285,286,287
WILLIE
  Charlie 159
  Mr 6

WILLY
  Charles 159
  Charles E 159
  Mary 158,159
  Minnie 159
WINTON
  Fagan 189
  James 185
  Jas 186
  Mansfield 189
  Martha 186
  Martha E 187
  Martha Elizabeth 196
  Minerva 185,186
  Mr 190
  William 185,186,187,188,190,
  191,192,193,194,195,196,197,198
  Wm 186
WOOD, Clara Mitchell 44,179,180,
220,307,308,316
WOODALL, *(Clerk)* 298
WREN
  Charles R 166,167,169
  Edward 166
  Edwin 165,166,167,168,169,170,
  171,172,173,174
  George H 166,167,169
  Kate 166,169,171
  Margarett 166
  William A 166
WRIGHT
  Levan 98
  S T 7
  Wyley P 98
WYLEY
  Alice 189
  Alive 189
YARGAIN, J C 57,58
YEARGAIN
  Claybe 54
  James 54,55
  James C 53,54,55,56,57,59,60,61,62
  Mary J 54,58,59
  Mary Jane 53,55,57
  Robert P 54
  Robert Percey 54
  Robert Percy 54,55

Index

Turner Alvin 54,55
YEARGAN, J C 58

www.ingramcontent.com/pod-product-compliance
Lightning Source LLC
Chambersburg PA
CBHW020244030426
42336CB00010B/605